Introduction to Digital Publishing

by David Bergsland

This is the introductory book to the digital publishing series teaching the practical aspects of print and Web production. The series includes this book, *Printing with Illustrator and FreeHand, Publishing with Photoshop,* and *Publishing with InDesign* — all from OnWord Press Thomson Learning.

Introduction to
Digital Publishing

by David Bergsland

THOMSON

™

DELMAR LEARNING

Africa • Australia • Canada • Denmark • Japan • Mexico • New Zealand
Philippines • Puerto Rico • Singapore • United Kingdom • United States

THOMSON
™
DELMAR LEARNING

Introduction to Digital Publishing
by David Bergsland

Business Unit Director:
Alar Elken

Executive Editor:
Sandy Clark

Acquisitions Editor:
James Gish

Editorial Assistant:
Jaimie Wetzel

Executive Marketing Manager:
Maura Theriault

Marketing Coordinator:
Karen Smith

Channel Manager:
Fair Huntoon

Executive Production Manager:
Mary Ellen Black

Production Manager:
Larry Main

Production Editor:
Tom Stover

Cover Illustration:
Nicole Reamer

Cover Design:
Cummings Advertising

Book Layout
Bergsland Design

Library of Congress
Cataloging-in-Publication Data

ISBN#0-7668-6326-3

NOTICE TO THE READER

*I dedicate this book
to my favorite person in the world,
The Rev. Patricia H. Bergsland.*

Acknowledgments

Over the years, many people have helped me along the way. Personally, I have to thank my friends at Nob Hill Foursquare, my wife's church, for their immense help in bringing me to greater maturity. Their love and support have been essential to my growth as a person, as a teacher, and as a writer. This wouldn't have happened without their prayers and support.

At school, I have to thank my Dean, Lois Carlson; my Associate Dean, Dan Valles; and Program Chair, Marcella Green. They have given me leeway to pursue this new style of teaching and a great deal of support and kindness. We creative types can be very hard to live with, but they have hung in there with me even though I am severely bureaucratically challenged. I am grateful.

Many thanks have to go to my students in my Business Graphics degree and certificate programs at Albuquerque TVI and in my commercial mentoring venture, Pneumatika Online School. It is horribly unfair to name names, so I won't. We've had a great deal of fun. They didn't volunteer as guinea pigs. In fact, most of them think I'm some sort of expert. But I know better...

At Delmar/Onword, I have had a wonderful crew. Thomas Stover has been a wonderful help to production – answering my many questions almost instantly. He kept the workflow smooth and solved all the production issues. My editor, Jim Gish, has been a joy to work with – as has his assistant, Jaimie Wetzel. Their professionalism is far beyond what I have ever experienced.

My copyeditor and tech editor did a wonderful job. This is the first book I have worked on with Mardelle Kunz. She has been a marvelous copyeditor with insightful corrections and an understanding of contemporary grammatical changes. Plus the speed of her edits was phenomenal. Melissa Cogswell is my technical editor. Her input saved me from several embarrassing passages.

The crew at TransContinental, our printers, have been very responsive, extremely professional, and helpful. It is a major task for an author to write, design, and format his own book. All of these people have made it much easier to accomplish. More than that, they have enabled professional output.

My major gratitude is reserved for my incredible wife, Pastor Pat as she is known by her sheep. Her ability to put up with my foibles is staggering. Without her love and support, I would have quit a long time ago. In addition to being my wife, she is also my pastor which, as you can imagine, is a fantastic help. Serving as one of her elders has given me a glimpse into true leadership and a teaching ability that has been the core of my inspiration as a teacher and mentor. Her friendship has been my stability. Our love is my reason for going on ...

June 1, 2002
Quail Meadow, New Mexico

This book was written, designed, and formatted on a 400 MHz Mac G4 with 576 MB RAM, MacOS 9.1. I used InDesign 1.5.2 and 2, FreeHand 10, Illustrator 9, Photoshop 6 and 7, Word 98 and X, and Dreamweaver 4 to create the pieces. My scanner was an Epson 636U. Everything was proofed on my old beat up Laserwriter Select 360 with PostScript Level 2. Each chapter was printed to disk from InDesign and distilled using TransContinental's settings in Distiller 4 and the Prinergy plug-in. I designed all of the fonts used, in Fontographer. They are for sale at MyFonts.com

Contents

viii: Table of Contents

5 • Software needs   127

x: Table of Contents

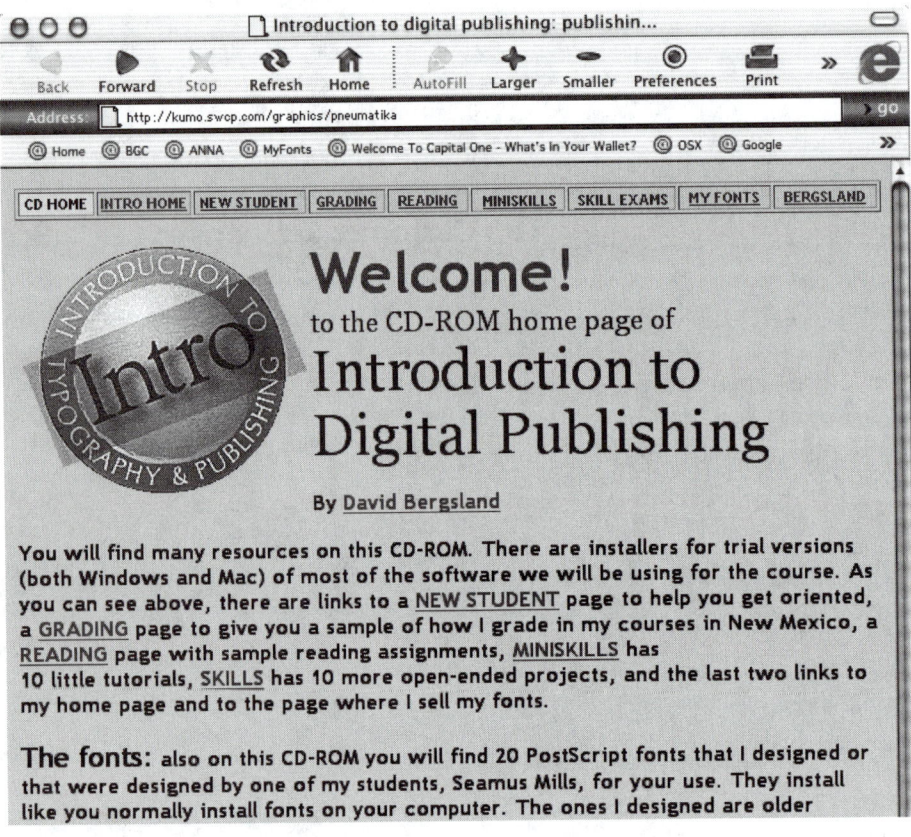

The basic instructions for the materials in this book are all found in the next six pages and on the CD linked to the home page. Simply open *CDhome.htm* in your browser and get busy...

Working the System

Concepts

1. Skill exams

2. Tutorials

3. Discovery learning

4. Reality orientation

Discovering the basic attitude and skills necessary to survive in the publishing industry

One of the largest problems with this style of learning is just getting you to start work. The procedure will probably seem foreign to you unless you are already working in the digital publishing industry — either print or Web. Then you will feel reasonably comfortable.

These materials are what is professionally known to educators as *discovery learning*. What that means is that you learn to do the exams by discovering what to do. The learning is in the searching and the practice. Try first, then ask for help. The knowledge you need only comes by experience. The materials in this book offer you experience in a safe environment.

Personal responsibility

You will have to determine what you need to know and then learn those skills. Your instructor is a resource person who has the skills and the resources to lead you to green pastures where you can graze on feed that will result in professional-level skills on your part. Experience cannot be force-fed. You must practice on real-world projects or the closest possible thing to it to gain the experience you will need in your career.

The learning goals

In reading industry trade magazines, perusing the many books available, and talking to employers in the new industry, it has become apparent that most current study offerings are not meeting the needs of either the employers or the students. Most books still just teach the software and assume that you know the publishing. To quote the former chairman of my advisory committee for my Business Graphics degree, which is filled with employers and working graphic designers:

"Software is a moving target."

This book assumes computer literacy and a basic knowledge of at least one of the page layout programs. You can do tutorials in any of the seven programs used by the professionals: PageMaker, QuarkXPress, InDesign, FreeHand, Illustrator, Photoshop, and Acrobat. At this point (mid-2002), all the other programs are lagging far behind InDesign, Illustrator, and Photoshop. You will certainly need the full version of Acrobat. The other three you will need because you will be getting documents from people who still use them.

Introduction to Digital Publishing teaches essential skills needed on a daily basis using the best tools for the task — as mentioned above. The concepts and skills taught work equally well with the following versions: Pagemaker 6.5 or 7; Quark 4.1 or 5; InDesign 1.5.2 or 2; FreeHand 7, 8, 9, 10; Illustrator 9 or 10; and Photoshop 5.5, 6, or 7. The newer versions streamline production with some of the new capabilities. However, the basic concepts work equally well on any version listed. The concepts and skill sets taught in *Introduction to Digital Publishing* are essential to professional production without the titillating illustration techniques that have little practical use once the student gets hired.

Five learning goals:

- **Basic graphic design knowledge, without the egocentric techniques traditionally taught in fine art and design schools that are so overly expensive to actually produce in projects for real clients who really need to communicate with their customers.**
- **Practical job skills covering the production requirements of offset lithography, screen printing, electrostatic printing, and inkjet printing — plus the needs of Web site creation.**
- **Strong thinking and problem-solving skills.**
- **Strategies to determine when to use FreeHand and/or Illustrator and when other types of software are appropriate.**
- **Basic working knowledge of how to integrate FreeHand and Illustrator with the rest of the software used by the publishing industry for projects in print, multimedia, and on the Web.**

The problem with tutorials

Introduction to Digital Publishing is easy to read, very practical, and a reference for basic techniques that will be used during your entire career as a professional desktop or digital publisher. These techniques cover concepts that are not going to change.

However, this book is not enough. A new method of instruction is necessary also. Current courses around the country are usually simply lockstep software tutorials teaching wow-factor techniques. These tutorial entrances are generally helpful, but they teach none of the learning goals listed here. They are boring to you and do not add the skills you really need on a day-to-day basis. They merely show software capabilities — not how to use that software. Use tutorials as little as possible.

A new method of instruction is necessary.

Lockstep tutorials are little help to you beyond a bare introduction to the software. They teach the location and capabilities of the various dialog boxes and commands. However, tutorials force you to think in the manner and order of the tutorial creator. The problem is that graphic design projects have thousands of different, equally competent and professional solutions. It is impossible for a designer to solve design problems by trying to think like someone else. Exams must be open-ended. Only when you are actively involved in problem solving can you be creative.

You will have some need for more directly guided tutorials when you first begin. However, my experience has shown that the sooner you can move on, the faster you will learn. We are definitely talking liberty here, not license. This style of teaching gives you freedom within the context of professional production standards. If any solution would not be sellable to a real client, you need to redo it until it is.

The procedure and conceptual basis of the Skill Exam approach

Instead of lockstep tutorials, *Introduction to Digital Publishing* includes open-ended projects in the form of Skill Exams and Miniskills. The distinctions between the two are arbitrary. The Skill Exams have been tested for many years to make sure they actually help internalize concepts in a production environment. After a tutorial, I could give you an almost identical project and you would not be able to do the work. After a Skill Exam, the skills are yours — and you can easily transfer those skills to real projects for real clients.

There are ten Miniskills and ten Skill Exams. They are all located in the HTML Web site on the CD. This is a copy of the Web site I actually use in my classes to teach online. I give my students relative freedom to pick the exams that will help them the most. This means that some will pick the easiest. We always have the lazy ones. However, you are better than that, I know. As you can see on the grading policies page on the Web site, you are required to do five of each type of exam. You can earn the additional points needed for a "B" or an "A" with additional Theory, Miniskill, or Skill exams. Plus, you are strongly encouraged to work on real-world projects.

Skill Exam rules:

The following are some simple guidelines to make the use of these Skill Exams and Miniskills as much fun as possible. The Miniskills are usually easier, with more direct, step-by-step instruction. You will find that

 This icon notes a tip to help.

 This icon locates a basic concept.

 This icon warns you that you are about to be assaulted by my opinion.
Have a fun ride!

May 2002

You may want to do the same skill in several applications.

This is encouraged. By doing this you come to realize how all PostScript applications do basically the same things. It will greatly help your learning. Unless the other versions are almost identical, I try to give the same points for additional skills done. However, they do not count for the five required Skill Exams.

there is still quite a bit of freedom allowed in them also. The Skill Exams are real projects for fictitious clients. You can always substitute real work if you have a client with a similar need. This depends on your instructor. I tend to make projects the focus of my courses (though projects are difficult to require because all students need the same opportunities).

There is no time limit, unless you are substituting real work with the accompanying deadlines. Regardless, you can practice as much as you like. Remember, these are genuinely Skill Exams, meaning that you will have to take the time to develop the skills. Please do not assume that you can just toss off the required finished product. (If you can, you are wasting your time taking this course.) Pick a skill that challenges you a little.

You can ask as many questions as you need to ask. These exams are designed to teach you needed skills. We are not interested in your methodology (if it's important, there will be specific suggestions). **The required steps of the Skill Exam are all there for a reason.** Read the instructions carefully. You can invent your own shortcuts later, on your own time. However, like all projects, skipping part of the project means angry clients and lost work. Treating these exams like job tickets will help you get them done professionally.

Unlimited demos and redoes

If you cannot figure out how to do any part of the Skill Exam, the instructor or one of the staff will demonstrate it for you. Feel free to ask one of your classmates (but remember they may not know any more than you do). This is discovery learning, so *figuring it out* is an important part of the learning process. This learning by discovery is what embeds the skills in your memory.

You will finish with a specific product (usually a PDF except in Photoshop where you send JPEGs or GIFs) that you attach to an email, which you then send to your instructor for grading and comments. The same skill in several applications counts more (up to an additional skill each, depending on the skill and your instructor's discretion).

If there is a problem with your final product, the instructor will annotate your PDF, or describe problems in the reply email, and send it back for corrections. There is no penalty for the second try (or third or fourth).

If you work in a team with other friends or classmates, you are required to be able to do the Skill Exam on your own, without help. You need these skills. If the instructor thinks you are trying to get away with avoiding some of the skills, you may be required to demonstrate the skills that have been submitted, at any time.

There is no way you can cheat on these tests. You have to be able to acquire the skills. At any time, if there is any doubt in the instructor's mind, all he or she has to do is ask you to do the skill while he or she is watching. Once you have done a Skill Exam, and acquired the skills, you should be able to redo any of these exams in just a few minutes.

The reason for the Theory Exams

As you well know, current teaching styles normally use multiple-choice testing for theory concepts. This style is used for ease of grading with no thought to its helpfulness in analyzing your actual conceptual understanding. (To rephrase, multiple guess is easy to grade and they don't care what you have really understood.)

Introduction to Digital Publishing includes a complete set of Theory Exams using short essay-style questions that enable your teacher to accurately assess your understanding of the basic concepts. These exams are the questions at the end of each chapter. All Theory Exams are to be typed (with the questions) into an email and sent to your instructor for grading and annotation. My experience is that the teacher's comments help more than anything to increase your knowledge. These concepts are important for you to understand, and they help your teacher know where you need help.

All of these exams are designed to force you to think.

Many of the theory questions are open-ended, with no right or wrong answer — just like the Skill Exams. They are designed to force you to think (although it is certainly more politically correct to refer to the process as strongly encouraging thought). This style of teaching gives you the opportunity to work together with other students on the exams. In fact, you are strongly encouraged to work together.

Robin Williams (in her extremely popular book, *The Non-Designer's Design Book*, Peachpit Press, 1994) calls it "Open Book, Open Mouth" learning. The questions are open-ended, often requiring careful thought and personal opinion to answer. Often there is no right or wrong answer, but a search for thoughtful opinion. The goal is to learn to think, not to regurgitate data. The process of writing the answers into the email and the annotated email responses will give you great reinforcement to help you remember and internalize the concepts. The very process enables long-term retention of the materials.

The importance of real world projects

In my courses, students move on (as soon as possible) to real projects for real clients with real deadlines. This enables them to apply what they have learned, making the new knowledge and techniques a permanent part of their skill set. You always have the built-in option to supply your own "real projects." You will learn so much on these projects (especially if you have trouble) that you really need to push past any fear. These projects will give you a chance to work on *real stuff* in a safe environment with professional help readily available.

When you graduate or finish the course, you will have to use your skills to satisfy real clients' needs. You cannot start this process soon enough.

The landmark

This is the beginning landmark used in all of my books since 1994. Hopefully, it will keep you oriented and on the straight and narrow. Please relax and enjoy your trip into publishing.

I always give grades to real paid projects, but that will depend on the policies of the school you are attending. If they do not allow it, please write me at graphics@swcp.com and I will try to help. I do online mentoring and consulting for any student who needs it, for a fee.

Distance learning and online training:

Introduction to Digital Publishing includes a complete generic Web site on the CD that has been used and tested since 1996. This site is set up for easy inclusion into the distance learning courses taught by any community college, business, or vocational school. If this course is not available online at your school, or if you are studying alone, on your own, please contact me at: http://kumo.swcp.com/graphics or email me at graphics@swcp.com

The Web site on the CD-ROM includes all the reading assignments, Miniskills, and Skill Exams developed for the course using *Introduction to Digital Publishing*. These materials were designed so you can do them online in your home or office on your schedule.

 Learning online or on your own requires much more self-discipline than many realize. You will have to set up a regular schedule to work on these materials. Every online student I have who fails does so because he or she was not willing or not able to spend the time necessary to learn the skills. You will have to work at this to be sucessful.

If you are studying on your own at home or in the office

Everything I just wrote applies to you also. Although most people find that working in a group like a class helps a great deal, many of us no longer have the time (or the money) for that luxury. With the self-discipline mentioned on the previous page, you will find these materials are really fun to use. If you have questions, feel free to write me: graphics@swcp.com at my private school.

Chapter 1

Digital Publishing

Concepts

1. Desktop
   publishing

2. Digital publishing

A BRAND NEW PARADIGM

Defining the difference between desktop and digital publishing

Chapter Objectives:

By giving students a clear understanding of the digital publishing industry, this chapter will enable students to:

1. explain the position of desktop publishing
2. describe the interaction of the Web with the industry
3. list the entry-level requirements of the career
4. discuss why multimedia is such a small part of the digital publishing industry

Lab Work for Chapter:

1. Become familiar with the computer you will be using.
2. Learn the file management procedures for your lab or set up folders for your use on your own computer.
3. Open the Web site for this class (or the version found on your CD) and explore the links offered.

If you are taking this class in a classroom setting, this is the time to learn the procedures set up by your school. You will not have time later, and many problems will be avoided by learning these things now.

Things have changed!

Here we see how much things have changed since the 1300s and earlier. This original form of desktop publishing was slow, laborious, and very difficult. However, it was incredibly beautiful, extremely subtle, and can barely be equaled in quality today.

There are only a couple of people in the world with the skills. The materials are priced far out of reach. A single sheet of real parchment could be a couple hundred dollars, for example, if it were available.

One of the first things you must understand in this industry is the long tradition of amazing quality that is no longer available. We simply cannot afford it anymore.

The exciting news to old professionals is that many of the old abilities are becoming available digitally. I will explain all of this as we learn what it means to be a digital publisher in the twenty-first century.

Why not desktop publishing?

"But everyone calls this desktop publishing!" I can hear the whining already. **Stop it!** IT'S TIME TO GET SERIOUS NOW. What do you think of when you think about desktop publishing? Most of you have images in your mind of secretaries doing newsletters in Word or Publisher. It is a correct stereotype, in most cases. Of course, some use PageMaker once a month to do those newsletters and such. However, it is a peripheral event in their lives and careers.

So, the problem is not the term itself. The problem is how desktop publishing is used in common speech. The normal conception of desktop publishing is nonprofessionals doing neat little things on their computers (usually to avoid paying a pro to do it right). A want ad for a desktop publishing job in a newspaper is often a secretarial position where the only digital tool is Office.

We will spend this entire book talking about the differences between the public conceptions and the professional reality of the career you are about enter. Often, you will discover, these differences are radical. As you embark, you need to realize that this is a strange journey, fraught with public misunderstanding. It is also some of the best fun you will ever get paid to perform.

This was formerly called commercial art.

As most of you know, things have radically changed with the digital revolution in all fields. Nowhere have they changed much more than they have in publishing. Commercial art was formerly an esoteric craft, known by few and understood by fewer. As an art director, I wouldn't have even interviewed you unless you had at least three to five years of practical experience in the industry.

The skills required were daunting. You were required to be able to hand render type (at an accurate point size), demonstrate remarkable drawing skills, and work exceedingly quickly. However, things have not changed beyond recognition. What has happened is the new norm in our culture. We build better and better tools so that we can handle (and be responsible for) more or more portions of the process. These tools enable the less skilled to compete on equal footing with those with traditional skills. At least that is the politically correct theory.

What we are talking about is professional production of digital documents that will be published. Prior to 1990, this meant printed pieces, and they were not done digitally. Now we have to include Web pages, Web sites, multimedia productions, and a great deal more. The key word, though, is *professional*. This is a career involving digital production of graphic communication, primarily for the marketing and advertising industry. It includes all types of publishing: flyers, stationery, logos, graphics, signage, editing, brochures, displays, newsletters, magazines, newspapers, books, Web sites, packaging, training materials, billboards, bus wraps, catalogs, skyscraper posters, and much more.

But we are getting ahead of ourselves. What we need to discuss as we begin is what has changed and how radical has that change been? Commercial art was formerly only involved with print production. What about the Web? How does multimedia figure into this? What has changed during the conversion from commercial art to digital publishing?

So, what's new?

The entire conceptual basis, that's what. We will talk briefly about the history of publishing in chapters 2 and 3. What we need to discuss now is where we are (as if anyone really knows). For not only have the rules changed, we are in a brand-new ball game. Certainly there are remnants of former careers floating around in this new world. However, they are all strangely realigned, combined, and synergized.

The problem is that our industry is so large and so far reaching that almost anyone can make a case for almost any scenario. In the backwaters of the country, there are shops and towns where nothing has changed. In some industries, print is no more. In between is anything you can conceive of in a larger portion than you might think. Think of what has happened to television since 1960. Back then, you were fortunate to get all four channels: ABC, CBS, NBC, and maybe PBS. The last time I heard there were nearly 2,000 different cable and satellite channels, with more being added monthly.

Here is the major difference. One person can now do it all. It is true that most of us have sense enough to get involved only with that which we can do well. It is true that larger companies are much more compartmentalized. However, there is no longer any limit, conceptually, to who does these tasks. Moreover, the projects themselves are very fluid in scope. Because the same hardware is used for it all, and the same software can do most of it, each individual project has the capability to vary wildly from the one done previously. It increasingly depends on the skills and interests of the individual doing the designing. I will ignore the abomination of design by committee, and wish it would go away (forlorn as that hope might be).

One person can now do it all.

This book, for example, is radically different from my first textbook. *Printing in a Digital World* (which came out in 1996) was a traditional textbook, at least in physical appearance. My books have evolved from a static traditionally-printed volume to an entirely new way of teaching which is commonly taught entirely online. It now includes a Web site in HTML on the enclosed CD-ROM, as well as a traditional printed book. It is all being done with the normal software tools of a publisher: some sort of word processor, Web access, InDesign, PageMaker, Quark, FreeHand, Illustrator, Photoshop, and Acrobat. Plus, most of us have Dreamweaver and/or GoLive, Fireworks and/or ImageReady, and Flash and/or LiveMotion. So part of the new paradigm is the wideness of options and the power of the choices.

However, it goes far beyond that. It all started at the beginning of the twentiethth century with the concept of a universal tool. The idea was a tool that could do anything—a calculating machine, but more.

The Digital Age

These original machines were all analog. If you think of a car's odometer, you are not far off. The big change came with what we now call the digital age, starting just after World War II. Based on a binary numbering system that uses only 0s and 1s, these new computers were only limited by the size and speed of their electronic switches. Once semiconductor chips were developed with their thousands, then millions, now billions of miniaturized switches, we entered a new era.

This is the revolution— much less boring repetitive work.

Don't misunderstand—it isn't the intelligence of computers that has changed our world. Computers are not smart. It is the ability to do stupid repetitive things very quickly, without mistakes. (The mistakes that harass you are almost entirely operator or programmer error.) The now ubiquitous pocket calculator is a clear example of this. We no longer have to waste our mental storage capacities to remember things like multiplication and division tables (we won't even mention such horrible nasties as sines, cosines, tangents, square roots, etc.). Even if we remember how to do those things, the pocket calculator is so much faster—and more accurate to boot. Of course, there is that tendency to become dependent on batteries.

We know that this freedom from repetitive tasks is not literally true. We seem to have an infinite capacity for boredom. However, this is the basis of the new paradigm. In the publishing industry, this has led to radical, fundamental change. There are no fond memories of drawing rectangles with technical pens, parallel rules, and triangles—then being forced to work for several minutes with a single-edged razor blade to clean up the corners. It was boring, drudge work.

Entire careers have been eliminated by software (which is simply a set of mathematical instructions that execute very difficult, yet precisely definable tasks). One problem with this is simple to explain (though hard for me to understand). Those boring drudge jobs that have disappeared were highly prized by those who find thinking painful. However, there are many who find the new creative freedom exhilarating.

The Business PC

The change was first noticed in the business community. It wasn't the word processor, wonderful as that was. It was amazing for secretaries to have editing ability, not to mention fonts, functional tabs, and the rest of the capabilities of the electronic typewriter. However, this did not fundamentally change anything. Secretaries still typed letters, reports, etc. They still looked like secretarial letters and reports—ugly fonts, bad spacing, no typographic controls, horrible graphics. (*Pssst! Don't tell anyone—but they still do.*)

The revolution in business was brought by the database and spreadsheet. Prior to this, business prognostication and planning was only done if an army of accountants could be afforded. Inventory was hit and miss, hand-counted, roughly known. Mass mailings were exactly that. Somehow lists were compiled, and then the list members were blindly mailed purchasing come-ons. All mass mail and financial planning was carried out by dedicated specialists with years of experience and specialized knowledge. This worked reasonably well for the giant corporations. Small businesses were left out in the cold.

The spreadsheet ended that CPA monopoly. Software enabled the small business owner to take control of her own financial destiny. She could now see trends, determine effectiveness, and guess about the future with much greater power and effectiveness. Finally, she had a way to determine where the money was going without much of it going to an expert who was hired to tell her.

The database increased the power of the new paradigm. This gave the owner much more knowledge about what was happening with inventory, who the customers really were, and which clients provided the best income with the most profit. It enabled targeted mailing to customers who really wanted to hear from the business—those loyal clients that deserved encouragement. Junk mail, or mass marketing, began to phase into communication with people who want to hear from you (as mass mailing grew too expensive). Now we talk about targeted marketing or direct mail. On the Web, it is the change from spam to opt-in marketing.

The Mac Revolution

However, all through the 1970s and early 1980s, things were still extremely crude. Secretarial work was still obvious—even to the visually illiterate. Small businesses were still clearly small. It could be seen in the crude output of WordStar and Lotus 1-2-3 on their 286s through their 9- and 24-pin dot matrix printers. I was forced to double my typesetting charges for copy provided from those 9-pin printers. It was just too difficult to read, and my typesetter's speed was cut from 110 words per minute to less than 40 words per minute. Often it was faster for me to drop what I was doing and sit next to the phototypesetting machine reading the copy to her while she set it.

We first began to see the shape of the new paradigm shortly after the Macintosh was released on us during Super Bowl 1984. The Mac was a cute, but very expensive, toy. The concepts sounded wonderful, but the output was the same as those horribly ugly DOS torture devices. Of course, we pros dismissed all of it as trash—crude, ugly, unsophisticated, and unusable in the professional publishing environment.

We hardly noticed the salvation of the Mac by PageMaker, PostScript, and the LaserWriter. Those that did (like John McWade,

What's a paradigm?

This is one of those words that has radically changed since the middle of the twentieth century. There was a man who had this great video that was shown to virtually everyone in the United States who worked at a company. It was about recognizing and coping with change.

He defined paradigm as: the normal way of doing something, the standard set of rules and procedures. He had many examples of a paradigm shift and what it does to an industry. The best probably concerns watches.

Prior to the mid-1960s, everyone knew what the paradigm of a watch was. It had incredibly intricate interactions of amazingly complicated assemblages of springs and tiny little gears mounted on jewels to reduce friction that were all made in Switzerland.

One of their scientists came up with the idea of using the vibration frequencies of a quartz crystal, but the idea was obviously unusable and not even patented. It didn't fit the watch paradigm.

They showed the idea as a curiosity at a show in Paris. It was so far outside their paradigm, that they thought it was humorous. Of course, Seiko and Texas Instruments did not agree — and put Switzerland out of the watch business. Watches entered a new paradigm without gears.

Deke McClelland, Sandee Cohen, David Blatner, Ole Kvern, and many others) were unknowns, far outside the power structures of Madison Avenue and the pressrooms of R. R. Donnelley. However, this was, and is, a real paradigm shift. It is as radical as Xerox or the quartz watch. It has brought fundamental changes to our entire industry, and is modifying all of civilization.

Desktop Publishing

Paul Brainard of Aldus, PageMaker creator, is credited with coining the term desktop publishing. His goal was to enable one person to publish from their desktop. The publishing industry treated the concept like a new video game for kids (which of course it was). But the rules had definitely changed. Up to this point, every area of publishing required a different specialist who performed tasks that were difficult and time consuming. Publishing was a labor-intensive industry.

Of course, we had already come out of the dark ages of letterpress into the light of photographic offset lithography, pasteup, phototype, and process color. However, the paradigm was the same: expensive equipment, extremely difficult handwork, and highly trained, very experienced specialists. In that earlier paradigm, as mentioned earlier, I never even interviewed prospective designers unless they could prove several years experience and had a portfolio that demonstrated they *knew the industry*. Talent was not enough—experience was essential.

In chapter 2, you will see a glimpse of the industry as it developed over the past 500 years. It became a giant whose power engulfed our civilization. It vastly increased its influence in the twentieth century with the advent of advertising and market research. There are many good reasons why the hot topic of movies in the 1950s was Madison Avenue. We became controlled by a marketing economy that was propelled by the publishing industry and its arcane, specialized knowledge. Capabilities that cannot be understood are often perceived as dangerous.

The crack in those walls was PageMaker on the Mac. Even though the original output was still very crude, the conceptual basis for desktop publishing was recognized very early by the pioneers mentioned above and many other men and women. These pioneers quickly became a movement of independence. Now anyone could publish—from the top of their desk. *Sure!* Those of you who have been trying know that this is possible, but not nearly as easy as the software marketers would like us to believe.

It was, though, a genuine shift in the basic rules of operation. By the late 1990s, the entire industry was radically different. Entire careers were gone—typesetters, hand letterers, pasteup artists, cameramen, strippers, and more. An entire industry of tool manufacturers and graphic suppliers has been wiped out—presstype, Magic Markers™, Format™ screens and rules, parallel rules, waxers, tech pens, stat cameras, and hundreds more. All of these things could now be done by a single person, sitting in front of their Mac, next to their scanner, laser printer, and inkjet color proofer.

This was, and largely remains, a Mac revolution. Only with Windows 2000 and XP are the PCs truly included in the game. Billy Gates is a marvelous marketer, and the hype has said PCs could do desktop publishing for years, but they were lying. Even Macs have only been at a truly professional level since the beginning of 1995, the PowerMac, gigabytes of RAM, and multiple-gigabyte hard drive space. Windows 95 and 98 just started to close the gap. PCs have only had font management software in the twenty-first century, for example.

Now it is possible for a single person, sitting in their converted garage, to produce publishing that is indistinguishable from the big boys on the coasts. My first textbook rocked my publisher. They had never had an author who wrote all the copy, created all the illustrations, shot all the photos, and produced the finished artwork that was sent to the printing company for production. Almost all of the problems with the final product (and there were many) were a result of their inability to deal with the new reality. I finally gave up fighting for a cover, for example. Their reason was simply, "Authors never do the cover." I didn't fit their paradigm.

The Web

At the same time, publishing was being attacked from a completely different direction. In the 1960s, the Defense department and military establishment had set up a data protocol that could use ordinary phone lines to provide communication that was basically unstoppable. The original idea was a computer network that would survive a nuclear attack. If any piece was destroyed, the rest took up the slack. The result was the Internet. The anarchy necessary for survival led to the freedom we now experience.

If possible, the original paths that were developed into the information highway were a worse joke than early DOS word processing. You thought DOS was bad—that's just because you hadn't seen UNIX. It was the haven of computer geeks—those nerds who really think that number crunching is important, those who can think in code. Of course, it is. But do you really want to talk to those people? The information superhighway was originally merely a series of well-worn paths from university to think-tank to defense lab.

One of the major benefits of a new paradigm is the fact that everyone starts in the new paradigm on equal footing. There is truly no advantage to experience because there is no experience.

There was a real reason for the well-publicized computer phobia of the seventies and eighties. The code required was gruesome. The Internet was stuck in a similar paradigm as the publishing industry. You had to learn code to do anything. It was a game for insiders and the experienced. Here the paradigm buster was Mosaic, now known as Netscape. They provided the first publicly popular tool to browse that new graphical portion of the Internet—the World Wide Web.

Navigator did to online communication what PageMaker did to publishing—it brought these capabilities into the Small Office, Home Office (SOHO) world that was emerging as a result of the new technology. What many of us wanted to do (after our downsizing or dot com failure layoff), we were now capable of doing. Even Aldus had not a clue where that desktop they were concerned with was actually located. They thought it was in a normal business office, like the paradigm said.

With a Web site, a computer, and some nerve, we could compete with the big boys on virtually even footing. In fact, many of us reaped one of the major benefits of a new paradigm—the fact that all start in the new paradigm on equal footing. Truthfully, those coming from outside the old paradigm often have an easier time adjusting in the early years of the new. Now that the old way of doing things is just memories, that early advantage has disappeared.

One person can do it all from their SOHO hideout.

Again the early efforts were crude and often annoying. Most of us, for example, quickly learned that most chat rooms are filled with teenage boys impressed with the fact that they can write f*** and get away with it. Most early Web sites were simply monuments to the designer's ego, and demonstrations of their obvious lack of design skill. However, this was a change like desktop publishing. One person can do it all from their SOHO hideout.

The advantages of the Web are rapidly emerging. *"An 800 number on steroids." "A friendly face available to your clients 24/7/365." "Your entire inventory available at the touch of a keyboard." "Communication that avoids the irritation of phone tag." "A worldwide presence from the comfort of your office (wherever that is)."*

This is still a very young technology. There are very few making any money at it (other than those who charge you to help you advertise over the Web). We have all watched the birth and death of the dot coms with fascination. The brick-and-mortar behemoths are assuming their position of power here also. The new Web giants are Barnes & Noble, KMart, and companies like that.

However, the synergistic addition of the Web to the Desktop makes SOHO much more viable. Again, the new paradigm has to do with decentralization, creative freedom, and the ability to break out of the corporate coffins. The result is fundamental change to the business world and the publishing industry.

The depersonalizing of society has grown to be too much to bear. The new paradigm offers the personal touch to the technological information age. In a society where we are forced to look far beyond our immediate environment for friends who think as we do, the new rules enable us to gather into virtual communities of support, friendship, and love. These new groupings have little to do with geographic or political boundaries. More than that, the new technologies are focused on enabling communication in the isolation of the technocracy. Of course, it is not as good as sitting and talking over a cup of coffee in front of the fireplace. However, it is certainly better than the sterile isolation of the seventies and eighties.

Multimedia & Interactivity

My students are completely focused on the joys of multimedia and computer animation. "Dude, it's awesome," or some such slangish drivel. It has become very hard to get them focused on the reality of making a living while they are seduced by the fun of the interactive virtual experience. However, at present, this is a very small area of endeavor in our day-to-day lives. Life experience and maturity will solve some of this problem.

However, there is no doubt that multimedia is growing phenomenally. Here we have not completely identified the "killer app" (that piece of software that will change us like PageMaker and Navigator). Many thought this might be Acrobat and the interactive PDF. Many think it might be Flash. Only time will tell. The key to the killer app is easy availability. Bandwidth is still killing PDF and Flash. The Web was not potent until we could all do it – cheap and easy. Desktop publishing was a joke until the hardware and software prices came into line and the workflow became predictable (from a production point of view).

At this point, multimedia is for entertainment. It can make training fun. There are many hooked on the games produced. The main thing here, like the rest of our discussion, is to recognize the new paradigm. That hasn't really happened yet. There are many exciting things being

Synergy

This is that interesting phenomenon, first talked about by Bucky Fuller, where the new whole is greater than the sum of the individual parts.

Digital publishing is the synergistic addition of desktop publishing, the Web, the cell phone, multimedia, and digital video.

The animated portion of the new digital publishing has not fully been brought into the fold yet. But it is coming quickly.

done with multimedia, but interactivity is extremely time consuming. It is a very specialized, extremely difficult field of endeavor.

However, as I write this, I realize that I could add the graphics and interactivity to this book with hardly a thought. With Acrobat, interactivity is easier than font adjustments (it certainly takes less training and knowledge). The seducing part of multimedia is animation, video, and sound. The problem is easy delivery to prospective readers/viewers/surfers.

At this point, there is little evidence that these things are cost effective outside the realm of entertainment. As much as we are influenced by movies, TV, games, and music, it is rarely an economic part of our work environment. However, as the ease of use grows, those things that help will simply be added—by you, the new graphic designers.

Plus, the world of those born after 1960 is radically new. Many of you have never seen a world with no television, or black-and-white TV—with no remote. Most cannot imagine life without cable's many choices. Many of you learn primarily from video. You've never lived in a world where almost all entertainment was on printed paper.

This is the basic of the new paradigm. All of the publishing tools, all of the communication tools, and all of the multimedia capabilities are available on my desktop as ways to help me communicate with you. The larger shops will still have specialization. But, even here we find single persons taking on entire projects. The old paradigm where I needed others to do the things I was incapable of doing for myself has become merely an expensive option needing huge budgets and lots of time.

Worldwide Fulfillment

The final difference between the new and the old is the area of influence. Over the past few days, I have had student and client inquiries from New Zealand, Alaska, Montreal, Texas, Nepal, New York, India, Virginia, St. Louis, plus several others who haven't bothered to mention their location. It no longer makes any difference. I use the same software and the same delivery method for my next door neighbor as I do for my student on the North Island of New Zealand.

I remember talking (via email) to my editor for my first book, back in 1995. She made the comment that she could communicate with me faster and more easily than she could with her colleagues two floors up, in the same building. Modern intranets have now solved that problem, of course. But the point was, and is, that she was in Albany, New York and I was in the midst of the high desert plains forty miles south of Albuquerque, New Mexico.

In this industry, where we are selling ideas and designs in a digital format, it is becoming common for the designer to be in one country, the client in another, and the actual production to be spread all over the globe. Book publishers no longer accept typed manuscripts. They want documents from word processors attached to email (although most of them will probably still accept a ZIP disk snail-mailed to them — grumbling while checking for powdery substances). The only problem for us is final delivery of physical art and proofs, but FedEx™ and its competitors have solved that. My real problem today is that I have to do an ad and hand-deliver it to the local newspaper. What a hassle! I don't have time for that kind of thing anymore. Why can't I just attach it to an email?

Companies like R. R. Donnelley, AlphaGraphics™, Sir Speedy™, Kinko's™, and many others now allow me to design anywhere and print anywhere else I need. The job tickets are all online. AlphaGraphics even built their digital production facility right next door to the FedEx hub in Memphis, Tennessee. I can place my order online and it is delivered the next morning anywhere in the country. Overseas delivery is simply a little more expensive.

Web publishing, of course, is instantly available globally. Sometimes it gets humorous. The other day two of my students sent an email to one of our nonprofit clients about a proofing schedule. The client's reply reached my computer before the carbon copy of the students' outgoing letter reached me. Such are the vagaries of the Web.

I've gotten to the place where I would rather deal with people out of state. In fact, I have eliminated all local clients (I hand them off to former students). The delivery schedules are much easier to deal with, and the communication is more reliable. At school, I have removed the answering machine in my lab in an attempt to force email communication. Phone calls (or should I say phone tag) is simply too time consuming. Things have truly changed.

Entry-level requirements

So, what is required of you as you begin this journey? Creativity will help, but it isn't essential. Drawing ability is often a plus, but it is not really needed. Artistic skills can be learned, but they are not central to the industry. More than anything, you need to be curious and have an eclectic interest in people, processes, and trivial information. You need to have a concern for good, accurate communication. You need to enjoy the production of graphics.

Beyond that, you need a basic computer literacy. You have to be able to open new documents and save them to specific, planned locations. You need to have a basic familiarity with what is available in hardware and software. You need to have some online experience—especially with email. We will review some of this in this book. Chapter 6, for example, is on file management. However, this is not the time or place to be sitting at a computer for the first time.

Current Realities

You will shortly discover that our industry is huge. Printing is the third or fourth largest manufacturing industry in the country (and probably the world). There are hundreds of thousands of jobs in the industry. However, for designers, the reality is that most of you (about 65%, according to an industry survey in 2001 by TrendWatch™) will earn some or most of your income freelancing out of your own office, from your own computer, printer, Web site, and so forth. Part of this is because we are never satisfied with our pay. Part of it is the result of our extremely low boredom threshold. Part of it is simply that creative people have need to be in control.

According to the Graphic Artists Guild in their *Handbook on Pricing and Ethical Guidelines*: entry-level designers need a solid typographic knowledge, Macintosh experience, QuarkXPress/Illustrator/Photoshop experience, and the basics of Web design. As we have already mentioned, Windows has come of age in graphics so the Mac is no longer essential (although it is still easy to prove that a Mac is much more productive).

You will discover that Quark is in serious trouble. Not only has its software been blown away by InDesign, the company itself is on a rocky road. Only time will tell if it remains dominant. It doesn't look likely at this point. Quark 5 is no big deal.

This book will give you a good entry into typography. More than that, my goal is to give you the beginnings of a feel for the industry. As my advisory committee is fond of telling me, *"We can find computer whizzes. We can find experienced print professionals. We can find excellent Web designers. We can't find people who can do all three, and that is what we need."*

The age of extreme specialization is past. As art director at a large printing company, I used to have a freelance relationship with a man (who we used regularly) who did nothing but produce air-brushed gradients. There was another who did nothing but handmade camera separations of color photographs. Another was an airbrush photo retoucher. This list of specialists could go on for a few pages. That era is gone.

The tools of digital production are amazingly powerful and extremely complex. They assume a huge amount of basic knowledge about a wide variety of subjects: typography, printing, the World Wide Web, color theory, halftone production, marketing, color separations, logo design, copyediting, graphic design, paper, advertising, printing technologies, computer operation and troubleshooting, software installation, plus much more.

What is required is good taste.

The good news is that none of this stuff is very difficult except drawing and painting. It is extremely complex, but that merely requires a bit of memory. Creativity cannot be taught. Some have it and some don't. However, it is really not needed in many cases. What is required is good taste. Good taste is developed by study, curiosity, and experience. Taste is a learned skill.

Resources to keep current.

This book (or any other) will never be enough for you to keep up with this industry. You will be studying and learning for the rest of your life. Here is a brief, limited list of resources.

Some of the best resources are Web sites. For software tutorials, tutorialhound.com is hard to beat as a starting point. Of course there are the obvious sites like adobe.com and macromedia.com. CreativePro.com is another excellent resource. MacDesignOnline is another. ZDNet has a lot of sites and publications. Just set up a search in Google or your favorite engine and start looking.

As far as print is concerned, we are talking primarily about magazines. Book production can barely keep up with the pace of change in the industry, and is primarily used, like this book, for training purposes. The best, most current, books (other than mine, of course) are found at PeachPit Press. They have absorbed (or at least distribute) all of Adobe Press and Macromedia's official books. Plus most of the best authors, Ole Kvern, Robin Williams, Sandee Cohen, David Blatner, Bruce Fraser, Lynda Weinman, and many others, publish through them.

The best magazines for industry information are mainly what are affectionately known as trade rags. This means they are mainly free to those in the industry. At present, some of the best are:

- *Publish*: Recently converted entirely to the Web industry.
- *Electronic Publishing*: Currently the best source for printing knowledge.

Where should you be by this time?

This is the introduction to your studies in digital publishing. If you are in a class, your instructor will be showing you what is expected with file management, which software and hardware is available, and so forth. Many of you will make very different choices in applications.

It is time to get yourself settled in. This would also be a good time to begin looking at the tutorials that are available to you. You will find them in your user guides, or www.tutorialhound.com is a good place to find resources online.

DISCUSSION

You should be meeting your classmates and finding out their history and goals. You will become increasingly convinced during your career in publishing that lone wolves make lousy graphic designers. Publishing is a team sport, and you might as well get started now.

Talk amongst yourselves...

- *Digital Graphics*: Serving the large-format inkjet industry.
- *PEI*: Focused on the newest in digital photography and stock imaging.
- *Computer Graphics*: For gamesters.
- *Mac Design*

There are certainly many others, dozens of others, depending on the industry portion on which you are focused. The field is in constant flux, so any list is out of date within a month or so. The point is that you need to check out these resources on a regular basis.

Knowledge Retention:

1. What is the place of multimedia in our industry?
2. What was the Web equivalent of PageMaker?
3. How is digital publishing different from commercial art?
4. Why do you think the Mac changed things so much?
5. How has the digital designer been empowered by the new paradigm of digital publishing?
6. Why don't we use the term desktop publishing?
7. List ten different products or documents commonly produced by digital publishers.

Chapter 2

Printing History & Technology

Concepts

A BRAND NEW PARADIGM

A technological history of printing

Chapter Objectives:

By giving students a clear understanding of the digital publishing industry, this chapter will enable students to:

1. describe a brief history of printing
2. list the advantages and disadvantages of offset lithography
3. list the advantages and disadvantages of electrostatic printing
4. list the advantages and disadvantages of inkjet printing
5. list the advantages and disadvantages of letterpress and its current usage

Lab Work for Chapter:

1. Complete tutorials in page layout.
2. Complete tutorials in PostScript illustration.
3. Read chapters 3, 4, and 5 for next week.

Printing has a long and colorful history.

The important thing for you to know is that you must know what technology and what press you will be printing on *before* you start designing. All technologies have different capabilities and requirements. You must be aware of them before you design something that cannot be printed at all. Or, that cannot be printed without entirely blowing your budget.

This is your responsibility!

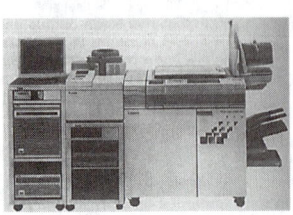

What desktop publishing became when it grew up!

Many people think that the personal computer destroyed printing as it was known prior to 1990. I would disagree with that. Plus, as mentioned, the computers were not even powerful enough to use in professional production until 1995 or later. However, the stories of printing as it was are fascinating. But most of them have little relevance to digital production. So why are we starting with history? Mainly to give you a perspective.

You know the old proverb: *Ignoring history condemns you to repeat the same mistakes made historically.* This is part of why we start here. More than that, the history of printing is one of the central factors in civilization as we know it. Until very recently, the knowledge we learned came from books. The decisions we made were often based on what we read. The joys of living are still often associated with printed matter (even if it is only a ticket stub souvenir).

Professional design requires the memory of fine printing.

From a practical design point of view, our clients and their clients base many of their feelings about a company or organization on historical printed associations. A fancy formal invitation done in bold, mechanical type is not appropriate and everyone knows it. A quality client does not use cheap paper. We'll get into this in depth later on. The point here is simply to make sure you understand the importance of historical context when using the printed word.

More than that, you cannot produce excellent designs until you know where printing came from and have a good idea of what excellence in printing looks like. What this means on a practical level is that you must begin looking at printing with a new eye of appreciation. Search out excellent printing: magazines, books, rare book sellers, and so on. **Educate your eye.**

Each type of printing has its own advantages.

While everything I just said about historical context is true, the real importance of this chapter comes with the distinctions between the different printing technologies. You will discover that the determining factor in a design element is often whether it will print or not. The determining factor for which technology is used is usually based on budget.

Every printing technology has its own requirements. Each has its own advantages and disadvantages. None are perfect. All have limitations. Your task will always be to design within those limitations. None of these different methods of printing is better or worse. They are different and each is the best choice in different circumstances. It is extremely important that you keep that in mind, but we are a little ahead of ourselves.

It all started in China, of course.

Often it seems as if virtually all the major inventions necessary to civilization came from the Far East, China in particular. This is certainly the case in printing. Their language made the idea of printing much more obvious. Instead of words being made of a certain number of characters, like our alphabet, every Chinese word is a single character. These characters were seen as art. And pages were seen as a large graphic.

An early Chinese press

It's just a low, flat table sturdy enough to handle printing pressures.

The Bettman Archives

Almost 1,500 years ago, the Chinese began carving blocks of wood into the shapes of characters. They carved an entire page at a time. Mistakes were drilled out of the wood plates, plugged and recarved. The concept of movable type was invented around the middle of the eleventh century. Robert Bringhurst (in his popular book on typography, *The Elements of Typographic Style*, Hartley & Marks, 1992) places this revelation in 1040 AD by a man named B' Sheng.

The concept of making characters a consistent size was the beginning. They were then able to assemble the characters in rows. Once they had the rows put together, all they had to do was ink them up, lay a sheet of paper on the blocks, press the paper into the ink, and peel the paper off. If they were careful not to move the blocks, many virtually identical copies could be made. Some of these character blocks were wood, most were baked clay.

However, typography like this never really caught on in China. Even in the nineteenth century, most books were still made by carving entire pages in one block of wood. However, the idea spread. It was in Korea by the thirteenth century and made it to Europe within a century or two. We'll talk about the developments in Germany in a bit.

 The idea here for the type of printing done is the rubber stamp, potato stamp, or linoleum block. The image is painted or exposed onto the surface of the block and the background is then cut or dissolved away leaving the image standing above the background. The image is inked up with a roller and pressed firmly onto the paper (or the paper is pressed onto the block with a brayer).

They had to invent ink and paper, too.

Of course, they had to have something to print on — which they also invented. This came earlier. Chinese writing was originally done with brush and ink on silk. The ink was a mixture of soot, glue, and water that was dried into sticks. The sticks were then ground into a pool of water on a fine grit stone, as needed. Modern India ink is still made from the same basic materials — except we add varnish or shellac to our glue to make the ink waterproof.

Ink was an easy concept compared to paper. We never did figure paper out in the Western world. All we had was *papyrus* and *parchment*.

Papyrus was made from reeds that were soaked, slit lengthwise, and then peeled like a long tubular onion. The pieces were dried flat. Then these long strips were glued together side by side. Not a very exciting paper stock — hard to feed through a press.

Parchment was a totally different story. It came from butchered lambs. When they were skinned, the hides were scraped smooth. Parchment was very smooth and so thin that it was translucent. Of course, it was a bit stiff, and rather expensive, too. Having to kill a lamb to make that flyer would make flyers rather rare.

The Chinese were writing on silk. It was an excellent surface to work with, but rather expensive. Then came a brilliant idea. Starting

Chinese writing

This little piece of calligraphy was done for me by a fellow student from China in my last graduate-level seminar on Chinese Art History in 1970. I asked him to write my name (I was going by Loose Man at the time). He wrote this and gently laughed. I suspect that this phrase was Chinese slang for hippy in the 1960s.

Quality compromises

The history of printing is a constant series of compromises in quality. The dominance of the bottom line is not a modern invention. Humankind has always looked for ways to do things faster and cheaper. The best way is often completely unaffordable.

Digital production, in general, is a result of this mentality. Its dominance is largely the result of economic factors. Our best efforts do not even come close to the quality of a medieval manuscript hand-lettered on parchment with illuminated initials. As gorgeous as type and color photography can be (digital or not), they are usually a poor substitute for excellence in calligraphy and traditional illustration.

with a fibrous material, such as mulberry bark or cotton, they chopped it up, threw it in a pot, and cooked it to mush (the consistency of soupy mashed potatoes). Then they rinsed it out and cooked some more, repeatedly, until they were left with just the fiber.

The genius came in how they used this gooey mess. They poured it on a screen of hand-tied bamboo splits — rather like the bamboo roll-up window shades we use, but much finer. When they shook the cooked fibers into flat sheets, the water drained through the screen, leaving a mat of interlocked fiber, much like blotter paper. The closest modern equivalent is high-grade, handmade watercolor paper or Japanese craft paper. Some of you have probably made paper something like this in a craft class using a blender.

This paper was smooth and flexible. It allowed brush strokes that flowed gracefully. The ink was absorbed into the surface, producing a rich, deep black. It may not have been quite as beautiful as writing on silk, but paper was much cheaper to produce (see sidebar). It was also stiff enough to be used for printing. Silk would not stay on the surface of the characters. It bent down around the edges.

Marco Polo

Even though Marco Polo is only a representative of the forces bringing technology from the East, his name brings understanding. Until he, those like him, and the Mongol hordes brought silk, paper, printing, gunpowder, porcelain, and spices, Europe was basically stuck in the Dark Ages. European culture was extremely parochial with little to unify it. Communication was a major problem.

The Renaissance

By the fourteenth and fifteenth centuries, Europe was in a state similar to today. New knowledge was turning everything upside down. All the old standards were being questioned and many were found flawed. It was an exciting time to be alive. The possibilities seemed endless. We could solve our problems! Mankind could perfect itself (by the way, I've got a bridge for sale).

In our industry, this is where it all began. In the mid-1400s, several people were experimenting with various printing techniques. Printing production did not exist, although the basic theory was understood. Fine art printmaking was becoming a mature art form. The concept holding everything back was availability of something to print on

The importance of paper

The 1400s were a fantastic time of intellectual excitement. Everything was coming together. The techniques for graphic reproduction had been in place for many years — in fact, many centuries. The Copts (a societal group in Egypt) had been using woodcuts to print textiles since at least the sixth century. Throughout medieval Europe, textile printing was common. Etching and engraving techniques were well known by metal workers throughout Europe.

Frank and Dorothy Getlein, in their analysis of fine art printmaking titled *The Bite of the Print*, Bramhall House, 1963, were convinced that everything needed for printing had been in place for some time. The factor that tipped the scales was the arrival of cheap, plentiful paper. The Arabs had paper in the eighth century. The Moors brought it to Spain by the twelfth. Paper mills were up and running, first in Italy, then in Germany by 1400. By the time Gutenberg was experimenting, paper was common and reasonably priced. This availability of paper naturally triggered the desire to use it.

The revelation needed was *movable type*. The concept required standard-sized letters that could be assembled and reassembled at will. By cutting letters into the surface of dies or stamps, molds could be punched. Then the individual letters could be cast. It became possible to assemble words. With enough letters, pages could be built — books could be printed.

Johann Gutenberg

Johann Gutenberg usually gets the credit for inventing the process instead of the Chinese. Actually, there were many men experimenting with the process. For our purposes, it is enough to understand the times and the invention, as we've already covered. What Johann developed was a method for making metal type which was much smoother than wood or clay and lasted a lot longer. He also developed a casting system that enabled relatively rapid production of type letters and characters. The main thing Johann contributed was a functioning production process.

The turning point was Gutenberg's 42-line Bible, the Latin Vulgate. In other words, he printed a Bible that used 42 rows of words per page. This came to about 5,500 letters, punctuation marks, and spaces per page. Two pages were printed at a time. Part of his success was because of the press he developed out of an old wine press. Michael Barnard argues that maybe he should have left well enough alone, but he readily admits that the communication resulting from the press was probably better with books than with wine.

Even this first book required many letters. While they were printing a pair of pages, they would assemble the next two. As you can see, the number of letters needed was well into five figures. With two persons working twelve-hour days, it took more than three years to produce a couple hundred copies. It was hardly printing as we know it. But it was enough to fundamentally change society. You may remember that the almost unanimous choice for the most important person or invention of the past millennium during the Y2K hype was Gutenberg or printing. Johann got it going.

The revolution began.

Before Gutenberg, a wealthy noble with a huge library might have twenty or so books. All books were hand-copied (by monks). When you ordered one, the wait was measured in years. Because they were hand-drawn, they were gorgeous. But, they were the equivalent of fine art originals. As a result, they were very rare.

By 1500 (forty years), libraries grew to thousands of volumes, as print shops sprang up throughout Europe. Popular fiction was invented, the first widely distributed romance novels. In the mid-sixteenth century, Bibles made it into the hands of ordinary people in their own language. This triggered the disruption of the Reformation. The Greek and Roman classics, in addition to the rest of the books being printed, enabled libraries which enabled universities. It became possible for an ordinary person to study masters long dead or a long way away. Reading became the central skill of education. Science became possible as people could now easily share ideas across continents.

The platen press: speed was the problem.

Gutenberg's press was revolutionary but slow. As mentioned, the original design was a modified wine press. By the early 1500s, a standardized form had been developed. The letters were assembled on a tray and locked in place. This tray was mounted on the press under a large pressure plate or platen. The type was evenly inked across the surface of the letters with a very stiff ink applied with a roller. A sheet of clean paper was carefully laid on the type. Once the ink and paper were positioned, the platen was screwed down with a strong pull on a lever into firm contact. The type had to be all the same height and the pressure even. With good, tight contact, a virtually perfect copy of the type was made.

When the press was opened, the sheet was carefully peeled off and hung on a line to dry. The form was re-inked, the new sheet of paper was placed in position and rolled under the platen, the lever was pulled, and so on. Working hard, two persons could make around 300 impressions a day. The design was so solid that Ben Franklin used virtually the same press 300 years later.

The major problems were speed and size. It takes 175 pounds of pressure per square inch to transfer ink to paper. The pressure needed to print an 11"×14" sheet is more than 13 tons. The presses had to be huge. I have an engraving of a platen press that printed a very large sheet of paper. It was two stories high and used horses to pull the lever.

Both the press and the composition of type needed a great deal of help. The press designs came first. Major advances were made by automating the paper feeding and eliminating the pull-and-release lever action.

This type of printing is called relief printing. The modern term is letterpress. Currently letterpress is mainly used for numbering, die cutting, foil stamping, embossing, scoring, and so on. Any technique that requires paper to be physically stamped is done on a letterpress machine.

The best graphics in history

At the same time Gutenberg was developing what we now call letterpress, fine art printmaking exploded. Some the best printmakers that ever lived were active in the hundred years following the 42-line Bible: Schongauer, Mantegna, Dürer, Holbein, Bruegel, and countless more. The next century brought us the master illustrator, Rembrandt van Rijn. If you have never seen his etchings, shame on you.

Many of us in the graphic industry are not impressed with modern, slick, process color printing. Works from the sixteenth and seventeenth century make it obvious why. There is a major difference between richness and slickness. The prints and printing from this time represent some of the finest ever produced. Digital process color

Platen press

A replica of the platen press used by Benjamin Franklin is very similar to Gutenberg's original.

Courtesy of the Smithsonian Institution. Photo No. 17539-B

LETTERPRESS
RELIEF PRINTING
The background is cut or etched into the plate surface, leaving a raised image. The image is then inked and printed.

An old engraving

This print of Lincoln's home is from *Century* magazine, sometime in 1887 (the way it is bound in my collected copies, I can't tell the date).

I had to use grayscale to reproduce the lines. They are too fine to scan accurately or print as well as they did with our currently available tools. I only have a 600 dpi Epson scanner and that is not enough.

perfection cannot attain the quality of those sheets — printed on 100% rag, handmade paper, delicately printed with the finest, hand-ground pigments, using hand-assembled plates. Only through extreme effort can we even come close. It is no longer cost-effective and many of the materials no longer exist.

Woodcuts — relief printing

Designs carved in wood were the easiest to add to printing. Many of you have made linoleum cuts in public school art classes. This is the remnant of an extremely skilled art form. Dürer's woodcuts, for example, raised symbolic storytelling to new heights.

The process is simple in concept. You take a block of wood, paint a picture on it, and carve away anything that is not part of the picture. This leaves the image raised or in relief. This is the same technology that Gutenberg used. As you can see, it became sophisticated.

The only difficulty with using woodcuts in printing concerned the size and shape of the wood block used. It had to be type high. In other words, it had to be the same thickness as the type slugs being used. The block also had to be rectilinear, in order to be locked into place with the type slugs. These were simple mechanical problems that were quickly solved. The eventual type height standard came to be 0.918 inches thick in America.

By the nineteenth century, an entire graphic career had developed. Paintings and other artwork were converted to relief blocks with incredibly detailed carvings. These were used as illustrations in the books being produced. It was still a laborious process. Picture books as we know them did not exist, but these woodcut illustrations are still extremely beautiful. The house on the other page was printed using letterpress.

The techniques were developed until the illustrations were being engraved, with exquisite detail, into laminated end-grain wood blocks. For durability, engravings were also done in metal. Copper engravings started replacing woodcuts as early as 1550. This type of engraving was also printed as a relief block. The delicacy of detail is almost unreproducible with current equipment.

Engraving and etching — gravure printing

Engraving and etching were also used for another method of printing. Known as *intaglio*, this technique was the major source of printmaking for fine art. It was not used by the printing industry until much later, due to the difficulty of using type with this technique.

Intaglio is the reverse of relief printing. Here the concept is to cut the image into the block or sheet of metal. The entire plate is thoroughly inked up with a roller. Then the plate is polished, leaving the ink in the recessed areas (where the image was cut or etched). The plate is then covered with slightly dampened paper and run through a press that squeezes the paper into the image to pick up the ink.

There were many advantages to this technique, especially with etching. For the first time, it was possible to reproduce original drawings. Because etchings were drawn directly on a coated plate, with the image etched through the scratches in the coating, hand-drawn lines could be reproduced in quantity. Rembrandt's etchings demonstrate a fluidity of line and a mastery of line control that has never been matched.

Intaglio was responsible for the development of the cylinder press. The pressures needed to press the paper into the recessed image are much greater than those needed for relief printing. The line of pressure created by a cylinder enabled a press to be designed that would print intaglio

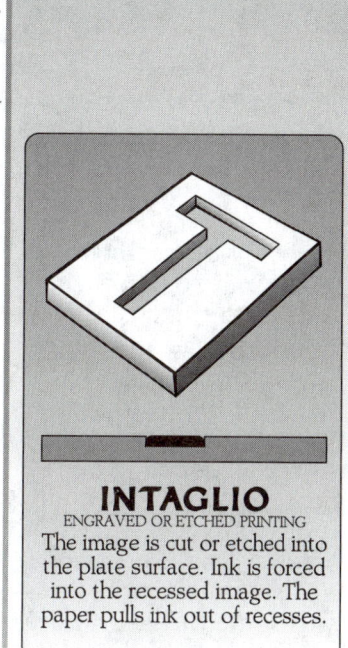

INTAGLIO
ENGRAVED OR ETCHED PRINTING
The image is cut or etched into the plate surface. Ink is forced into the recessed image. The paper pulls ink out of recesses.

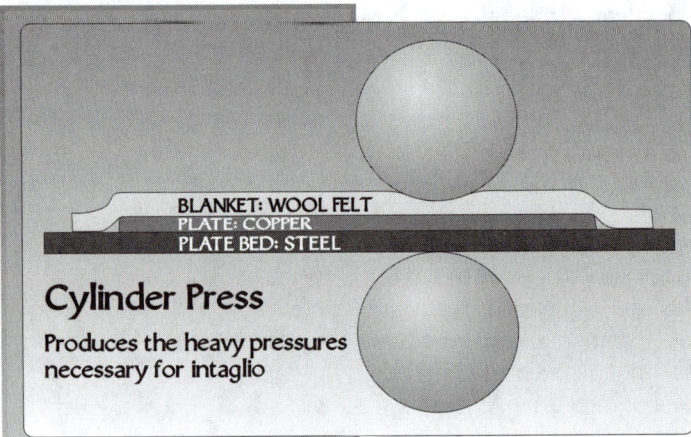

BLANKET: WOOL FELT
PLATE: COPPER
PLATE BED: STEEL

Cylinder Press

Produces the heavy pressures necessary for intaglio

Litho's invention

The invention of lithography supposedly happened this way. Al was working on his ideas. His wife hollered into the shop, "Hey, honey, when you go to the store, pick up some bread and butter." Having no pen handy, Al just scribbled a note on one of the stones with a grease pencil. Shortly after that, he accidentally knocked over his glass of water on that same stone. While blotting up the mess with some of his printing paper, he noticed that he was getting an excellent copy of the note onto the blotting paper.

I believe the story.

plates. The plate was mounted on a bed that was rolled between opposing cylinders held together by strong springs. The dampened paper was laid on the plate. The plate and paper were protected by a thick felt blanket. These presses are still used for fine art etching today — still cranked by hand.

Intaglio is a very high-quality technique. Careful inking allowed very fine lines and dots to be printed. Lines this fine would break or flatten when pounded by a platen press in relief printing. As a result, intaglio was definitely preferred for illustrations. The obvious problem was that the type was all printed in relief. So, intaglio illustrations had to be bound in as separate pages or glued onto pages left blank (termed tipping in an image).

No movable type in intaglio.

Relief printing allowed for movable type. Because the letter shape was raised from the background, the seams between the slugs did not print. In the case of intaglio, these seams would hold ink and print. There was no practical way to use intaglio for anything other than illustration until the nineteenth century. At that time, photographically produced gravure plates became possible.

Stone writing — lithographic printing

In the late 1790s, a man in Austria named Alois Senefelder was experimenting with an extremely fine-grained limestone from a local quarry. His idea was to draw on the stone with etching ground (a mixture of asphaltum and wax) and then etch the background. This created a slight relief that could be printed. It was much cheaper than copper.

This idea was no big deal, however. With the advance to rotary presses in a few short years, his technique would have become merely an interesting sidebar. Limestone makes lousy cylinders (though they tried). However, after further experiments, Senefelder discovered that coating the background with a water solution of gum arabic made it repel ink. In fact, he learned that keeping the gum damp enabled him to ink up the stone with no etched relief at all.

On a perfectly flat stone (with the image created with a greasy ink and the background protected with gum), he could dampen the stone and ink it up by simply running an ink roller over the entire surface. A sheet of paper laid on the inked stone picked up a virtually perfect image with very little pressure. In fact, I remember printing a very good image in college by merely rubbing the paper onto the stone with the heel of my hand. Senefelder called this process lithography, from the Greek for stone writing.

Reversed images

There was a major problem with relief, intaglio, and lithography. Because the paper was laid on the plate and peeled off, the image was reversed. This meant that any handwriting had to be written in reverse. Leonardo Da Vinci's writings could be printed (though apparently they never were). I suspect he developed the skill from etching. Normal persons' handwriting could not be used. Several artists did develop the technique, but it was always clumsy at best.

The industrial revolution

Printing developed a rich history of beautiful work. Relief printing, or letterpress, on quality paper has a richness of surface that is hard to describe. The image is slightly debossed, or recessed, into the surface of the paper. Intaglio flattens the paper leaving an embossed, or raised, image. Wood-pulp paper did not exist, the sheets used were of a quality that can hardly be found anymore except in hand-made, 100% cotton, watercolor paper.

The problem was the slowness. Type was composed by hand. Illustrations were carved by hand. Sheets were printed very carefully, but very slowly. In addition, the quantity of illustrations was very limited. Printing was totally dominated by type.

Cylinder presses for letterpress

The cylinder press solved some of the press problems with letterpress. By rolling a cylinder over the plate, several things were accomplished. Because a cylinder's contact and pressure point is in a narrow strip, sufficient pressure to transfer the ink could be reached more easily. Cylinders could also be rolled much faster than a pressure plate could be lowered, squeezing the paper onto the ink. Adding inking rollers just after the impression cylinder increased the speed by automatically re-inking the plate. Production reached thousands of pages a day.

At these speeds, weekly newspapers became possible. Newspapers became the community lifeline, vital to community life, although

The gray limestone

The original quarry where Al found this exceedingly fine-grain limestone was the only source. The quarry was used up long ago. Every time an image is made on a stone, it has to be ground off to allow for a new image. As a result, these stones get thinner and thinner, eventually breaking into smaller pieces.

Almost all the stones are gone. The largest collection of these stones is probably the Tamarind Institute in Albuquerque where stone lithography for fine art is still produced. They do printing runs for artists, and artists come to directly image the stones themselves.

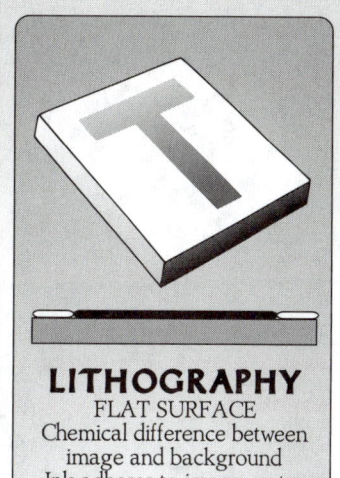

LITHOGRAPHY
FLAT SURFACE
Chemical difference between image and background
Ink adheres to image, water repells ink on background

production was still very small by our standards. A few pages, weekly, was a major effort for several people. They began appearing in the early seventeenth century. In America this happened about 1622.

Rotary presses

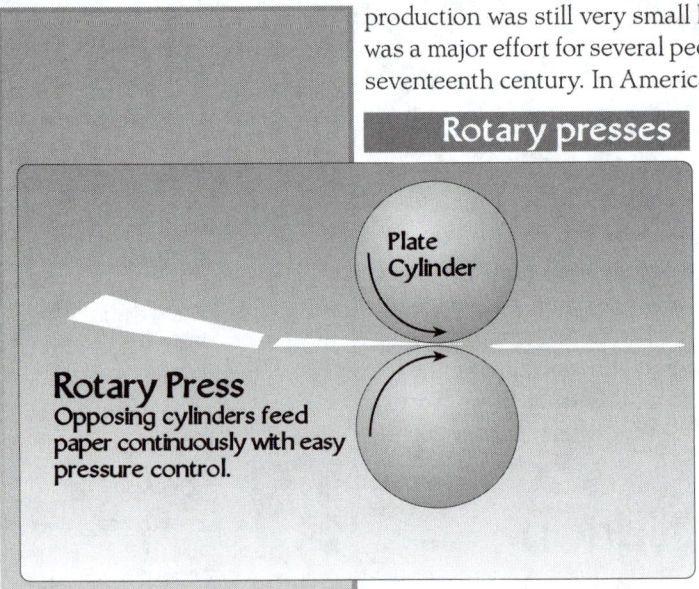

Rotary Press
Opposing cylinders feed paper continuously with easy pressure control.

Plate Cylinder

By the middle of the nineteenth century, the next major advance in press theory was discovered. By using two cylinders rotating in opposite directions, it became possible to feed paper continuously. Cylinder presses only rotated through less than one rotation. Then they had to be reversed back to the starting point. This wasted half the time. With a rotary press, 12,000 impressions an hour (instead of a couple thousand a day) became commonplace. The limiting factors now were type assembly and paper quantity. Paper was the first to be solved.

Paper production

Up to this time paper had been entirely cotton fiber. This is still the best kind of paper. The cotton paper used for intaglio in the fifteenth century is still clean, white, and bright. However, the rag pickers just couldn't keep up. Even chlorine bleach only helped a little. There were two inventions about this time that brought us to the next step.

First, in France in 1802, the Fourdriniér brothers introduced the continuous paper machine. Their idea was to change the screens upon which the fiber was shaken out to dry, and expanding them a little. If they could just make a screen, like a long conveyor belt, that would enable the water to drip out before the fiber reached the end of the screen, paper could be made continuously. It worked.

Secondly, machines were made that could grind up trees to produce a much larger source of fiber. The resulting paper machines were huge. The current incarnations in the northern woods (where the trees are) can cost a billion dollars, have screens that can be thirty yards wide or more, that are a quarter to a half-mile long, with sets of drying rollers at the end that make the entire machine up to a mile long or more. The output is a huge roll of paper the width of the machine and several feet in diameter called a *log*. These paper logs could be slit into narrower rolls or sheeted into paper usable in sheet-fed presses.

Web presses

It soon became obvious that rotary presses eliminated the need for feeding a single sheet at a time. A web press feeds rolls of paper, in a continuous stream, through the press. The paper is not sheeted until after it is printed. This concept allowed daily papers to emerge. By the end of the Civil War, with speeds passing fifty thousand impressions an hour, huge presses could even print morning and evening newspapers. Magazines and books became much more available because the reduced costs and greater speeds significantly increased printing quantity.

Setting type

The major bottleneck was rarely the presses. In fact, presses dominated production, and they still do. It takes many people to keep one press fed with work. In the latter part of the nineteenth century, the major problem was type — all those tiny little slugs of lead cast into letters. A major focus of this book is typography. For now, though, we are only concerned with the practical production problems.

The technique was tedious at best. Letters were assembled, word by word, line by line. The labor was called composing and the words were composed a line at a time on a *composing stick*. The composed type was then locked firmly in place in a clamping frame (which became

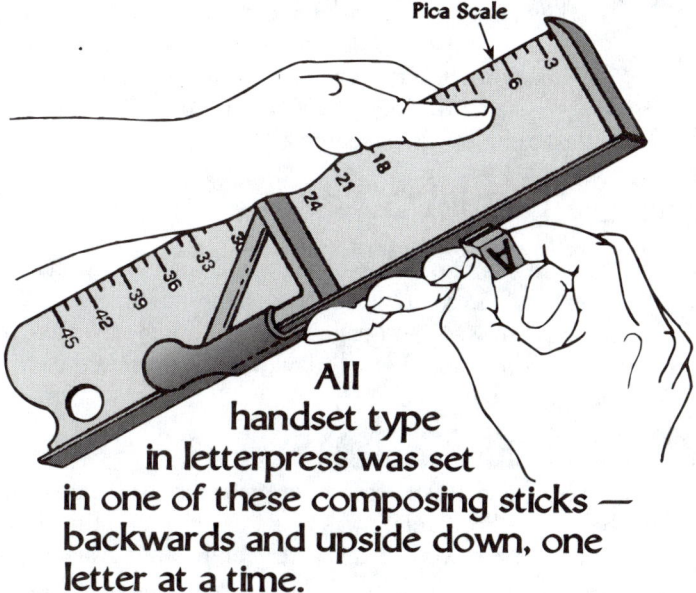

Pica Scale

All handset type in letterpress was set in one of these composing sticks — backwards and upside down, one letter at a time.

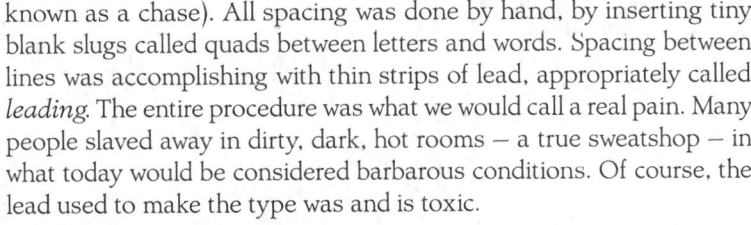

known as a chase). All spacing was done by hand, by inserting tiny blank slugs called quads between letters and words. Spacing between lines was accomplishing with thin strips of lead, appropriately called *leading.* The entire procedure was what we would call a real pain. Many people slaved away in dirty, dark, hot rooms — a true sweatshop — in what today would be considered barbarous conditions. Of course, the lead used to make the type was and is toxic.

Automatic typesetting

The major breakthrough came in 1886 with the demonstration of the first truly automatic typesetting machine at the *New York Tribune*. Invented by Ottmar Mergenthaler, the Linotype has been called one of the ten greatest inventions in the history of humankind. It was the enabling technology for modern periodical literature such as magazines, newspapers, and so on. For a marketing economy like ours, the absence of typesetting equipment would be crippling. It could be argued that a marketing economy is nothing without printing.

The concept is simple. Rather than assembling letters individually, the Linotype assembled molds or dies, called a matrix or matrices. The type was then cast line by line. The matrix was dropped into position by hitting a key on a board that looked similar to our keyboards today. The matrices were recycled. Teams of typesetters made it possible to cast up to 150 characters a minute. It still took many typesetters to keep up with one press, but a great stride had been made. Print production soared again.

The Linotype machine

This has been called one of the top ten inventions of all time — up there with the wheel.

Courtesy of
Mergenthaler Linotype Company

Photography

As we have mentioned in passing, up to this time in the mid-1900s, there basically were no illustrations as we know them. What illustrations were seen were hand-engraved. Photography changed that forever. It took a while, but photography eventually made the entire page a graphic illustration.

Photography's appeal

Photographic processes were discovered early in the nineteenth century. The name photography was coined in 1836 and the French released details of a process called Daguerreotype on 19 August 1839. The hype made clear the attraction of the process: *"requires no knowl-*

edge of drawing..." and that *"anyone may succeed...and perform as well as the author of the invention."*

Basically, photography uses a machine to cause the real world to draw its own image. It's a simplistic definition, to be sure, but it helps to underscore the difference between rendering by hand and photographic reproduction. It takes incredible skill and experience to illustrate realistically. Photographic illustration is a photomechanical process that can be done completely by machine. The skill becomes one of selection rather than creation. There are many people with good taste who have no illustration skills. As a result, mechanical means of graphic production are extremely popular.

 Digitally, we see the same thing in the difference between PostScript illustration software, like FreeHand and Illustrator, and image manipulation software, as we see in Photoshop. Photoshop is much more common and much more popular emotionally. It takes quite a bit of work to realize the advantages of FreeHand and Illustrator. Most are not willing to make the effort. The ease of manipulating scans as opposed to drawing your images is very compelling.

It doesn't matter how photography works, at this point. Digital imaging is making photography a historical fact and a fine art technique again. However, between then and now, photography totally revolutionized our industry. No longer needed were entire careers like engraving, die cutting, letterpress, and so forth. It took 150 years to effect the change completely, but the change was total.

The halftone

The first major photographic change was the halftone. The problem is that presses can only print ink or toner or nothing. The solution was developed in the 1880s by breaking the image into variable sized dots. Tiny dots left a lot of paper showing and produced the highlights. Large overlapping dots produced the shadow areas.

The first major use of halftones was found in *Century* magazine in 1886 or 1887. They looked terrible next to the engravings. But the attraction of photographic production was so strong that halftones were common by 1900. Photographic halftones greatly helped the developing advertising industry.

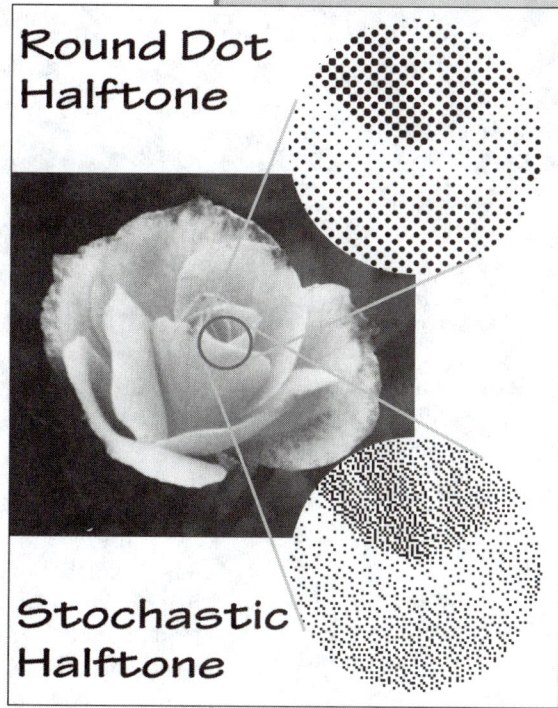

Round Dot Halftone

Stochastic Halftone

Photographic offset lithography

Lithography developed slowly until three key discoveries were made. One, images could be made on thin, flexible metal plates. Two, these images could be produced with a photographic emulsion. When this emulsion was exposed to light and developed, the image became ink-receptive and the background washed away, leaving the bare metal. The background could then be coated with gum.

The blanket: offset printing

The third discovery solved the remaining problem. That was the reversed images. This could be solved photographically, but proofing was laborious at best. In 1904, the final discovery was perfected to ensure the domination of lithography during the latter half of the century. Ira Rubel, an American, announced offset lithography on paper. By printing the plate first to a rubber blanket cylinder and then to the paper, several gains were made. The reversed image problem was solved. More importantly, the paper damage from all the water was greatly lessened and the blanket allowed lithographic printing on textured paper.

Lithography using photographically imaged plates, offset onto a blanket using rotary presses, took over the printing industry in the last half of the twentieth century. By the 1980s, letterpress was reduced to a trade service for offset. When die cutting, foil stamping, embossing, or other services that required hard physical stamping action were needed, many smaller shops sent that work to the few remaining letterpress operations.

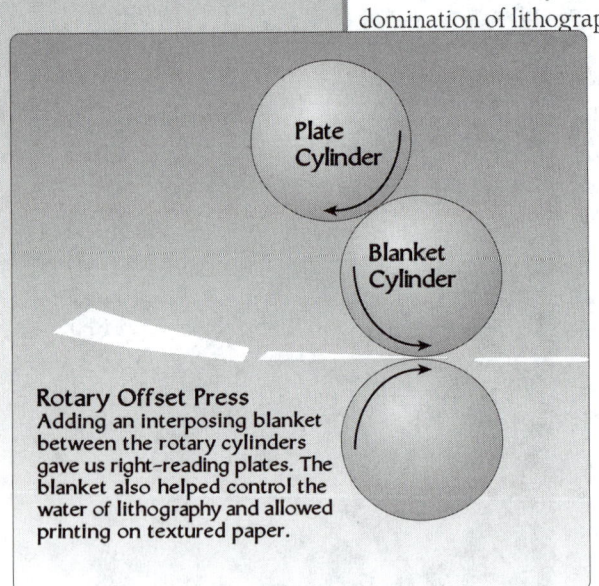

Rotary Offset Press
Adding an interposing blanket between the rotary cylinders gave us right-reading plates. The blanket also helped control the water of lithography and allowed printing on textured paper.

Plate Cylinder

Blanket Cylinder

By 1990, virtually all type was set photographically, and all artwork was photomechanical. All plates were produced photographically. Roger Black called it "the age of the X-Acto™ knife." This age started about 1960 or a little earlier. Photographic pieces were cut, moved, arranged, trimmed, and cleaned up with technical pens and #11 craft knives. Some of the old codgers back East still used single-edged razor blades, but they were merely tolerated. Pasteup ruled the industry.

By this time, offset lithography had 80% of the industry or more. Printing kept getting more and more complex. Designers became the bane of printers as they asked for more and more difficulty. Commonly, designs were impossible to print — or nearly so. It was a time of highly skilled, specialist artisans. Printing was manufactured by finely tuned teams. In some places, it still is, but only by the larger companies. Digital production is as revolutionary now as photography was then.

Screen and sign printers

Screen and sign printers normally use a totally different technology — screen printing. This technology is relatively modern, coming out of the experiments during the Depression. The Getleins date this to 1938 in the W.P.A. art projects. Screen printing uses stencils adhering to support screens for the production of signs, T-shirts and clothing, uniforms, and many different types of product manufacturing. Screen printing inks are opaque (unlike lithography) and screens are flexible. This allows screen printers to print on metal sheets, wooden plaques, clothing, bottles, control panels, dashboards, and the like. The opaque inks work well on colored surfaces.

Screen printing is relatively slow. Often each piece is hand-printed with a squeegee and screen. For extremely short-run, multiple-color work, screen printing is often the only economical method. This is especially true if the printing is to be done on materials that cannot be fed through a printing press, such as wood boards, shirts, and so on.

Sign printers used to be sign painters. Signs were hand-painted by one of the last holdouts of hand-crafted tradition. Digital production has largely wiped them out with computerized vinyl cutters. The same software that produces graphics for "normal printing" can be used to produce files that operate plotters with knives that cut type and illustrations out of pressure sensitive vinyl. In some areas, this technology was first used to produce the sponsor graphics on race cars. It quickly took over the sign industry. Not only was the type quality much better, but it was also much cheaper.

It turned out that vinyl-cutter technology could easily be used to cut screen stencils also. It was natural for screen printers to absorb the sign jobs left by traditional sign painters as they went out of business.

Xerography

In the mid-1930s, Chester Carlson came up with a method that he called dry writing. As was fashionable, he used Greek, so the name of his process became known as xerography. The process uses the

SCREEN PRINT
Image is cut or exposed into a stencil. The stencil is adhered to a support screen. Ink is squeegeed through the openings onto paper or whatever.

Vinyl sign cutting

One of the most common digital printing technologies used today is the vinyl sign cutters. You do have to be careful. Many of the old sign painters bought a proprietary system for a company like Gerber. These are really not very satisfactory for graphic designers.

What you are looking for is a company that can use the EPS you bring in from FreeHand, Illustrator, or CorelDraw. This is one of the small industry segments so PC-driven that it actually prefers CorelDraw files (although any EPS will usually do).

Chester's new paradigm

Mr. Carlson's invention is often used to show what can happen to entrenched sets of rules and ways of doing things. Evidently, no one in the photographic industry could see the advantages of dry writing. What we now call electrostatic printing has now almost put many of the traditional photographic companies out of business. Virtually all of the digital production presses are electrostatic. What is rapidly disappearing (largely due to environmental considerations) is photography. Chester's invention will likely be the dominant printing technology of the early twenty-first century.

ELECTROSTATIC
FLAT SURFACE
Electrical difference between image and background. Toner adheres to positively charged image, negative charge repels toner on background.

photoconductivity of a selenium-coated plate. This material has the property of holding an electrical charge in darkness, but losing the charge when exposed to light.

According to legend, he took the process to Kodak to see if they were interested. They escorted him to the door. His crude process would never come close to being competition to film and photography, So Chester went out and started Xerox.

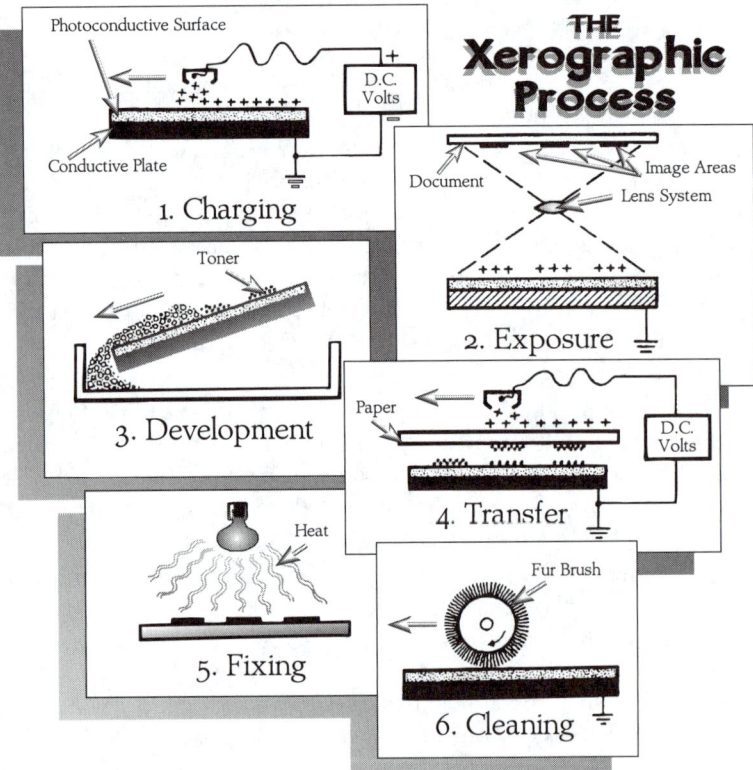

THE Xerographic Process

1. Charging
2. Exposure
3. Development
4. Transfer
5. Fixing
6. Cleaning

By now, there are countless methods of exposing the plate. Plates have been made into drums or continuous belts. Exposure comes from strobes, LED light sources, lasers, and the like. The process remains basically the same — the charge left on the plate in the image areas is used to attract toner. Toner is currently made of very finely ground plastic with embedded metal. The toner sticks to the image only. Paper is then passed close to the drum surface.

A stronger electrical charge of the same type (negative or positive) is given to the paper. This causes the toner to transfer from the plate to the paper. The toner adheres to or is "fixed" to the paper by heat. A lamp or a hot roller melts the toner, which is absorbed into the paper. Finally, the plate, drum, or belt is thoroughly cleaned by a blade, brush, vacuum head, or a combination of these tools. This is necessary to allow a new image to be created and to recover unused toner.

This is the basis of the entire copier industry. Xerography forms the foundation of the modern quick-print segment of our industry. The same technology, conceptually, is now called electrostatic or electro-photographic. Its dominance in quick print was given a huge boost in the mid-1980s with the PostScript LaserWriter.

The laser printer

Laser printers use the same technology, electrostatic, with one major difference. Instead of using lens systems to capture camera-ready originals, laser printers use a laser to precisely expose individual tiny dots on the drum. This laser can be controlled by a computer. With the advent of lasers, we finally had a computer printer that could output high-quality prints. Almost all new digital presses are electrostatic, or some variant. Most use lasers.

Inkjet printers

Recent years have seen the inkjet printer evolve from printing address labels on magazines as they fly by at 30,000 or more per hour to a quality alternative that is preferable in some areas. Scitex brought out an inkjet printer that will print 250 feet per minute, 18 inches wide — that's 15,000 11×17s per hour. That is true press speed. But, then, it is only 144 dpi. A couple of new ones are up to 240 dpi.

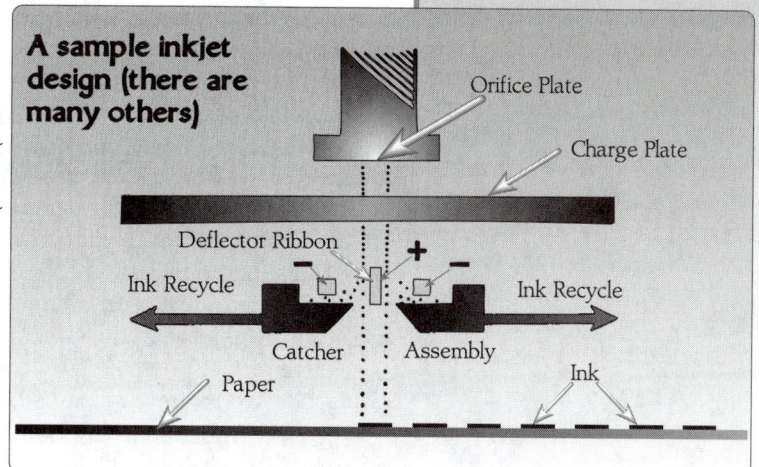

A sample inkjet design (there are many others)

Orifice Plate

Charge Plate

Deflector Ribbon

Ink Recycle

Ink Recycle

Catcher

Assembly

Paper

Ink

Basic inkjet technology involves spraying drops of ink or dye directly onto the paper. There are many varieties: continuous drop, drop-on-demand, bubble jet, and piezoelectric using single jets or multiple jets. This technology is rapidly growing in sophistication.

Though it was originally greatly restricted in resolution, it has now reached acceptable levels. It is still held to a maximum of 400 dpi or so. Piezoelectric technology allows manufacturers like Epson and Roland to control very tiny dots to give the equivalent of 1440 dpi.

Inkjet papers

Papers made for use in inkjets are one of the modern anomalies of printing. The coatings used to make them are some sort of plastic. Be careful never to use print-ers' glossy paper in inkjets (or laser printers). As we will discuss in chapter 14, these printers' papers are coated with clay which will clog your print heads or ruin your toner cartridges faster than you can stop yourself from printing.

Glossy paper for inkjets is too expensive and only available in small sizes. So it is never used for professional production printing unless you are actually using an inkjet for production work. This is rarely done except for large format work. The consumables cost is simply too high. Inkjets are the most expensive way to print.

Because the ink has to be liquid enough to form the tiny droplets, it tends to bleed into the paper. Special coated sheets or ultrasmooth paper give exceptional results with rich, saturated color.

More and more these tiny ink jets (that cost less than $100 for process color) are used for cheap proofs. The problem with them is the expense of consumables. I have an Epson 1520 that prints up to 13 x 19 inches at a 720 dpi equivalent. I thought it was a great deal at less than $700. However, photo-grade paper at that size is $2-$3 per sheet. And a $60 set of ink cartridges with full coverage on the sheet, gives me 16 prints. That is over $6 per proof. My tabloid-extra (13 x 19) laser printer, on the other hand, costs less than 50¢ per print. Of course, the printer cost $5,000. As you can see, technology decisions are not minor.

Fine art inkjets

One of the top-end inkjets, the Iris inkjet, is very high quality. It is commonly used for contract proofs in process color workflows. In addition, there are many studios which are using this for fine art prints. The process is often called giclée (pronounced zhe-clay). These fine art prints are often printed directly on watercolor paper with pigmented inks. The result cannot be easily discerned from traditional fine art. The prints cost about $150 each, but they are commonly being used for limited editions. The original giclée inkjet from Iris is no longer in production so this portion of the industry is in great flux, again.

Large and grand format inkjets

One of the areas that was never serviced well with traditional printing was posters and billboards. Posters worked fine unless you wanted less than a thousand copies. At that point they became too expensive because the setup charges never were less than $600-$700. Large format inkjets can do a remarkable job at about $60 per print. These large format prints are also commonly mounted of translucent plastic and used for trade show displays.

Grand format inkjets print from 8 feet wide on up onto rolls of substrate — usually plastic. If you have been curious about what appears to be large prints stretched around frames on the billboards you pass, these are them. They are also used for truck- and bus-wraps. When printed on mylar screen (like coarse window screen) they can be stitched together into prints that are thirty yards wide and a hundred yards tall. These are commonly hung on the sides of tall buildings in our larger cities. The bus-wraps have become very common. When producing for them, just call the printer and ask them what size and resolution they want. They are just normal digital documents.

Dryography

During the 1990s a new technology appeared. Most of us call it waterless offset. It uses plates with multiple coatings. The top coating repels ink. The undercoating is ink-receptive. The best examples of this technology use lasers to burn tiny holes in the top coating. These dots can be much smaller than any other technology allows. Many of the platesetters use a random dot structure that allows for six-color process or hi-fi color.

The image quality of these presses is exceptional. The cost of prints is quite a bit higher than normal commercial printing. As a result this technology is still a small niche in our industry. It remains to be seen how far it goes.

Flexography

This is a variant of letterpress on flexible plates. Originally the plates were rubber and the process was very crude. Because the plates stretch on the press, a special computer program is needed to compensate. Circles are made into ovals so they will be circles after they stretch, for example. Again, talk to them first, before you start designing.

Regardless, this has become a major force in our industry. Flexography has taken over the corrugated box industry. Plus it prints a huge percentage of our packaging, like soda cans and such. The only other alternatives for irregularly shaped objects are labels or screen printing. Flexography is much cheaper and the new presses can even do process color. I have seen figures suggesting that flexography is now 16% of the industry. I do have a hard time believing that, though.

In the midst of change

Our modern printing industry is a vastly different place than it was a mere decade ago. Even in 1994, the Graphic Arts Technical Foundation (commonly known as GATF) listed 17 different industry segments:

- Bank stationers
- Book printing
- Business forms printing
- Catalog and directory printing
- Commercial printing
- Corrugated box printing
- Financial/legal printing
- Flexible packaging printing

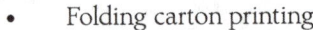

- Folding carton printing
- Greeting card printing
- In-plant printing
- Label printing
- Metal decorating
- Newspaper printing
- Periodical printing
- Quick printing
- Yearbook printing

Even though GATF claimed to have the latest knowledge of the industry, by the time it published its book, the digital revolution was breaking up those neat categorizations. Even those categories that still remain are being radically altered by the paradigm shift.

Forms printing is almost gone, and most of bank and legal work is now printed in triplicate directly from the computers in offices all over the country. As you can see, there is no mention of large and grand format printing, because it did not exist. Digital printing is not mentioned, because there were no digital presses yet. This was only seven years ago. We have seen a lot of change.

The democratization of the craft guild

Traditional printing was a guild populated by highly skilled specialists. These wizards practiced a difficult and obscure craft in a rarefied atmosphere outside the understanding of normal folk. Unless a person was part of the industry, communication with the industry was very difficult. A different language was spoken: picas and points, leading, gripper, guides, negs, seps, lineart, stats, Matchprints, halftones, linescreen, and so on. If you didn't speak the language, you couldn't join the club. Many companies that produced a lot of printed matter hired one special person who could communicate with "those printers."

Beginning in the mid-1980s, this world was shaken to its roots. The problem, of course, was that the industry did not recognize the new paradigm. All of a sudden, all those things that could only be done in darkrooms or under special lighting by highly skilled masters became accessible to designers. Now it is available to the general public.

Predictably, the result was chaos. The industry passed off the new phenomenon as a joke or a passing phase of new entertainment. The new breed assumed that the old masters were archaic relics with no relevance to modern desktop publishing.

For a while, desktop publishing was ignored by the industry. Everyone lamented the passing of huge industry segments, but the ostrich approach was ubiquitous: *"If we ignore it, it will go away."* Of course, it didn't. The economic pressures were too great.

An economy based on marketing cannot ignore a technology that requires yearly upgrades. Digital production is a marketer's dream come true. Every year, upgrades are released that are genuinely needed. Once a person enters the digital arena, she is at the mercy of marketing pressures that are unprecedented in the history of humankind.

The printing industry is huge.

By now, you should be getting a glimpse of how large the printing industry really is. Virtually every segment of modern society requires printed materials. The advertising industry claims that every individual sees thousands of ads every day. Many of these ads are printed. Just thinking of printed advertisements brings huge industries to mind: magazines, newspapers, product labels, and packaging pop up instantly. A modern discount bookstore has selections that boggle the mind in sheer quantity as well as quality — but that stock covers only a very small portion of the printing industry.

Think of lawyers with their legal forms and documents; bankers with their numerous forms and disclaimers; and small businesses with letterheads, business cards, envelopes, purchase orders, invoices, shipping receipts. Add to that all the printed matter that floods your mailbox every day, plus posters, bumper stickers, CD packaging and labels, textbooks, software documentation — the list is endless and still growing.

In the period from 1994 to 2000, printing went from the fifth largest manufacturing industry to the third largest (just under automobiles and appliances). It is still the fourth largest. Plus this size does not include all of the materials printed on the desktop. Here is a recent list from Frank Romano in *Electronic Publishing* magazine in March 2001. The Federal statistics making us fourth largest only include the third from the last category: prepress, printing, and finishing.

Creative services for print	$100,000,000,000.00
Print-related consumables	$140,000,000,000.00
Print and related equipment and software	$22,800,000,000.00
Equipment maintenance and service	$2,700,000,000.00
Print buying, administration, and consulting	$1,400,000,000.00

Prepress, printing, and finishing	$534,000,000,000.00
Distribution and storage of printed products	$191,000,000,000.00
Print-related training and education	$5,100,000,000.00
Total: not counting new sources	**$997,000,000,000.00**

Frank also saw $200 billion in new revenue streams in e-commerce and variable data printing. That brought the grand total to nearly $1.2 trillion per year. That's more than for many small countries!

GATF stated in 1994 that out of the 20 major manufacturing groups in the U.S. Government's Standard Industry Classification system, we are first in the number of establishments with more than 60,000. But even this does not cover the huge number of printing centers made up of a secretary, a word processor, and a laser printer. Designers, with all of our software and several desktop printers and proofers, are also not included in these statistics.

Blue collar to white — a whole new image

As large as it is, our industry has made a paradigm shift. By leaving the guild of wizards behind, much else has changed also. Printing used to be a dirty industry filled with ink and dust and huge piles of paper scraps. Before the modern era, with OSHA, EPA, and industry safety standards, it was very dangerous.

Printing companies used chemicals that not only stunk, but also ate skin. They were filled with tremendous mechanical devices that commonly ate fingers, if not whole hands. There was no sense wearing decent clothing. It could get ruined in a day and often was. It was commonly said that *"printing gets into your blood"*, and that was literally true. The hands of a pressman could be recognized at a glance by the uninitiated — ink-stained and callused. Back then there were no presswomen. The entire industry had the reputation of being hard drinkers with girlie calendars plastered on the walls. Printing was perceived as hard work done in sweatshops by uneducated mechanics. It was seen as a process that was close to magic.

Digital production is an entirely new ball game. It takes place in carpeted, air-conditioned offices with windows. There are pictures on the walls. Most of the participants are educated, often college graduates. Printing is no longer a craft handed down by apprenticeship. It is a technological skill learned from books, videos, and specialized training, practiced at computer terminals, and no longer bound to any location. Even in the traditional segments of the industry, all that is left are the presses and bindery equipment. The concepts are still handed down, but the equipment is radically different. Even presses have changed dramatically as digital production has entered the mainstream.

The tremendous variety

As mentioned earlier, there are more than 60,000 printing establishments employing more than 1.5 million people — without even considering office production. These range from one-person home offices with a press in a converted garage to multibillion-dollar corporations. The industry is dominated by small firms employing from one to twenty-five people. A two- or three-person shop can easily generate several hundred thousand dollars worth of printing a year. A company with 25 employees can produce several million dollars worth of business. The industry as a whole is well into 13 figures (trillions of dollars a year) with the largest printers grossing many billions a year.

Normal printers:
seen by the public

There are four subcategories in this group:

- Quickprinters
- Digital printers
- Commercial printers
- Screen and sign printers

What these four have in common is direct contact with the general public. Even here, commercial printers often remain relatively invisible. These four types are the printers most people think of when looking to meet their own printing needs. If they need *quality printing*, they look for a commercial printer. If they are motivated primarily by price and quick turnaround, they seek out a quick printer or digital printer (which are often called copyshops).

It could be argued that screen printers do not fit here, but they are not perceived that way by the public. Quick printers, digital printers, and screen/sign printers often have reasonably close ties simply because of the constant referrals back and forth of their walk-in customers. Often customers walk into an offset shop looking for 10 or 20 bumper stickers or a dozen signs or whatever. They are usually sent over to the local screen printer — although, increasingly, they are sent to a digital shop with a vinyl sign cutter or laminated large-format inkjet.

Expensive printing

The public perception of printing is that it is far too complicated and far too expensive. The inexperienced have no idea how difficult the process is. They have no concept of the equipment expenses necessary. What those of us who have been in the industry for a long time perceive as a drastic lowering in quality is often seen as a move toward sanity by the purchasing public.

Quickprinters

Quickprinters and commercial printers used to share a common technology — offset lithography. Quickprinters handled the low-quality, fast-turnaround clients. The original ads in the late 1960s and early 1970s often revolved around, *"Come in, have a cup of coffee, and take your printing home with you."* They were built on a new technology — *photo-direct plates*. These plates were made of paper or plastic. They were produced directly from the original camera-ready copy on special copy cameras called platemakers.

Because these plates stretched and could only be crudely lined up on the press, multicolor work was almost out of the question in the beginning. In addition, because all photos and artwork had to be on the original pasteup, only very coarse reproduction techniques could be used. Platemakers usually had cheap optical systems, and the tight focus necessary to copy fine lines was just not available until digital production arrived recently.

Quickprinters were considered a joke by many traditional commercial printers. As a result, they quickly took over huge segments of the printing market almost totally unhindered. They were offering a service many people really wanted. Most people were not going to pay $100 or more for 100 copies that took a week to print when the neighborhood quick printer could do comparable work for less than $5 in less than 10 minutes.

Quick printers worked on much higher profit margins by severely limiting their output to a few standard ink colors on a few standard sizes of a few brands of paper. The other enabling technology was the offset duplicator. Duplicators eliminated much of the mechanical perfection and minute adjustments found in printing presses in favor of ease of operation and speed of turnaround. A photo-direct plate could be shot and hung on a duplicator in less than 5 minutes for less than $3. Since duplicators ran at 6,000 to 9,000 impressions an hour, a thousand black-on-white letterheads could be produced easily in 15 minutes.

The copier invasion

The electrostatic copier created havoc in the printing industry. Based on Chester's new printing method, a large percentage of printers initially saw it as little threat. These copiers were very crude, but able to make a single copy for a few pennies. In the beginning they were restricted to black toner, but now they can print in process color or any of a number of colored toners. At first, they could not do halftones, at all. Now they print marvelous photos.

Before very long, industry giants like Xerox, Kodak, Canon, and many others brought out printing-quality copiers. Soon there were printing-quality color copiers. Originally, these had the same limitations as early quick print, but they rapidly grew to be very sophisticated. Copiers added in-line bindery capabilities like collating and stitching. In many ways, they produced better quality than the duplicators: larger and denser solids, more consistent color, and very small setup costs. At this point, the better digital color presses produce output that is virtually indistinguishable from traditional offset.

Again, because these so-called photocopies were only economically viable for short runs, printers ignored them. As a result, quickprinters utilizing copiers grew like weeds, and were set up to be the first to capitalize on digital production. Much of the new technology is the logical descendent of the copier. They print better, faster, and larger, but the concepts are the same.

The first digital printers

Desktop publishing was made possible by four factors in 1984 and 1985: Apple's Macintosh, Aldus PageMaker, Adobe PostScript, and the Apple LaserWriter PostScript printer. Ah — the light dawns as you realize that laser printers use the same technology as copiers — electrostatic printing. Originally, laser printers were too coarse, but soon they were producing output that surpassed quickprint quality. At present, quickprinters can be totally digital. There are a few holdouts who use the old technology, but they are being forced into the digital arena by economic pressures.

The old duplicators are rapidly being replaced by small presses using digitally produced plates to produce the spot color work that is still unavailable on copiers. Tabloid extra, black and white, 1200 dpi laser printers can output excellent plastic plates with excellent 100-line halftones in place for a couple of dollars or less. The quality is far better than the old vacuum frame platemakers. The new digital platesetters output plastic plates very quickly that are very high in quality.

Since plain-paper copiers and high-resolution laser printers have become common office equipment, quick printers have had to add design and color capabilities to stay in business. Copyshops converted to digital printers like Kinko's™ have become major forces in our industry. In reality they have become digital printing companies. Even in spot color, some digital duplicators have added up to fourteen standard colors at 7,200 copies per hour. It may not have the variety of custom-mixed spot color, but most customers aren't aware of the differences.

Commercial printers

You are not far wrong if you assume that commercial printers are commonly kin to dinosaurs. The ostrich approach mentioned earlier has caused many companies to die and others simply to fossilize. But commercial printing is not dead. Many commercial printing operations are growing faster than they ever have. In fact, this is where much of the excitement is – digitally. The thriving printers are focusing on the new and exciting quality advances. Many have added digital presses for short-run and variable data printing.

Commercial printing is not dead!

Commercial printers are the top of the heap in printing in terms of quality, versatility, and price. This is custom manufacturing at its best. Every run is custom product, produced to exacting standards, under tight deadlines, with uncommon teamwork. In larger traditional industry segments, we find huge printing giants specializing in very limited markets. In commercial printing, versatility is the key and quality is the byword. In a single day, an average commercial printer might produce full-color rack brochures, two-color business cards, a three-color poster, product sheets, greeting cards, some letterheads, a newsletter or two, flyers, booklets, fine art reproductions, calendars, catalogs, programs, or virtually anything else you can think of – all to a quality that most people consider perfection.

Typographic errors, color variability, pieces out of square, or similar problems often result in customer rejection and reprints at the printer's expense. Printing clients demand and receive a level of perfection that is difficult to comprehend outside the industry. On a printed piece with literally thousands of elements, one misspelled word causes total rejection of the job. All of this is done at great speed under ridiculous deadlines. The level of craftsmanship is superb.

Why would anyone in their right mind even bother to try? It has often been argued that no printer is in her right mind – by definition – but we'll ignore that attitude. The real reason is the sense of satisfaction over a difficult job done well. Printers are in the business of meeting client needs. Producing a gorgeous printed piece that not only meets the client's needs but greatly surpasses her expectations is a feeling that cannot be explained. It must be experienced. Be careful – it can be addictive! It gets in your blood. Many designers are surprised at how strong the attraction is from finely printed product.

Big iron and high tech

Commercial printers have done all of this with an incredible array of equipment. Huge, multicolor presses costing millions of dollars are the norm. A medium size press (5-color 40"; printing 26" x 40" sheets of paper) is around 12 feet wide, 12 feet high, 40 feet long, and weighs in at around 60 tons. Full-color (hereafter correctly called process color) printing requires tolerances of a couple thousandths of an inch. Skilled prepress person-

nel assemble photographic negatives to a perfection obtained with 12x magnifying glasses (called loupes). Imagesetters and platesetters can easily cost hundreds of thousands of dollars. It is euphemistically called a capital-intensive industry (meaning the machines cost a lot!).

Largely because of equipment costs, many commercial printers have been hesitant to convert to digital production, but the benefits cannot be ignored. In addition, over 95% of all artwork for printing is produced on a computer. Now, some companies even charge extra for artwork produced traditionally. Many have eliminated their process cameras and platemakers. They have no way to convert traditional mechanical artwork into negative form, unless they have a copydot scanner. The result is go digital or perish.

Top-end digital printing

Because of the quality requirements of commercial printing, digital production was not even possible until the mid-1990s. Personal computers did not have the necessary computing power until then and digital printers (called imagesetters) could not reliably process all the data. Most of those problems have been solved, however.

At this point, a majority of commercial printers use digital production from design to final film (even plates are increasingly produced with platesetters). There are still many holding on to the old technology, but as equipment is replaced, it is being replaced with the latest digital gear. Some of the new presses (often called DI presses) hang blank plates that are imaged on the press with lasers.

Press size

When we installed our first 5-color, 40" press (at the last commercial printer I worked for), it was a major event. First of all, it cost a million dollars. Second, we had to tear a huge hole in the floor slab and replace it with three-foot-thick, reinforced concrete that contained a well where the press operators could go under the machine for service and repairs. Third, we had to install 400-amp service on a new pole outside to handle the electricity necessary for the infrared dryers.

It took a week just to move it into the building and assemble it. And this is considered an average press, on the small side. It looked much like the Miller seen above. That palette full of paper, on the floor, has 26"x40" cover stock on it.

Normal summary

Of the 60,000 establishments mentioned earlier, probably 50,000 to 55,000 fall under these four categories. Your neighborhood printer is probably a quickprint shop or one of the new digital shops like Kinko's™; your local printer is probably a commercial printer. Screen printers are not quite as common, but they are readily available. Except for rare cases, all of your printing needs can be met by these skilled people. Your career will probably center in these establishments. They vary widely in size, equipment, attitude, and clientele. You can almost certainly find an excellent place to work that matches your personality.

THESE HAVE CHANGED ALSO

Traditional industry segments

Printers in traditional industry segments cater to specific industries that produce huge amounts of printing. In most cases, the concept of custom manufacturing is almost gone. For example, let's look at one that demonstrates the specialization clearly — business cards. Very early in my career, I received this advice: *"The most economical way to deal with business card customers is to hand them a $50 bill and tell them to go down the street to your competitor."* It was not told to me as a joke.

The labor required to produce custom business cards means that you must charge $100 a color for 500 cards or you lose money. There are several companies who have capitalized on this fact by providing business cards as a trade service to printers for approximately $20 per 1,000. They do this by limiting color and paper choices and printing either hundreds of designs at a time or by printing on precut paper that is slitted rather than trimmed on a paper cutter. They make very good money and provide a real service to commercial and quick printers.

Most traditional segments use the same concept. Usually they are built on specialized technology. Often this technology is simply a web press as opposed to a sheetfed press. Web presses print on continuous rolls of paper rather than feeding individual sheets of paper through the press.

Web presses allow for several major savings. First, they are faster. Second, they can print on thinner and therefore cheaper paper. Third, they can often print both sides at the same time, often in process color. In addition, many web presses can do all of the finishing in-line. This means that they can produce finished product that is labeled, folded, collated, bound, trimmed, wrapped, sorted into ZIP codes, and palletized. The labor savings alone are considerable.

Web technology is the basis of the following segments:

- Book publishing
- Newspapers
- Periodicals
- Catalogs and directories

Several other segments are built on technologies that produce packaging. Some have to feed very thick paper like corrugated boxes and folding cartons. Some have to print on unusual surfaces like flexible packaging and metal decorating. Some require specialized die cutting, like label manufacturing. Check printing requires very powerful numbering capabilities. Still others have artistic considerations with extremely complex production, like the enormous greeting card industry. All of these have gone digital to some extent. Most use at least digital artwork. Some of the web segments have gone completely digital.

What these portions of the industry have in common is a specialized labor force. Even though the principles are the same, the production methodology is very different. People working in newspapers, for example, have a very different set of rules. Daily deadlines are the most obvious difference; but printing on newsprint causes many others. Newsprint and newspaper presses require much coarser reproduction techniques because of the blotter-like characteristics of the paper and the speed at which the presses must run. Magazines, in contrast, require printing that almost matches top-end commercial printing. Both newspaper and magazine production are virtually totally digital, from design through plating, but they use far different criteria.

The training in this book is geared toward producing digital documents for quickprint, digital printers, and commercial printers. However, you can supply art to any of these traditional segments. Just remember, these portions of our industry have specialized needs. Before you start designing, contact them for specifications. CD production, for example, usually uses process color for the covers and two-color screen printing for the CD itself.

The newcomers

There are several blossoming industry segments that have no counterpart in traditional printing. Digital production is the enabling technology for them. There will certainly be others. This portion of the industry also includes many traditional segments that have been taken over. Vinyl sign cutting is but one example.

Let's look at five that have emerged so far:

- Service bureaus
- Short-run color
- On-demand printing
- CD production
- Variable data production

There will almost certainly be others. New color and multimedia capabilities allow options that have not even been recognized yet. For example, book publishing is likely to radically change. Maybe it will be e-books. Some books will go to on-demand, some to multimedia, some on the Web, and who knows what else?

Service bureaus

Service bureaus rose almost like a phoenix from the ashes of defunct typesetting and prepress houses. Until desktop publishing, type could only be produced by highly specialized operators on highly specialized equipment. Early digital type appeared extremely crude to the professional community. This is no longer true and all of the former typesetting professionals have had to find other work. Traditional type houses are no more.

The same is rapidly happening to prepress houses. These were companies that provided top-end stripping capabilities to the quick printers and smaller commercial printers. Virtually everything they did is now the normal output of professional-quality publishing programs on personal computers.

As these highly skilled people looked around for survival possibilities, the imagesetter appeared. An imagesetter is a high-resolution printer that outputs film instead of paper. They were, and usually still are, necessary for professional-quality artwork. The platesetter, which outputs plates instead of film, is normally found at printing companies. Service bureau imagesetters, however, are commonly used by designers to control the quality of their output. It also allows designers to use a wide variety of printers who have not digitized yet.

The skills of typographers and separators uniquely enabled them to become the experts in imagesetter operation. They had the finely honed skills necessary to enable them to help digital designers. These designers are mostly newcomers to printing and often are totally ignorant of our history, techniques, language, and technical requirements. Imagesetters are far too expensive to be owned by normal designers. They are normally $50,000 to $500,000.

Service bureaus filled a much needed niche. Although they are rapidly fading away as imagesetters are moving in-house to the printing companies or being replaced by platesetters, they will be around for a long time. However, they will be much less common, and certainly not so necessary, as the digital design portion of our industry becomes printing-literate. Many service bureaus have become digital printers in the following categories, simply to stay alive.

Short-run color

This brand-new capability, short-run color, is basically process color quickprint. It has been enabled by digital presses. Process color used to be the dividing line between normal and top-end commercial printing. The technical requirements were very demanding, the equipment was very expensive, and the labor costs were very high due to the skill levels needed. This has all changed. Color has been made available to everyone, with some limitations.

Digital presses

This now antique digital press made by Indigo is sheet-fed, six-color, and costs about $500,000.

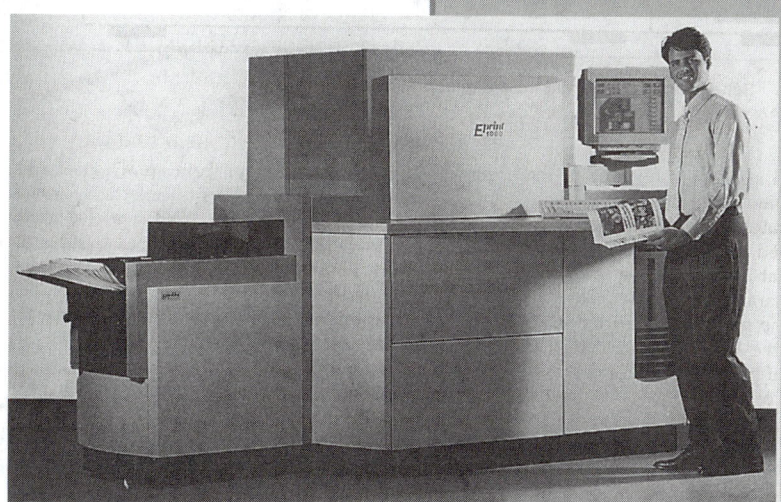

Digital process color basically means using a very fancy printer on your computer. Digital presses range from process color laser printers to top-end digital presses costing $500,000 or more. There are also traditional presses that are hung with blank plates that are laser imaged directly on the press. The result is process printing that is very economical, with turnaround times of a day or less. Entirely new products, like baseball cards for Little League teams, have become possible.

Most prognosticators expect this to be one of the fastest growing segments of the printing industry for years to come. This may be true, but much of this growth may be in the on-demand segment covered next. However, one thing is certain. With almost all black-ink printing being taken care of by copiers and laser printers, short-run color will be increasingly in demand. The industry predictions of digital color prints for pennies will greatly accelerate this process. Instead of having pieces typeset to avoid the typewriter look, people are having pieces printed in color to avoid the laser printer look.

In addition, process color is so easy on a computer monitor that designers are often not satisfied with less. In *Publishing with Photoshop*, we discuss at length the difficulties of dealing with a design population working in full color with no knowledge of printing. For now, simply understand that process color is growing like crazy, and it will grow even faster.

On-demand printing

On-demand printing is yet another brand-new capability enabled by digital production. By coupling a powerful computer to a digital press with in-line bindery ability, it is possible to produce custom books. We are not talking about short-run publishing here. We are looking at a customer who asks for chapters 1-6, 9-11, 14 and 27 with this foreword and those illustrations — and wants 25 copies. On-demand printing can do this at close to the current cost of a traditional book.

On-demand books is also radically changing the boutique book publishing markets. Many of these books are self-published, by the author. With no distribution channels, many of these books only sell a couple hundred copies. Now the books can be stored digitally and printed as sold.

Variable data production

Additionally, there is the prospect of blending data with templates to print customized mailings for an entire list of clients. Variable data has not become commonplace yet. But the capabilities are amazing. A million pieces, all personalized, is now more than a theoretical possibility. We are not simply discussing personalized phone bills. We are looking at custom brochures based on data gathered by telephone operators containing only the information asked for.

The possibilities are enormous. Professors can have textbooks custom-tailored to their curricula. Catalog publishers can produce custom catalogs for specific demographics and even very small targeted groups. In the near future, you may call a large retailer like Sears, Lands' End, or Spiegel and have a catalog sent to you that contains only the products you are looking for in the sizes you wear.

The ultimate in on-demand printing may come with print configured, script assembled, vector-based Web downloads. At that point it may become viable to go to a Web site and have a custom brochure or catalog ready to download in full color and high resolution. At this point the only limitation is bandwidth. Bandwidth problems will probably be eliminated by satellite delivery in the near future.

CD-ROM/multimedia

This area of design is still looking for that killer product. The economic pressures are tremendous, however. CDs that can be produced for a couple of dollars may contain several full-color catalogs, amazingly realistic games, or stock photography. With CD-RW now standard on all Macs and most PCs, a single person with a personal computer can output a CD containing almost any digital content.

An industry in flux

In general, now is a time of great opportunity in publishing. Our industry is growing rapidly, especially when including the Web. New technologies mean new possibilities and new economies. The word is go digital or die, as mentioned. For many this has not been pleasant. For those of us involved, it is very exciting.

Welcome to an industry on the move!

Where should you be by this time?

By now you should be heavily involved in tutorial entries into the software you will be using. Tutorials for PageMaker, QuarkX-Press, InDesign, FreeHand, Illustrator, Photoshop, or Acrobat are appropriate.

Also, bear in mind that many of the miniskills on the CD-ROM that comes with this book are really tutorials that are hopefully a little more entertaining than the normal fare.

DISCUSSION

You should be talking about excellence in print and Web, sharing excellent Web links, bringing samples to class that you have found, and so on. What you are involved in is the training of your eye. You will have to work at it a little. However, if you are truly a designer, you have probably been doing this all your life anyway. Focus on looking for excellence in print, for now.

Talk amongst yourselves...

Knowledge retention

1. What took Europe so long to print books?

2. Why was intaglio virtually unusable for book printing until photography was discovered?

3. How did the Linotype change printing and where was it first used for what type of publication?

4. What is the major time saving with a rotary press?

5. What are three major reasons why quickprint grew so large?

6. What happened to the traditional image of the printing industry and printing presses?

7. Describe the conceptual importance of on-demand printing.

Chapter 3

The Digital Revolution & Online World

Concepts

1. Quickprint

2. Commercial printing

3. Service bureau

4. On-demand

5. Variable data

6. Bandwidth

7. Gamma

PRINT PLUS WEB

Current printing setups plus the synergistic addition of the World Wide Web

Chapter Objectives:

By giving students a clear understanding of the digital publishing industry, this chapter will enable students to:

1. describe how the Web fits with printing
2. explain why traditional printing is disappearing
3. explain how the Web is friendly
4. discuss current printing setups

Lab Work for Chapter:

1. Complete tutorials.
2. Begin miniskills.
3. Read chapters 4, 5, and 6 for next week.

Print versus Web:

As you can see, the quality differences are extreme.

This really is a revolution!

The paradigm shift still has many confounded. With digital publishing, our industry is no longer tied to the manufacturing section of town. Desktop digital presses are available. At this point, a printing establishment could rent the corner office or simply set up behind partitions in any office. I have printed projects in the digital presses in my classrooms while lecturing. The entire operation would be simply hooked up with Ethernet or something even faster.

The days of a secretary completing a new price list and then hitting Command/Control P, 1500, then Return/Enter are here. These 1,500 copies can be printed at 6,000 to 10,000 copies per hour. So, in 15 minutes, those price lists are ready for distribution!

This is the key to understanding the new printing paradigm. For most uses, the new technology is more than good enough for the vast majority of customers. With color prints currently limited to about 2,500 per hour, 12×18 inches, duplex, at about $.50 each in materials, traditional printers still do not see them as a real threat. After all, traditional presses can do 13,000 to 50,000 copies per hour at prices approaching a few cents each — assuming that the run length is long enough.

Cost-effectiveness of digital printing

Many traditional printing companies just blow off digital printing with a quick, *"They are only cost-effective for run lengths of less than 1,000 copies."* In 2002, that is almost true. However, DRUPA 2000 had speakers claiming that the cost of full-bleed, duplex, tabloid color would be down to the current cost of black and white before 2010 — maybe 2005. At that price, traditional printing is almost gone. Even in 1996 run lengths of 2,000 or less comprised nearly 50% of the printing market. That percentage has gone quite a bit higher, as far as I can tell.

Traditional printing has major setup expenses.

One of the major differences with digital presses is the fact that setup charges are virtually eliminated. Traditional printing required camera shots, negs, flats, rubylith, and so on. For example, we used phenomenal amounts of masking sheets, tape, and X-Acto blades. All of this is gone. With it has gone much of the labor.

For traditional work, the setup charges (not counting printing) are about $50 per color for small presses, and $150-$200 per color for large presses. Yes, these prices are very generalized. No, I am not looking for arguments. What I want you to understand is that these setup charges are the same if you print one copy or if you print 150,000 copies. And that you have to pay for these setup charges whether you print anything or not. If you find a mistake in a plate, you have to redo all of the setup.

At this point, traditional printing usually uses 20×24 to 24×36 negatives (or somewhere in that area) to eliminate a lot of the film assembly. But the negs are still $25 to $100 for each side and for each color (depending on the size) and the plates imaged from those negatives cost almost the same. Many shops are still arranging 12×20 negs onto the larger flats before plating. In this case you still have to pay an imposition charge.

At the last traditional shop I worked at (a commercial printer), we charged the same for any job under 2,000 sheets. The setup charges made the paper charges and printing time negligible. If the negs and plates cost $50 to $150 per side per color (depending on the press size), the $5 to $25 for paper is not really a part of the equation.

Small amortized costs for digital

Digital printing has minimal setup charges. It is commonly $5 to $25 to load the files on the computer and preflight them. Many shops just include this cost in the per print figure. This is why you often pay quite a bit more for less than 100 copies. Other than that, every print costs the same.

As a result, digital printing makes most of its saving in the first few hundred prints. Instead of everything under 1,000 copies being the same cost, with process color from a digital printer we have $0.75 for one copy, $7.50 for 10, $75 for 100, $750 for 1,000, and so on. Of course, many of us are still paying $2.00 per copy or more. But that price will be dropping rapidly.

If we eliminate color (and well over half of all printing is black and white), we have costs $5 or less for loading the files and then $.02 to $.04 for one copy, $.20 to $.40 for 10 copies, $2 to $4 for 100, $20 to $40 for 1,000, and so on.

Traditional printing spreads the startup charges thin enough to become less expensive than digital at somewhere between 1000 and 2,000 copies. By 2,500 to 5,000 impressions, offset is clearly cheaper. Of course that's at present rates. Process color digital presses are getting into the $0.25 per copy range for consumables. A Riso digital mimeo-

Preflight

This is a process developed for and by printing companies and service bureaus that enables them to open submitted documented to see if they will "fly". Nearly two-thirds or all digital documents submitted for printing are unprintable as received.

graph can print at a penny per copy per color or less. Offset cannot compete against that. There are still quality differences, but even they are being dealt with rapidly.

Most printing is short-run.

The statistics show an interesting figure. Frank Romano's *Pocket Guide to Digital Prepress*, Delmar, 1996, has a table showing run lengths as a percent of the market. He is using it to show that long-run printing will be around for quite a while. He talks about 56 percent of commercial, book, and office printing falling in the 500 to 5,000 impression category. This is true.

What he failed to note is that over 86 percent of the market is fewer than 10,000 impressions. If it is true that digital presses will become the equipment of choice for everything up to 10,000 impressions, our industry is in for more shock. (Many owners are quite depressed.)

What is ignored in a lot of the speculation is the fact that many, if not most, people outside of our industry consider printing to be very overpriced. There seems to be a perception by the general public that printing is ridiculously expensive. Very few people outside our industry know how difficult quality offset lithography is. Even fewer know how complicated digital publishing is. Many people are more than willing to take the slight quality reduction of some digital technology for the return of more reasonable printing bills. The pressure to lower prices is incredible and will not be going away.

Also forgotten is that fact that people can now buy four-color process printing for what they formerly paid for two-color work. It is true that this only applies to short-run projects. But, even if we cut things off at 5,000 or less, we are still taking about almost 73 percent of the market. Digital is getting much larger than anyone thought sooner than they imagined.

Press operator crisis

One of the largest factors in the digital revolution is the growing shortage of qualified press operators for traditional printing. There is an increasing tendency toward button pushers who fix machines by part swapping. Computerized control is nice, but it breeds operators who cannot function without it. Press operators have to be able to fix their presses. In many cases, they will need to find someone to cut new parts out of tool steel. The death knell for the current press technology may well be the lack of operators. (And the corresponding lack of small independent machine shops.)

As mentioned, the Tamarind Institute in Albuquerque is one of the last remaining stone lithography printers. Many of the reasons why it is almost the last are technological, to be sure. However, they are also psychological. It simply takes too much human effort to get an excellent print. It is easy to see the same thing happening to traditional printing. No one wants to get their fingers dirty.

We were forced to completely shut down our traditional commercial printing degree at my school. This was not due to lack of demand, for the printing industry in New Mexico is still clamoring for more trained help. It was shut down because we could not get any students to take the courses. In fact, I have trouble getting students to take my courses (until they start seriously thinking about employment). Most of them are infatuated by computer animation and multimedia.

No one wants to get their fingers dirty.

In the not-too-distant future, commercial printing as we knew it in the 1970s and 1980s will be little more viable than letterpress is now. Its niche will be a bit larger. It all depends on whether they can find the personnel. What happens when the hourly rate for an excellent four-color press operator goes over the $100 per hour rate — if there are any applicants for the position the company needs to fill? Obviously, the price of traditional printing will skyrocket unless the labor problem can be solved, and soon.

Reasons for digital dominance

There are many factors pushing digital publishing to dominance. They are almost unavoidable. This will make twenty-first century printing and publishing a totally different market. Among the goads toward change are:

- The economic pressures to cut costs far below the present levels, to get a competitive edge, continue to increase. This trend shows no signs of slowing down.
- The ability to get what is perceived as free information off the Web is increasing these pressures. A lot of printing is now being done in our homes and offices from downloads or off Web sites. Very small print centers are becoming common.
- A global economy requires global marketing. The Web has increased that tendency. Global delivery of published materials is simple with global printing networks where the same artwork is sent to printers all over the world via email.

- Our current nonmechanical labor force wants and truly needs fully automated equipment. Repair personnel who can make a needed part are long gone. Most traditional printing will migrate overseas. If you have the time, it is already much cheaper to get coffee table books printed in Korea, Hong Kong, or Singapore.

- The pressure to get things done in ever-shorter periods of time to keep ahead of the rush of society is only going to increase. Only digital production is fast enough to even begin to keep up.

- The need for personalization in an overpopulated society is growing critical. Variable data printing is one solution. On-demand printing allows for complete customization. The Web really creates the ability to develop personal communication and service for millions of customers.

The equipment costs are phenomenal.

Printing realities

Before we get into commercial printing output levels, remind yourself that top-end printing is not desktop. More and more, all of the artwork and digital documents are being done with desktop computers, but much of the input and output equipment is much larger than the desktop definition allows.

The computers themselves are now powerful enough (with the G4s and the slightly slower gigahertz Pentium IIIs and IVs, dual CPUs, gigabytes of RAM, and so on). But even these cost in the $2,500 to $5,000 range with all the RAM needed.

The peripherals are a different story. In professional printing we are entering the realm of equipment from $50,000 on up to millions. Printing professionals are used to dealing with multimillion-dollar presses. Here a $10,000 color proofer is considered very cheap. A $50,000 scanner is entry-level for most printing companies that are serious about quality and/or that have a 28-inch or 40-inch press. Imagesetters and platesetters cost hundreds of thousands of dollars.

Imagesetters and platesetters

The real problem with the digital printers you have experienced is the toner or inks used. Toner particles simply are not fine enough to render the resolutions necessary for top-quality traditional presses.

RIP: Raster Image Processor

One of the issues that we have not dealt with yet is the absolute need for PostScript in printing. This is the standard in the industry and cannot be avoided. Even PDFs are PostScript-based.

PostScript printing involves having the software generate vector-based code to send to the printer, imagesetter, or platesetter. This code is then converted to a custom bitmap that fits that output device. These bitmaps are called raster images. And the hardware or software that makes those conversions is called a Raster Image Processor or RIP.

Relatively speaking, inkjet droplets are huge compared with toner (not to mention film). Film or fine-grained emulsions are required to make the plates using dot structures that need tightly controlled dots measured in microns. And ink is required to get the particle size down small enough to print these dots.

To create professional-quality work, the printer needs to output very small, precisely controlled, hard-edged, well-shaped dots. In a word, film is required, at a minimum. Most imagesetters use normal high-contrast photographic film imaged with a laser. The laser can produce dots that range from 5 to 20 microns. In fact, the smallness of the dot can be a real problem. A 15-micron dot is about the equivalent of a 1% dot at 150 linescreen or .0007 inch! Very few companies have good enough equipment and personnel to print dots that small.

The price differences

One of the main differences lies in the hardware RIP (see sidebar). The RIPs that come with imagesetters are typically much higher in performance than anything used in digital printers and most digital presses. This means that they are faster and more accurate — plus they are much more expensive, of course. Higher resolutions become available, which enable finer screens. For imagesetters and platesetters, low resolution is 1200 dpi, normal is 2400 dpi, and high resolution is 3000 dpi or more.

Stochastic

Top-end imagesetters are also where stochastic imaging first appeared. Stochastic imaging produces what appear to be random dots as opposed to the normal rigid grid pattern of traditional halftones. It requires a specially powerful RIP to calculate the location of the dots. Every spot has to be precisely placed to achieve accurate color. In fact, stochastic is a blend of two Greek words meaning skillful at aiming, and to aim involving random variables or probabilities.

For many reasons, stochastic will probably become much more common in the not-too-distant future. There are many dramatic benefits that cannot be ignored. The modern platesetters using plastic plates all have a large-spot stochastic option. The disadvantages are merely changes in the paradigm.

Stochastic advantages:

Many of these advantages use terminology that some of you have not seen before. These terms will be covered in depth in the more advanced books and courses, like *Publishing with Photoshop*:

- Images look smoother with more detail.
- There is better color reproduction.
- There is no possibility of moiré patterns.
- It is much easier to run on press; has much faster makereadies, reduced drying times, and easier ink/water balance.
- There is no midtone tonal jump in halftones.
- Registration (the ability to keep multiple colors aligned on the printed piece) is not a factor in color balance with process color. With traditional halftone grid structures, poor registration (where the colors do not line up properly) can cause severe color shifts.
- Touch plates, spot color additions, and hi-fi six-color printing are possible for far better color.
- Gradients can be much smoother and longer. Banding cannot happen with random dots.
- Less dot gain, especially with waterless printing (waterless has typically 10 to 15 percent less dot gain than lithography).

Stochastic disadvantages:

- A slight graininess appears in the highlights and upper midtones reminiscent of mezzotints (it looks different — if you look very closely with a magnifying glass).
- Top-end systems use extremely small dots (less than 10 microns). This makes reproduction very difficult without excellent equipment and careful quality control.

Large-spot stochastic

This is where the industry is probably headed. By increasing the spot size to 45 microns or more, all of the disadvantages are eliminated except for a slight graininess. With the exception of the highest quality printing, customers cannot see the graininess. What they see is the improvement in color reproduction and saturation. The press operators see the ease of printing.

Large-spot stochastic (100-line and 133-line equivalency) makes it possible to print process on any press that can register. It has the capability of bringing process into quick print. A duplicator with a T-head can handle it easily. These printing machines are extremely common, as are the new plastic platesetters.

Inkjet printers are all large-spot stochastic. In fact, they are a little lower in quality than that, using diffusion dithering instead of true stochastic. However, the random dot solves many problems.

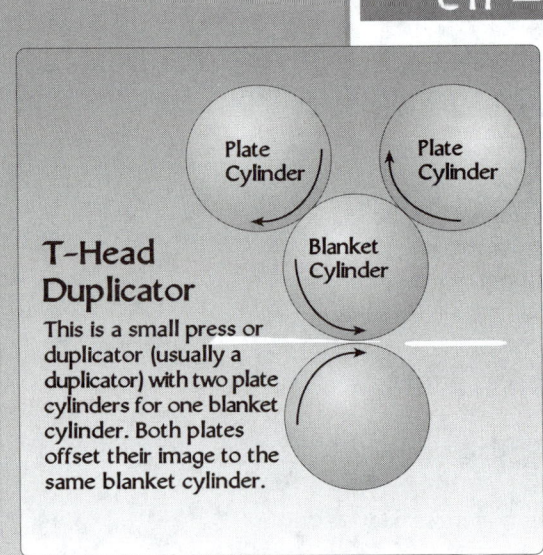

T-Head Duplicator

This is a small press or duplicator (usually a duplicator) with two plate cylinders for one blanket cylinder. Both plates offset their image to the same blanket cylinder.

T-Head importance

The simple fact that these cheap duplicators can place the images of two plates on the same cylinder means that these cheap presses can handle tight-registration, two-color spot printing. I have not found accurate stats for two-color spot printing, but it is somewhere around **25%** or more of all printing currently produced.

With the new small press platesetters and their plastic plates, these machines have become a major factor in digital quickprint.

CTP — Platesetters

Computer-to-plate (CTP) technology has been around for a long time. Beginning in the early 1970s with special plates output by phototypesetters for the phone company, there has been a dream of plate production directly from a digital file with no human intervention needed. The time and labor savings are obvious. Some of the new medium press platesetters can produce a plate in a couple of minutes.

In the mid-1990s, CTP had become the rage. At DRUPA 95 (the twice-a-decade printing mega-show in Germany), it was joked that there was now a CTP manufacturer for every printer. By mid-1995, there indeed were almost as many manufacturers as there were installations.

Frank Romano gave top-end platemakers until after the year 2000 before they are commonplace. He expects the top 1,000 printers to install very quickly, but at more than $400,000, the other 60,000 will lag a little. Frank was pretty accurate (as usual). Digital presses have become more common, much quicker than predicted, but that's another story.

The fact is that CTP is a reality, now, for many printers. By Romano's figures around 90 percent of the industry is producing black-and-white or spot color work. Computer-generated plates have been a reality here for some time. The only thing that is new is the ability to output top-end metal plates for process production.

These plates do not have to be metal either. Companies like Printware™ make platesetters for medium sized presses that output plastic plates which are very high in quality. Platesetters are still less than 10% of the market, but their use is growing fast.

Black plates

Almost any imagesetter has the option of black plate production. Here black plate is used as a generic term for polyester and/or photopolymer plates. These have been available since the early 1980s when 3M came out with its Onyx line. They have been the standard in quickprint for almost two decades.

There are presently several manufacturers of plastic plates. These plates used to have a severe problem with stretching. By increasing the thickness to seven or eight mils, the stretching problem has been almost eliminated. Plastic process color is not a big deal on modern top-end imagesetters/platesetters as long as the press can handle the registration. One problem for these machines is accurate, inline, punching of the plates so they can be hung on the presses easily. Printware™ and others have solved these problems.

Paper and plastic plates

What many do not realize is that the better 1200 dpi tabloid-extra (13×19) laser printers have output plastic plates for years. In fact, one of the best uses for high-resolution, plain-paper printers (1200 to 1800 dpi) is the plastic plate. These sheets of plastic print out beautifully. They work normally in quickprint duplicators and they are good for up to 10,000 impressions. If you have a longer run, just print another one. At less than a dollar and three to four minutes, a new plate is no sweat.

These plates can be output as composites. This means that the halftones and tints are first-generation, so plastic and paper plates can now handle professional quality halftones with relative ease. With high-resolution, plain-paper printers priced at less than $2,000, the future of quickprint is not in doubt. It will be totally digital through plate.

Thermal imaging

This applies to imagesetters as well as platesetters. The market is being pushed very hard by federal safety agencies (EPA and OSHA) to eliminate hazmat chemistry. Plates have gone to aqueous processing, which helps a lot. Thermal imaging appears to solve the problem entirely. A new imagesetter outputting thermal film and plates compared to a high-resolution laser printer is only a little larger and outputs 12×35 film, 2400 dpi — no chemistry, no smell, no hassle.

What this means is that imagesetting can move into the office. One of the reasons for separate service bureaus was the hazmat chemistry associated with film processing. To give you an idea (in 1994, before we eliminated photoprocessing), it cost my school $600 to dispose of a 55-gallon barrel of spent fixer. This was because the nearest hazmat processor was around 600 miles away, at the time. It's a little cheaper for those in more populous areas, but it is still a major problem.

Finally we can describe the new industry.

It is now possible to describe the shape of the industry in the twenty-first century. Publishing will be increasingly digitized and automated. There will still be drudge jobs for those who refuse to get educated, but there won't be many in printing. Printing will become a highly educated industry. It will require computer-literate personnel trained on the job in the specific software used by the specific company.

Pasteup

Do not make the mistake of thinking that pasteup is totally gone. Especially for copy shops, pasteup is often the only practical solution to assembling the pieces to be copied.

Even in traditional shops, many companies still have to put up with camera-ready copy because of customers who bring in artwork in printed form for their magazines, newsletters, and programs.

One solution is copydot scanners that can scan these camera-ready ads into a high-quality TIFF. It may be true that digital output is absolutely dominant. However, in older printing companies with customer relationships that are decades old, smaller towns, and outlying areas, you will find many workflows outside the new digital norm. This will be true for a long time in the future.

By 1995, it was almost impossible to even get interviewed without Mac experience with PageMaker, Quark, FreeHand, Illustrator, and Photoshop. The maturing of PDF and the release of InDesign are the first real changes we have seen since then. In those years we have seen thousands of traditional shops go out of business or be transformed into all digital or partially digital operations. For designers, it's been all digital for quite a while. The only thing that has changed is that Web design experience is now required, usually in Dreamweaver and Flash.

For designers, it's been all digital for quite a while.

We will look at workflows in three areas: commercial printing, quick print, and digital printing. There is no way we can cover all the variables. However, we can give you a good feel for what is out there.

The changes to traditional shops

The first thing to note is the disappearance of cameras. Some firms that have them still use them, a little. However, there is often an extra charge for camera-ready art because of the expense of firing up the film processor again. What this means on a practical level is that several careers have disappeared also. Camera operators and strippers (film assemblers) are gone. In many shops, even platemakers are gone – replaced by platesetters or presses that image blank plates while they are hung on the press.

In addition, cameras are no longer needed in the art room because PMTs are no longer needed for enlargement and reduction. Pasteup has vanished as a career now that everything comes out composited. Typesetters are also gone with everything becoming part of the new digital publishing. Traditional shops have been decimated. Over half of the traditional career positions are gone.

The closest to traditional

Digital commercial printing

First of all, there are shops that are still tied to some of the old technology. Basically, we are discussing establishments that are still using their old presses. They may be still using their platemaker. That would depend on whether they have an imagesetter or a platesetter. Even if they have an imagesetter, there have been radical changes.

Front office

One of the things that has broken down is the white-collar versus blue-collar segregation that existed before 1990. It is possible that only the pressroom staff still qualifies as blue collar, and maybe not even them. This is due, in large part, to the fact that most jobs are coming on disk (about 95%). Commonly, there is a department of customer service representatives (CSRs) charged with handling all the incoming data and taking care of the overall file management for the entire operation. This data room covers those responsibilities, plus basic preflight and electronic job ticket writing.

The rest of this office has not changed a lot. The estimator now sends her data to the CSRs after the quote is accepted. The CSRs and all sales personnel have to be digitally literate and at least functional on an entry level with the publishing software. Everyone communicates by email and cell phone. Many jobs come in as electronic job tickets off the Web site with the digital files attached, and this will increase with Adobe's new solutions. Some companies provide clients with specialized software and a dedicated ISDN or DSL line for placing orders and approving proofs.

The entire shop is networked. There may still be separate nets for office and production, but even they are connected in the data room. All the computer areas run both Mac and Windows, even though Macs still vastly outnumber Wintel machines in design and production areas.

Digital design and production

The art department does not even look the same. It is air-conditioned, quiet, and decorated. The walls are lined with workstations. They are still using Macs primarily, but they have Windows machines to handle customers working in Wintel (at least to translate them into usable Mac format). All jobs are sent first to a workstation run as a translating station. Here all data is translated to formats that are readable by the software used in the shop. Both the word processing files and the graphics have to be checked, preflighted, and converted, if necessary. When everything is ready, it is placed into an appropriately named folder which is noted on the job ticket folder.

The art director's career has changed a lot. It has become much more administrative. She is a traffic manager and handles all customer relations. Customer conferences are easier that way, and nonadministrative, production employees waste too much time if they are overly involved with customer relations. Her responsibilities are creative supervision, job assignment, and layout approval.

Terminology

I apologize for the use of so many terms that many of you have never seen before. They are all covered in my more advanced books. They are defined in the glossary at the back of this book.

After receiving a job and getting the client to answer any necessary questions, the art director gives the projects to the graphic designer whose skills best fit the client's needs. The graphic designer is charged with producing a layout, a graphic needs list (with sizes and general typographic decisions).

The designer gives the graphics, outside his personal expertise, to the creative director. The creative director's responsibilities include all illustration, scanning, and tracing plus halftone production. Even those done directly by the graphic designer need to be approved by the creative director. His personnel include illustrators and a scanner operator who runs the tracing program and produces halftones. Tracing printed logos and converting them to EPSs is a major duty. The halftone producer may be an additional Photoshop specialist who is also charged with the production of *duotones* and the commodity separations.

Once the graphics are assigned, all copy is sent to the copyeditor. He cleans up the converted files and keys in any additional copy. He is responsible for fixing spelling, grammar, typos, extra returns, extra spaces, superfluous tabs, and the like. He is also a reasonably good copywriter for those projects needing those services. Finally, he adds headlines and subheads when required.

Once the graphics and copy are finished (or brought as far as possible), they are returned to the designer. After an approval conference with the art director, production begins. There may or may not be a rough. Sometimes the client provides a layout. Sometimes the project is a redo with changes. Regardless, the art director has to approve all layouts and *art proofs*.

The designer sets all the defaults, flows the copy, and drops the graphics into place. If any additional pieces are needed graphically, she sends them to the creative director for assignment. Simple pieces she does herself (although her machine often does not have enough RAM to work effectively in bitmap). Increasingly, production designers are PostScript masters using Illustrator or FreeHand for their production graphics. The bitmap (Photoshop) graphics are handled by the specialists. When complete, the job goes back to the art director with a laser art proof that will be shown to the client for approval.

After art director approval, the rough is sent on to the software specialist. This person is typically a computer nerd who can fix any software problem in a heartbeat. He is also charged with keeping production flowing, installing software, and maintaining the creative network. His job is to open the folder containing all the pieces to make sure that all the pieces are there. After ensuring that all pieces are present, in the proper format, linked correctly, and in the right folder with a proper name, he generates a prepress PDF. Then he prints a contract art proof, marks it up, and sends it up front. Then the properly named folder is stored in the correct place on the correct drive until approval arrives, with the PDF ready to go if there are no changes.

Image assembly

After the client signs off on the proof, we enter the world of the production manager. Her task is to produce what has been created. She gets all approved jobs as a PDF from the design department plus all the projects that come in already designed, on disk. The first step is serious preflight on outside jobs. The CSRs simply look for missing pieces. Her preflightist just graduated from a local vo-tech and she's checking him out. The word is that he is not creative, but he's a hard worker and a Photoshop wiz. She's hoping that he'll have an eye for color correction — those are really rare.

After checking to see that everything is in working order, the preflightist sends the folder back to the production manager. She sends it on to the separator. By now the job is on a definite schedule. Everyone has a digital schedule that shows where every job is. Before image assembly, a delivery date was only an approximate guess. Now everything is scheduled to the half hour.

On the critical color projects, the separator scans color images and separates them — sending low-res placeholders back to the designer or the art department. She also performs the *OPI substitutions* for the low-res images after they return. This is where the appropriate *GCR* adjustments are made, where the *neutral gray levels* are balanced, and the image is sharpened. In some shops this is the same color specialist who works in the design department under the creative director. When complete, a *contract color proof* is made and sent back to the production manager.

After the color proofs are approved (sometimes by the client, sometimes not), the production manager sends the folder to the plating department. All projects arrive here as PostScript files or PDFs. Here the *trapper* and/or the *impositor* assemble the pages into *sigs*, and the *traps* are applied (if required). After determining that everything is in order, *blueline* or low-res proofs are made. Once the proofs have been signed off by the production manager, either *negs* or plates are output. They are thoroughly checked by the system manager and then the digital components are stored away. Some shops keep an old prepress master who lays down the prepunched composite negs on standard master

These workflows

All of the sample shops presented here are composite, fictional presentations of possible solutions to the new paradigm. You will see countless variations. These specific solutions mentioned here probably do not exist. However, they would work well — and you will run into all of these variations as your career progresses.

sheets and burns the plates. He also makes all the laminated proofs. The old printing expertise is still extremely helpful for quality control, and for producing patches in areas of the negs having fit problems or needing last minute changes.

Pressroom and bindery

The pressroom has not changed much. They do have a new waterless press, but they are still using the same old plates that have worked so well for so many years on the rest of the presses. Rumor has it that the plates are not going to be made any longer. At that point, the plan is to get a new stochastic platesetter and convert the rest of the presses to waterless.

The bindery is also the same. Here the same people are still working as they have since the mid-1980s. There are no plans to change and no need to do so. They don't go up front much. They don't feel like they belong. It's really alien up there these days.

This shop has changed a great deal, but it still looks a lot like it did. The techniques are still the same conceptually. It's just that everything before the composite negs is digitized. The huge horizontal camera has been outside in the rain because they tore out the darkroom. The huge racks of negatives, flats, and plates have largely been digitized, although there are still several old clients who reprint enough to keep the old plates around.

The new quickprint

Here's an industry segment that has changed a bit more radically. When you walk in the front door, nothing looks very different. After all, quick print led the way into desktop publishing. Because they could work with 85-line screens, laser printers were able to output camera-ready copy years ago. Even here, though, things have changed. First of all, there is now a preflight station next to the front counter. It is presided over by our trusty software guru, who examines all incoming projects that arrive on disk and confers with the customers. Although many jobs come in from the automated Web site.

This guru is a bit spiffier and friendlier, in keeping with the retail nature of the shop. It's almost a guru-as-CSR position. She is also kept busy helping the people at the rental computers in the corner. There's a couple of G4s and a Wintel workstation with a couple hundred megs of RAM and a good flatbed scanner available for those who can't afford to buy one. Some customers prepare their files and then come in to rent

Old equipment

There are many old shops with a lot of that million dollar equipment that is already paid for. It still works well so why get rid of it? Many don't.

However, those that don't tend to go out of business fairly quickly unless they adapt. We, as digital designers, have been one of the pushing factors.

At this point, you need to be very aware of what terms your printing company does not know. If you ask how they want their PDFs and they reply, "What's a PDF?", you know you have a real problem.

These older shops with their old equipment may win the bid wars, but in many cases they are more trouble than they are worth. Be careful!

the computer to add their halftones and separations under the watchful eye of the guru. (The sad state of affairs is that most designers do not know much about their technology.)

The digital publisher is in a little room by himself. He does a lot more keyboarding than the copyeditor in the last shop. He had to pass a typing test to get interviewed, but his 45 words-per-minute rate was sufficient. He had explained that even though he wasn't a very fast typist, he was a very fast editor and an experienced user of OCR. In most cases, fast editing and formatting is worth far more than typing speed. He is responsible for all artwork production: word processing, illustration, halftone production, and page layout.

In most cases, fast editing and well-designed formatting is worth far more than typing speed.

Formerly, he helped a lot at the front counter, but he got so busy that they hired the guru to manage the CSRs at the front desk. Once he has completed a project, he proofs it, and gets it approved by the customer (quickprint business usually doesn't rate the term client — go figure). Increasingly, he sends PDF proofs to the customer attached to an email for approval and annotation. When the project is approved, he does any imposition or trapping needed (rarely), exports it as PDFs or PostScript files, and sends it to the sign cutter (it still works from EPSs) or the print area (they prefer the PDFs).

The sign cutter is new. The boss decided to get what she saw at a demonstration at a big print show. From the day they got it, business has grown phenomenally. It has become a major profit center. The new employee in the sign shop has done some wonderful pieces, including a huge eight-color graphic covering both sides of a new delivery van. The main source of business seems to be two-foot by eight-foot coated canvas banners announcing sales, openings, and so on.

On the other side of the shop are the largest changes. In the print room, all the smelly old duplicators are gone. They've been replaced by a 600 dpi digital mimeograph, a large production black-and-white copier with limited spot color capability, plus the trusty old 12 page-per-minute color copier, with a powerful new RIP workstation controlling both laser printers. The room is quiet, decorated, odorless, and clean. Everything is controlled by the system manager with her workstation. She runs the files through preflight software, queues them up on the RIP, prints them, and stores them for future use, if necessary. As customer files build up in size, she burns 500 MB at a time for long-term storage on CD-Rs, deleting the hard-copied files to free up the server. She is also responsible for maintaining the hard-copy storage of samples for each job. Several times this has saved all of their necks by enabling rescanning and OCR of the sample.

The only other addition are the paper handlers, who work under the system manager. They load and unload paper from the presses, do the preventive maintenance, and move everything back to the bindery after it's printed. Maybe a better name would be print gophers. The bindery has not changed.

The service bureau printer

The digital print shop

Now we have finally arrived at a type of company that could not have existed before 1995 or 1996. Our sample is built out of a service bureau. Service bureaus rose from the ashes of old typesetters, separators, and prepress houses. Some simply saw an opportunity and grabbed it. The best were often started by a desktop computer wiz and an experienced separator. Maybe one hired the other, but these are the ingredients.

The shop we are going to look at was started by the city's digital pioneer. This is the guy who saw it coming back in the early 1980s. He had a copy of PageMaker and a LaserWriter in 1985. Being absolutely fascinated by the process, he kept soaking it up until people started asking him how to get things working. After several years of consulting, he tired of the rat race and looked for a comfortable office and people he could train to do the running around. About that time, one of the local color separators was going broke from payments on equipment.

Our pioneer ended up buying most of the equipment at far less than cost and hiring the separator as his production manager. It sounded screwy to everyone else, but they had a chemistry that worked. The front office is a beautiful reception area with a receptionist, a CSR and/or job ticket writer, and a huge office for our man.

The production manager runs the back shop. Her preflightist is more experienced than any of the others mentioned so far because he is also in charge of file repair. Over 60% of the files come in with broken links, missing fonts, spot color mixed with process, bad bleeds, and so on. When he is preflighting, he fixes what he can immediately.

There are three scanning stations. Two are huge. In this shop that means G4s with a gigabyte and a half of RAM and 75 GB hot swappable RAID arrays. All three have dual monitors, all color calibrated. Each station does its color-critical work on huge Barco monitors (one of them cost over $10,000). Even the small station has 768 MB RAM and a RAID array. The shop has two top-end drum scanners (one will scan up to 17 inches by 22 inches) and a top-of-the-line flatbed that has an automatic document feeder they use for production OCR. The production manager runs the color correction station with her years of experience.

The entire shop is hard-wired with 100BaseT Ethernet which is starting to really cramp their style. So far they are covering their need by using the hot swappable RAID modules as a massive sneakernet. They'll be forced into gigabit Ethernet by the end of the year.

The entry-level positions are where this shop's staff assembles the scans for client use. They do a lot of high-res scans for clients, plus artwork and difficult image repairs. They have had to add a station where the newest person is broken in, doing nothing but assembling files in folders for copying to removables and for proper storage.

One of their niches has become composite negatives of imposed and trapped sigs for the 40-inch presses in town. Several of them have refused to go digital, so our group prepares the composite negs for them. They all prefer to burn their own plates, but the town can only support one eight-up (24×36) imagesetter, so far. This shop is thinking of getting out of it because of the chemistry problems in their down-town high-rise. One of their most experienced women has expressed an interest in moving the photochemical portion of the business to an industrial area just outside of downtown. It looks like this might work, and the phone company will help them install a hard-wired fiber optic connection between the two locations.

On-demand capabilities

The fastest growing portion of their business is on-demand print-ing. They have a 22-inch Agfa Chromapress, an Indigo six-color label printer, a large Iris inkjet for proofing and fine art giclée prints, and two large-format inkjets (one is a hi-fi color Roland). They are seriously considering adding two Docutechs to complete their full-service produc-tion capabilities. Because they are in the middle of downtown, near the phone switching building, it has been easy to network to clients with high-speed ISDN phone lines. They also offer T-1 Web access for their clients, in keeping with their plan to provide everything their customers need. Their shop is the digital hub of downtown.

They have had to lease most of the floor below for file storage, hardware, and file management. They have four huge RAID arrays down there; one is just under a terabyte. They have every type of removable drive that exists. The room is radiation-proofed and has its own protected power supply with a small generator run on natural gas to back up the power company. Their Web server is in there also. Recently they moved the Chromapress and the Indigo down there, leaving room for the proposed Docutechs. This will be a massive change because of the sheer quantity of printing they will putting out. Even with virtually automatic inline binding, an amazing amount of complexity is being added to the operation.

Increasingly, they are doing variable printing. One of the real estate companies has paid to keep a fancy full-color brochure stored on their server. The brokers come in and get what they need weekly. Because their RIP can handle changing two of the eight pages on each brochure, the brokers can add all of their listings for the week. The real estate company bought a nice digital camera, based on the printer's suggestions, so the brokers can just bring in the shots of the newly listed homes on 250 MB ZIP disks. The template is set up to drop these in almost automatically. The brokers can order as few as one brochure, if they wish for a dollar a piece. The real estate company pays for all the setup charges and paper costs.

Design department

Probably the biggest change recently is the addition of a design department. It is pretty stripped down. They have an incredibly creative art director and her husband, who is the town's leading PostScript illustrator, plus a woman who is amazingly fast with document assembly. If the art director can get this person an accurate rough plus all the pieces, the document is basically done.

This has enabled them to offer full-service, on-demand printing. With their new design services, they are thinking of adding a sales department. At this point, however, they can barely handle the business they already have. They keep adding equipment to supply almost anything their clients request.

Large-format business

For example, their large-format inkjet business started years ago with one of the early large-format inkjets. They saw it as a way to offer simple posters. They quickly grew into the largest trade show display producer in the city. They haven't gotten into video or multimedia yet, because of their alliance with one of the best design and production shops in town. But their video displays, surrounded with huge photos, are awesome. Now they are starting to design them. Is seems obvious that there will be much more interaction with the video and multimedia studio in the near future.

Beyond this, the PostScript illustration skills have enabled an easy entry into Flash. Many of their customers have Ethernet intranets, so the designers are increasingly producing very Flashy internal sites for their clients. So far, they have not really entered the Web design arena, but they have been discussing the fact that all they really need is a geek to do the database management and the scripting needed.

They are getting a lot of requests, and they do see this as an income source. There is just not enough time. They figure they would need to hire at least two more people. It will probably happen.

The wide variations in reality.

We could go on and on, but you have the idea. I haven't mentioned the worldwide access offered by AlphaGraphics™, Sir Speedy™, and Kinko's™. There are online Web printing services that are growing like mad – able to ship anywhere in the world. The new digital job tickets enable accurate service ordered from the SOHO and delivered directly to the client – anywhere in the world.

Web design versus print design

This does not really exist. *Publish* magazine published some stats in 2000 that lead us all to believe that print designers spend half of their time designing for the Web and vice versa. Publishing is publishing. Except for technical considerations the same design personnel do both. Obviously some are better at one or the other. Both areas have very different design considerations. But those differences are simply part of the fun. Surely you see the concepts.

Sample production times

Let's give you some sample production times. Obviously, these have to be modified by circumstances and complexity. If you are working in process color for a company making a national push for new markets, you can quadruple these times. If you are working for a small printer, these are pretty accurate. Process color will probably take twice as long. The main thing to remember is that this is always a deadline-driven industry. If you want time to be creative, you will have to produce at this speed or faster to free up enough time. Most small customers do not want to pay for thinking so you have to make your own time. In general, however, this is what you will be expected to produce:

Need for speed

The main thing I want to impress on you is the need for speed. The deadline pressures in our industry are enormous. There is immense satisfaction in producing beautiful work under these pressures, but you need to be fast enough to cut it. Otherwise you'll be dropped from the team.

- 12-page newsletter — 12 hours
- Halftone production — 5 to 7 minutes
- Separation production — a half-hour or less
- Scan and trace logo — 15 to 30 minutes
- Name changes on four-up business cards — 15 minutes
- Small flyer — 30 minutes
- Produce clipping path on product shot — 30 minutes or much less
- Typographic headline manipulations — included, no charge

In general, you can figure that you have an hour to produce a letter-sized document, 40 minutes for a half letter, 1.5 hours for a tabloid. Creative charges are in addition to this, obviously. If you are marketing your design skills and marketing solutions, clients will be willing to pay for your creative time. In many cases, however, clients need and expect creativity on a deadline or creative production.

You do not get involved in digital publishing because *"you like to draw."* You have to love print, typography, and beautiful graphics. You have to enjoy pleasing a client. You must take it seriously and learn your craft. This is a highly competitive field. Only professionals survive.

The Web: a different world?

This is where many designers with a print history will begin having a rough time. On the World Wide Web, we are entering a world of coarse, crude graphics, with little layout control, no color calibration, and no output control. However, like all design problems, this is just another problem to be dealt with. There is hope. Some of the new software, like Dreamweaver™, Flash™, Fireworks™ and the Adobe variants, promises layout control. But, it is still dependent on the defaults of the individual browser that is reading the site.

The software only changes a little.

The best software applications for Web graphic creation are still FreeHand, Illustrator, and Photoshop. Fireworks and ImageReady are more specialized. Flash offers new and powerful animation capabilities, but bandwidth is still inadequate. Graphic communication is about using graphics to communicate, and the FreeHand/Illustrator/Photoshop combination is the best for graphics no matter what the medium.

This is the primary reason why Web site design and creation are still dominated by desktop publishers. It is basically the same skill set. The drawing and creative skills are almost identical, compromised only by the limitations of the formats used. The layout and design techniques are still largely the same, except for the fact that many normal options are no longer available.

Limited by the environment

First of all, the Web is severely limited by its output device – the monitor. Although it is true that the Web looks better on high-resolution monitors, most people do not have them. Even if high-res monitors are available, the graphics are still limited to 72 dpi. Most people still use 640×480 pixel monitors.

Beyond low resolution is the problem of color depth, or the ability of the monitor to display enough colors to satisfy the designer's desires. As of 2000, the average monitor was still 8-bit, at best. Average means that many are less and many are more. If your client's customers are mostly graphic designers, then you can almost count on resolutions of at least 1024×768 with 24-bit color depth. If those customers are small business owners, you'd better design for 640×480 and 8-bit color. If you are marketing to ancient bureaucracies in small towns or dated agencies, you'd better allow for 4-bit or less. The subtlety we take for granted in print is simply not available on the Web.

Platform differences with monitors

On the Web, you have to be cognizant of the vast differences between PC and Mac. It sounds like a simple difference. PC monitors use a gamma of 2.2, and Macs use a gamma of 1.8. In practical terms, gamma makes your monitor look lighter or darker. So, here's a translation of the gammas just mentioned. Mac monitors are much brighter, and usually much higher resolution. Images created on a high-res Mac, that look great there, often look very dark and dingy on a PC – not to mention that they look huge. Images created on a PC, that look fine there, are often far too light, with all the highlights blown out; often they are also much too small.

This is even true of type. On my high-res monitors, I usually use 14-point type or larger to make it legible on the screen. The type looks absolutely huge on a PC. This is also why many Web sites created on a PC are completely unreadable on a Mac, because the type is too small to be read – especially if it uses small, light type on a dark or graphic background. (Backgrounds usually don't print. So, white type on white paper hurts your readership.)

Page layout for Web

Both Quark and Adobe are pushing hard to make you believe that PageMaker, InDesign, and QuarkXPress are excellent HTML layout programs. Do not believe it. You may be able to use these programs for Web design, but you certainly cannot take your print document and simply export it as HTML. The design needs of the two media are just too different. The writing style must change as much as the layout.

Graphics turned off

This is probably not the place to mention all those who surf with the graphics turned off. Most of you do not want to hear this. The figures I saw most recently, in early 2001, were that somewhere between 15% and 30% of surfers browse with the graphics turned off because of the speed of their connection. We have to remember that the average modem connection is still 40 kilobits, or less. In fact, virtually all of us who access the Web over a phone line are limited to that speed by the phone line. Modems are slow.

Free color

However, this is an environment where color has no penalty; you can always work in color, if you want to, at no extra cost. Although we are not talking about the impact of four-color process on cast-coated stock with the photos popping off the page, highlit by gloss varnish in front of a dull varnish background, the color available is good enough to get the reader's attention — 256 colors are definitely better than black and a spot color. All we have to do is design within the medium's capabilities. Careful attention to detail still provides excellence of design. Don't fuss about the limitations. Design within the medium.

The limiting factor is bandwidth!

This problem is actually worse than the limited palette and low resolution. The average surfer has a 33.6 modem at best. Normal phone connections max out at about 3K to 4K per second. Even the 56 kilobit standard is glacially slow when we consider that normal color separations are dozens of megabytes in size. At 28.8 kilobits (which is well under 4K per second), a 10 MB graphic would take forty-two and a half minutes — minimum (if there is not a break in communication that requires you to start over). In general, modem connections over phone lines work at 28.8 to 48.0, no matter what hype sold you your particular modem.

Surveys often state that the average surfer cancels out and moves on if the entire page takes more than thirty seconds to appear. I have read articles that suggest anything over ten seconds is a problem. An informal study of my students indicates that fifteen seconds is a practical limit. This means that the entire page must be less than 45K (though many agree with me that less than 30K is wiser). Even at the community college where I teach (where we have a T-1 line on an Ethernet network), I consider myself fortunate if I can download at 30K per second, although an excellent connection will work at more than 200K per second.

Surfers leave in ten seconds!

Of course, there are always the storied cable modems and even satellite modems. I'm sure you have one? I know something of that ilk will probably come in the next decade, but it's not here yet. So the sum of the limitations is that your Web graphics have to be 72 dpi, usually 8-bit, and always less than 30K in size (3K is obviously far superior).

The best thing I have ever read about the Web was on a Web design site several years ago, and it went something like this:

People do not come to your site to see the killer Web site — they come for easily accessible data.

Your customers (or your clients' customers) are not looking for amazing digital dances to amuse and pass the time. They want to know what you are offering, why they need it, and how to get it. The fancy stuff does not help. **It irritates!** It's the same reason why most of your printed projects are still black and white. In printing, process color is the fancy stuff — and even that is much easier to justify than that incredible animation with the embedded row of changing interactive buttons where you have to wait seconds for each new image.

A word on friendliness

Web sites are unique bits of graphic communication. On the one hand, they are very cold, uninvolved, impersonal assemblages of digital data. For pixel pushers like us, they are great fun and global on top of that. Some may tout the Mac as friendly, but it is not alive and cannot relate to us. The same is true of the Internet, that incomprehensibly vast and intertwined network of most of the computers on Earth.

On the other hand, our Web sites reach our customers on a very personal level in a quiet time, where they are isolated within their computer environment, often in the apparent safety of a bedroom, den, living room, or office. Like a Mac, the Web seems friendly, responding easily to our command. More than that, it is a communication medium. Good writing counts.

What this means in practical terms is that the Web is a strange type of uniquely personal communication. I've written this book in first person, but none of you really think you are communicating with me. However, if you go to my Web site, find out where I am coming from, and we start an email dialogue, we can develop a pretty tight relationship relatively quickly. This is true no matter where you live.

In my commercial online school, I have students from all over the world. The geographically farthest one, so far, is from the North Island of New Zealand, but I've had many inquiries from India, Nepal, Malaysia, Singapore, Japan, all over Europe, and the Middle East. Normally, I don't even find out where they are from until we have talked to

Copywriters

On the Web, well-written copy is even more important than in print. Those punchy ten-word headlines are hard to write, but they make all the difference. The tightness of the writing style necessary for the Web is very difficult to pull off. Get a good writer with Web experience.

each other several times. It really does not matter at all. The only differences I have noticed with my student in New Zealand are: their year is very different, being south of the equator; they use metric (but most do that); they spell words differently (colour, cheque); they hyphenate words differently; and they use plural verbs with companies. Those small differences are merely enough to make things fun.

The other interesting fact is that I know her better than I do most of my students who are in my classroom for a few semesters. The Web seems to promote that. It seems to have something to do with the safety of distance and the relative anonymity of computer-to-computer communication. This has increased a lot with anthrax in the mail.

The visitors to sites you design really need to touch a human there. They want to know names, email addresses, history, background, and so forth. One of the original successful sites was for a small hotel in London. It was phenomenally successful via the simple technique of letting prospective guests wander through the hotel in their imaginations. If they wondered about meals, there were pictures, menus, a picture of the cook and her background. The designer said he regularly got bookings from people who made statements like, *"I've been wandering around your site for nearly two hours now, having a marvelous time. I guess I'll book a room."* The last time I heard, nearly 75% of the bookings for that hotel were coming from the Web site. How did he do that?

The answer is actually very simple. First of all, his writing style is cheerful, friendly, unpretentious, and believable. This is very important. However, more than that, he has a real gift of letting a surfer answer any question he or she might have. Upon visiting the site, you are left with the feeling that the hotel really cares for you — that they genuinely want you to have a wonderful experience staying with them.

The friendliness, openness, and genuine trustworthiness of your site are primary!

This needs to be your focus in Web design. Seems like normal stuff for any type of graphic design, doesn't it? Just as with print, if the surfer reacts consciously to the neat graphics and your incredible design, you've lost him as your client. The best designs are not only invisible, they should also enable the surfer to feel like she can go anywhere she wants and get the answers she needs — quickly and easily.

Most of your Web design problems will be solved if you simply remember the reason for the site in the first place. If you are getting paid to design the site, the client needs to make income from it. So, you immediately go back to the same old questions:

- What's the product?
- Who's the client?
- What does the client want the reader to do?

- What's the message?
- Who's the reader?

With the answers to those questions, you can design a clean site that downloads fast, is easy to understand, and is easy to negotiate. The client's readers will happily do what is desired because you will have helped them to see that the client's product is something they really need – plus it's easy to purchase, remember, or use.

By using normal digital publishing software, and starting with printable graphics, you will not have too much trouble when your client says, "I love the site! Make it into a brochure."

Where should you be by this time?

By now you should be almost finished with tutorials for PageMaker, QuarkX-Press, InDesign, FreeHand, Illustrator, or Photoshop.

By this time, you should have finished at least one or two of the basic Mini-skills. Push yourself a little. It's the only way to grow and learn.

DISCUSSION

You should be talking about excellence in print and Web, sharing excellent Web links, bringing samples to class that you have found, and so on. Focus on comparing print and Web design, for now.

Talk amongst yourselves...

Knowledge retention

1. Why do commercial printers keep as much of their old equipment as they do? (Give at least two reasons.)

2. How can the Web possibly be personal?

3. Why were quickprinters the first to go digital?

4. How does gamma affect the monitor differences between PC and Mac?

5. Why are the new digital printing companies the technocrats of our industry (why do they have the newest equipment and software)?

6. What is the maximum usable size in kilobytes for a complete Web page, including the graphics?

7. Why do designers spend about half of the time on print design and half on Web design?

Chapter 4

Hardware Needs

Concepts

THE EQUIPMENT NEEDED

A discussion of the hardware you will need to produce professional digital publishing

Chapter Objectives:

By giving students a clear understanding of the digital publishing industry, this chapter will enable students to:

1. explain the problems with ZIPs
2. discuss RAM requirements
3. purchase a usable scanner
4. explain the advantages and disadvantages of inkjet and laser printers

Lab Work for Chapter:

1. Work on miniskills.
2. Begin skills.
3. Read chapters 5, 6, and 7 for next week

Registration Mark ➔ ⊕

Saturday Only!
CLEARANCE SALE!

The typical temptations to spend more money than you have! Plus luscious pictures and supposed cash savings.

Logo/address

The dotted line is the actual trim size of the document.

BLEED   TRIM

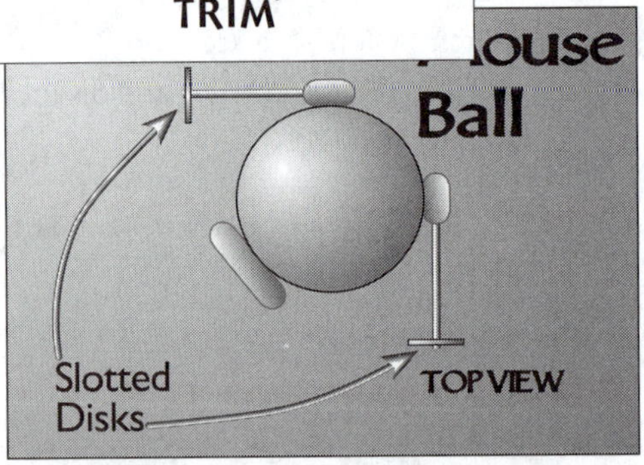

Mouse Ball

Slotted Disks

TOP VIEW

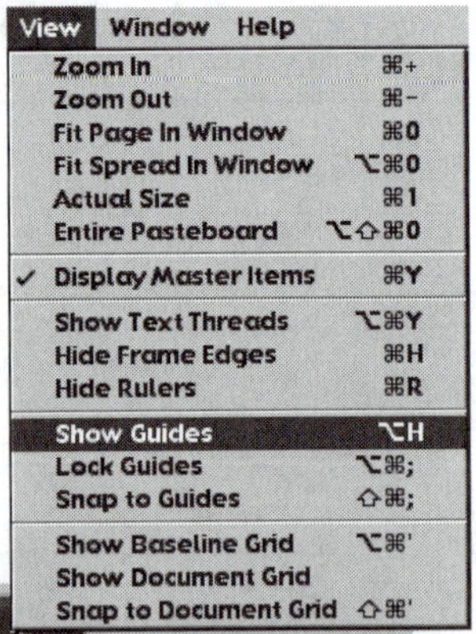

View Window Help

Zoom In	⌘+
Zoom Out	⌘–
Fit Page In Window	⌘0
Fit Spread In Window	⌥⌘0
Actual Size	⌘1
Entire Pasteboard	⌥⇧⌘0
✓ Display Master Items	⌘Y
Show Text Threads	⌥⌘Y
Hide Frame Edges	⌘H
Hide Rulers	⌘R
Show Guides	⌥H
Lock Guides	⌥⌘;
Snap to Guides	⇧⌘;
Show Baseline Grid	⌥⌘'
Show Document Grid	
Snap to Document Grid	⇧⌘'

The new paradigm in action

Please be aware that we haven't touched on the core of the new paradigm. In late summer 1999, *Publish* or *Electronic Publishing* magazine (I really can't remember which – it may have been the Department of Labor) offered a survey on designer compensation which claimed that over 60% of graphic designers are self-employed. Where I live and work, the figure is closer to 85%. Freelancing is the norm in digital publishing. It isn't mentioned commonly in trade media. All the training and verbiage is directed at the old paradigm of huge printing firms and design agencies employing dozens or hundreds of designers doing highly specialized work under the dictatorship of the account executives and art directors.

It is true that there are huge design firms in the larger cities. However, even here the publishing world is in constant flux. Creative people change jobs far more often than most, and they are much more motivated to have their own business. The fact of the matter is that most of you (more than half) will probably be working in your own office, often at home – in equal competition for the design projects in your area (or worldwide on the Web). Even if you have employment, the pay for artists is so low that you will normally be freelancing to supplement your income. The survey mentioned above quoted something like 24K to 36K as the normal spread of employed income unless you get into sales or management. Freelancing is necessary.

Freelancing is necessary.

So, what I think we need to do next is talk about what is needed to set up for business – hardware and software needs, mainly. We will leave software for the next chapter. This will give you a quick handle on where your equipment stands now, what your needs are, and what you must purchase next. The question, in our fast-growing marketing economy, is never "*Do I need to purchase more?*" but rather "*What comes next?*" Your employer will be providing this or more. If not, you'll have to buy your own. Even if you are employed, these will be your needs.

Hardware purchases

This will be a constant issue for the foreseeable future. Every time you update your operating system, you will be faced with purchase decisions for peripherals. You will regularly buy new software that will require a new CPU. Clients will demand certain peripherals. The list is endless. Be prepared.

Personal computers

Remember that personal computers today are more powerful and faster than the supercomputer mainframes of the 1970s and 1980s. We are not speaking of toys; these are full-fledged computers small enough to sit on a desk and be used by only one person. Apple's G4 is not allowed to be sold in China because it is so powerful that the State Department considers it a super-computer. It's as fast and powerful as a Cray mainframe was a short time ago. Several years ago there was a minor push toward workstations manufactured by companies like Sun and Silicon Graphics. These workstations were never common, and the new Macs and PCs are much more powerful.

PC: also called Wintel

The genius of IBM's PC, back in the very early 1980s, was its use of off-the-shelf pieces stuck in a box. The CPU came from Intel. The operating system came from Microsoft. It was certainly not the first personal computer. Kits were sold in the early 1970s. Apple Computer brought out the Apple I and II in 1976 and 1977.

Probably because of IBM's position in the industry, the PC was taken seriously by business. As a result, the PC had over 75 percent of the market very quickly. By 1984, IBM seemed invincible – a dangerous place to be. The first crack in the armor came with the PCjr, which was introduced about the same time as the Macintosh. The PCjr was a disaster, giving a toe hold to others.

The PCs used the Intel chip. Each new CPU was two to ten times faster than the previous model. These machines became essential business equipment. Beginning with the 8086, then 80286, 80386, 80486, and then the Pentium, Pentium II, Pentium III, Pentium IV, PCs and their clones took over the market. Because IBM did not protect its machine design, competitors were able to take the same pieces and make computers that worked almost as well.

IBM clones and semi-compatibles

The key word is almost. We don't talk about clones much any more. This is because there is no longer any original. Everything is anarchy in the PC world. Wintel machines are usually about 75% to 85% compatible. Because everything was in DOS, hours were spent configuring systems to make clones work with the software being used. DOS is still the basic problem with all Windows operating systems except Windows 2000 and supposedly Windows XP. By the time your custom configuration works, it often looks very different from other PCs.

Of course, when you upgrade, the configuration problems start all over. It can take months to get a new system running well. It can take a week or two to get that new CD-RW running properly. This works for specialized setups. It is a real problem for industry-wide standards. Uncontrolled clones can quickly degenerate into anarchy. PC shops must have computer experts on staff to keep things running. Individuals spend amazing amounts of time talking to tech support personnel.

The PC's biggest advantage is the freedom to configure what you want. It is also its biggest disadvantage.

PC owners are often computer freaks — that is, they like playing with computers. They enjoy learning about them, configuring them, creating batch files, setting up macros, souping up their machines, and so on. The problem for normal folk (especially creative types) is that they are required to do this kind of stuff in the Wintel world.

Most PC owners have all their tech support numbers memorized because their computers will not work without regular help with the code and configuring. Their focus is on the process of getting the computer to function. When I hear my students talking in class, the owners of PCs are usually talking about setup and configuration problems.

Mac

The Mac was introduced with a commercial shown during Super Bowl 1984. Did it turn the computer world on its ear? Not really. The PC contingent thought it was a toy. After all, you could not dig inside and mess with it. Besides that, it was slow and very expensive. Because it used a totally different chip made by Motorola and a radically different operating system, nothing hooked up with PCs. Still, the Mac developed a small cult following that became almost a religion.

Mac owners were and are intensely loyal. The Mac was sold as a way of life. No one took it seriously as a production tool though, which is strange. From the beginning it was set up primarily for production, even though no one seemed to know that. It is still not commonly understood how much time is wasted by having to configure cards, using two clicks

Tech support

There are many real reasons why Wintel setups require tech support and entire tech support departments. One of the reasons why Macs tend to dominate graphic setups is that tech support is not nearly as necessary.

For example, in the past eleven years, I have set up dozens of computers, peripherals, networks and so on. I have never had to call tech support. I have only had two minor problems with the computers and they were fixed immediately, on site, by Apple's warranty. I don't have time to set up and configure computers. This is one of the main reasons I remain completely Mac.

War stories

I teach about 500 students a year. I live in an Intel town and teach in an Intel school. (Actually it is a state school but they refuse to support Macs.) About 65% of my students have their own PC at home. Maybe 15% have their own Mac at home. From PC students I regularly hear stuff like, *"I couldn't get you the exam because my computer crashed and I lost my hard drive." "A virus crashed my email program and I lost everything."* Most of them have their PCs in the shop at least once a term. Mac owners' problems are almost always about learning software applications and design problems. They almost never have trouble with their hardware.

to execute a menu command, manipulating that document window inside the application window, and so on. These sorts of activities consume a major portion of the PC operator's time every hour of every day.

Plug'n'play, ROM, and the intuitive interface meant that anyone could learn a Mac with almost no training at all. The packaging and documentation are works of art. Apple quality is the standard by which personal computers are measured (although with the iMacs, G3s, and G4s, Apple started using some of the same lower quality components as the rest of the industry). In addition, Apple's exceptional system software always stretched the poor computer to the limit. PCs couldn't do near as much, but what they could do they did fast.

The Motorola chips followed the same progression as Intel's. As they became faster, Apple became slower in implementation, designing every computer from the ground up. Apple model releases were lagging a year behind. PCs went totally modular. By the early-1990s, PCs were much faster and cheaper than Macs. It didn't matter that Macs had a cleaner, more elegant, and more functional system. Bottom line won out. The number-crunchers won with their short-sighted viewpoints.

Cost comparisons

Of course, the Wintel world still thinks that Macs are much more expensive. That hasn't been true for years. When Steve Jobs came back to Apple to get it running again, most of Apple's hardware problems were solved. The largest selling PC model for a couple of years was the iMac. Macs are still not quite as modular as PCs. However, they now have five slots, three bays, and so on. But what they can change is incredibly easy to access. With comparable equipment, Macs are the same price or cheaper than PCs. The thing still confusing the issue is the inferior quality PC parts that seem much cheaper to purchase. But then, the cheap ones are much more expensive to keep running.

A new strategy

It wasn't that Motorola chips were lesser chips. In fact, they matched or exceeded abilities every time: 68000, 68020, 68030, 68040, and 68060. (The computer classes and programming instructors at my school teach their students that the Motorola chip is superior for programming and handling software routines, even though the school is solidly PC due to price alone.) The difficulty came with production. Even though the 040 Quadras were as fast as the 486s, 486s were available in 1989. Quadras didn't appear until late 1991. The 060s never saw consumer reality.

At the same time, IBM was having real trouble. It is so large that it had trouble keeping up with the rapid changes. In addition, it continued to focus most of its efforts on mainframes. Apple was not gaining ground on PC dominance, at all. Something new was needed.

In 1991, IBM, Motorola, and Apple joined forces to develop what became the PowerPC CPU. They realized that the X86 and oXo chips were peaking out. They could not be made to go much faster. The size necessary to make faster and more powerful chips caused overheating. In addition, these larger chips took too much power to run.

CISC to RISC

What the consortium did was use IBM's experience with mainframe and workstation chips. These processors used an entirely different chip architecture. The 486 and Quadra were both CISC chips. By the way, the Pentium chips are still CISC chips.

CISC stands for Complex Instruction Set Computer. These chips use relatively lengthy instructions. This means that programs can be fairly small, but it limits the speed with which a CPU can process them. The CPU regularly has to stop and go back for the rest of the instruction. CISC chips have to use microcode to tell the chip how to process some of these lengthy instructions.

RISC (Reduced Instruction Set Computer) chips use a smaller vocabulary of shorter instructions. It may take several instructions to do the work of a single CISC instruction, but the processing time is much faster because the chip can deal with the instructions much faster. The only problem is that much more working memory (RAM) is required. All the PowerMac chips since 1995 have been RISC chips.

The current official CPU minimum, according to software manufacturers, is a Pentium II or a PowerMac G3. **They are joking.** Even a G3 is a little slow if it is less than 400 MHz and the same is true of any Pentium slower than 450 MHz – this, of course, depends quite a bit upon the RAM you have available. You definitely need a G4 or a fast Pentium III or Athlon. The word is to avoid the Pentium IV, and Celeron chips are compromised for tough graphic applications (like we use).

Beware of comparing MHz

One of the things you must be careful of is CPU MHz speed claims. In most tests using the graphics software we use all day long, the 300 MHz G3 is roughly the same speed as a 600 MHz Pentium II. A 1 GHz G4 chip is much faster than the fastest Pentium with a trillion calculations per second. Any relative slowness on a Mac is a result of gigantic software and an operating system straining the system.

The office metaphor

As you have seen, the windows GUI (graphic user interface) uses a basic metaphor: the desktop. The Mac may have invented the windows interface, but the latest Windows operating systems do it well also. You are asked to believe that working on a computer screen is analogous to working on the top of a desk. It's not accurate, but let's take it as far as we can. It is certainly useful to describe computer operations.

You – The operator – CPU

You are analogous to the CPU. You make all the decisions. You decide what to do and when to do it. You have to make sense of the mess. Finally, you as CPU have to decide how to work, where to work, where to store things, or whether to pass the data on to another CPU.

The desktop – Working memory – RAM

The desktop is where you work. In hardware terms, this is RAM (Random Access Memory). Everything you are doing is dumped onto it. It may be a clean and organized work area, or total chaos. You may have folders and documents strewn all over the place, or tidily stacked materials allowing clear work areas. The operator determines methods. The desktop is where you work.

What you do on the desktop is very volatile. That means that anything can be changed, moved around, thrown out, combined with other pieces, and so forth. In addition, this desktop is different from a *normal* desktop in one very important way. Every time you leave and turn out the lights, a janitor hoses off your desktop with a flamethrower. Every document in progress left on the desktop is vaporized.

It may seem cruel, but that's the way it is. Your desktop is huge. It has access to tremendous tools. In fact, the top of your desk has access to all the tools in your desk drawers at the click of a button. You can do amazing things. The problem is that janitor. Sometimes she just shows up and tosses a tarp over everything you are doing, locking it in place. So far she hasn't flamed things while you were there, but sometimes she has to mess with the fuses and power supply. Sssshphoooom! Everything you are working on is vaporized again!

The file cabinets – Storage memory – Drives

The saving grace is your file cabinets. In hardware terms, these are the hard drives. These are incredible things. First of all, the file drawers (partitions) are almost infinitely malleable. You can add and subtract drawers almost at will. In fact, you can add or subtract the cabinets themselves almost as easily.

Best of all, you can file things with incredible ease. With the click of a button, you can navigate the file cabinets without ever leaving your chair. You can file items or pull items onto your desktop almost entirely from your position at your desktop. Plus, that darn janitor normally leaves your file cabinets alone. Sometimes your files get vandalized, but not by the janitor — unless you ask her to, in writing.

The folders – Organizing storage – Directories

The folders are equally amazing. (Wintel calls them directories.) They are almost infinitely expandable. You can put folders inside of folders; drag a folder from one cabinet to another; and rename or refile these folders at will. Folders can just magically appear in your hand, at the click of a button, or the stroke of a shortcut, as you place a new document into the cabinet, for instant categorization.

Briefcases and cartons – Portable memory

You have many things with which to move these documents around. We call them ZIP, JAZ, CD-R, DVD-R, and so on. They have all the capabilities of the file cabinets, but they are also portable. Some of them are just as large as the largest file cabinets. To call them cartons really does them an injustice. The only problem is that some cartons are not only pretty small, but they are made of cheesy materials (think ZIP, which is just a souped-up floppy).

They are all like the best briefcase you have ever had. These cases have direct access to your desktop (just like the file cabinets). They have the same type of folders. Even more miraculously, you can simply toss a file cabinet at one of these cartons. If the cabinet hits the carton, it copies itself into the carton (if there is room) and then goes back to where it was. You can throw folders and documents at these cases also. In each situation, the original remains in its original position and is not damaged. It simply places a copy of itself into the briefcase or carton. The ability to make backup copies of things is crucial to working with digital documents.

Protection – Type, lock, and encryption

Some of the cabinets and cases cannot be damaged by radiation. Normal storage is susceptible to radiation damage. These special storage units use a different technology that cannot be hurt by radiation (CD-ROMs). In addition, all cabinets, cases, folders, and documents have locks that can be locked with a button click. You can also purchase combination locks that can be opened only after a password is typed into them. Of course, the best protection remains a second copy locked in another building. All you have to do is drag a picture of your folder to another cabinet and the copying takes place automatically.

Connections – Networks, faxes, and modems

All in all, it is an incredible office. As recently as two decades ago, this office (now contained in your computer) would have taken many people to operate and all operations would have been done by hand. Now the entire office fits on your real desk, with room to spare. You can handle the entire operation yourself. With networking, you even have direct access to other offices. The largest network, of course, is the World Wide Web.

These other offices become, in effect, additional file cabinets for you to use. Some companies have a huge storeroom called a file server. Sometimes you have to argue with the other operators (or CPUs) for printer or network access and the system gets jammed up. Sometimes they speak another language. Sometimes the other office is in another country. It's getting more amazing all the time, isn't it?

Converting to digital reality

This chapter is not concerned with protection. We are concerned with the documents themselves: both production and storage. In computerese, the concept is called memory. There are different kinds of memory that correspond to the desktop and storage items mentioned earlier. It is extremely important that you have enough memory. It is even more important than a super-fast CPU.

Volatile memory — RAM

This is normally called RAM. RAM is an acronym for Random Access Memory. This is where you are working when the operator (CPU) pulls a document from a cabinet or case (hard drive, floppy disk, or removable cartridge). This is also where you are working if the CPU pulls a toolbox (program or application) from a cabinet, opens it up, and starts creating.

RAM is very fast memory. Its speed is measured in nanoseconds. A nanosecond is a billionth of a second. In RAM, you can freely create, change, or move around millions of bytes in seconds or less. Without RAM, your computer would be so slow that you would move back to your old desk and start dong things by hand again.

An excellent example concerns Photoshop. Photoshop works in RAM if at all possible. Even there, it is relatively slow due to the incredible amount of information being manipulated. Photoshop documents with 100 million bytes of data are common. If you have gigabytes of RAM, things go fast. You don't have to wait at all. If you are short of

RAM, then you can only work with little pieces at a time and things slow to a crawl. This is because Photoshop has to spend all its time putting document portions into file cabinets and pulling out new portions to work on. Cabinets and cases work in milliseconds, or millionths of a second. In other words, the storage units are a thousand times slower than the desktop.

Storage memory is a thousand times slower than RAM.

Other programs, like FreeHand, work entirely in RAM. If you use up all the RAM, these programs just lock up. Everything freezes and you have to pull the plug. There's not even an opportunity to save and no warning. You are forced to restart (warm boot) or at least force-quit the application. This brings up the other important aspect of RAM. It is volatile. This means that it is very fast but as soon as power is cut it is empty — absolutely! Any power surges or shutdowns wipe out RAM just like it was hit by a flamethrower — and at billionths of a second, it is gone fast.

SIMMs and DIMMs

RAM is supplied to the computer in SIMMs and DIMMs. SIMM stands for Single In-line Memory Modules. SIMMs are pretty rare. DIMM stands for Double (or Dual) In-line Memory Modules. These are little printed circuit boards with semiconductor chips soldered to them. These chips can be freely written on and manipulated at will. This is where you work to write the code.

They come in many sizes and configurations. SIMMs are rarely used any more because they were so small. The current standard is various DIMMs: 32 MB, 64 MB, 128 MB, 256 MB, and 512 MB.

These DIMMs are used for several things. First of all, they are the working space on your computer. This working space has been growing almost faster than we can keep up. When I wrote *Printing in a Digital World*, 16 MB of RAM was a lot. I wrote that entire book, created all the graphics, and produced all the digital documents for printing on a small Quadra with 8 MB RAM.

Last year I was telling my students that they could get by with 32 MB of RAM but they really needed 64 MB. Now I am telling them that 256 MB is the minimum and you really need 1.5 GB. Hopefully a gig and a half will keep us going for a couple of years. But I wouldn't hold my breath. I'm using a gig of RAM for now.

Photoshop needs

To work effectively in Photoshop, you need five times the largest document you normally use. Remember, every time you add a layer you add the original size of the document. In other words, 1 layer > 2 MB; 2 layers > 4 MB; 3 layers > 6 MB; and so on. In print, single layer, full color documents are commonly 50 to 75 MB. If we add the 24 MB or so it takes to load Photoshop into RAM, this means we can't really do much in Photoshop without 512 MB RAM. In fact, you can consider that the current functional minimum for RAM in your computer.

VRAM

There is a special category of RAM called VRAM, short for Video RAM. This RAM is used to hold the images being written for your monitor. The more colors you need to display and the larger your monitor, the more VRAM you need. Because digital printing normally requires 17-inch monitors or larger and uses 16.7 million colors or more, 8 MB or more of VRAM are installed (usually on the video card) to handle the image rendering necessary.

This has also grown a lot. Currently, you are really limiting yourself if you only have 8 MB of VRAM. Most if us have 32 MB of VRAM with the new super-fast cards that come standard with the new G4s and Pentium IIIs. It is really needed.

Other places you will find RAM are obvious once you think of them. PostScript printers have their own CPUs so they have their own RAM. Any peripheral that has its own processor will have its own RAM. Get as much as you can afford.

Hand input devices

The extended keyboard

The most common way to access computer innards is by hand. In fact, most personal computers are little more than glorified typewriters. Our industry is one of the few that pushes far beyond that. The most common input device is the keyboard. Before the Mac and a GUI using a mouse and windows, the keyboard was basically it. Nothing else was needed — because normally nothing else was available.

We need to examine them a little. First of all, they are assemblages of switches. There are no levers to pull, no keys to strike the paper. Because they are piles of switches, it is possible to make them silent and easy to press. However, keyboards like that are very difficult to use. We need the auditory, tactile, and digital (remember, fingers are digits, too) feedback to increase our speed and control.

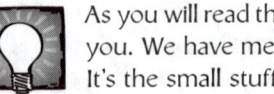 As you will read throughout this book, it is the details that kill you. We have mechanisms for dealing with major traumas. It's the small stuff that drives us nuts. It pays to find input devices that fit your style. They should be comfortable, durable, and (preferably) good looking. Your hands need to be comfortable on the keyboard. Carpal tunnel damage is rampant. A cheap clumsy keyboard can slow your production speed by a factor of **20%** or more.

In general, the Mac keyboards are excellent in most ways (except for those lousy three-quarter-size boards that came with the first iMacs and G4s). In Wintel, there is huge variation, with the cheaper comput-ers receiving much cheaper keyboards. You really need to check out keyboards at your local super store. You will be using yours a lot and it needs to be comfortable. We will just mention the problem of carpal tunnel damage that some say affects nearly a third of computer users. I just spent a week with a student who couldn't get her iMac to work. It turned out that her keyboard was the problem. It was a cheap after-market board that was not compatible with her new operating system.

On some keyboards, the keys rattle a little. There are large varia-tions in pressure needed to strike the keys. Here's a simple example of what can become a major problem. Some cap lock keys do not click down. In fact, they do not click at all. As a result there is no auditory, tactile or visual feedback except for a tiny light next to the on switch. It is very irritating not to be able to tell if that key is locked or not. You have to hit and check a couple of times to determine. Worse yet, all of a sudden the line starts appearing in all caps. Other keyboards have cap lock keys that lock half way down with a click. You can see it, feel it, and hear it. It saves a couple of minutes a day plus the aggravation.

So who cares about minor foibles concerning keyboards? My point is this. These kinds of little irritants can greatly slow you down in the long run. Production efficiency is largely involved with saving seconds on oft-repeated tasks. A keyboard that is not comfortable can cost you a great deal of time over a period of months and years.

Traditionally, printing professionals carried their own toolboxes. If you were working in a print shop or design studio today, you might want to bring your own mouse (if necessary). If you are having trouble with your wrists, get your own ergonomic keyboard or wrist pad and bring it. Quite possibly, you might want to supply your own software utilities, if the boss would not buy them. In most positions, you will be getting paid (hopefully with regular large raises) primarily because of your speed and efficiency.

Many bosses couldn't care less about your design skills. Creative style is entirely too subjective. Printers are primarily concerned about printability, as long as the clients do not complain. Ad agencies and design firms are concerned about cash flow. They hired you for your production abilities. They need someone who can produce artwork on schedule and within budget. All you have to do is please the client. They aren't looking for the Mona Lisa. As a hired gun, you need good tools. Increasingly, they are not only essential for production speed but for personal health.

As you can see from the following illustration, computer keyboards are complex. Most use the extended board with a layout like you see in the capture. The only time you will run into anything less will be on a laptop or those tight three-quarter boards that came with the original iMacs and G4s. Thankfully they are long gone.

In general, you should always be looking for ways to increase speed. One of the first things you need to get straight, as students, is this: your future employers might like your artistic abilities, but they are paying you for production. Efficiency is the key. Production is the way to get paid. Efficient production is the path to profits and growth.

10-key pad

The 10-key number pad to the right of the extended board often has very different use in professional publishing programs. Several software publishers use these keys to directly select tools from the toolbox. FreeHand is especially good for this. All the drawing tools can be selected with the number pad. This makes it possible to work with one hand on the number pad and the other on the mouse or pen. It is a very efficient way to work.

InDesign requires that you use modifier keys with the numerical keypad to select paragraph and character styles. You probably need to get out of the habit of entering numbers with that pad.

Arrow keys

The arrow keys between the QWERTY pad and the 10-key pad are also extremely useful. They are by far the fastest way through text when editing. Also, they are used in many keyboard shortcuts. Option/Alt–left arrow or Option/Alt–right arrow are often used for kerning (which we will talk about in chapter 10). Adding the shift key increases the amount letters are moved closer together or farther apart. Increasingly, companies like Adobe are using the arrow keys to move through pages.

Modifier keys and shortcuts

Let me state emphatically, keyboard shortcuts are not an option. They are a production necessity. With the production speed required by our industry, there is no way you can keep up without fluid use of keyboard shortcuts. However, shortcuts are a very personal thing. I could offer my set of shortcuts, but they would probably help only a few of you.

Increasingly, applications allow you to customize your interface. Software manufacturers are seemingly coming to realize that the level of production speed you can achieve with a customized interface is very impressive. FreeHand has, by far, the most control. InDesign is second, with Illustrator a close third with Version 9 or later.

Keyboard shortcuts are a production necessity.

One of the many real differences between Macs and PCs is the number of modifier keys available to use for shortcuts and other special options. Macs have four modifier keys: Command (Apple), Option, Control, and Shift. PCs only have three: Control, Alt, and Shift. The Control key is not used too much on a Mac. It is located in the same place as the Control key on a PC. It is used to access the contextual menus PCs access with the right-button. However, it is available for customized shortcuts in Mac programs.

You will use these modifier keys so often that you will develop the habit of using your dominant hand for the mouse and your other hand for the modifier keys. To rephrase, while I am working in the programs we use, my left hand draws with the mouse and my right hand lightly rests on the Command and Option keys. This will switch if you are right-handed (though many more creative people are left-handed than the norm). If you are using a PC, the keys your "other" hand rests on will be the Control and Alt keys.

 You need to recognize that for the programs we use, the shortcuts are almost identical cross-platform (at least until you customize them). If you are from a PC, going to a Mac, most of the shortcuts you learned that use the Control key will use the Command key on the Mac. The Option/Alt difference is even easier because these keys are in the same location. If you use a right-click on a PC, it is probably a control-click on a Mac (unless you have bought a 2-, 3-, or 4-button programmable mouse).

Hand input devices

Rodents, tablets, and pads

Mice

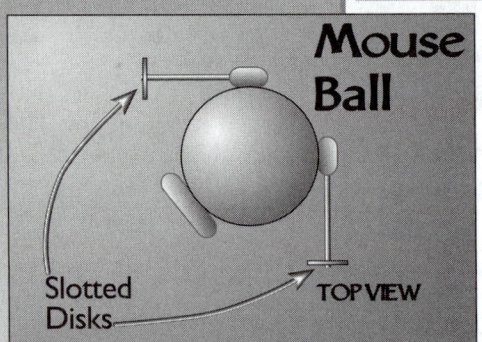

Mouse Ball

Slotted Disks

TOP VIEW

An older model

This drawing ignores the new laser mice, but it still gives the concept of normality. A light shining through the slots is read as it flashes. Dirt on the rollers is a real problem.

Clean your mouse!

The mouse is a major part of the GUI revolution introduced by the Mac and borrowed by Windows. It is really a simple device. The mouse ball drives three rollers that calculate the cursor's location horizontally and vertically. The important thing to remember is that the mouse does not draw or highlight or create anything. What it does is calculate a screen position for the cursor. It merely redraws the cursor around the screen moving it horizontally and vertically by measuring how much the ball rolls.

The cursor is simply a rough visual indicator of where you are working in the code you are writing. If you use the mouse to click on a handle, and drag that handle to a new position, you are not drawing. What you are really doing is rewriting the code that described the original position so it describes the new position. The mouse is used to nudge the cursor to locations on the monitor screen, which are used to activate specific locations in the code.

Trackballs

Notice that trackballs are in my artificially conceived "rodent input" section. A trackball is simply a mouse flipped on its back — same rollers and usually a larger ball. Instead of moving the container, which causes the ball to roll, you roll the ball directly. Many feel they have more control that way. Controlling a large ball with your fingers is more tactile and does seem to offer tight control for small movements. It is a matter of personal style.

This is often a choice for people looking for relief from carpal tunnel. You can rest your arm and work just using your fingers. Of course, what you do when your fingers go — I don't have a clue.

Buttons

For years, Wintel people have gloated over their two-button mouse. Mac mice that come as standard equipment only have one button. We have mentioned the fourth modifier key that Macs use instead. However, both of these options are the result of limited thinking. Apple assumes that you will buy a real mouse, if you need one. The same is true on the Wintel side.

Button quantity is your choice

Both mice and trackballs can have any number of buttons. Several have two, four, six or whatever instead of just one or two. Buttons cause the rodent to do special actions. The buttons on the multibutton rodents can be programmed to do almost anything. Basically they are simple macro producers. You can make them save, print, save and print, or whatever you think you need most. Many pros just use a *normal* mouse, but in the interest of efficiency, as mentioned earlier, you should check out all your options. If any of these rodent options appeal to you, use them. *We are not playing games – this is a career.*

I am currently using a two-button mouse, with chording, plus a scroll wheel. All of the buttons and the chord are completely customizable with the software that comes with the mouse. So in reality, I have a four-button mouse. For example, my left button is normal. My right button is an Option-click. The chord (both buttons at the same time) is a Control-click for contextual menus. The scrolling button works as a page down or up. It's just a little Kensington USB mouse that works on PC or Mac and costs $19. I'm assuming you'll get something like this ASAP.

There are dozens of choices: Mac, PC, and both. The most complicated I have heard of has eight buttons, but don't quote that at a store clerk. In my personal experience, the best software comes from Kensington. You will all have your personal choice. You may have to buy several before you find one that fits your style of work.

Graphic tablets: the "artistic" choice

Another important form of hand input uses a pen and pad. The analogy is supposed to be pen and paper. In reality, graphic tablets are powerful tools, but they are as far from pen and pad as the keyboard is from the typewriter. They allow direct input of hand actions. Handwriting becomes possible, as does freehand sketching.

The technology is simple in concept. The tablet contains the electronic equivalent of pixels or points. As the pen moves over the tablet, it activates points that tell the cursor where to be so you can rewrite the code.

With a tablet, you have a very different situation than with a rodent. With a mouse or trackball, the ball moves the cursor. If you pick it up and move the mouse without rolling the ball, nothing happens. With a tablet, every point on the tablet has a specific relationship to the pixels on the monitor and the location in the code. Picking up the

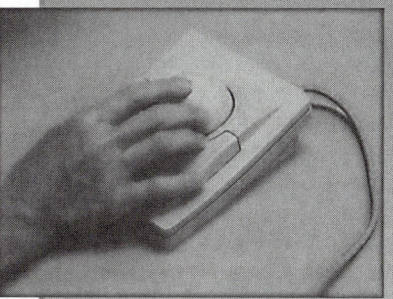

Two-button trackball

This is an very simple example of what is available. This trackball has two buttons, one on each side. Many have many more options than that. They are also available in ergonomic models. However, most ergomomic things are only for right-handed people.

A quick tablet signature

pen and touching a new location moves the cursor to that new location. The cursor is tied to the tablet, not to the pen. The pen just activates cursor movement.

Pens come in various shapes, sizes, and weights. They can have buttons like a rodent that serve the same purposes. Some of the pens look and act almost exactly like a traditional airbrush. Some have ballpoint pens so you can cover your tablet with tracing paper and draw directly on the tablet – while the cursor follows your hand on the screen.

There are also pucks for placing coordinates as in CAD. It is primarily used for drafting and engineering. There are also cordless mice. There are many manufacturers, but the common advice is anything other than a Wacom tablet is a waste of money. Wacom has up to 95% of the market and all others are going broke quickly. Do not be sucked in by the spiel of some young salesperson with no practical experience.

Pressure sensitivity

Good graphic tablets have pressure sensitivity capabilities. This means that the pens have a point that moves in and out of the tip according to how much pressure is placed on the pen. Increased pressure makes the line wider or heavier, changes its color, and/or changes its opacity. Capabilities depend on the software used. Like all good computer tools, digital pens can be configured to do whatever you need. They have amazing capabilities.

 BEWARE! The problem is that the pens have a very different feel from traditional artist's tools. They are an exceptional tool, but they are unique. The degree of difficulty is very similar to that of a large, fine sable, round, watercolor brush. They take a great deal of skill and experience. Expect to practice a lot before a digital pen becomes a fluid tool under control. It takes years to learn to control a brush — be forewarned!

In many cases, it is still preferable to use scanners to bring in artwork. Digital pens have a long way to go before they can match the feel and versatility of all the different pencils, pens, markers, brushes, and other hand tools. All the traditional hand tools can be switched in an instant. More importantly, most artists and illustrators have had years to develop skills with the traditional tools (and it takes years).

Tablets greatly vary in size. The smallest are 4"×5", and are used exclusively for drawing with a pen. The largest are several feet in dimension. Wacom's entry-level tablet is a small 4×5 USB tablet with a pen that has a side button (normally used for the double-click), a pressure sensitive tip (for drawing lines that vary in width, color, and/or opacity), and an eraser on the other end. It also includes a cordless mouse. It is under $100 (less than $75 refurbished at wacom.com).

Wacom's professional line, called Intuos, have all the other options. A 6×8 is about $200 and they go up to several thousand dollars. Wacom also offers an LED monitor as a tablet where you can draw directly on the tablet. Obviously, that one is not cheap.

Trackpads

One alternative is the trackpad. It looks like a miniature graphic tablet (1"×2"), but your finger is used directly instead of an electronic pen. It has buttons like a rodent. On some you can double-click by tapping twice with your finger. They are standard equipment on laptops. Most people find them to be clumsy. That's an understatement.

Monitors

Monitors use a technology similar to that in your television set. Instead of processing electromagnetic waves coming through the air, they process the binary code created by all the input devices. The processing is done by video boards or cards.

The software that actually produces the image on the screen is part of the system software. Mac OSX has introduced the use of PDF to produce the graphics. Earlier operating systems used many different formats.

Video cards change the digital code to analog signals that control the electron guns in the cathode ray tube of the monitor. This card enables you to see what you're doing with the code — what you see is what you get (WYSIWYG). The goal was an inch on the screen equals an inch on the paper. With high resolution monitors now standard, the inch measurements have little to do with the size of the image on the screen. If you are producing a CD-ROM, a video presentation, or a Web site, what you see on the screen is it.

24-bit color

This is now the norm, at least for designers. Normal people still average 16-bit color or less. Macs have been color since 1987 and 24-bit monitors have been commonplace since the early 1990s. Almost everyone wants to work in color, although a small minority (including me) think it's vastly overrated. Nevertheless, you will be working in color. Most of you will be working with large two-page, 24-bit color monitors. They are nice, but for those of you doing without — never fear. Most

Color depth

When we are talking about hardware like monitors and scanners, we have to know how many bits of information are used to describe each pixel produced by that equipment. This is called the color depth of the hardware. Since each bit has two possibilities, color depth doubles with each bit added:

1–bit:	2 colors
2–bit:	4 colors
3–bit:	8 colors
4–bit:	16 colors
5–bit:	32 colors
6–bit:	64 colors
7–bit:	128 colors
8–bit:	256 colors
16–bit:	thousands
24–bit	millions

24-bit is 8×8×8 or 16.7 million to be a little more exact. That sounds like a lot, but remember we are comparing it to the human eye which can distinguish trillions of colors (if you are not color blind).

people will tell you that you have to have the largest 24-bit monitor with the fastest video accelerator you can afford. In fact, you are better off buying RAM and storage.

 Unfortunately, 24-bit color is greatly overrated. No matter how well it is calibrated, a monitor will never look like a printed page. The monitor is a light source. The printed piece is not. You need to learn to do the color by the numbers as opposed to what you see on the screen. Even though it looks lavender on the screen, if the color is not made with light tints of cyan and magenta (with the cyan 5 to 10 percent stronger), it will not print as lavender.

Calibrated color

The only solution is a calibrated monitor. At this point, it is unlikely you have one and unlikely you will ever pay the money to purchase one. There is a hope that by the second decade of the new millennium, calibrated monitors will be the norm. But don't hold your breath. They are much more expensive to manufacture. Plus, most people do not think they are worth the money or the hassle.

Calibrated monitors are very new to the Wintel world. Microsoft didn't really offer effective color calibration until Windows 2000. They have been available in the Mac world since the early 1990s. The standard here is probably Apple's ColorSync, but Kodak's Digital Science is still used by some of the older programs and Adobe has their own, of course. Use what your printer uses.

A true calibrated monitor has a standardized color target that you can scan and print. It also comes with some sort of color densitometer or photospectrometer. You take the print and get readings off the various targets with the meter. Then you attach the meter to the screen and adjust the color on the screen until it matches. Of course, the screen is RGB color and the print is CMYK color — so this is not even theoretically possible. Light will never match pigment. But these monitors do a credible job for several thousand dollars. Most commonly, computer retailers do not even offer them.

Monitor size

The original Macs had nine-inch black-and-white screens. This was like looking through a keyhole instead of a window. The norm now is 15- or 17-inch screens with 24-bit color. This is tolerable. The solution is to use the higher resolutions available. Most Adobe products now require pixel dimensions of 1024×768 minimum. Many of us, like me, are using 1280×1024 on our 17-inch screens. 21-inch monitors are very nice, but they are still expensive. Using the 17-inch monitor at the higher resolutions enabled me to buy an extra 256 MB of RAM.

LCD screens

These are becoming much more common. Pixel dropout is now much less of a problem. They are still a little expensive and the resolutions are more limited. Viewing angles are still a little narrow so you cannot easily look over a coworker's shoulder, but they are impressive. They will probably become the norm, although there are newer technologies rumored in the wings.

Other digital input

Scanners

Scanning devices have become as necessary to our industry as a keyboard, mouse, and monitor. Anything can be scanned, digitized, and used by publishing software. Printed pieces are obvious things to scan, although there are serious copyright issues with scanning printed materials. Original artwork is the most common scannable material: photos, drawings, paintings, and the like. What some are not aware of is 3–D scanning. Real objects can be scanned very well with many scanners. At the very least, a flatbed scanner allows you to capture images of hands, leaves, fabric, or textured items by laying them on the scanner glass.

Scanner types

Technologically there are two types of scanners: CCD (charged–coupled devices) and photomultiplier. CCD arrays are used in flatbed scanners, slide scanners, and digital cameras. Photomultiplier tubes are used in drum scanners.

The CCD array is made up of a group of overlapping metallic electrodes layered on silicon crystal. When light strikes the electrodes, electrons are excited and react with the silicon. An analog-to-digital converter reads the electronic signals and uses them to assign a color value to the electrode location. The array can have several thousand electrodes and measures a couple of inches. Because of their small size, direct digital output, and low price, CCD arrays are perfect for small scanners and digital cameras. The cameras now have little CCD rectangles of approximately 3000×2000 pixels or 6 megapixels.

Larger monitors

You may wonder about 20" monitors or larger. Many people love them. I'm not very impressed my self. The real estate on those screens is so large that losing the cursor becomes a real problem. Also, it is hard to move the mouse quickly from one corner to the other.

Dual monitors

One common solution on a Mac is dual monitors. Just by adding a second video card, you can set up a second monitor next to your current one. The Mac OS has supported this for a long time and Wintel began supporting them with Windows 98. What you get is a huge monitor. The second monitor can be used for storing palettes, for example.

dMax: maximum density

dMax stands for the maximum density that can be seen by the device. Density is measured in a scale like the Richter scale for earthquakes. Going from 1 to 2 , or from 2 to 3 in density means that the higher number is ten times darker. Densities range from 0 (zero) which is white to 4.0 which is the maximum possible black. To give you an idea of density levels, here's a short list for photos and art:

dMax	artwork
0.7	pencil
1.1	printing ink
2.0	snapshots
2.7	pro print
3.1	transparency
3.8	Ansel Adams contact prints

Scanners

2.5	consumer
3.3	pro flatbed
4.0	drum

A photomultiplier is a highly refined version of the photoelectric cell used to open supermarket doors. When light hits the cell, electrons are emitted. This electrical current is analog (i.e., it varies with light intensity). Photomultipliers do exceptionally accurate scanning with finely focused lasers. The original art is placed on a drum that rotates at high speed over or in front of the laser beam. Transparencies allow the beam to shine through. Reflective art (opaque) reflects the beam. Because the information gathered is analog, the data has to be processed with an analog-to-digital converter.

Dynamic range

Photomultipliers have a much higher dynamic range than CCD arrays. In other words, photomultipliers can "see" many more levels of gray or color between the deepest black and purest white. This enables them to capture higher quality images with better tone and finer detail. As you can see below in the sidebar, drum scanners can see detail much better in the darker shadows.

This comes at a price, however. Because of the complex optics, the accuracy of the tracking, the computer power needed, and other factors, drum scanners are much more expensive than CCD flatbeds. Excellent quality flatbeds can be purchased for a few thousand dollars (a couple less than $1,000), whereas drum scanners are in five digits. Even cheap drums are $20,000 or more. Many reach $100,000 or more.

Of course, this is nothing compared to the original laser scanners back in the 1970s when seven-digit prices were not uncommon. The first scanner I used in 1978 cost 2.5 million dollars. The point is that these new desktop scanners are phenomenally cheap and incredibly accurate. Traditional graphic arts copy cameras that cost $50,000 to $100,000 are being sold for metal scrap. Desktop scanners produce images that are comparable in quality, in close to the same time, for much less than 10 percent of the price of a traditional camera. This is one of the clearest examples of why the industry has gone digital. Never forget that economics and the bottom line are the real reasons for digital production. Desktop publishing is truly a marketer's dream.

Consumer scanners

Many of you are reeling. You thought that $100 scanner you just bought at the super store was really more than sufficient. In reality *"good"* basically eliminates any scanner under $500. Actually, it nearly eliminates anything under $1,000. The best consumer brands are: Heidelberg, Agfa, UMAX, Microtek, Epson, in that order (IMHO). The main thing needed is a good Photoshop plug-in. These five brands have good plug-ins. The rest don't. HP is an excellent scanner, but its scanning software has always been clumsy, inadequate, and slow. Some of my students claim this has gotten better in recent years.

Scanner brands like Relisys, Tamarack, Mustek, and the other off-brands of that ilk can take up to an hour to do a poor-quality scan. (However, even Heidelberg and Agfa have slow, cheap consumer scanners.) In Heidelberg's and Agfa's defense, slow for them is maybe a minute per scan and the color is excellent. The off-brands often take 30-50 minutes per scan and the color is unusable.

I am not ignoring the reality that most of you (and this includes me) are forced to use these cheap consumer scanners due to pure financial constraints. Also, the better scanners are much harder to find. However, you must accept that these consumer models are quite restricted in resolution, density range or dMax, and image size.

Resolution requirements

It is important that you check out the optical resolution. That is the first number listed when they say a 600×1200 dpi scanner, for example. The 600 in this case is the actual count of sensing devices per inch in the scanning array. The 1200 simply means that the scanning bar is calibrated to cover 1/1200 of an inch at a time down the length of the scanning bed.

For now, let's just say that the minimum is 600 dpi optical. Most companies are now offering 1200 dpi to even 2400 dpi in their lower priced scanners (up to $2,000). Read the magazines for reviews. Some companies fudge the figures a little. UMAX has been accused of this for years, but their scanners are excellent, and their scanning software is a superb plug-in.

Slide scanners need much higher resolution. A 35 mm slide is about one inch square. You commonly have to enlarge these images to 8×10 or larger. To do that you need at least 2400 dpi, and really you need 4000 dpi to have any control. There are many excellent slide scanners on the market in the $1,000 to $3,000 range. Nikon and Polaroid seem to have the best reputation on the lower end.

Color depth

As we have mentioned, the standard is supposedly 24-bit color. This uses three 8-bit channels: 256 colors of red, 256 of green, and 256 of blue. This gives a total of 16.7 million colors. CMYK (or printed color) needs 32-bit. The problem is that 24-bit CCD arrays are very limited in dMax and general sensitivity. As a result, most consumer scanners

---

What are you looking for in a scanner?

Let's make it short and sweet. Here's a list:

1200 dpi

dMax of 3

36-bit color

8.5×14

Photoshop plug-in

3-minute scans

If it is at all possible, try it before you buy it. It has to fit your style and not irritate you. I have a little Epson, for example, that is pretty good, but the plug-in is obviously a PC port to Mac and I do not like the way it works. As soon as I can afford it, I'll probably go back to UMAX. I just like them.

use many more bits to scan and then use those extra bits to produce a much better 24-bit image in Photoshop.

It is hard to purchase a scanner at this point that doesn't have at least 36-bit color. Let's consider this the minimum. However, we have gone far beyond entry level here. You need to read *Publishing with Photoshop* and take a production Photoshop course to get that knowledge. You will understand those terms better before we finish, if you don't now. If you have the money and the business, it should be obvious that a professional scanner is greatly preferred. However, these are expensive (from $3,000 to $300,000) and are really necessary only if you have a lot of business or a lot of high-end process color business — CMYK or hi-fi color. The better scanners are not only much better in the shadows, with much more accurate color, they are also much faster. Many can claim an average of a scan a minute. The more you get into Photoshop production, especially print, the more you will want and eventually need a professional scanner.

The revolutionary part

Desktop scanning

Desktop scanners have radically changed our industry. Flatbeds are now *"normal"* equipment. Top-end drum scanners have lowered prices, and there are now desktop drums. Printing color photos was always an extremely specialized field, and the skills necessary are still enormous. In addition, it takes a well-trained, extremely critical eye to produce top-end color while converting photos to digital files that can be used to make printing plates.

However, most normal, single-color artwork can easily be scanned on the cheapest flatbed scanners. Even quick-print-quality color is relatively painless with one of these machines. It used to take a graphic arts camera (normally with a darkroom) plus photochemical processing (with all its potentially toxic chemistry) to make artwork or photographs usable.

With an extremely cheap flatbed sitting on your desk, you have many capabilities that a camera operator never dreamed of. As long as you have at least 1200 dots per inch (dpi) capacity, you can handle almost anything except 35 mm slide transparencies (for them you need at least 2400 dpi). Sometimes the process is slow, but this is usually caused by operator experimentation with the endless possibilities of image manipulation.

Artwork categories

Lineart

Lineart was traditionally defined as camera-ready copy in black and white. In other words, we are talking about single-color artwork with no grays or tinted colors. With a flatbed scanner and Photoshop, the art no longer has to be camera-ready, so the new definition of scanned lineart is artwork that has been converted to one-bit color. It is relatively simple to convert colored art to black and white with Photoshop. If necessary, you can scan it in color and convert it to grayscale. Then you can clean it up, sharpen it, gradually take the contrast to the limit, and save it as a black-and-white bitmap.

In normal production, scanning a logo and converting it to digital form is a common task. Flatbed scanners are perfect for this. In fact, this is one place where cheap hand scanners work very well. If your plan is to trace the logo to produce PostScript artwork, 400 dpi is often the finest resolution tracing programs can handle (memory-wise). If you are hand-tracing, 72 ppi is often sufficient (this is the monitor resolution). For printing purposes, lineart should be scanned and printed at the resolution of the printer or imagesetter. If you are outputting film on a 2400 dpi imagesetter, your lineart should be 2400 dpi. You may be able to get away with 1200 dpi, but anything less will compromise the image.

Lineart is was also called inkwork. Until computers, most lineart was generated with technical pens. These are ink pens carefully designed to produce constant width and constant-density lines. Everything was black or white. It was also called camera-ready art because it could be put directly into a copy camera and the resulting negatives could be used without modification.

Digital lineart: This is what I usually call PostScript illustration. It is vector-based artwork produced by FreeHand and Illustrator. This is the new digital lineart. This PostScript output is also camera-ready once the colors are separated. All the shapes are hard-edged and crisp. It is not used for realism. These are the fast graphics necessary for production. They are an essential part of digital publishing — for their versatility if nothing else.

Continuous tone

Continuous tone art is any other kind of art: photographs, paintings, pencil drawings, marker art, real objects, and so on. Any artwork that has any shading, gradations, grays, or color changes is continuous tone. This kind of artwork is the heart of what scanners are about. Hand input is usually lineart (with the exception of paint programs). Scanners produce continuous tone. Even lineart is often scanned in grayscale, for reasons we cover in my other books.

This image to the left is the original continuous tone ink painting that the lineart landscape on the previous page was traced from.

This is where scanner types become important. Flatbed scanners are questionable unless you are working with grayscale or commodity color. For commercial printing quality or better process color, drum scanners are the way to go, although flatbeds are rapidly closing the gap. Color scans are becoming a commodity that flatbeds can deliver much cheaper. Top-end, critical color will continue to require the dynamic range supplied by drum scanners (with corresponding cost increases).

Consumer color

Question: When was the last time you tossed a brochure or a magazine because the color wasn't accurate?

Industry segments requiring critically accurate color, such as fashion catalogs, national print advertising, and the like, will continue to blanch at the idea of commodity color. The fact is that digital color has gotten so good that the average user cannot tell the difference. Most users welcome it with open arms as a way to add color to their production without the horrendous costs of traditional process quality.

OCR — Optical character recognition

OCR is the incredible capability of software to analyze a scan made up of tiny dots and recognize type from those dot patterns. Humans have a very highly developed sense of shape recognition. We can recognize a tree whether it is a silhouetted spruce at sunset, a gaudy red maple in the fall, or a Christmas tree. Computers, in contrast, *see* these images as collections of dots. Computers do not see shapes in scanned images. They have to be taught to recognize patterns of dots. This is a very complex process. OCR software does this simply (often at the click of a mouse) with close to 100 percent accuracy — assuming you have good copy.

 When using OCR software, there are several things to keep in mind. First, italic type distorts the patterns to a point where OCR usually cannot recognize them. The same is true with fancy typefaces and tiny type. Finally, try to make sure that you have high-contrast, consistent-color type to scan. Anything less than that causes real problems. Actually, anything other than Times and Helvetica is probably going to cause at least some problems in reading accuracy.

Faxes, for example, are difficult. Even here, the software authors are working hard. It is possible to get fax software that reads faxes in grayscale and recognizes them with OCR. This allows faxes to be received as editable type that can be dropped into your word processor.

OCR has made a radical difference in production. It is no longer necessary, in many cases, to rekey last year's brochure (even if it was printed a thousand miles away and the artwork is gone). The problem of cleaning up and professionalizing typewritten safety booklets is also gone. In a lot of scenarios, it is better and faster to scan a secretary's non-PostScript document than it is to redo the nonprofessional formatting on a word processor. Using OCR to scan it in saves hours.

Digital cameras

Digital cameras are the current hype in publishing. They use no film. They directly capture digital images with CCD arrays. This is the future of photography. For many, it is the present. Many top-end photographs will still be photographic for a long time. Studio shots will be mostly digital in a short time. Professional photographers are increasingly going to digital cameras.

The main thing to remember is that you will need at least a 4 megapixel camera, unless you are doing Web work exclusively. There are quite a few of these available now at reasonable prices. The thing to look for is the quality of the lens and the software. Buy a camera that uses a lens made by a company with a lot of experience in traditional optics: Nikon, Zeiss, Canon, Pentax, Minolta, and so on. Read the magazine reviews to find out software problems. I had one that took an hour to download pictures — plus all shots were green and they were fuzzy.

An antique
This is the original Apple QuickTake that started it all. It was the first digital camera to be taken seriously even though it was only 600×480 pixels.

An excellent digital camera still costs several thousand dollars. They usually are camera backs for excellent SLR traditional cameras. Camera backs for a Hasselblad are super quality, for example. But they can still cost $5,000 or more. Increasingly, there are excellent cameras for around $1,000. Just check the reviews and the specs carefully.

Digital video

Video images are easily digitized. This works great for the Web, multimedia, and presentations. Monitors and televisions are very low resolution devices. Even high definition television is a long way from printing quality. Printing requires a lot more. For printing, video capture is a long way from usefulness. It just does not have high enough resolution to be useful. A 72 dpi image is garbage for printing, regardless.

Sharing the goods

Unless you are producing CD-ROMs or screen presentations, you are still nowhere. At this point we can create documents, save them, and make copies of them. We are still stuck in our little environment, however. We have discussed nothing outside our CPU except for ways to input digital data and ways to view the code WYSIWYG on a monitor. We have not covered ports or slots, at all.

There are several different types of ports. There are ADB, printer, Ethernet, modem, video, sound input, sound output, parallel, serial, SCSI ports, USB, and FireWire (IEEE 1394) among others. Check the owner's manual for your computer to find out which ones you have. These ports are used to connect your computer to the outside world.

At this point, every type of port is leaving except Ethernet, USB, and FireWire. Unless you assemble a PC yourself, you will have a hard time even finding a machine with these older standards. Macs have not had anything but USB and FireWire since the late twentieth century. Basically, USB is much faster than ADB, parallel, or serial ports. However, it is quite a bit slower than SCSI, the old Mac standard. FireWire is quite a bit faster than almost all SCSI except the newer, more exotic flavors. The new USB-2 is as fast as SCSI. 100BaseT Ethernet has become the norm for the networking port. 1000BaseT is standard on new G4s. Increasingly, technologies like Apple's Airport are being used. With their infrared connectivity, cables are no longer needed at all.

Hot-swappable, cross-platform

Probably the most important aspect of both USB and FireWire is that they are hot swappable. This means that you can plug and unplug from these networks without shutting down, with no problem, no lost data, and no corrupted disks. More than that, almost all of the new USB and FireWire peripherals work on both PC and Mac. This means that they are excellent devices for cross-platform document movement.

Slots

Except for consumer machines like the iMac, all computers these days have slots. We do not want to get into a discussion of slots. The main thing to remember is (if you have a PC) that most of the things that come standard on a Mac will have to be purchased separately for your PC and installed in a slot. You may well have to buy a USB card, a FireWire card, an Ethernet card, a super-fast video card like the NVidia GeForce, a SCSI card for your old peripherals, or maybe even a parallel port card for your old ZIP drive. On a Mac all of these things come standard except for the SCSI card for old peripherals, and SCSI cards are just an option when purchasing your new computer. Buying one aftermarket usually causes compatibility problems, Wintel or Mac. Get your cards installed by the factory.

Upgrading

OPINION: In the Wintel world, the concept of upgrading motherboards is rampant. IMHO it is a foolish thing. It compromises the quality of your machine and will cause you trouble. Even additional cards in your slots often do not work after upgrading a motherboard. I know it sounds like sour grapes because Macs normally do not have motherboard upgrades. However, most of my student problems with computers are because they build their own and are regularly upgrading their motherboards. Like I said before, most of my Wintel students spend more time keeping their computers running than they do designing. **Buy a new machine!** The old one can be used as backup or to burn CDs or whatever.

Storage: long- and short-term

Storage devices are the file cabinets. They basically are highly refined versions of your audio and video recording equipment. They use the same technologies: magnetic, optical (CDs), or a hybrid. Let's start with magnetic storage first.

Hard drives

Hard drive devices use the same type of emulsion that coats the brown plastic used in cassette tapes. Just like cassettes, the data is written on the emulsion by magnetic impulses that align the molecules in certain ways. A hard drive has the emulsion coated onto hard disks, usually made of aluminum. Larger hard drives have many of these disks (also called platters) stacked on top of each other.

To read or write the data, hard drives have heads that are essentially highly refined versions of the old needles used to read vinyl long-playing records. These heads move back and forth over the disks like a group of phonograph needles reading and writing data in magnetic impulses. Crashing is when the head hits the disk.

Hard drives come in many sizes and prices. The smallest now available are about 2 gigabytes; the largest weigh in at nearly a terabyte (a trillion bytes). Usually, the larger the drive the faster it is. Hard drive access times are less than 10 milliseconds. The fastest drives have access times way below 4 milliseconds. The faster drives have transfer rates of almost a gigabyte a second. Prices range from a couple hundred to many thousand dollars.

RAID arrays

There are many variations on the hard drive theme. For example, hard drives can be configured as RAID arrays. RAID is short for Redundant Assortments of Inexpensive Disks. Basically RAIDs are groups of hard drives that are software-controlled to act as one drive. They can be used for simultaneous backup and/or the data can be broken up into parts that are simultaneously written to multiple drives. Writing data on two drives at once is almost twice as fast. Some take the even bytes onto one disk and the odd bytes onto another. They are reassembled when read. There are RAID arrays up to a terabyte in size.

Fail-safe, hot-swappable backups

Some redundant setups automatically switch to the backup drive if the first fails. This way there is no loss of production time. This is the best way to protect your data. If you can afford it — you'll need several thousand dollars — study before you buy. There are basically six variations of the RAID theme. RAID 0 is pure redundancy — duplicating the code on two hard drives at the same time. RAID 1 is pure speed — splitting the code into two parts that are written to two machines at once. Levels 2 through 5 are combinations of the two. Most of these more sophisticated scenarios split the code between several machines with an encoded backup that can reconstruct any lost data. Some allow for hot-swapping. This means that a failed drive can be tossed and a new one hooked up without even shutting down the computer. This can be a critical advantage to a high-volume, high-pressure shop.

This is the first opportunity to begin hammering on you to back up all your data. When your hard drive fails — notice we said "when" as opposed to "if" — everything you have done since the last time you backed up will be gone. If you have never backed up, everything you have ever done will be gone. More than that, you really need to have a backup off site. During the L.A. earthquakes in 1997, many companies suffered huge losses because their backups were in the next room. The only ones who did well had multiple backups, with one at home or in another county. Then there are those of us who have a machine stolen. That's great fun with no recent backup.

You need to establish a regular backup schedule. Wise folk back up daily. There is software that will do it automatically. At the very least, back up all the documents you are working on. When I'm writing a book, I back up at the end of every session on a ZIP disk. A few times a week I do a complete backup on a JAZ disc. At least twice and maybe more, I'll copy all the files to a CD-R.

Floppies

Floppy drives use the same technology as hard drives. In fact, it's more accurate to say that hard drives use the same as floppies, because floppies were first. It was a large step when personal computers began providing two floppy drives so backup was possible. The original floppy drives were found on phototypesetters. They used 8.5-inch floppies that stored up to 400K.

Floppies are much closer to audio cassettes, in that they use the same brown plastic to record on. Floppies are basically a disk of the brown stuff encased in a shell. The original shells were made of cardboard and bent easily — hence the name floppy. A 3.5-inch HD floppy holds around 2 MB (less after formatting) or around 1.4 MB usable storage. A ZIP disk holds 100 MB or 250 MB. Surprise, surprise — yes, **ZIPs are floppies.**

Floppies have a few problems. First, they are not very permanent. They are easily damaged by heat, magnetism, or static electricity. Also, the plastic itself wears out fairly quickly. Experience shows that they are good for a year maximum — much less if they are used a lot or reformatted often. ZIP disks are as bad as the old 1 MB floppies. If you get a few months out of them you are doing well. In fact, because of the cheap prices, even ZIP drives are very prone to failure.

Secondly, they are very slow. They are about a tenth as fast as a hard drive or slower. Primarily this is because they have to spin so slowly (again because of that flimsy plastic disk). Hard drives spin at 3,600

Working off a removable

You really need to realize that removable cartridges are not meant to be worked on. In other words, they are used for backup only. If you receive a file on a ZIP, the first thing you do is copy it onto your hard drive. Then eject the ZIP so you do not accidentally work on the copy on that ZIP. Not only is working on a floppy very slow, you will ruin the drive very quickly. I know people who have worn out up to four ZIP drives in a year (not disks, but drives). The same is true of JAZ drives — backup only.

Here's an old 88 MB SyQuest. It was actually a hard drive in a cartridge. But at $600 per drive and $50 per cartridge, they were overwhelmed by the ZIP — even though the ZIP is a radically lower quality drive and cartridge.

to 12,000 rpm or more, whereas floppies rotate at 360 rpm. Of course, multiple disks or heads are impossible with floppies.

The old 1 MB floppies are almost never used anymore (except by nonprofessionals). If the files are small enough to fit on one of them, they are small enough to attach to an email. Even ZIPs are too small for many projects. This book will be around 550 MB when it is done. A color magazine can easily be 2–14 GB. ZIPs are still used primarily because they are so cheap (around $10) and small enough to carry easily. Because they fail so easily, always make two.

 One of the real advantages of ZIPs is that Macs can read PC ZIPs. This makes PC formatted ZIPs the current best solution for cross-platform use.

Removable cartridge drives

Finally, we come to cartridge drives. These have changed a lot in recent years. Prior to 1998 or so, the only removables worth much were SyQuest drives. These were actual hard drives in a cartridge. They were very well made, even though the software was a little fussy. However, Iomega drove them out of business with the ZIP. Cheap is not better, but most people do not care.

For a removable hard drive, Iomega offers the JAZ drive in 1 GB and 2 GB flavors. They also offer the Peerless, with 10 GB and 20 GB cartridges. I haven't used a Peerless, but the JAZ is a pain. At irregular intervals, the cartridge starts coming up to speed (for no known reason) and stops your computer dead until it makes it up to speed. Also, working off a JAZ (instead of using it for backup only) can cause the drive to fail in a few months. In addition, JAZ cartridges are just a little less than $100 each. Peerless cartridges are $150 to $200 each.

There are several other options, but they are not common enough to even remotely be called a standard. There are super-floppies, and Castlewood's Orb drives, and so on. Many sound really good. The problem is that unless everyone supports them and has a drive on their machine, they are functionally useless. At this point, the only universal standards are 100 MB ZIPs and CD-Rs.

Tape drives

Tape drives are used almost exclusively for backup. They work like your audio cassettes (if you still have any). By using minicassettes, they can record from 2 gigabytes to over 25 gigabytes of data. The problem is the same as audio cassettes — access time. Since you cannot simply move a head over the surface of a disk, tapes have to be fast forwarded or rewound to find the next pieces of data. This makes them very slow, but they do hold large amounts of data very cheaply. However, the medium is magnetic and therefore not very permanent. As a result, optical storage is taking over here also. There are optical juke boxes that can handle almost a half a terabyte of data. That should keep most of us going for a couple years anyway.

Optical drives

The next category of storage is optical. These drives use the same technology as audio CDs. There are several major advantages with optical drives:

- **Size**   - **Permanence**   - **Portability**

The basic CD is 600 MB. This allows for a large amount of storage. For this reason they are used for encyclopedias, dictionaries, and other large documents. They also work well for clip art storage. In fact, CDs are the primary source of clip art. Instead of using dozens of floppies or six ZIPs, everything fits on one CD.

Optical technology is also very permanent. You are looking at decades instead of months (unless you leave it in a hot car on a summer afternoon). Because the data is written with lasers, and protected with a thick plastic coating, static and magnetic fields have no effect at all. Even scratches are a minimal problem unless they are very large. Because they are on the surface of the protective coating, they are usually out of focus and ignorable as far as the laser reader is concerned.

Finally, CDs are almost as portable as floppies, even though they have the capacity of 400 floppies or more. They are almost as small (maybe not pocket size, but they'll certainly fit in a purse). More than that, CD-R disks are commonly only a dollar.

CD-ROM, CD-R, CD-RW, DVD-RAM, DVD-R

The original optical drives were CD-ROM (you know – Read Only Memory). They work well for storage, as mentioned, but they cannot be used for backup because they cannot be rewritten on. The original CD-ROMs were almost as slow as floppy drives. They now have 32x speed drives with access times approaching 20 milliseconds. They are still slow, but they are reaching tolerable speed. DVD solves the problem. They will hold up to 4 GB at much faster speeds. They are not ubiquitous yet, but they are coming on fast. DVD also started out as ROM only, but is also changing rapidly.

CD-RW drives that can burn CD-Rs and CD-RW disks are the new standard for portable storage. The standard for top-end Macs is the SuperDrive which can read and burn CD-R, CD-RW, and DVD-R, plus it can read music CDs and movie DVDs. CD-RWs can be rewritten so they can be used for backups, sorta. In reality, CD-Rs are so cheap, they are quickly tossed off like floppies used to be. CD-RW, because they require a stronger laser, are slightly problematic. DVD-Rs will probably become the new standard, but only time will tell.

The only real problem is that old cross-platform bugaboo. Macs can often not read PC CDs and PCs can never read Mac CDs. Most of the decent CD-burning software can burn cross-platform disks. But it is still a problem that has to be dealt with. I do find that PC-burned CD-Rs often do not read on Macs.

Finally, something we can touch

Hard copy: printers

Finally we arrive at our goal. If you recall, our goal is usually printed materials. Even Web sites should be built from graphic pieces that are printable. This is one of the real advantages of Flash. The first thing most surfers do when they arrive at the information they are seeking is print it. Printers come in all shapes and sizes, but this book is concerned solely with professional-quality printers.

Secretarial devices are a waste of our time and space. Most of you already have one or more. They may work well for you at home. The problem is when you try to make a contract proof that you get signed by your client. You must have a proof that the client will promise to pay for and the printer can guarantee can be duplicated. Secretarial machines cannot produce these proofs.

Basic printer types

There are three types you need to consider if you are purchasing a printer. If you are working for a graphic production facility, only two of the three are usable. The one to ignore is the non-PostScript printer. Professional printing requires PostScript. It is the absolute standard. You may run across — specially if you're seduced by apparent bargains — HPL compatible (Hewlett-Packard LaserJet) printers. These can also be ignored. They cannot do usable halftones, gradients, knockouts, crop marks, and so on.

Non-PostScript printers can be used for rough proofing, but little else. They are what I call secretarial equipment. For those who cannot tell type from typewriters, these printers work well. In addition, they are very cheap. You get what you pay for. They are low-resolution print-ers plagued with strange nonreproducible anomalies. They cannot be used for camera-ready artwork — even by the lowest quality print shops. More seriously, as mentioned, the proofs produced by these machines cannot be duplicated.

PostScript

Everything in printing is done in PostScript, and probably will continue to be so for the foreseeable future. A few short years ago (the late 1980s), books talked about how helpful it would be if professional desktop publishing ever developed a standard. We have, and it's PostScript. This has largely been driven from the service bureau and commercial printer end of the industry. The computer does not need it.

Everything in printing is done in PostScript

PostScript is a page description language. It was developed by Adobe and released about a year after the Macintosh was announced. It, along with PageMaker, was primarily responsible for the salvation of the interface and the development of desktop publishing. Before PostScript, there were simply too many quality problems with printed output. This is the main reason why only the Mac was taken seriously by professionals. Windows did not support PostScript at all until Windows 3.1 and it doesn't support it completely now, except for Windows 2000 and possibly XP. Windows 95, 98, and ME have varying problems.

PostScript liberates the document from the monitor. Non-PostScript software and hardware usually just print a screen dump. Because the monitor is stuck at around 72 ppi, this is a major quality issue. PostScript describes the page mathematically. Mathematical formulas are used to describe shapes as outlines. These outlines are then rasterized or filled in by the printer. Ultimately, everything done digitally is bitmapped. In a bitmapped image, every spot, dot, or pixel is defined individually. PostScript allows printers to draw their own custom bitmap of an image. The result is that PostScript documents print at whatever the resolution of the printer is.

The genius of PostScript printers is simple in concept. Give the printer its own computer so it can generate images that are the best that printer can produce — in a couple of words, *resolution independence*. This printer computer is called a RIP. RIP stands for Raster Image Processor. A RIP takes the PostScript code and makes a custom bitmap specifically designed to use the printer to its best capabilities.

Comparison: bitmap vs. vector (PostScript)

BITMAP TIFF: 284K, cannot be resized without blurring, cannot be enlarged without pixelation, difficult to edit, a collection of pixels, 300 dpi.

POSTSCRIPT EPS: 180K, can be resized up or down at will, very easy to edit. Each shape is a separate object, no specified resolution. Resolution is determined by the printer and can be anything from 72 dpi to 4000 dpi, if needed.

Because every PostScript printer has its own computer (RIP), it always generates images for itself. PostScript printers are sent mathematical descriptions that are rasterized at the resolution of the printer. This means that the same document can be proofed on a 300 dpi printer and output for plating on a 2,450 dpi imagesetter. Each printer produces its own customized bitmap that works best on its own printing engine.

The problem, of course, is that RIPs are not cheap. With my DocuColor 40 at school, the printer itself cost $50,000. The RIP for that digital press cost $65,000. A tabloid extra (13×19) color laser printer costs at least $4,000. Of that, the RIP is about $2,500. The cheapest letter-sized HPL laser printer is less than $300. The cheapest letter-sized PostScript laser printer is still nearly $1,000 because of the RIP.

 Always purchase genuine Adobe PostScript. Currently that means PostScript 3. There are PostScript clones, and they always cause some sort of problem. This is the main reason I never recommend HP printers. They have clone RIPs. If it doesn't say Adobe®, it will probably cause problems (unless it's over $200,000).

What's available

Printer species

For many reasons, which I cover in other books, 600 dpi PostScript is the minimum professional standard. Many hold that even this is only good enough for rough, internal proofing. Actually, the market determines the standard. A 600 dpi PostScript printer will give minimum-quality photographs and tints. For newspaper and quick print, this is fine; it would stand out like a lacerated thumb in a quality magazine like *Smithsonian*.

There is much equipment that meets this standard and far exceeds it. Let's cover the basic technologies.

Ink jets

Consumer machines – these are almost entirely non-PostScript. Now that piezo-electric printers (from companies like Epson) can give the illusion of 1440 dpi or better, the output is gorgeous. However, these gorgeous prints are the bane of professional printing companies.

First of all, with one rare exception (no longer available), the color produced is not calibrated. This means that if you take your gorgeous color inkjet print to a printing company, they will probably scream at you, cut off your thumbs, or laugh hysterically. When the documents that made your uncalibrated print are output professionally in PostScript, and converted to calibrated CMYK, the colors will change radically. You will be upset.

Secondly, because inkjets are really very low resolution (around 400 dpi) with the ability to make extra, tiny dots from those coarse jets, they cannot even be scanned. Any image that is already printed is broken into dots. The dots used by inkjets are not reproducible.

Consumables

The major problem with inkjets is the cost of consumables. There is nothing more expensive to use than inkjets — with the possible exception of dye-sublimation. These printers are cheap. However, photo-quality paper and large coverage can make these prints over $2 each for letter-size and over $5 each for tabloid proofs.

This brings us to that trite proverb: pay me now or pay me later. Any compromise on equipment quality will be paid for in service and setup problems. Or, you will pay for it in the cost of consumables.

Top quality inkjets

These are rapidly becoming the standard for art reproductions and color proofing. They are very expensive (mid five figures to low six figures). They produce outrageously good images. It is almost impossible to distinguish them from real watercolors, if they are printed on watercolor paper. Even at a cost of $150 per print or more, they have become the new rage for fine art prints and limited editions.

Large- and grand-format inkjets

Even though these machines also have very high consumable costs, they have become the standard in industries where only one or a dozen or fewer images are required. Large-format printers come in 24-inch to 96-inch widths. The length is usually limited by the length of material on the roll. Grand-format machines come in seven-foot to sixteen-foot widths and the rolls limit the length to about 50 yards.

- Tradeshow displays are now done with large-format inkjet prints on translucent substrates and backlit.

- Banners are commonly done with large- or grand-format prints that are laminated.

- Billboards are now usually done with grand-format inkjet prints that are stretched over the billboard frame.

- Skyscraper prints are done with grand-format inkjet prints, using Mylar screen as the printing material. These long strips are then sewed together into those huge 100-foot by 300-foot

Large-format flatbeds

The latest trend is for large format work to be done on flatbed printers that can print directly on foamcore, plywood, and so on. By using dye sublimation inks they can print on rugs and many kinds of unusual materials and surfaces.

(or larger) images that are hung from the sides of large buildings in the major cities.

- Truck and bus wraps are done with grand-format inkjets printing on self-adhesive vinyl, with screen covering the windows.

These images are not cheap, but they are much less expensive than hand-painted images. Plus they are of photographic quality with rich color. The going rate is about six dollars per square foot or less. Of course, skyscraper prints and bus wraps have high installation costs on top of that. Nevertheless, in the rarefied world of large budget advertising, these prints are considered a bargain. Remember, a thirty-second TV spot can cost a million dollars to produce for the big boys and girls.

Laser — plain paper

In most cases, you really want to get a good electrostatic solution to your proofing needs. If you get a laser printer with PostScript 3, these rough proofs will be all you need in most cases. The key is getting good enough resolution. There are several machines which offer genuine 1200 dpi and produce excellent 100-line camera-ready copy and separations for quickprint. The key is getting PostScript 3. Genuine Adobe® usually is best although I have heard excellent things about Harlequin RIPs.

If you have a color laser, these will even work for short-run projects. In many cases, the color is good enough for a rough proof, although a contract proof will still need something that the printing company is willing to sign off on.

The major advantage of laser printers is the cost per print. For black-and-white this is usually around 2¢ a copy per side of an 8.5×11. For color, the cost is usually about 25¢ per side of an 8.5×11. The cost of color prints is dropping fast. There is a reasonable hope of 11×17 duplex, full coverage for a quarter in the near future.

600–2400 dpi

These can be used for quick-print operations. They produce excellent camera-ready copy for these situations. The only problems come in linescreen production. Tint screens and halftones can be mottled because of the blotchiness that results from ironing toner onto the paper. Toner does not produce crisp, accurate dots. However, companies like Xanté have excellent reproducible dots.

You do have to be a little careful. There have been many companies over the years who promise 1200 dpi and actually give you an interpolated 300 dpi or 600 dpi. This is the source of most screen blotchiness. It is a self-healing problem though. The companies that were doing that are mostly out of business.

Color laser printers

These work well for proofing. As the calibration gets better, color laser prints become more usable. They are also used for commodity color production. The usual problem is that most of these printers are actually 300 to 600 dpi with 8-bit dots. This results in excellent color but strange halftone structures. As a result, many printers do not like to use them for proofs. However, if you are printing the final product at a Kinko's™ on their DocuColor 40™, you might as well get a proof from that machine.

Digital color printing

There are many machines to choose from. Xerox is working hard to corner the market, but they have a lot of competition. The main thing to remember is to ask the company doing the printing what they prefer for a proof. The press operator shortage will ensure that most of our printing in the near future will be done on machines like this. For black-and-white work, 600 dpi machines like the Docutech™ are already the standard. The linescreen is relatively crude, but the clients are usually not looking for fine art. They are just trying to get information to their customers.

Paper platesetters

Plain-paper laser printers can output plates if they are large enough. Paper and plastic plates used to be a joke from a quality viewpoint because they stretch so badly on the press. They could also do no continuous tone work – tints or halftones. Now they can produce output with photos and screens in place. This makes them an excellent choice for single-color quickprint, as they cost much less than a dollar a plate.

Laser printers normally come in letter or legal size. For truly professional use, tabloid size is highly recommended. Oversized tabloid (Tabloid Extra: 13×19) allows you to print 11"×17" two-page spreads that bleed with crop marks. As you can see, we've gone far beyond secretarial. Non-PostScript printers can't even do marks.

Printers' marks

The illustration below only shows a few of the possible printers' marks. The trim marks show the sheet size after it is finished. A bleed goes beyond the edge an eighth of an inch so the ink always goes to the edge without leaving little white slivers of blank paper. Registration marks are used for aligning multiple colors.

Registration Mark →

Saturday Only!
CLEARANCE SALE!
The typical temptations to spend more money than you have! Plus luscious pictures and supposed cash savings.

Logo/address

The dotted line is the actual trim size of the document.
BLEED   TRIM

Negs

The offset lithography process uses transparent negative images to burn their plates. These are called negs, and they are specifically right reading, emulsion down. This means that when you can read the image, the emulsion of the film is down. Like this, the emulsion is in direct contact with the plate as the plate is imaged in a vacuum frame giving exact reproduction of the neg.

These things differ by technology. Screen printing, for example, used right reading, emulsion up positives. Some letterpress images need right reading, emulsion up negatives. Your printer will tell you what they need if it is important.

Laser — film

These are usually called imagesetters. To achieve the fine detail required by commercial printing, film is usually necessary. The standard resolution is 2400 dpi or more and toner really has trouble in this range. The film is usually exposed with lasers. Sizes range from 12×18 to 24×36 or larger. 2400 dpi is necessary for printed process color.

1200–4000 dpi photochemical

These have been the backbone of our industry. The problem is the photochemistry, which uses toxic and hazardous chemicals. Many of us ol' f**** really like those smells, but that's another story. You can expect these to disappear as soon as possible. In many areas, you need a license to operate a darkroom. With 55 gallon drums of spent fixer costing several hundred dollars in disposal charges, the days of this type of chemistry are numbered – IMHO.

1200–4000 dpi thermal

At this point, these offer the best hope for environmental functionality. Because these image thermally, the hazardous chemistry is eliminated (at least as far as we have been able to ascertain). But then mankind has a long history is causing severe problems in ignorance.

Both of these imagesetter types output composite negs (see sidebar). This means that the entire career path of stripping (hand assembly of photographic negatives into an image that is burned onto plates) is gone. The new term for these people is not clear, although I like *impositors* personally. Their main task is now imposition, because the only task remaining is to assemble the composite negs into signatures. Signatures being that arrangement of multiple pages onto a single sheet of paper so that when the paper is folded and trimmed the pages are in the proper order and orientation.

Laser — plates

This is usually called CTP for Computer to Plate or Press. Here all the intermediate steps are done digitally and output directly on the plates to be printed. This is the only real hope for traditional printing like offset lithography. CTP is becoming fairly common, but platesetters are still quite expensive.

Platesetters

This is the obvious path to economically viable digital production. By directly outputting plates, all handwork is eliminated. In addition, the imposition is much more accurate. The only problem at this point is proofing, and that is rapidly being solved. As long as the same RIP is used for both proof and plate, contract proofs work well.

As mentioned, one of the major growth areas of platesetting is in the high-quality plastic plates. The original platesetters, like you see above, were major productions costing hundreds of thousands of dollars. Now, there are many smaller platesetters outputting excellent quality plastic plates for small- to medium-sized commercial printers. Because these plates cost around three dollars, many of the old setup charges are eliminated. These will keep the old traditional presses viable for a lot longer (*IF* they can find press operators).

Presses

This is the final step. By either imaging the plates while they are hanging on the press or by hanging the digital plates automatically, the remaining human sloppiness is eliminated. The problem? Without human interaction, the details cannot be tweaked to perfection.

DI presses, introduced by Heidelberg in the mid-1990s, use lasers to image blank plates hung on the press. They can burn an image on a plate in a few minutes. Registration problems are largely eliminated by the preciseness of digital production. DI presses are the best economically in the 500 to 3,000 impression market. They are actually traditional presses dolled up — they still require press operators.

Other color printers

Most of the other technologies are being left in the dust. Inkjets have taken over the cheap machinery and laser printers have grabbed all the cheap output. These other technologies are only mentioned so we can say we covered it all.

Thermal wax

These printers create color by melting tiny droplets of colored wax onto the paper. They provide brilliant color, but the wax can melt if left in a hot car in the summer. But then that may be an exclusively southwestern problem. Xerox does give theirs away free if you buy the wax sticks from them. Plus, they give free black wax for the life of the

Dye sub

As mentioned, large-format inkjets are now being used with dye sublimation inks to print photo-quality images on many new types of surfaces. Usually they print onto a transfer sheet for mounting on the final surface or material.

printer. Those kind of desperate measures should give you a clue as to how popular they are. However, the people I know who have one love them. I think it is what I will get next, even though it is only letter-sized. The prints are gorgeous.

Dye-sublimation

These work much the same as thermal wax printers. The temperature is higher, so the dots bleed more into the surrounding area. As a result, the prints look photographic. The difficulty is the lack of a halftone screen. Printers do not trust them because no dot structure is visible. They make gorgeous photographic proofs, but crude type. Plus, the prints are expensive — around $10 each.

There are also printers that produce slides or transparencies, CD-ROMs, video, and a host of multimedia output. They have not been considered part of printing until very recently. Now, more and more printing firms are adding these capabilities to the arsenal. Once the document is in digital form, you can output it any way you wish. In many ways, multimedia is easier to deal with. First, it is much lower in resolution. Second, it is RGB output (like scanners and monitors) and never has to be converted to CMYK (process color) for printing.

Break on out

Communications help

Most people in this day and age connect communication, computers, and cyberspace. For printing professionals, the Web is a major area of concern. More and more, information is placed on a Web site for 24/7/365 access. Of course, the first thing surfers do is print the page, but the printing costs are then born by the surfer and not your client.

Email is used a lot. Increasingly, proofs are PDFs attached to email. There is more talk, all the time, about using graphics downloaded off the Web. Flash enables printable quality. Normally, the Web is 72 dpi and horribly crude. Publishers now transfer almost all their copy via the Net (as long as it is unformatted or word processor text).

 The current state of affairs (according to a survey in one of the trade rags) is that most designers spend about half their time in print projects and half in Web work. The thing to remember is that there are very few who are making any money off the Web (except for those of us who design for the Web). The Web, at present, is primarily a fulfillment option for traditional marketing which is mostly print and mass media. This is not likely to change too much.

Networking

Connecting your computer to another (or dozens more) is one of those intellectually enticing things that has become commonplace. Macs come with built-in Ethernet. All you have to do is plug all the computers to a hub or switch. Plug'n'play is a reality here.

The basic techniques are really simple. In a nutshell, you plug the machines together with Ethernet cords, turn on AppleShare, and then access each other's storage units. That's it! There are reports of computer networks being set up (including the initial opening of the shipping cartons) in less than a half-hour. Actually, that report comes from me.

Cross-platform

Ethernet works at ten to a thousand megabits per second. This is what is commonly used. Larger networks spread out over several floors or buildings. At this point, your company will be forced to hire a full-time network administrator to keep track of all the network-induced problems. *Beware of the IT thugs!*

The real problem comes when you add Windows to the mix. Every company using Microsoft operating systems has to have full-time technical support to simply deal with the Windows and networking issues. Thankfully, we are designers and can hire the geeks to get that done. Gratefully, Macs don't usually need that kind of structure.

Satellite hookups

The larger printers are increasingly using satellite connections. *USA Today* has sent its copy to its printers by satellite for many years. The larger image assembly or separation houses have their own satellite link and assemble pieces produced worldwide.

This book skips over networking. For production purposes, networking is assumed. It should be invisible and done by someone else. If you have to fuss with it, production times are being damaged. There are many other networks, both other types and other protocols. The largest, of course, is the Web. You will be using these networks; everyone is or will be. It has very little to do with digital production (any more than telephones, mail, or overnight delivery services do).

The Web and online services

Online services will become more and more of a factor in our industry. In this general category are online services, the Web, satellite hookups, and so on. Most of these require high speed phone links like

Where should you be by this time?

By now you should be finished with tutorials for PageMaker, QuarkXPress, InDesign, FreeHand, Illustrator, or Photoshop.

You should have finished at least a couple of the basic Miniskills. Push yourself a little. It's the only way to grow and learn.

DISCUSSION

You should be talking about excellence in print and Web, sharing excellent Web links, bringing samples to class that you have found, and so on. You need to settle your printer needs. Talk about that...

Talk amongst yourselves...

ISDN, DSL, T-1, lines, and cable modems. The thing to remember is that most of the world is still on a modem and they are very slow. The average is still barely 33.6 kilobits a second (4K).

 One of the most important choices you need to make is your ISP, or Internet Service Provider. Here reliability and service are more important than hype. Many of the larger providers are so large that their service is terrible. Make sure you find someone who can grow with your needs and who can answer all your questions. In most cases, that means someone local. Millions of fellow customers is usually a recipe for trouble.

You really need fast Web access. You will do well to have ISDN, at minimum. Simple phone line modem access is frustrating, at best. It is virtually impossible to work in publishing anymore without fast Web communication and the ability to attach or ftp proofs and files for printing. WhamNet! was basically designed for our industry.

DSL, cable delivery, or satellite each make good SOHO access. All of our software now have the ability to work in a PDF workflow. Illustrator and FreeHand are fair PDF editors. A PDF workflow greatly simplifies the Web transfer of documents. Increasingly you will work online.

My current hardware list

 Having said all of this, here is my current list — just to satisfy your curiosity. I am doing this book with an old 400 MHz G4 with 1 GB RAM and an old Epson 636U scanner, plus a ZIP, a JAZ, and a FireWire CD-RW. I'm still proofing on an old LaserWriter Select 360, PostScript level 2, I bought with my first Performa back in 1994 for $2,000. I have a color inkjet, but I never use it. The same with my Graphire tablet.

Knowledge retention

1. Why do you need PostScript?
2. What is the problem with ZIPs?
3. What are the monitor requirements of digital publishing?
4. How has the Web impacted our industry?
5. How much RAM do you need?
6. Which is better, PC or Mac?
7. Why would you want to buy a new mouse?

Chapter 5

Software Needs

Concepts

1. Vector-based

2. Bitmapped

3. Image manipulation

4. Page layout

5. PostScript

A discussion of the software you will need to produce professional digital publishing

Chapter Objectives:

By giving students a clear understanding of the digital publishing industry, this chapter will enable students to:

1. describe PostScript illustration software
2. explain the difference between painting and image manipulation
3. explain what page layout is and what it is used for
4. discuss the interrelationships of the Big Seven

Lab Work for Chapter:

1. Complete tutorials.
2. Continue work on miniskills.
3. Read chapters 6, 7, and 8 for next week.

DIGITAL DRAWING

HIGH ON THE MESA

The software we use

We begin a new great adventure, learning how to use several powerful publishing applications. I wish I could tell you that we have finally found the Holy Grail, the software application that does it all. However, that program does not, and will not, exist. Current programs are already very large. Digital publishing now requires, and will always require, at least four software applications to do it well. As we go through this chapter you will soon see that, in reality, you will be using about seven applications all at the same time, not counting utilities. Any software large enough to do it all would consume your computer.

Nothing is enough

The basic fact of publishing remains: we need a suite of programs to do what we do. In the early-1990s, this was called the Big Five. Now, we have to add two more to the mix. The programs necessary for us to work in this industry are: InDesign, PageMaker, QuarkXPress, FreeHand, Illustrator, Photoshop, and Acrobat. You will also need a word processor, and several utilities. Web design is a definite part of the mix which adds at least one other program. We cannot do without any of these. Even if we do not use them all, we will receive pieces of our documents produced with all of these programs.

Digital publishing is the new paradigm of several old industries: marketing, advertising, publishing, and printing. We are the service industry for marketing and advertising agencies. Or, we are doing all of the marketing, advertising, and public relations for a company. Or, we are working for a printing or design firm who services these people. As part of this industry, we are responsible for producing the artwork and digital documents for printing projects from business cards to billboards, from brochures to books, from envelopes to point-of-purchase displays.

In addition, we are commonly responsible for the graphics and page production of Web sites. Often, we are also responsible for simple multimedia in the form of simple interactive CDs and PDFs. Finally, because we are often the only artist in the place, we also produce all the graphics and set up the PDFs or HTML for presentations.

PageMaker

Although elitists in the industry have made outrageous assumptions about the inferior capabilities of PageMaker, they have ignored the fact that PageMaker always outsold QuarkXPress two to one. Currently there are more copies of InDesign in use than either of the others. The elitists mutter "secretaries" like they are spitting. But reality is truth, in most cases.

There may well never be any version beyond PageMaker 7. From what I have heard, the code it too old and no one can remember what it was coded in. That is why InDesign was written.

The fact remains, even though Quark is an assumed necessity in publishing, it is a very dated piece of software. It feels old, looks old, and acts old. There is no solution for Quark either, except to totally rewrite the code. It remains to be seen whether this happens or not.

This is not the time to be learning how to run your computer.

No wonder that there is no one program that will do it all. In fact, in some shops there is no one person who is allowed to do it all. So, before we can go on, we must discuss the software that we must use to do the things we do. I will try to mention all the options.

 Please keep in mind: I offer many of these rather strongly stated opinions for several reasons. One is obviously to entertain. Another is to provoke discussion. A third is to give a hint of the wide variety of publishing solutions used in the industry. If you think I am wrong, good for you. What is important is that you think. Focus some time on software that is available, holes in your capabilities, and purchases you need to make.

However, we have gotten ahead of ourselves. There are a couple of basic issues that need to be taken care of before we can really start talking about the programs we actually use on a day-to-day basis'. First, let's mention an absolute necessity.

Basic computer literacy

Duh! This is much more important if you have a Wintel machine — although Windows 98 was nearly functional, Windows 2000 solved most of the remaining problems, and XP is supposed to be the salvation of the world. Windows machines require you to have a lot more computer hardware and software knowledge because they are much more complicated to set up. It is true that you can add whatever capabilities you like. The problem for most designers is that you have to do this.

Wintel needs tech support. When you add peripherals and change software — especially system software — there will be multitudinous configuration problems. The only useful advice is to save often and keep a list of your tech support numbers next to your computer. There will be nothing you can do about the infancy of color calibration, the plethora of inadequate hardware sold to the unsuspecting, or the ugly interface. The main thing is to be very careful about upgrades once you are running well. An upgrade can take a couple of months or more to integrate into your setup. You probably need to take a class in Windows.

If you have a Mac, you made the wise choice for graphic designers. You will have far fewer configuration and operating problems. However, if you have hardware problems you are in deep doo-doo (repairs are more difficult — I usually toss the computer, but then the problems are all on very old machines). Regardless, you still need to know how to run your computer. You need to rebuild your desktop regularly (it's a Mac-only thing, OS9 and earlier — restart and hold down the command and

Option keys until the dialog box comes up asking you if you want to rebuild the desktop). In OSX you can rebuild with the click of a button in the Classic 9 System Preference. If you haven't done it yet, you need to buy and read the appropriate version of Robin William's *Little Mac Book* series. Most of your operating systems will be covered. She is a marvelous writer — very clear and very easy to understand.

In both platforms

With both platforms, you still need to save often, clean up your filing messes, and name your files with real names that can be remembered (in other words, names that can be figured out by your replacement when you call in sick). You need to be able to load system software, install programs, and set up a functional filing system. We will cover filing in detail in chapter 6.

Beyond that, you need to have developed a basic troubleshooting methodology so you can figure out what went wrong. To say that computers are sensitive and complicated is understating the obvious. Remember, it is not *if* your hard drive crashes, but *when* it does. The same is true of corrupted files, failed floppies (including ZIP floppies), and all of the host of things that can and do go wrong with your files as you work on them. It may happen a little less often on a Mac, but it still happens on a regular basis. Your task is to learn to deal with it quickly, without getting upset over the unavoidable.

This book assumes prior knowledge.

Although we will cover basic reviews of all topics you need to know, I must assume that you have some word processing experience. Most of you have never learned or been taught basic file management techniques. We will spend an entire chapter on that after this software overview. Basic mouse usage, simple text editing, Clipboard procedures, and so forth must be assumed.

In other words, I expect you to have a basic working knowledge of your computer and how to use it. My experience suggests that many (if not most) of you were poorly taught in these areas. In many cases, you were taught lies. Students in the computer literacy classes at my school are actually taught to work off their ZIP disks. In fact, it is quite possible that my euphemistically named reviews will be brand new knowledge for many of you. But we will cover those things as we go.

Please notice again that I am not using desktop publishing. That phrase has become meaningless for most of us — having only nostalgic meaning for those who remember Paul Brainard and the early days of Aldus and PageMaker. In most cases, desktop publishing currently

We have to assume that you have done a little word processing, at least.

refers to what I would call secretarial use. Those front office people, who spend most of their time with business correspondence and materials, who are called upon to do the monthly newsletter for the personnel or customers. These people have no publishing knowledge, and certainly little printing experience.

Where it all started

Office software

Originally, personal computers were merely toys for techno-freaks. No one took them seriously. There was no need. All they were was a fancy calculator. The missing piece was software. After the last chapter, you assumed that we were ready to go, right? Not really. You could have the most recent computer, hundreds of megabytes of RAM, huge hard drives, all the input devices you could imagine, and a 1,200 dpi, tabloid extra, color laser printer. You would still be dead in the water, unable to move. You need tools to write the code that we deal with.

Our specific tools

Applications, commonly called programs, are the drivers that make the computer move in a planned direction. The computer becomes a specific production instrument when a program is fired up and loaded into RAM. The application is what tells the computer what to do, when to do it, and how to output it. It is a series of instructions written in programming code. (Rumor has it that PageMaker 6.5 used over two million lines of code.)

Business tools

The original personal computers could not do much except math, which they could do very fast. Big businesses had huge accounting departments to keep all their financial statistics, balances, and projections. What turned the personal computer around was the applications that were written to take the power of an accounting firm to the masses — those millions of small business owners who could not afford anyone more expensive than a bookkeeper.

The tools for business management thus became available off-the-shelf. These analytical tools were well known and used powerfully by big business. They enabled management to accurately understand the customer base, the market, and the financial picture, and, above all, to project growth much more accurately. They make financial management much easier, especially for small businesses.

The database

The simplest example of a database is the mailing list – but what a mailing list! Entries were made, normally, by keying them in. Once made, any entry can be found again with powerful search tools. The lists can be rearranged at the stroke of the enter key – alphabetically, by Zip code, by state, by age, by sex, by size of purchase, by purchase frequency, and so on. For example, it became simple for a catalog merchandiser to design a sale brochure targeted at only females who purchase every month, always use a credit card, aged 25-40, exercise regularly, and spend more than $300 a month.

It became possible to effectively manage lists with tens of millions of names. Customer analysis became a science instead of an art governed by hunches. All this analytic power became available to the small business owner with a few thousand customers and a limited budget. List management and list purchases are now a huge business.

The spreadsheet

Spreadsheet programs did for statistical and financial analysis what databases did for mailing lists. These were financial reports with a difference. That change was automatic calculation. The spreadsheet report enabled users to add mathematical equations to forms. Interest and payments could be calculated automatically. Sales personnel could be automatically ranked by performance. The month could automatically be compared to last month.

In addition to automatic calculations, charts and graphs were generated by menu commands. Sales and marketing meetings became precise planning sessions instead of guesswork. Costs were broken down into useful categories. Expenses could be analyzed to determine where the capital was going or why the cash flow was not there.

Maybe the most important use came from modified spreadsheet programs coupled with databases that provided automatic inventory control. It finally became possible for a business to track product usage, as well as thievery. Cash flow became a line item that could be calculated and accurately planned in advance.

Our real beginnings

The destruction of the typewriter

It didn't seem like much at the time, but the major change as far as the printing industry is concerned was the word processor. The first ones were merely fancy typewriters. (Actually, they still are.) However, typewriting is the least of it.

Office is the bane of our existence

You will discover that you will spend a lot of your career fighting the inadequacies of Microsoft Office. None of the software in the package can do what we need it to do for professional publishing. In fact, most of its output requires that we basically toss the documents we are given and start over to make a printable file. At the least they have to be radically edited and watched closely.

Word processing

Having said what I have about Office, word processing skills are the basis of editing which is one of the main skills needed in digital publishing.

The real revolution centered on three phenomenal capabilities. One, you could throw the whiteout away because these documents were editable. Second, you could print multiple copies without needing a copier or a print shop. Third, you could archive letters and documents for later retrieval, printing, and/or modification.

Early on, the problem was the printers. Dot matrix printers were almost illegible. To fit within the very limited parameters of their capabilities, letter characters had to be deformed, and the result was often unrecognizable. Many typesetters at the time could not read the stuff at all. A second person had to read it to them, so they began charging double. I charged triple rates because I had to drop my work and slowly read to my typesetter to get it done. Not only was my schedule set back, but Carolyn certainly couldn't maintain her 110 words a minute while I dictated. Many in our industry developed very prejudicial attitudes against "computer art" — primarily because of these printers.

However, the new capabilities were too much to ignore. The die was cast. Secretaries could no longer stand copy that had to be retyped because it could not be edited. Form letters became a snap! You could simply call up the document, change the address, and print out the new copy. Even that became automated with mail merge.

Limitations and abilities

Early word processors had many inadequacies. There were very limited choices of type style or size. As mentioned, the printers were of horrible quality, slow, and loud! All you saw on the monitor were screen characters that represented the final type, so you had little idea what your document was going to look like when printed. The screens showed green or orange type on a black or brown background. The cursor had to be moved with arrow keys. In general, comparing those early word processors to the latest version of MegaWord 13.0 is like comparing a Model T to a brand-new, top-of-the-line Ford sedan.

The programmers knew they had a hot item and worked like beavers. They began a cycle of improvements and additions that has not ceased, to this day. By now the programs are beginning to collapse under the weight of the embellishments, like the cars of the late 1950s that almost collapsed under the weight of their chrome ornaments. However, many additions were true improvements.

Find and change

The first — and probably most powerful — is the ability to find almost anything and change it to almost anything else. For example, the word *floppy* can be changed to *high density disk*. You can do that in all the selected copy, the entire story, or the entire document. You can check each occurrence one at a time or change them all at once.

You are probably less than impressed. How much can this simple tool really help? Well, change all double spaces to single space; all double returns to single returns; tabs to spaces; a lower case *n* to an open ballot box (□) by switching it to Zapf Dingbats; all returns followed by a tab to a simple return (thereby eliminating tabs used as first-line indents; and countless others. Now you've got something that really helps! You can find and change one font to another; change a font to outline style; change sizes; and on and on. Again, you are limited only by your imagination.

Take some precautions, though. For the lower case *n* example mentioned previously, it would be wise to check the "whole word" box. Otherwise, *every □ i□ the selectio□ will be cha□ged.* As you can see, this might cause a problem. The only problem is determining a specific find description that will find only the occurrences you are seeking to change. But that simply takes some thought.

Another thing to do is find the list of invisible character codes in your documentation. For example, in PageMaker and InDesign, ^*p* means return, ^*t* means tab, and ^*n* means soft return. Some programs make you select these special and/or invisible characters with the mouse in a menu. InDesign has a pop-up menu in the Find & Change box.

Thesaurus

A thesaurus is purely a writing tool. It enables a writer to look up synonyms and antonyms in the midst of writing without leaving the processor window. Here word processors beat page layout in making spontaneous written creation much easier. Page layout applications do not offer thesauri. But then, they are used to format and assemble copy after it is written.

Several stand-alone thesauri are available if you find that you end up writing a lot. These utilities can also offer a book of quotes, an encyclopedia, and/or an almanac. All of these things make writing easier and faster.

Grammar checker

This is really what we need — right? Nope! Grammar checkers are one of those things that sound wonderful but are really almost useless. First of all, we must go back to the evolution of language that we mentioned before. We said that English is a living language, and that is true. Some might argue that the early twenty-first century is seeing anarchy in grammar.

As a result, things are changing all the time, grammatically. Far beyond that, our language is falling apart. The fashion for the past forty years has been, "Do your own thing, man!" This tendency is increasing. Now we euphemistically call the phenomenon "taking responsibility for yourself," but the result is the same. Almost everyone has a different idea of correct grammar.

Grammar checkers try to apply someone else's ideas to your copy. Most people rebel. However, this is the least of the problems. First of all, grammar checkers miss many obvious things. Secondly, they tend to flag almost everything. Every sentence, or maybe several times a sentence, the computer says, "do you really want to do that?" If you are not careful, that warning might be coming with a halt to production and a dialog box. Irritating does not begin to cover it!

Most grammar checkers come with word processors, or are included free with some other software. If you like them, good for you. Very few folks can claim that they increase productivity. They seem to appeal to that type of person described in a recent British sitcom, "He's so tense that he's in constant danger of sucking himself inside out."

Spell checker

Spell checkers, in contrast, are a modern-day necessity. Spell checkers are the prime weapon countering the woeful spelling abilities of today's employees. When they are run, they flag any word they do not recognize. Some dictionaries are better than others and recognize more words. Regardless, almost none recognize proper names, place names, or technical terms.

However, this really does not matter. All you have to do is add those terms to your user dictionary. You usually simply click on the Add or Learn button, check the hyphenation, and it's done. Hyphenation is the second use of the dictionary. Unless you are forced by your software to use hyphenation by algorithm, your program uses the spell check dictionary to determine where to properly place hyphens.

Do not think of user dictionaries as an unusual requirement. Every field has its own jargon, and none of these specialized terms will be in the dictionary. It is possible to buy a few specialized dictionaries, such as medical or legal, but generally, you should be prepared to add words for a long time before your dictionary will finally work well for you and the clients you serve.

Spell checkers also have their problems. They are not grammar checkers or hyphenation checkers. As a result, sentences like the following pass with flying colors:

I went two the store too sea if eye could by for roles of film four my camera.

The preceding sentence would cause no problem for a spell checker. A spell-check command will not flag wrong words that are spelled correctly. A spell checker is no substitute for careful proofing. It does eliminate many errors, but it also misses many. You'll be amazed at how many typos spell real words that the spell checker misses.

Drag'n'drop editing

One of the nicer writing tools added in recent years is the ability to select copy and drag it to a new location. By holding down the Option/Alt key you can add a copy of the selected copy anywhere you like in the document. This is a great time saver when writing.

Bells and whistles

Word processors have many other capabilities, but most of them are useless to printing professionals. There are word counters, index generators, table of contents generators, and many other functions. They all become useless when you flow the type into your page layout document or, like the word counter, they make no difference beyond a means to identify quantity for payment. Our concern is: how does the copy fit the document size the customer is paying for? Within wide variables, we can adjust the type to fit. As graphic designers we often quote prices by the page — never by the word.

In addition, many good and necessary things were automated, such as headers, footers, automatic numbering of footnotes, tables of contents, indexing, and all the accoutrements of writing. Limited graphics capabilities were added. Table creation and powerful tabs became normal.

No matter what you do with a word processor, it is still not capable of professional-quality printing. The line spacing is often limited to space, space and a half, or double space. There is little or no control over word spacing, letterspacing, or kerning. For now, let's just say that word processors can type well but they cannot print professionally. All things considered, although they are incredible writing tools, they are still just fancy typewriters. In the hands of a professional, type can be preformatted easily. Word processors are essential for us, but they must not be considered a graphic tool.

All things considered,
it's still a fancy typewriter.

Professional usage

Today word processors are used professionally, but strictly for writing. They are used for producing the copy to be used by the page layout programs. In fact, if you use a program like QuarkXPress or InDesign, you have to set the copy in a separate word processor. Secretarial pools are still there, but now they are keying in raw copy.

Secretarial formatting

In fact, without a great deal of training, most secretaries and typists are incapable of producing formatted copy that will work in a professional environment. If they are capable, they are normally too valuable to be wasted on strict keyboarding. In many cases, it is usually better to simply ask them to type in the words with a return at the end of every paragraph. It is often difficult enough to get them to avoid returns at the end of every line.

You'll probably have to spend some time explaining word processing paragraph concepts and how the needs of publishing differ from secretarial work. It is important that there be only one return in a paragraph. If typed correctly, paragraphs can be resized and reformatted at will. If there are extra returns, reformatting becomes a laborious task at best. One of the major strengths of desktop publishing is the ability to reformat copy freely.

Regrettably, it is often necessary to spend many minutes (if not hours) removing all the secretarial formatting before copy can be flowed into a page layout with any degree of freedom. However, a word processor in the hands of a trained operator can save a great deal of time by preformatting everything. Imported text simply flows into place. All the indents, tabs, headlines, subheads, and so on just appear as planned. The designer merely has to massage the type to perfection and add the graphics and sidebars. Word processors provide the raw material for the graphic professionals to manipulate.

Basic word processing techniques

Usually the first thing you do before editing text is make sure that the invisible characters are shown. You usually set that with a check box in the Preferences dialog box or a menu command. When you show invisibles, you can see all the word spaces, tabs, soft returns, hard returns, and so on. The invisibles are a great help when proofing.

This is the first opportunity to explain printing realities. For many reasons, your customers expect perfect work. A single typographical error (always called a typo) can mean a reprinted job and a major loss of money and credibility. Proofing is extremely important. At least three people should proof everything. You will normally not find your own mistakes. That is why you made the mistake in the first place — you couldn't see it. If you missed it the first time, you will usually miss it the second.

Keyboard selection shortcuts

This is one place where it really pays to read the documentation. For example, in InDesign and Quark a single click places the insertion point, but a double-click selects the word, a triple-click selects the line, a quadruple-click selects the paragraph, and a quintuple-click selects the entire story.

In every program the shortcuts are a little different, but they really save time when you learn them. For example, in InDesign and PageMaker, Shift–Right Arrow selects the next letter, adding the Command/Control key selects the next word; Shift–Down Arrow, the next line (the same combination with the left or up arrow selects the previous word or line). Repeating the command extends the selection. Command/Control–Down Arrow takes you to the beginning of the next paragraph, and so on.

Some final comments on word processors

Word processors are designed for the business community rather than the printing industry. As a result, their abilities are geared for business at the expense of professional type. These programs are very powerful, but they are to be used for writing, not for design decisions.

These programs are very powerful, but they are to be used for writing, not for design decisions.

Dealing with secretarial copy

Many jobs will come with a disk containing the copy. For the moment we will assume that it is in a format you can read and import. Often, though, the copy will have been input by a secretary with no training in printing requirements. It will be filled with multiple spaces and returns. Copy that should be italic will be underlined. The tabs will be made with multiple spaces. Centering will be done with the space bar. The list is almost endless. Here is a procedure that will eliminate most common secretarial typos in a few brief steps:

1. Use the Find and Change command to change all double spaces to single spaces.

2. Use Find and Change command to change all double returns to single returns.

 Steps one and two may have to be done several times. Many typists center headlines by using the space bar. This could use 10 to 20 spaces. Each time you run the command, you will halve the number of spaces until there is only one left. The same is true of returns. Often spacing on the page is accomplished by adding many extra spaces. Moving to the next page is often done by holding down the return key until the page changes.

3. Select All (Command/Control A) to select the entire story. Then format everything to your body copy paragraph style. This is why the style is called body copy, because the vast majority of the copy is set in this style. This will enable faster formatting because all that will have changed are the heads, subheads, and special paragraphs.

This will eliminate most of the foreign formatting, which is probably littered with type styles not found on your machine. In addition, the formatting that is there probably contrasts greatly with your approved layout and your sense of style.

Junky tabs

The only problems remaining should be with tabs. Commonly, secretaries have no idea how tabs are used in setting type. You will regularly have to replace all tabs with a space and retab everything by hand. Often, first line indents are done with a tab that has to be eliminated. In general, indents and tabs are not effectively taught in secretarial word processing courses.

Extraneous spaces

In addition, you will probably have to eliminate all spaces before and after a return. These spaces commonly litter secretarial copy. They are not a severe problem, except for the obvious fact that your copy will not line up correctly. Centered copy will be off center and first line indents will vary.

Now you are ready to format everything with your style palette. Edit your styles after eliminating all the imported styles from the palette. Often the fastest procedure is to eliminate all styles and then import or append styles from a template you have set up properly. Eliminating all styles automatically changes everything to No Style. Step three would still be needed after you import the new style palette.

Although this process may seem like a real hassle, it is much faster than anything else. Ideally, your copy will come in properly formatted. In reality, this rarely happens except with regular clients; even then you often have to train them. A general guideline is this: if the copy was not keyed in by a trained typesetting professional, all formatting probably should be eliminated before you go to work.

The problem with word processors

Normally, the first step in digital production is word processing. This is only the first step because word processors simply do not have the typographic capabilities required to produce professional-looking documents. Interestingly enough, InDesign has left this capability out of its environment. Like QuarkXPress, it basically cannot do word processing. That is, it always works in WYSIWYG page layout view. Multiline composing and screen redraws make writing in either Quark or InDesign a pain.

Watch out! Here comes another of many opinions. You will do well to get rid of the normally accepted word processors like Word and WordPerfect. What publishing professionals need in a word processor is speed in the writing and editing of copy. All the fancy bells and whistles of the modern word processing behemoths are useless in a professional publishing environment anyway. In addition, that copy of Office you have on your machine is using huge quantities of disk space and your precious digital fluids (RAM). Is it really necessary?

I strongly recommend that you purchase (if you haven't already) a dedicated word processor that has drag'n'drop editing and style palette capabilities that can be assigned with a keyboard shortcut. My preference is Mariner Write. It takes barely 3 MB of hard disk space, less than 2 MB of RAM, is lightning fast (opens in less than 3 seconds), and has all of the powerful text editing tools needed (plus the list price was less than $80). I have also heard very good things about Nissus Writer. On the PC side, I do not know names, but it wouldn't surprise me if there is a freeware word processor that will do the job.

Publishing software

For some of you, this is review. Even for you power users, the conceptualization of how our software is used will be helpful. Many of you do not know why we use the programs we use. It is not because

CMYK color

Full-color printing uses four colors: cyan, magenta, yellow, and black. One of the larger frustrations you will be dealing with on a regular basis is reproducible color. You can only reproduce CMYK, and you can only do that with calibrated PostScript. Business software is RGB. Cheap inkjets cannot be calibrated.

they are popular. Keep in mind that if popularity were the issue, Quark would be out of business. PageMaker has sold ten times as many copies. In fact, last time I heard, Quark was in third place for page layout after InDesign and PageMaker as far as quantity is concerned.

Professional requirements

There are several important distinctions to be made concerning publishing software. First and foremost is the quality level. Software suitable for professional-quality publishing is top-end stuff. It has to support PostScript fluently and resolutions of 1,200 dpi or higher if it produces bitmapped lineart; or have the ability to produce a halftone screen frequency of at least 100 lines per inch for tints, halftones, and separations. Most professional work is at 133 linescreen or finer and 2,400 dpi or more. Also, this software must be able to read and use the common formats for graphics and text. At the minimum, this means support for EPS, TIFF, PDF, and the various word processing formats in common use, especially Rich Text Format. In addition, it has to support HTML, GIF, JPEG, and (increasingly) SWF and PNG.

We must have high-resolution CMYK PostScript.

A larger issue is the fact that programs like Word™ and Publisher™ cannot produce CMYK color. CMYK, or what we usually call process color or 4-color process, is what full-color images are actually printed in. Office programs work in RGB. This is the color space of light and is used by your monitor. It cannot be printed. Therefore, documents printed from these programs suffer radical uncontrollable color shifts when printed.

Professional standards

It must be remembered in digital publishing we are not competing against in-house secretarial productions, but slick "Madison Avenue" photographically imaged pieces. This takes a fast computer with a lot of memory (both RAM and storage) plus top-level software. (We covered the hardware needs in chapter 4.) Your competition is *Time*, *People*, *Smithsonian*, and the like as opposed to the *National Enquirer*.

Printed pages are amazingly complex images that use both conscious and subconscious techniques to communicate. We live in a culture that has received printed perfection for years, with clients who often refuse to pay for anything less. Courier and a spell checker will not cut it. We need kerning, tracking, various fonts, virtually infinite size, leading, and width controls, and we need them at the touch of a key or mouse button.

The need for PostScript

One of the most important things you must understand to work in this industry is PostScript. It is a page description language brought out by Adobe in 1985 that was part of the enabling technology (along with the LaserWriter and PageMaker) that created desktop publishing and saved the Mac. There were other competitors, but PostScript won out and became the absolute standard. Some others claim that their software can do as well – don't believe them. The problem is not in the creating software – there are many competing programs that can produce results that superficially appear professional (even Word, if you are very careful). The difficulty is in the final output. For the foreseeable future, all professional-quality output devices will continue to use PostScript. Even PDF is a streamlined PostScript variant.

For example, CorelDraw™ is not used much in our industry. That says nothing about the power and quality of the software. Right or wrong, there are basically three reasons: one, it was not available on the Mac for a long time; two, it does not use the standard industry terminology; and three, it does not produce files that can be relied upon with imagesetters and platesetters (it writes PostScript code that causes printing problems). Supposedly Versions 8 and up have solved the PostScript problem, but many of us are justifiably leery. When talking to printing professionals, the mere mention of the name causes very strong negative reactions. That alone is enough to make it unusable for our purposes.

The important thing to remember is that PostScript works by describing pages in terms of shapes. These shapes are described mathematically in a page description language. Even bitmapped images must be put in a box that is described mathematically, with screens and separations described in PostScript code. It is the focus of my book on PostScript illustration called *Publishing with Illustrator and FreeHand*. At this point, all you need is a firm grasp of the concept of pages as assemblages of shapes written as mathematical equations.

The software we use

Publishing software has at least three major categories: illustration – PostScript and paint; image editing or image manipulation; and page layout. To produce professional results, you will need at least one program in each of the categories. As mentioned, you probably need all of the Big Seven.

Illustration software

PostScript illustration

This book uses the term PostScript instead of other terms, such as vector drawings or object-oriented software, for a simple reason already mentioned. PostScript is the standard in our industry. Future developments will likely be improvements on PostScript. Even if there is a radical change, it will probably be called PostScript. The much discussed PDF workflow uses a cleaned up and streamlined PostScript. The concept we are discussing involves creating shapes by describing them with a mathematical equation of the outline and various fills.

This sounds much more clunky than it actually is. The equations used work elegantly. They are exquisitely precise and can be modified easily. It is a new way of working, but all the programs we use are PostScript. The major drawing tool, the Pen tool, is available in all publishing software. It takes awhile to learn how to learn the tool, but the precision and control are definitely addictive.

If there is a problem with this type of illustration, it is this precision. PostScript illustration can easily be too perfect. This is why much computer art is easily recognized. There is a perfection that cannot be found in the natural world. There is a matte smoothness that cannot be produced with a buffer or even hand polishing. There is no dirt, no breaks, no randomness, unless the artist works at it (and draws it in). For clean work with little or no visual distraction, PostScript software is the ideal solution. Adding the human touch is more difficult in these programs. All the dirt and abuse of reality must be drawn.

EPSs are smaller

A major advantage is that EPS (Encapsulated Postscript) graphics are generally much smaller than bitmap images like TIFFs (unless they are used to enclose bitmapped art). Because a large shape can be described with an equation instead of a huge, laborious list of each pixel or dot, vector drawings take up much less space in RAM, in storage, or in modem time. They can become so complicated that output is impossible, but this can easily be avoided with simple compassion for the imagesetter operators. EPSs are more portable by far.

Freedom of manipulation

In general, PostScript illustration is used because of the ease of manipulation. Any part of a vector drawing is treated as a separate object. As a result, any piece of a drawing can be cloned, duplicated, flipped,

---

PostScript illustration

This little graphic was done in FreeHand for the wrapped type and for the brushstroke, and InDesign for the finishing of the Intro band with transparency and shadow. Because the screen redraws were irritating, I eventually rasterized the PDF in Photoshop, saving it as a PSD file — to size.

INTRODUCTION TO TYPOGRAPHY & PUBLISHING
Intro

skewed, rotated, scaled, or filled with an almost infinite number of patterns, gradients, or tints. The professional programs allow layers to be built that can be moved above or below any other layer and turned on or off at will. Layers can be locked, grayed out, and made nonprintable (so they can be used for tracing). These layers can be directly exported as Flash animations. The creative freedom is totally exhilarating.

 The only problem is that illustrations can become so complicated that no image-setter can handle them. If you have a PostScript Illustration that approaches or exceeds 1 MB, it is far too large. In fact, it may not print. You need to be very careful about excessive complexity in PostScript illustrations. All it requires is a little planning and forethought.

Since the early 1990s there have only been two real competitors, FreeHand and Illustrator. The also-rans, primarily CorelDraw and Canvas, never quite matched up. Draw completely changes the technical language the rest of us use, plus it has always had problems with graphics that would not print. Even though it is possible to export as an Illustrator file, resave, and re-export as an EPS, this is obviously a bit clumsy.

Canvas has always advertised itself as the one-stop-shop, with many neat tricks. However, all reports indicated that, until very recently, Canvas lacked some of the basics and had trouble with PostScript. There are currently rumors that both Draw and Canvas are now professionally usable. No professional I know is using either.

I think the problem now is that pros are all deeply invested in FreeHand and/or Illustrator. Plus, increasingly PDFs are the deciding factor. There is no reason to change, and we don't want to take the chance. If they work for you, go for it. For most of us, the frustrations of getting things to print the way we desire eliminates anything but FreeHand and/or Illustrator.

FreeHand/Illustrator differences

As far as the two majors are concerned, Illustrator has always had the reputation. FreeHand has had the ease of use and most of the innovations. In my experience, Illustrator has been a lot like QuarkX-Press. It takes a great deal of memory and constant use to remember the keyboard shortcuts necessary to function in both these programs. They are not very intuitive until you have learned to think like they think. Without the shortcuts and constant use, the amount of mousing required greatly slows production.

However, once the shortcuts are learned, Illustrator is universally acclaimed as *the most elegant* PostScript illustration program. Illustrator is undeniably the choice of full-time professional illustrators. Its use will probably increase a little now that it is so strongly fit into the standard Adobe interface of PageMaker, InDesign, Illustrator, and Photoshop. It does have what is commonly called a steep learning curve. In practical terms, this means that it is a real pain to learn.

FreeHand, on the other hand, is very easy to use. Its functions are both easier to understand and easier to access. Its capabilities like drag'n'drop gradients, multiple pages, perspective grid, 25,600% enlargements, and 222-inch square pasteboard are not matched by any one else. No other program can handle type so fluidly. There are also direct interface ties to Dreamweaver, Flash, and Director that appeal to many Web designers. Beyond that, until InDesign, FreeHand was the only program that allowed the almost complete customization of the interface to fit your needs. FreeHand can almost do the Adobe interface better than Adobe, if that is your desire.

FreeHand is the clear winner for people who are responsible for the entire process of digital publishing – working with several programs open, every day, on a constant basis. Illustrator will probably remain the favorite of people who specialize in drawing and illustration, exclusively. FreeHand is probably the best choice in production environments. There is a real reason why the news wire services settled on FreeHand for their graphic delivery to newspapers – production. Both UPI and AP specified that several years ago.

The final software in this group would be MultiAd Creator. I know very little about it. All reports make this an incredibly powerful, extremely functional tool in the intensely production-driven newspaper and magazine environment. I have no idea why it isn't used more. But then I have never figured out why VHS beat out Beta, or why Iomega put SyQuest out of business. Often, the best simply does not win out.

Though the possibilities are amazing, many illustrations can still be done only by the other type of graphic illustration software, a painting program that works with bitmapped images.

Paint illustration

This discussion will separate paint from image editing because of the complexity of the tools. In this case, we are talking almost exclusively about Painter, now sold by Corel (or the 3D paint programs). Painter tries to emulate traditional fine art tools and techniques with remarkable success. It uses "real" brushes, like a Sumi brush or a round sable, doing a remarkable job of mimicking the look of the tool. In fact, fine art is the key to understanding this program. It uses fine art language and a fine art attitude for an interface that is nearly incomprehensible in its complexity. The learning curve is very steep in the beginning. This is a program for full-time illustrators. No one else really has the time to learn the interface.

Once you are in and working, Painter has amazing power. You start by specifying the surface to be worked on — watercolor paper in smooth, rough, hot press, cold press, and several variants; canvas of many kinds and textures; and so forth. Then you pick the color of the surface and the direction of the prevailing light source.

The tools have fine art names — brushes, markers, pencils, pastels, crayons, and so on. Unlike Photoshop's limited, single brush of varying size and color, Painter offers watercolor sables, worn bristle brushes, Sumi brushes, and so on. These brushes actually give the same results as their namesakes. Painter 6 has brushes where each bristle or hair produces an individual line.

Plus, most of the options available to fine art materials are there. You can drop water on a wash and produce the same bleeding and hard edge found in watercolors. All of these have many variations, and the penetration and saturation of the colors can also be controlled. The erasers come in ink, fine point, gum, dry, kneaded rubber, plus a full set of bleach tools. The erasers take you back to the surface color. The bleaches take you to white.

The tools can get rather exotic — spinners, rubber stamps, airbrush, smudgers, and so on. In addition, there are cloning tools, selection tools of many kinds, and blending tools. It becomes relatively easy to produce multiple strokes or multiple image parts. There is complete control of transparency and blending. Many fine artists are now producing watercolors in Painter and printing them out on large Iris inkjets on watercolor paper. It is virtually impossible to tell whether they were done by hand or by computer.

The only limits are your imagination and coordination. The main thing, as in all fine art, is practice, practice, practice. It is obvious that virtually any type of picture can be produced digitally **IF** (this is really a large if!):

- you have a lot of time
- you have a lot of RAM — 512 MB or more (1 GB RAM is commonplace in this rarefied arena)
- you have a lot of storage — RAID arrays and huge multigigabyte disks are normal
- you have a fast CPU — G3 or Pentium III or faster (a multiprocessor GHz G4 would be nice)
- you have a lot of skill and much experience

This is the major problem with painting. These bitmapped documents commonly run into hundreds of megabytes. Gigabyte paintings are not unheard of. Most of the applications require that there be three to five times the size of the file in RAM and the same amount available on the hard drive for manipulation purposes. Some of the three-dimensional paint programs still take days to render the image on the screen, even in the time of Pentium IIIs and G4s.

It is certainly possible to cover the surface of a shape with textures ranging from shiny metal through any fabric, stone, tile, whatever. It takes time. Often it takes a lot of time. With digital production time measured in minutes, painting is often a luxury that must be forgone. Often, there is only time for much simpler solutions.

Portability difficulties

Another problem that is often forgotten is, "What do you do with that admittedly gorgeous image when you are done?" If the document reaches several gigabytes, how can it be transported to a service bureau, unless you simply unplug your hard drive and carry it there? In fact, the current crop of pocket-sized, hot-swappable FireWire drives is one of the few solutions, so far. This is the reason for Iomega's Peerless drives.

Even these technological wonders only hold a dozen or two gigabytes. Huge multipage, process-color pieces like programs, magazines, or annual reports can easily total several gigabytes. It is too late to prepare for this when the document is finished at 2 GB and your largest removable is an old 1 GB JAZ drive. This part of the reason why DVD-R will probably become the norm at 4.5 GB or more.

A final concern with painted images is the need to create them to size. Unless you calculate accurately, resizing a bitmapped image can produce a severe case of the "jaggies." At the very least it will be softened. Transformation tools do the same. Unlike PostScript graphics, which rasterize the image at the printer, painted images have designated pixels. The image is modified in page layout at the risk of the designer. As a result, you should plan carefully in advance and produce an image that is transformed and sized for the final output directly in the creating software. Then it will print with no problems – easier than many EPSs.

Scan manipulation

Image editing software

Technically, image editing software could be called painting programs, but their purpose is different and the tools are more limited in quantity, though not in scope. In reality, image editing software can be called Photoshop (even though Corel's PhotoPaint is a distant also-ran). The major purpose of image manipulation software is to work with scans of photographs, artifacts, and continuous tone artwork. They do this extremely well. Beyond that, image manipulation software does an amazingly powerful job of compositing multiple images.

Professional manipulation software can work in color up to 48-bit. They can produce RGB or

CMYK, grayscale, and bitmap images. They can export the finished images in a very wide variety of formats including the required EPS, TIFF, GIF, JPEG, PNG, and PDF. In fact, one of Photoshop's common uses is converting strange formats into something more acceptable to the software being used for page layout. Unprintable TIFFs, from non-professional software, can simply be opened and resaved in Photoshop to fix them, for example.

Halftone and separation production

Photoshop can produce halftones, duotones, tritones, quadritones, and CMYK color-calibrated separations. It can produce virtually any screen frequency or angle in a wide variety of dot patterns, including round dot, square dot, elliptical dot, line, mezzotint, and custom dots. It provides complete control over color, tint range, highlights, midtones, or shadow dots, and so on. (If this paragraph seems to be in a foreign language, you need to read *Publishing with Photoshop* which teaches Photoshop production techniques.)

One of the major abilities of this type of software is another result of the paradigm shift. It has become relatively easy to blend many photos or scans into one. We are not talking about simple collages where images are pasted together into a single image. This is a brand new ability: New York balanced on the edge of Crater Lake with the Matterhorn looming in the background. You may have noticed my goat, Walter, in the window of the arch on the previous page. This is the technology used for all the reality distortions in movies and commercials. Or maybe you think that guy really carried in the Honda on his back, flipped it off, and drove it away.

Every image can be placed in its own layer. That layer can be infinitely doctored up with color modifications, feathering, and transparency control. When all the layers are flattened into a single image, it is impossible to tell that the image has been messed with — except for the obvious fact that it no longer has any attachment to reality known to mankind.

In addition, image manipulation programs offer a huge variety of filters to blur, sharpen, twist, pointillize, distort, lighten, darken, or otherwise play with the image. Because it is easy to edit at the pixel level, it is relatively simple to put one person's head on a different person's body, and so on. I remember a magazine cover showing Hillary as a dominatrix in leathers and whip, for example.

Retouching photos has taken on an entirely new meaning. In fact, it has become an ethical problem. Are we required to tell when we've removed a deformity? Photographs can no longer be considered legal evidence, as they used to be; no one can tell whether the photo has been modified.

You have not seen a real photo in a magazine for many years. We routinely take off zits, stray hairs, double chins, and so on. Of course, you take your life in your hands if you remove that beauty mark, thinking it to be a blemish. Ethically, we should probably be putting a little byline next to each picture stating that it has been modified. But that would still not stop the plague of anorexia caused by these images in the minds of immature girls.

The major source of *professionally ugly* design

The filters and multiple layers of various images have become a real visual problem. In recent years, many illustrations have become mere filter and compositing demos with little artistic merit. They are bad design covered with fashion. At its worst, modern image manipulation illustration becomes what could be called professionally ugly — distorted collages of images whose sole purpose is to convince the viewer of the creator's sophistication. John McWade calls it "grunge collage." What most fail to remember is that this style of image is often appealing only to their fellow Photoshop video warriors. In fact, many schools and most books teach Photoshop like a true video game — fun and games.

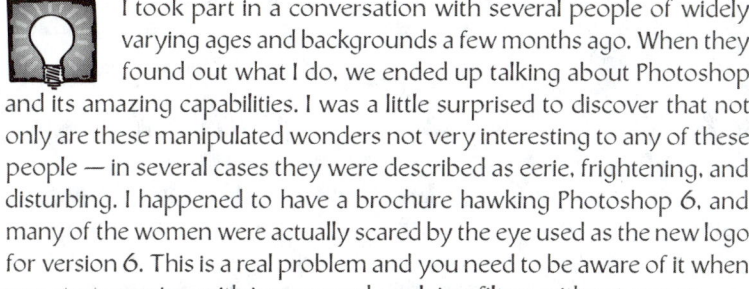

I took part in a conversation with several people of widely varying ages and backgrounds a few months ago. When they found out what I do, we ended up talking about Photoshop and its amazing capabilities. I was a little surprised to discover that not only are these manipulated wonders not very interesting to any of these people — in several cases they were described as eerie, frightening, and disturbing. I happened to have a brochure hawking Photoshop 6, and many of the women were actually scared by the eye used as the new logo for version 6. This is a real problem and you need to be aware of it when you start messing with images and applying filters without reason.

Fancy Photoshop images are usually liked only by Photoshop users.

The size and transportation problems are the same as for painting programs. The hardware requirements are very stiff. Photoshop professionals are always complaining about memory even at the norm of 256 MB of RAM. Every new version of Photoshop requires more RAM. The

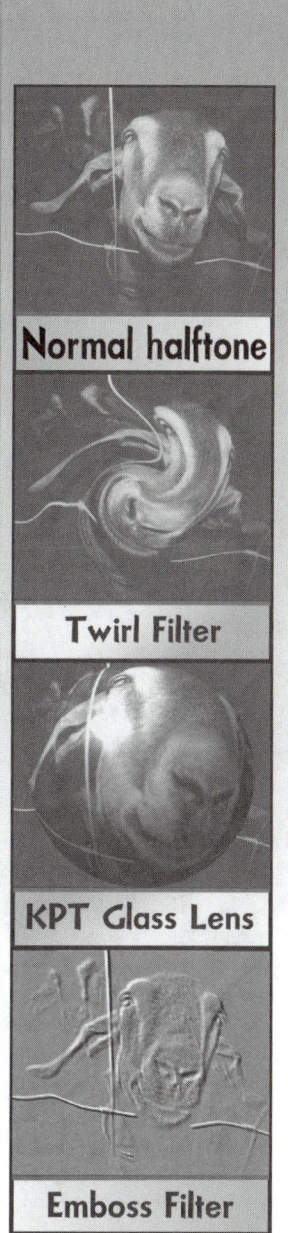

Normal halftone

Twirl Filter

KPT Glass Lens

Emboss Filter

minimum requirement, according to the user manual, is now 32 MB. Even then you can only work on small, simple images. In reality, the minimum is more like 256 MB.

Document assembly

Page layout

We have finally arrived at the pinnacle of digital publishing. Though it can be argued that image editing takes the most skill (PostScript illustrators can squeal now) and digital image assembly takes the most computing power (let's hear the whines of the animation crowd), page layout software is the cream of the crop, the top of the heap, the end of the chain. This is where the document comes together for print.

Though image assembly or prepress comes after page layout, creativity truly ends with layout. The master designers work in page layout. Illustrators can be hired, separations can be subcontracted out, and image assembly can be handled by the printer as a separate contractor. Page layout creates the publication in a very real way. Though writers and illustrators are often more creative (as classically defined), page layout is what ties the document together and creates the overall image. Writing is not read unless the publication convinces readers that they want to read it. Illustrations usually make little sense unless they are tied to the writing that goes with them in a way that communicates clearly and accurately.

Creativity ends with page layout.

In a lot of ways, page layout software is like a Jack or Jill of all trades, but a master of one: document assembly. You can write in them, but writers prefer a good word processor. You can draw in them, but many of the good abilities are missing. It is even possible to do some image manipulation, but only at the expense of quality. What page layout does better than anything else is final production of the artwork. Once a document leaves page layout, the rest of the production is concerned with duplication rather than creation.

Creative freedom with ultimate typography

A document in the hands of a master designer has the fluidity of paint. Type can ebb and flow like water into the channels prepared for it by the creator. Graphics become points of inspiration and clarification. The concepts of the writer communicate clearly, and the reader is powerfully motivated to respond as intended. Professional page layout software uses type, graphics, and color as malleable media. The freedom of photographic pasteup is nothing compared to our new digital expression possibilities. Document contents become fluid.

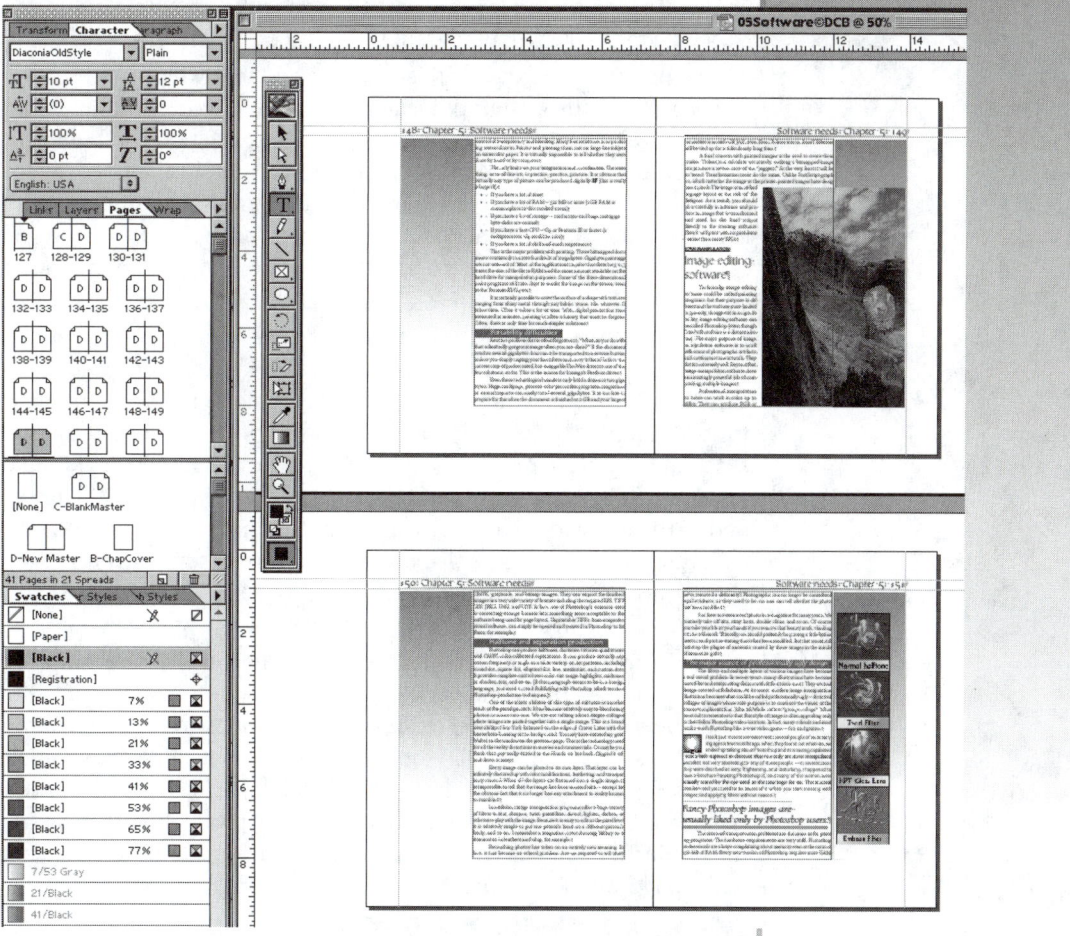

These applications allow a control of type size, leading, tracking, kerning, scaling, and positioning that is astonishing to traditional professionals. You can vary these from a few points to hundreds at the touch of a couple of keys or the click of a mouse. Paragraph styles can be preformatted to allow text to be imported and automatically flowed into place with an exciting amount of control. Character palettes allow for consistent typographic accents. Tables can be added with the same types of controls. InDesign even has full transparency to play with.

Graphics can be linked to the text so that reflowing the words brings the pictures along with them. Colors can be assigned freely and applied precisely. Everything can be "snapped" to a predefined grid to provide creative freedom with an underlying structure that prevents chaos. Type sizes and leading can be changed by minute amounts to eliminate extra lines or paragraphs.

Beyond all of these are such things as text wrap, which allows the designer to drop a graphic into the middle of copy and watch the words fit themselves around it automatically. Linking is so complete that you can open the original graphic directly from the page layout software. When changes or repairs are made and saved, the image is simply updated in the final document. If the wrong graphic is imported or you simply change your mind, relinking allows you to bring in the one you really intended to use.

When the body of the document is complete, tables of contents and indexes can also be created automatically. The chapters or sections can be tied together with automatic page numbering and "continued to" or "continued from" tags. Multiple master pages can be set up that automatically place repeating elements on every page as needed while remaining completely editable. Columns, guide lines, margins, alignment, and virtually any other element of a publication can be controlled with exquisite precision, often with the nudge of an arrow key. Power users can control all of these techniques on the fly with a complete set of keyboard shortcuts that can be adjusted to fit the designer's working style.

When everything is complete, the document, all linked graphics and text, fonts, and whatever else is necessary can be automatically assembled into a final folder for easy transportation to the imagesetter, printer, image assembly facility, or platesetter. For even more streamlining, everything can be condensed into a universally usable PDF. The creation is complete and packaged — all that remains is production. The rest of the production team is charged with duplicating the artwork produced in the page layout software.

The varieties available

Within the constraints of PostScript, there are four page layout programs that can work professionally: FrameMaker for the scientific, technical, and long document market; PageMaker for spontaneous creation where the designer is also writing or editing all of the copy; QuarkXPress for process production with automatic assembly into precise templates; and the most advanced, InDesign. FrameMaker is rare though it has several unique capabilities (footnotes, equations, and so on).

PageMaker, QuarkXPress, and InDesign

The three primary page layout tools are PageMaker, QuarkX-Press, and InDesign. As we just mentioned, FrameMaker is used for long technical documents and governmental tomes. It's relatively rare. FreeHand can also do page layout, but it doesn't handle long documents very fluidly. It's mainly used by people coming from Web design.

As far as ease of use is concerned, PageMaker is still the best. It uses the pasteup metaphor and is relatively easy to comprehend. Quark is a real pain. Everything is a two-step procedure, at least. Documents have to be thoroughly planned because readjustments often mean you have to trash the document and start over. On a scale of one to ten with one being the easiest to use, the following numbers would be pretty close: PageMaker–1; FreeHand–2; InDesign–4; FrameMaker–6; and Quark–8 or maybe even 9.

PageMaker was first, in 1984. Quark took over in 1991 when it could handle CMYK. PageMaker passed Quark in capabilities in the late 1990s, but by then Quark was firmly established as necessary for professional printing. Remember, fashion and reputation often have little to do with reality. InDesign was created in 2000 as a total rewrite of PageMaker, solving most of its problems.

Currently, PageMaker is still dominant in the business world. Quark still has the reputation, but there are equal numbers of people using InDesign. Quark, the company, is so busy shooting itself in the foot that InDesign will almost surely be the standard by 2005. At this point, with PageMaker 7, InDesign 2, and Quark 5, all are almost equally capable. However, InDesign is far superior in typography, interface customization, and PDF workflow. Its drawing tools are also far superior to the other two. Plus it has transparency, feathering, and drop shadows. Quark is probably still superior for pure repetitive production. However, it still requires many expensive Xtensions to do that (often thousands of dollars worth). PageMaker is really short on drawing tools. But for pure spontaneous production, it is still the best. It is being targeted at the business community though – so it will become less common in our industry.

Astonishing complexity

The realities of skill

Professional publishing software is complex enough to make it virtually impossible for anyone to be expert at all of it. Attempting to do everything usually compromises the quality of the finished product. If at all possible, the norm should be to let writers write, illustrators illustrate, and designers design. Try not to expect creativity out of pre-

Training time

You need to have training time, where you can explore and expand your knowledge. It must be regularly scheduled or you will fall behind. You will need two to four hours a week or you will get in trouble sooner or later.

press wizards— it will reduce their accuracy (and you are paying them for their accuracy and technical skill). Technicians in the image assembly department are chastised if they change the image without signed prior approval from the artist, at least, and usually the client.

Training requirements are huge

Finally, no matter how much talent one demonstrates, it takes a fair amount of time for anyone to become proficient at any one program. Expect that close to 200 hours of practice (not work!) will be required for power use of each program (much more than that for publishing novices). This is specifically 200 hours of practice and experimentation, as opposed to routine production, with each program. Also remember that the yearly upgrades often take considerable time to assimilate. This time should be planned for. Compromising training time will mean shorting your company (or yourself) on production speed and accuracy. If your superiors do not understand this, it might be appropriate to look for a new position elsewhere.

Beyond that there is the problem of wetware storage. It is the rare brain that can be truly expert in all areas of digital design. You are a fool to try. The adage is true: the jack-of-all-trades is rarely master of any of them. Look at your personal strengths and head in that direction, spending your training time where it will do the most good. You really do not have to do everything. It is the wise person who subcontracts his weaknesses (having people available to help).

PDF workflow

Recently there has been a huge amount of excitement about the last program in the Big Seven. There really is good reason to believe that it is about to become the center of your workflow procedures. Most of you have at least heard of PDFs by now. So, what's the big deal? From our point of view here, we will not get into the entire procedure for using a PDF workflow.

For now, let's just describe what they are. PDF stands for Portable Document Format. It was one of a group of formats developed in the late 1980s and early 1990s to solve the cross-platform dilemma. The basic idea is a universal format that can be read by anyone on any platform. PDF does this well. Acrobat Reader is free. You have a copy of the installer on your CD and it can be downloaded free from http://www.adobe.com for any platform you need: Mac, PC, UNIX, Sun, Silicon Graphics, Next, and others. This reader can read any PDF regardless of what platform it was created on (provided it is recent enough). You do have to stay current. And Reader is not enough for us.

One of the real problems I had when I first installed InDesign was that none of my students could read the PDFs I produced until they installed Reader 4.0.5. I still find that I do better with the full version of 4 than Reader 5. Acrobat comes in several parts. The three that matter to us are: Acrobat, Distiller, and Reader.

Acrobat is the full version of the software. It can edit and annotate PDFs. It can add links, adjust the cropping, and so on. Distiller is the program that produces PDFs. If you have trouble with PDFs exported directly, this is what you use. You have to print your file to disk — save the PostScript code generated for printing into a file. Then you open that PostScript file in Distiller. Distiller has many options and you will have to set it up carefully. Reader just reads PDFs and is used by our clients. Only Reader is free. The rest you must pay for.

Printable PDFs

However, PDFs go far beyond universal readability. Because they embed the graphics, PDFs produce an extremely accurate view of the original document. They can even be used for contract proofs. More than that, the image will be crisp, clear, and will not suffer badly when you enlarge it to see things better (as long as the bitmap graphics have high enough resolution).

More than that, the pages will print much better than they look on the screen, because they will print at the resolution of the printer. This is because the PDF format is a streamlined, cleaned-up version of PostScript. All the fonts can be embedded, so you do not have to convert them to paths — and once the fonts are embedded, they show up perfectly on PC or Mac. This solves the major cross-platform issue: the fact that Macs cannot read PC fonts and vice versa.

PDF annotation

During the process of creation, I regularly use PDFs for proofing. I send PDF proofs to each of my proofers and they add the corrections in the form of annotations. These are little notes that can be added to PDFs with Acrobat. These notes have the proofer's name on their title bar. When I get the proofs back I can assemble the notes from each of my proofers into a single PDF file. This makes adding the corrections extremely easy. The annotation procedure is not detailed enough for my copyeditor — after the book is completed. However, it makes a wonderful visual proofing medium for catching layout errors and so forth.

Beyond that, PDFs have proven to be the enabling technology for teaching these materials on the Web. Without the ability of students to easily send in projects in a complete package, online critiques would be impossible. More than that, without a way to annotate those projects as they work their way to professionalism, it would be impossible to offer suggestions or help that could be understood.

Compression

I have mentioned that PDF is a streamlined PostScript, but that would not be enough in itself. For Web delivery, we have to go much further than that. So Acrobat offers very powerful downsampling and compression capabilities. It offers both lossy and lossless compression to what printers would consider ridiculous extremes. But then the Web is ridiculously crude from a printer's point of view.

 You really need to remember that PDF was developed for Web delivery, among other things. The default when you install the Distiller package is for Web graphics. This means heavy downsampling (to 72 dpi) and extreme lossy compression (using JPEG at the maximum). Distiller 4 offers three job settings: Screen Optimized for the Web and CDs; Print Optimized for your laser printer or inkjet; and Prepress Optimized for your service bureau, imagesetter, or platesetter. You will need to carefully set up your job options when you start using this software regularly. You will need to save custom settings for your printers. My printer for this book, for example, wants me to be sure that I only use lossless compression and no downsampling.

Do not be dismayed, the Web *is* ridiculously crude from a historical designer's perspective. Extreme JPEG compression cannot even be seen online. While it is true that JPEGs can hardly be used in printing because of the compression artifacts, at 72 dpi those artifacts are not even rendered on the screen. However, the Save For Web command in Photoshop now makes lossy GIFs that are often far superior to JPEGs.

Interactivity

Beyond all of this, PDFs can be made interactive very easily. Internal linkages are made as fast as you can type. Links can be added to external URLs. Clicking on the Web link opens your browser and goes to the link. You can embed Quicktime movies that will play with a click on a link — or music. There is really nothing better for the generation of electronic books at the present time.

The front cover of one of my chapters for one of my early PDF books can be seen to the left. That Table of Contents is linked to the locations in the book. If I click on a TOC entry, it takes me to that page at an

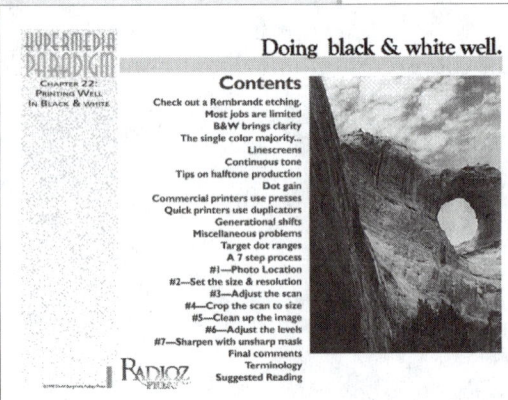

HYPERMEDIA PARADIGM

CHAPTER 22: PRINTING WELL IN BLACK & WHITE

Doing black & white well.

Contents

Check out a Rembrandt etching.
Most jobs are limited
B&W brings clarity
The single color majority...
Linescreens
Continuous tone
Tips on halftone production
Commercial printers use presses
Quick printers use duplicators
Dot gain
Generational shifts
Miscellaneous problems
Target dot ranges
A 7 step process
#1—Photo Location
#2—Set the size & resolution
#3—Adjust the scan
#4—Crop the scan to size
#5—Clean up the image
#6—Adjust the levels
#7—Sharpen with unsharp mask
Final comments
Terminology
Suggested Reading

RADIQZ PRESS

appropriate enlargement. There are also many interactive links inside each chapter. The glossary on the last page of each chapter is linked directly to the definitions in the chapter, for example. References to illustrations are linked to those illustrations. Most importantly, all of the linkages were added in about 15 minutes. It really makes a marvelous method to publish exploratory or limited edition books.

We haven't even talked about Apple's change from QuickDraw to PDF for monitor graphics in OSX. How far they go with that remains to be seen. There is a reasonable chance that PDF will become the standard for all monitor graphics in addition to becoming the output standard for digital publishing. It is easy to foresee all of publishing becoming dependent upon PDF as we are now dependent upon PostScript.

Web design software

Almost all of you will have a WYSIWYG Web page creator. Some of you will insist that Dreamweaver or GoLive is essential. Some will argue just as fervently that FrontPage or PageMill are more than sufficient. Many of you will have a dedicated Web graphic creator like Fireworks or ImageReady. Most of you will at least be tempted by Flash or LiveMotion. Many more will realize that when you only design a few Web sites a year (less than 500 pages or so), FreeHand, Illustrator, and Photoshop work just fine for the creation of your Web graphics.

The industry standard right now is Dreamweaver from Macromedia with about 85% of the market. There is also huge interest in Flash, a vector-based Web program providing amazing animation and interactivity relatively easily. Many people claim that Fireworks, which finishes out Macromedia's Web suite, is the best bitmap image editor on the planet. It doesn't do anything printable so it is still far behind Photoshop.

We don't talk much about Web design in this book because type is currently impossible on the Web. In fact, Web copy pulls us back to the bad old days of typewriters, WordStar™, MacWrite™, and other nontypographic word processors. Nevertheless, most of you will be spending almost half of your time designing for the Web. Most Web design is actually database management and programming. But the graphic portions will be done by people like you. It takes the same skill set you learn for print production.

Font management

You will definitely need font management software. Sadly, this is one of the areas where Windows is still far behind. Recently, Wintel font management software has begun to show up, as the need becomes more apparent. Currently there are Adobe Type Manager Deluxe and

WYSIWYG menus

One of the real advantages of font management software is that they all (except for Adobe) come with a utility that lets you see what the type actually looks like in the font menu. Adobe keeps trying to thwart that, for some stupid reason which they will not explain.

Suitcase. On the Mac, there are several choices. Suitcase was formerly the standard, but it has fallen behind. MasterJuggler has almost disappeared. Adobe Type Manager Deluxe works very well, but it will not be supported for OSX. There is a newer one with great reviews called Font Reserve. I like it and use it, but it's not that much better. For OSX there is Suitcase and Font Reserve.

With fonts, there are two things going on. First of all, almost all designers end up as virtual font collectors, for reasons you will understand by the end of this book. The longer you work in the industry, the more you are seduced by the beauty of excellent type. Both MacOS and Windows have limits to the number of fonts that can be installed (active) at any one time. The font managers allow you to keep the actual fonts used to manageable levels, giving you the capability of making font sets for your various clients and projects. You only turn on what you need for the project you are designing. If you find a specific need for your project, you can then add to your active set.

The second reason has more to do with production. When you start a project like an event program, a small magazine, or anything where you will be placing a lot of advertising, fonts can quickly get out of hand. PDFs are helping with their embedded fonts. However, many designers are not as enlightened as we are. Some have not even heard of PDFs. Most are self-trained and clueless.

You will receive ads as Quark EPSs with embedded Illustrator EPSs and Photoshop TIFFs. You will receive raw FreeHand pages. You will get PageMaker pages. You will get everything imaginable. Every ad will bring two to ten fonts to the mix. I remember doing a little sixteen page, process color, fine arts magazine (a year ago or so) where each issue had over 200 different fonts, just from the advertisements. Every agency sent a different set. They sent over 700 fonts; I only used 200.

Font management is not an option.

At this point, font management is not an option. That many fonts can quickly overload the resources of your machine. The scenario just mentioned was complicated by a printer, in Juarez, (old) Mexico who had never heard of PDFs. I'm not sure I would like to try to make a PDF out of a sixteen-page document with over 200 fonts and over 600 MB of imported graphics, anyway. (And for those of you asking, the deadlines precluded most repairs and the option of converting most of those fonts to paths.) Without a good font manager, that project would have quickly gone down the tubes.

Miscellaneous software

Cross-platform compression software

One of the regular problems you will run across is the fact that Wintel uses ZIP compression and Mac uses Stuffit. There are other compression options, but these two are the platform standards. Most PC people use WinZip. Most Mac people use Stuffit. Macs can't read ZIP files and PCs cannot read .sit or .sea files (the output of Stuffit). Both programs have utilities you can buy that enable you to compress for either platform and to extract compressed files from either platform. You need to buy one. The best on the Mac is Stuffit Deluxe. On a PC there are many options. Most do not do anything about Mac files.

Viruses

Hate to say it, but this is a Wintel problem. Last time I heard there were only a couple dozen viruses on a Mac and none of them were malicious. In fact, I have only had one virus on any of my computers in eleven years of hard use. I don't even use anti-virus software. I have in the past, but I never found anything. On a Mac, the anti-virus software causes more problems than the rare viruses. On a PC, viruses are a huge problem. Get a good anti-virus software package and keep it updated.

Utilities

In addition, all of you will have software that you are certain you cannot do without. It might be something as simple as a macro-maker like QuicKeys. It may be a less common program like Canvas or MultiAd Creator. (I even saw someone on the InDesign list the other day talking about using ReadySetGo side by side with InDesign.) It might be as complex as 3D bitmap illustration software. There are chart creation software, table makers, database converters, tag generators, and so forth. I can't function without dedicated screen capture software (Snapz Pro). The real criteria is that you are enabled to save your graphics in a usable format (EPS, TIFF, PDF – GIF, JPEG, PNG, SWF).

Quite a few of you will quickly discover that you simply cannot survive without barcode creation software. Several will be using Fontographer to solve font problems and to create custom fonts for yourself and your clients. The list goes on almost forever. We haven't even mentioned your copy of Director, Authorware, Premier, and After Effects – or maybe you prefer Final Cut Pro, Alias, or LightWave or whatever.

The point I am trying to make is simple. Every one of you will have your own personal hardware and software configurations that work well for you. You need to add the pieces that help you do the things you do best. If you don't like to work in Photoshop, don't be ashamed. On the other hand, if you haven't tried PostScript illustration (FreeHand and/or Illustrator) you are missing out on a great tool. Almost all of us use both bitmap and vector — to varying degrees. The key is not allowing yourself to be seduced by the video game nature of much of the software out there. There is a time for gaming, but it will certainly mess up production. Find software that improves production efficiency.

Timing concerns and benefits

Adobe and Quark do not do toolbars. Macromedia does have this option. In FreeHand, especially, you can completely customize its toolbars. This is not the place to get into specifics. However, we need to review basic production speed issues. The figures I am giving here are only approximate, but they are proportionally accurate.

- Mousing menu commands: 2 to 4 seconds
- Selecting tools by mouse: 1 to 3 seconds
- Mousing toolbar buttons: 1 second
- Using palette (if it is open): 1 second
- Keyboard shortcut: 2/10 of a second or less

To give a practical example, used many times a day: selecting the Type tool, so you can set type. In FreeHand, InDesign, Illustrator, and Photoshop, you can select the Type tool by typing the letter T. In an eight-hour day, you might do this 200 to 400 times. If you mouse to select the tool in the toolbox, this will take somewhere around 200 to 400 seconds or 3.5 to 7 minutes. By using the shortcut, it will take 80 seconds at most, and probably more like 20 seconds. This saves you 3 to 6 minutes per day. If you select all of your tools with the shortcuts, you can save almost a half-hour per day.

In a more dramatic example, let's use Photoshop. You will regularly be opening the Image menu to the Adjust command and then off to the side to select Curves. Grabbing the mouse, dragging down the Image menu and then accurately going off to the side menu for Curves can take 3 seconds or more. If you are producing a long series of halftones for a directory, for example, you might need to access this command 100 times in a day (minimum). By using a shortcut for Curves (Command/Control M), you can save another 3 minutes.

That time might seem insignificant, but there is a real reason why we ol' fogies can beat you young whippersnappers by hours. The going rate for formatting a book like this one is about 10 minutes per page. This includes importing the copy, formatting it, dropping in the graphics, eliminating widows and orphans, spell checking, and printing a proof. I can do an average of nearly twenty pages per hour. Without the shortcuts, I would be lucky to do a half-dozen. Remember, your fellow students are not your competition in this industry, it is people like me (and I'm not all that fast).

Learning shortcuts

So, with this short intro, what do I expect you to do? After all, you are in a state of panic because you do not know any of these programs. **Relax!** What is required at this point is a change in thinking and the beginning of observation. This will take some time. It might take you a year or two to get yourself set up. I still regularly modify my setup and my shortcuts. It is the first thing I set up when installing new software.

You need to watch yourself work. This is why this diatribe is in an early chapter of this book. Notice which commands and tools you use constantly. Learn the shortcuts for those commands and tools. If you find yourself regularly using (or starting to use) a command from another application by mistake, change FreeHand, InDesign, or Illustrator to match your normal usage. Do whatever you are enabled to do to make your shortcuts common to as many programs as possible.

You need to watch yourself work.

Obviously, this will take some time and effort. Of course, you will not be able to do this until you are in a daily creation and/or production environment. However, to survive in this industry, this is not an option. All of your competitors are doing it (especially those who can out-produce you by a factor of two or three times). The key is learning to watch yourself as you work.

Now you need to note, I have a photographic memory and I can retain about 500 shortcuts in my active memory. In addition, I teach these materials five days per week which refreshes that memory. Most of you will have a great deal of trouble remembering more than a couple hundred shortcuts, and it takes over 200 to run any one of the Big Seven: PageMaker, InDesign, QuarkXPress, FreeHand, Illustrator, or Photoshop. You must be selective to avoid overloading your memory.

Left-handed shortcuts

I will mention this heresy (to the normal world) because it is nearly normal in the design community (probably over half). All shortcut setups are right-handed. By this I mean that for those of us who use the mouse

Where should you be by this time?

By this time you should be producing simple documents. If you have previous experience, you should be producing complex documents.

By this time a few of you will have finished the minimal course requirements and will be working on projects to start building your portfolio. This is a good thing.

DISCUSSION

You should be talking about benefits of various software combinations. If you are an actual student, you should be buying educational versions for your computer at home. If you do not have a computer at home, sell your car and get one.

Talk amongst yourselves...

with one hand and execute the shortcuts with the other, lefties have a problem. (The compromised Mac keyboard is even more strongly right-handed with the elimination of the modifier keys on the right side.)

All I need to do is remind you of all of the shortcuts built around A, S, D, Q, W, Z, X, C, V. All of those keys are found at the left of the keyboard. Seemingly these would work well for lefties. However, in most cases, they mean we have to drop the mouse. As a result, I have experienced large production speed increases by simply basing many of my shortcuts on the ,./l;'iop keys on the right side instead. For example, in InDesign I access the selection tool with Command+', the direct selection tool with Command+\, and so on. This works for me, but it makes my shortcut set much different than the norm. In fact, I can leave both right and left shortcut sets in place to be used interchangeably — depending on which hand is using the mouse at the time. Yes, most of us lefties are at least partially ambidextrous.

The faster you can produce the more time there is to create.

Beyond the Big Seven, there is no right or wrong. Software decisions are based on what you like and what helps you produce more, faster and better. Take manufacturer hype with a grain of salt. No matter what you hear, Word cannot do page layout. No matter what you hear, FreeHand cannot do booklets and magazines. No matter what you hear, CorelDraw still has trouble making printable graphics (it is still the most common complaint I hear from service bureaus and Kinko's™).

Finally, typos are absolutely forbidden!

Knowledge Retention

1. What is the purpose of page layout?
2. What are the main problems with bitmapped files?
3. Why do we use PostScript?
4. Why can't we use word processors for page layout?
5. Why do we need font management software?
6. What is your procedure for learning shortcuts?
7. Why can't we do everything in one software application?

Chapter 6

File Management

Concepts

Keeping track of your digital litter

Chapter Objectives:

By giving students a clear understanding of the digital publishing industry, this chapter will enable students to:

1. assemble documents into a folder for printing
2. maintain good link management
3. name a file clearly
4. work off their hard drives, using ZIPs and the like only for backup

Lab Work for Chapter:

1. Make sure you are working on a wide variety of tutorials from different software. This is your opportunity to discover which software works best for you.
2. Continue with miniskills
3. Read chapters 7 and 8 for next week

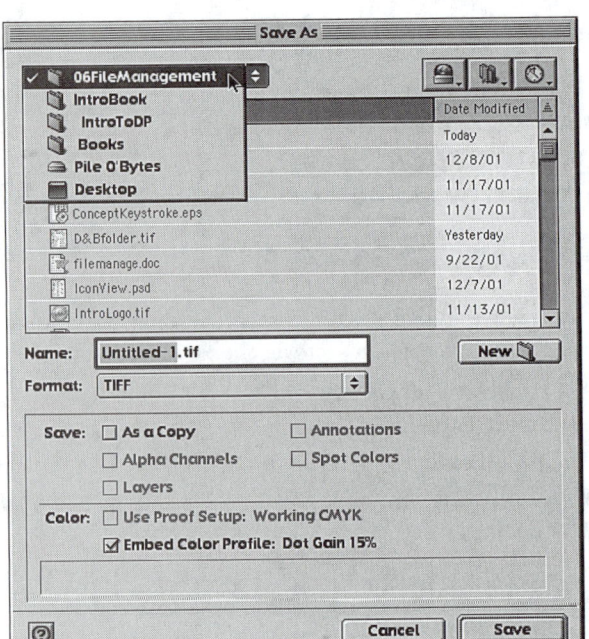

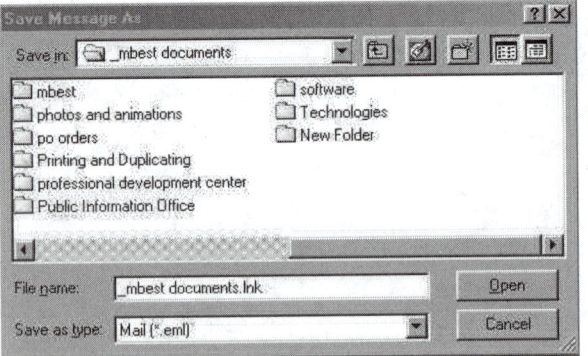

File management

What a bore! Can't we do something else?

As mentioned, Apple Computer changed the face of computing in 1984. What they introduced was based on technology that had been around for a long time. Prototypes that were similar in concept were floating around in places like Xerox's Palo Alto Research Center (PARC).

The concept was to eliminate the code by using graphic analogies. The goal was a computer that was "friendly" — easy to use and understand. From the second the Mac was booted, you knew something was radically different from DOS. Instead of a stream of unintelligible computerese gibberish rolling across a darkened screen, a cute smiling picture of the computer flashed on the screen, followed by the words, "Welcome to Macintosh."

Today, the Mac legacy totally dominates the computer world. Microsoft paid Apple $150 million and admitted it stole the Windows idea from the Mac interface a few years ago. Every year Wintel brings out *radically new* system software that longtime Mac users merely chuckle at. Things they have been using for years are finally available.

Interactive reality

The Mac interface was initially totally graphic and still remains almost entirely so. Instead of arcane code, the operator sees graphic analogies — the graphic user interface or GUI. Even though OSX is UNIX based, the code is well hidden. The Mac's clearest difference is intangible: how it feels.

> *The Mac has its own personality, one derived from a design that emphasizes not programmer's needs but human expectations, through the use of desktop and folder metaphors.* MacWorld, February 1994

Windows has come along nicely. With Windows 2000, Wintel has an operating system that actually works. XP is also a good step — although many are really worried about the Big Brother looking over their shoulders as they work. However, leaving code behind has brought its own problems.

Paths and naming

Instead of being required to exactly type paths locating documents in root directories and subdirectories, you are able to see a tiny drawing of a folder with a clear name in English. Merely by rapidly clicking twice on the picture with the mouse-controlled cursor, the folder lying on a metaphorical desktop opens into a window that displays all the contents of the folder. Names are in English and 31 to 45 characters long. We no longer have to reduce file names from March 1985 Financial Statement to MARSTA85.DOC.

WYSIWYG

What You See Is What You Get — almost unprecedented stuff. The concept was again simple — make what is seen on the screen match what is output on the printer. The execution is trickier. Even today, the truth is that what you see is almost what you get. Colors are very hard to match. Resolution differs greatly. Many other problems exist that we will cover as we go.

Original EPS   **Screen capture**

Basically, however, WYSIWYG was and is a reality. What appears in front of you on the monitor screen is remarkably similar to what will be output. In the example above, these illustrations give you a real feel for WYSIWYG. As you can clearly see, they are different. However, they look identical on the screen.

In my other books, we talk quite a bit about how to deal with the differences. *Publishing with Photoshop*, in particular, deals with the color shifts from original to monitor RGB to printed reality. This is a very thorny problem that can only be partially saved by throwing a lot of money at it. Accurate color management takes a lot of time, money, and work. That's all I'll say here, but read the sidebar.

Intuitive reactions

Apple's goal was a personal computer that could be figured out. To a great degree, they succeeded. Assuming a basic conceptual understanding, most problems can be solved with a small amount of trial and error. In code-driven systems, you must know the code — exactly. With a GUI, often you can simply play around and arrive at a solution. Even you Wintel users are helped here because all of the graphics programs currently in professional use started as Mac programs. This means that they all conform to the standardized interface software designers have to subscribe to when designing Mac software.

Because all Mac programs share certain basics, the interfaces tend to build on each other. If you know PageMaker or Quark, you can figure out InDesign. If you can draw in FreeHand, you can draw in Illustrator, and so forth. Photoshop shares the Adobe interface with PageMaker, InDesign, and Illustrator. All of these programs have New, Open, Close, Save, Save As, Print, and Quit under the menu called File. They all have Undo, Cut, Copy, Paste, Clear, and Select All under the menu next to the right called Edit.

Mac programs are judged by how intuitive they are. Ones that are not usually disappear. Ten years ago, I learned the basic operation of SuperPaint one afternoon while waiting for a professor to show up. I started up a computer in his lab, saw an icon labeled SuperPaint, double-clicked on it, and experimented for about ten minutes. By the time he arrived, I had it pretty much figured out by playing around.

The Clipboard

The Clipboard is one of the basic parts of the Mac operating software that we all take for granted. This is probably the first place you will memorize keyboard shortcuts. What we are talking about is the Edit menu. On virtually every menu bar, the Edit menu is to the right of the File menu.

Although the Clipboard is technically the Cut, Copy, Paste portion only, let's start with the top of the list:

Undo –Command/Control Z

 Get in the habit of always holding down the modifier key(s) before you go after the shortcut key(s). If you hit the QWERTY key first, that key will simply print. You will become very adept at holding the Command or Control key with your thumb as you reach for and touch the shortcut key. Often, you will hold down the modifier and type a series of letters to execute an operation. It gets very fast.

Undo – what a joyful word! If you make a mistake, you can undo it. Undos are roughly determined by mouse action. If you use the mouse after the action, chances are good that you will not be able to undo it. In PageMaker and QuarkXPress (those old has-beens), you only get one chance – there is only one undo. With InDesign, Illustrator, and FreeHand programs there are virtually unlimited undos. Most programs have some things you cannot undo. In InDesign, you can undo anything.

Photoshop has what is called the History palette that lets you undo outside the restrictions of linear order. You can step back and forth in history with Photoshop — while taking a pretty hefty memory hit.

If you are not able to undo, you are stuck, unless you can save the day by using Revert from the File menu. Revert takes you back to the last version Saved (this, of course, assumes you are saving at regular intervals). You will know you cannot undo if you see a grayed-out command line. Any inaccessible command will show as gray type.

Cut and paste

Now we enter the Clipboard proper. The basic idea is this: anything selected (within very wide parameters) can be cut or copied to a storage area. From there it can be pasted anywhere else (within very wide parameters). Some programs can use anything within the program, but the elements will not transfer outside to another application.

The problem is that the Clipboard does two things you need to be aware of. First of all, it copies the image in a certain format. Type, for example, is usually captured in Rich Text Format. Graphics used to be a much larger problem because nonprofessional formats like PICT, BMP, or WMF were used. They are still used a lot on the PC. Mac has gone, or is going, to PDF which works anywhere.

The main conceptual idea to remember is that the Clipboard can only hold one item at a time. When the next item(s) is Cut or Copied to the Clipboard, the one already there is deleted.

It is a good idea to only keep something small in memory requirements on the Clipboard. Otherwise, you are wasting precious RAM. Remember this after you cut or copy something huge. Then copy a single letter or something.

Cut – Command/Control X

This command cuts the selected item(s) from the document. It removes it entirely and places it into the Clipboard storage area in the system software.

Copy – Command/Control C

This command copies the selected item(s) from the document. It creates a copy of it and places the copy into the Clipboard storage area. The original remains in the document.

Paste – Command/Control V

This command pastes the selected item(s) from the Clipboard. It inserts it into the document at the insertion point, if you are working with text, or onto the top layer of the document you are working on.

Sometimes it pastes into the center of the page, the center of the window, or offset a little right and down from where it was clipped.

It depends on the application you are using. For example, PageMaker allows you to hold down the Option/Alt key and paste. Command/Control Option/Alt V pastes the item into exactly the same location on the page, even if you cut it on page 5 and pasted it on page 75. It will get confused if you copy from a right (odd-numbered) page of a spread and paste it into the left (even-numbered) page.

Clear

This command allows you to cut with no option to paste. In other words, you can eliminate something. It works just like the Delete key. In fact, some people never use Clear once they discover the Delete key.

Step and repeat or multiple paste.

Page layout programs have the option of pasting multiple copies at one time. Quark and InDesign calls this Step and Repeat. Multiple Paste is PageMaker's command. This is very handy for setting up multiple business cards on one sheet, or for making a grid (see Miniskill 5). The only limitation is that you can repeat the copies only in one direction at a time. So, for a grid you'll have to do this command twice.

Select All – Command/Control A

This command has some very helpful uses beyond the obvious. The obvious is it selects everything. Usually this means everything on the page and everything on the pasteboard or drawing board to which the document is taped. There are many uses for this capability. You can consider it sort of a maxi-marquee.

A less obvious usage includes finding hidden pieces. Let's say you created a white box with no border to cover up an area. Later that purpose was gone, but now you cannot find that darned white box to delete it. Command/Control A lets you see the handles of the white box. Deselect everything and click in the space where you saw the white box. As soon as it is selected, do with it as you will.

The Clipboard has its limitations, but you will use it a lot.

Another use comes with text handling. For example, if I hit Command/Control A now while typing, the entire story would be selected. This is true even if I can see only five paragraphs on the screen. I often bring in type with the Clipboard, to avoid messing with links to an outside document. If you are stuck with software that allows only one document to be open at a time, the Clipboard is the only way to move items from one document to another.

The Clipboard or import?

One of the real problems you need to deal with is the fact that using the Clipboard, as easy as it is, is usually the wrong choice. This seems to be one of those areas that most digital publishers have the most trouble with. The Clipboard does have its purpose and we will talk about that in a bit. However, normally you want you want to Place, Import, or Get Picture (depending upon the application you are using).

Importing

Importing was developed to solve two specific problems. The first problem is the huge size of most printable graphics. If you actually put the graphic into a page layout document, that page layout document quickly gets so large that you cannot manipulate it — or do anything with it. When page layout files get much larger than a couple of megabytes they get very clumsy. A single 8×10 color photo is around 50 MB at the resolutions we need — 300 dpi.

Linking

The solution that was developed is called *linking*. The basic idea is that we will just use a low-resolution placeholder in the page layout document to show us where the graphic is. A path will be noted to the location of the storage site of the graphic. When it comes time to print, the printer will search along that path and print the graphic at the far end of it. Because the monitor is only 72 dpi, the little 72 dpi placeholders look fine on the screen, but they are much smaller than the actual graphic file.

The graphic is not in the document.

The biggest problem newcomers to the trade have is understanding that the graphic is not in the document. All that is in the document is that low-resolution placeholder.

What is imported?

All graphic formats have a *screen preview.* This is that low-resolution image we have been talking about that interprets the high-res image as well as it can at monitor resolutions. When you import a graphic into another program, only the preview can be seen. The high-res image is not used until the document is output to a printer, imagesetter, or press. This causes all kinds of problems:

- The inexperienced (like you) are constantly frustrated because the screen image does not look like they expect. After all, it was *gorgeous* in the originating program. The obvious reason for this has already been mentioned. The imported image looks bad on the screen because it is a low-resolution bitmap. It has to be low-res to make screen redraws tolerable. InDesign does a much better job with this than most programs because it draws its own previews, but it is still a problem.

- Because the image on the screen is only a low-res preview, the high-resolution image has to be available for the document to print. You have to keep the high-resolution image in the same folder as the document, especially when you move the folder. Many assume that because the image has been imported, it is in the document, and the original can be deleted. This is certainly not the case. In most cases the low-res preview is the only thing in the document. The high-res image is only linked to the file.

- When the document prints, the printer or imagesetter searches for the original high-res file. If it does not find it, the printer either quits in disgust or simply says, "The heck with you — I'll just print the low-res screen garbage." It is very important to make sure that the imported file (or a copy of it) is contained in the same folder as the final document. You might get away with it if everything stays on the computer where you assembled everything. If you transport everything to another computer (as is usually done), all linking is broken. Printers and imagesetters are instructed to look in the same folder as the final document. If they do not find the high-res original there, the output is messed up — one way or another.

- When a scan is placed into a drawing program for tracing purposes, the preview is so crude that tracing is very difficult. Often it helps to make a black-and-white version of the scan. These tend to be more visible in the preview. Previews are always crude, however. For tracing purposes, a high-resolution preview helps a lot. It can seriously slow down redraw, though.

Platform glitches

Here you have to understand what is going on with the previews as well as the originals. The Wintel world has dozens of formats. Many of these are not even understood by most PCs. For our purposes in print, there are really only a few formats that work. EPS and TIFF still work well. EPS is the normal output of Illustrator and FreeHand. TIFF is especially portable. It is the normal final output of Photoshop. (Yes, Photoshop can also output EPS files, but that we'll leave for the Photoshop book.) InDesign has messed up the tradition by now directly importing Photoshop (.psd) and Illustrator (.ai) files. This means you have to be even more careful with file management.

TIFF works because the screen previews are also TIFFs. Our professional programs read these well, in most cases. EPSs are another story entirely. Here the problem is the previews. DOS EPS uses Windows Metafile (.wmf), and Mac EPS uses PICT. These are both file formats that the other platform refuses to recognize. Generic EPS usually does not have a preview at all. As a result, EPSs brought to another platform usually only show a box with an X through it. This box is the size of the frame holding the graphic.

The problem, of course, is that you cannot see the cross-platform graphic on the screen. It will print fine, but it is very difficult to properly arrange a graphic if you cannot see it. Most illustration software allows you to control the type of Preview used. Make sure you are using a format that can be seen on the platform and in the software in which you will be assembling the document.

 When working cross-platform, you have to regress to using the old 8.3 naming conventions. Wintel still requires the dot three extensions to know what type of file is being dealt with. (Even if Windows 95 and 98 no longer seem to require that, they simply make the required extension invisible.) However, to open a PC file on a Mac, the dot three extension for the format is required. To open or use a Mac graphic on a Wintel machine, it must be saved in a PC version of the format, the extension must be there, and the name will be truncated to seven letters followed by a tilde unless it is eight characters or less. This can cause severe problems when trying to make cross-platform CDs, for example.

The dot three extension for the format is still required, practically speaking.

This kind of digital acrobatics is irritating, but it works. It is relatively easy to open and convert PC graphics to Mac graphics. On a Mac you can simply change the name to add the dot three extension to open or use a graphic. (It doesn't always work, but it works most of the time – if you have any idea what the originating software was.) The opposite is not usually true. Cross-platform work must be planned and practiced. Wintel machines required specially purchased software to read Mac files. Every PC is different. Once you know a particular PC machine's foibles, cross-platform graphics are simple to deal with.

Link or paste summary

Let's sum up quickly. When you want to add a graphic to your document, use Place, Import, or Get Picture. This places a low-res preview in the document for viewing and establishes a link to the high-res graphic for printing. This is what you always want to do for printing. You do not want to embed the file or bring it in using the Clipboard.

If you use the Clipboard to bring in a graphic, you will have no link to any high-resolution graphic. The Clipboard will also change the file format to one that it can use: WMF in Windows, PICT in Mac OS9 or earlier, or PDF in OSX. This is usually not a good thing.

 The only time you want to copy and paste is within an application where you are creating a graphic that will be used in another document. If you import a graphic, in this situation, you end up with a linked graphic within a graphic. This is called a *nested graphic.* Nested graphics (or links within links) often do not print correctly.

File management

The problem with file storage is this: if there is no plan, you will not be able to find it anyway! Novice computer operators commonly have no clue about file management. They barely know that you should save regularly. As a result, they just save wherever the defaults take them. Often they do not even title the documents. After a week or so, they begin to realize that the hard drive is filling up with documents called untitled-1, untitled-2, and so on. Worse yet, they do name their documents, but they try for cuteness ("BIGBOBSHOLE" or similar nonsense); later they cannot figure out what they meant when that spasm flitted across their brain. This book gives one plan. Modify it to your heart's content, but remember this one rule: "Any brain-dead idiot should be able to make sense of your filing system." That is certainly who will have to figure it out when you call in sick.

Much of this little subsection is review. Nevertheless, it will help you to get this thoroughly absorbed into your habitual work methodology. File management is one of the most basic skills used in desktop publishing. It has nothing to do with design, production, or any kind of artwork, but causes more problems than you can imagine. More digital jobs are destroyed in this manner than any other. It has to do with what is called Saving. Saving is writing a copy of the code you created in RAM to the storage device of your choice.

There are several parts to this basic operation: naming, icons, and drag'n'drop filing. We use many visual metaphors, as you already know. The metaphor used here is the typical file cabinet/folder setup used in the traditional office, as discussed earlier.

You know the routine. All documents are placed in folders alphabetically. The folders are arranged alphabetically in drawers. The drawers are stacked in series of file cabinets. We vary this only slightly. First of all, you do not have drawers, because they would be too limiting. (The closest thing we have to drawers is partitioning which simply divides a large cabinet into several smaller cabinets.) Instead, you are allowed to nest folders; that is, you can place a folder inside a folder, which is inside a third folder, which is inside a fourth folder, and so on. Secondly, the digital equivalent of the file cabinet is your hard drive or removable.

In the traditional office, one of the major problems is alphabetization. Everyone seems to have a different method of alphabetizing. Like everything else, there is a correct way. However, in the chaos of the late twentieth century, everyone does what is right in his or her own eyes. Mac solves this by automatically alphabetizing. Apple has added a couple of new twists, though. Wintel users will find their own system.

This is a small portion of the Mac alphabetical order:

1st Names with a space in front: two spaces before a single space; three spaces before two, and so forth. These are alphabetized as a group.

2nd Names with a period in front: two periods before a single period; three periods before two, etc. These are alphabetized as a group.

3rd Names with numbers in front. The order is 0, 1, 2, 3, 4, 5, 6, 7, 8, 9 with doubles before singles, etc. These are alphabetized as a group.

4th Normal names made up of letters. These are alphabetized as a group.

5th Names with a bullet (•) in front, alphabetized as a group.

6th Names with an ASCII tilde (~) in front: two ASCII tildes after a single ASCII tilde, etc. These are alphabetized as a group.

The advantage of this setup is the ease with which you can arrange

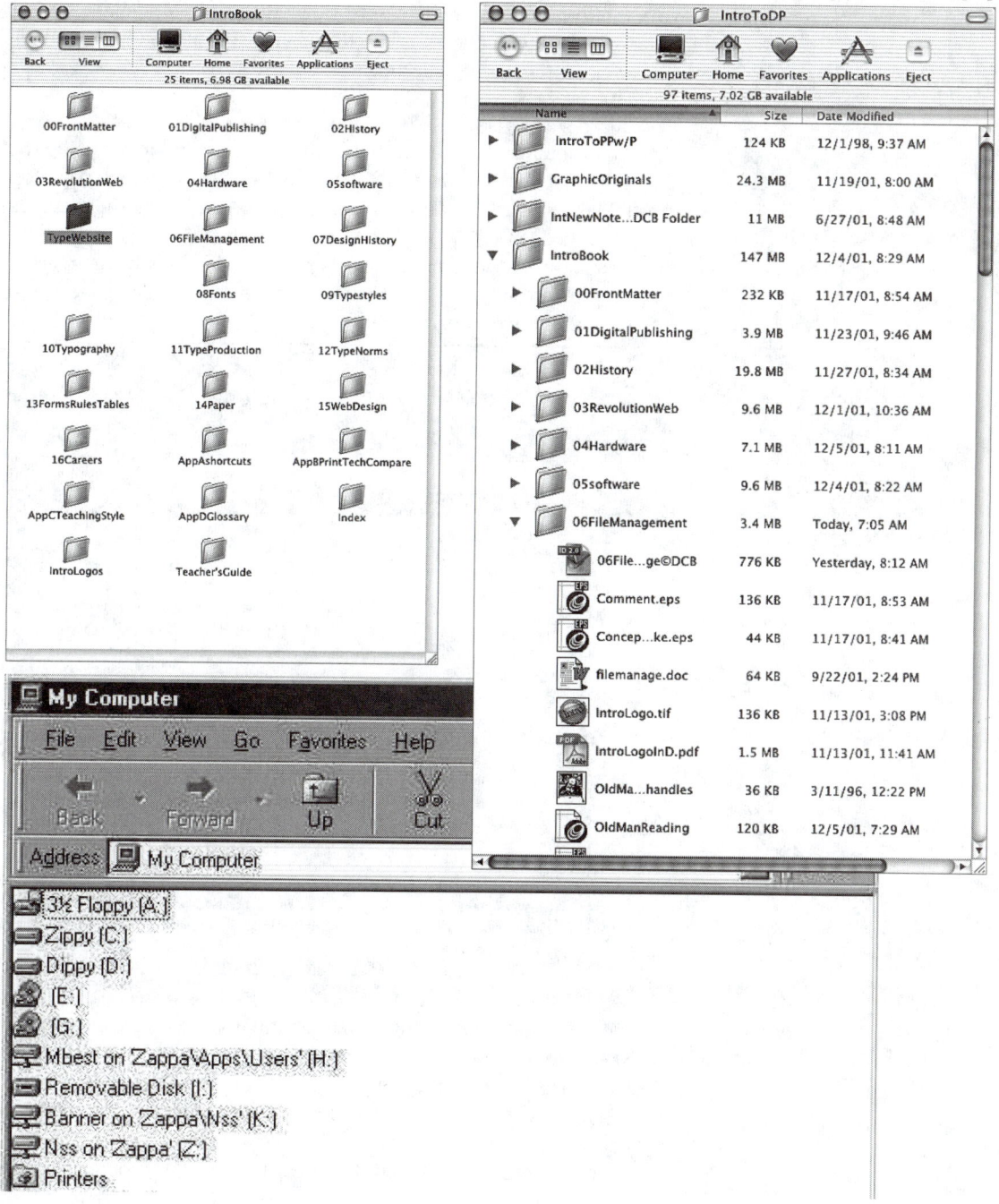

your windows while keeping a universally understood alphabetical order. For example, if you need a folder first on the list, all you have to do is type spaces in front of the name.

List view

As you may have noticed, I am assuming that you are using the list view for your windows (OSX's list view is on the previous page top right). Many still use the Icon View, like you see top left on the previous page. For those of you in Windows, your list view looks a little different. There's a copy of a My Computer window from Windows on the previous page at the bottom right, which is sort of a Icon view. Here is a capture of the Windows view in Explorer.

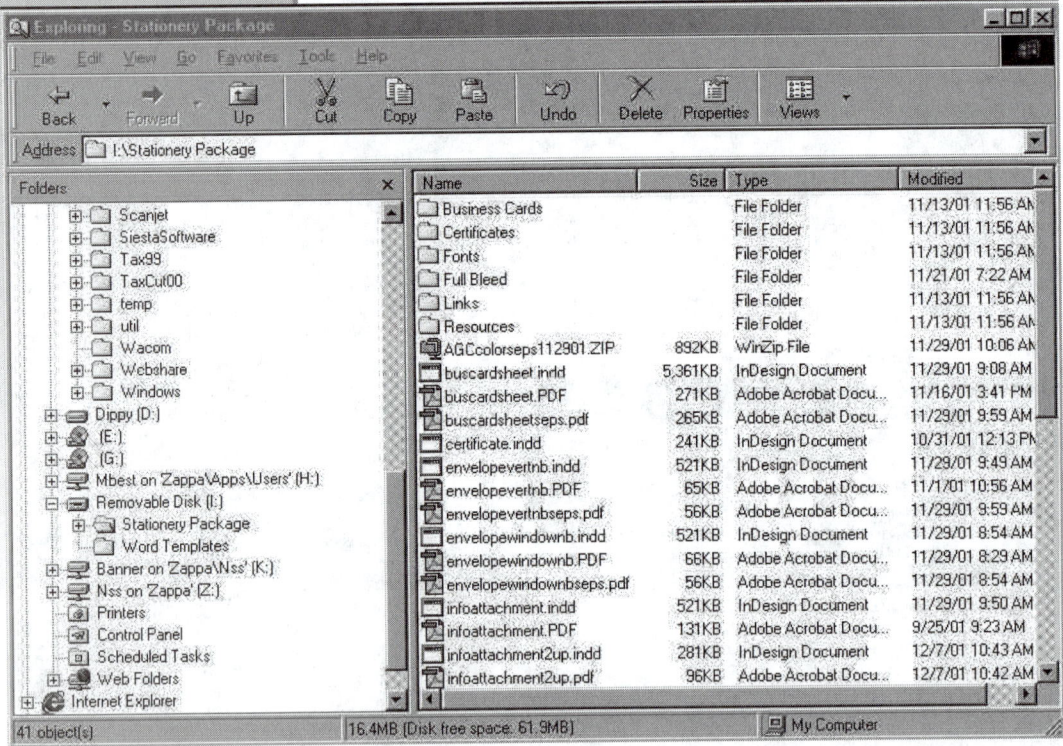

The point I am trying to make is that you need to do what is necessary so that you can see what is in all the storage as quickly and easily as possible. Negotiating your files is one of the major time-consuming tasks you do every day. Accessing these things is continuously improving. Mac OSX, for example, offers what they call the Column View (which you can see at the top of the next page). Personally, I am

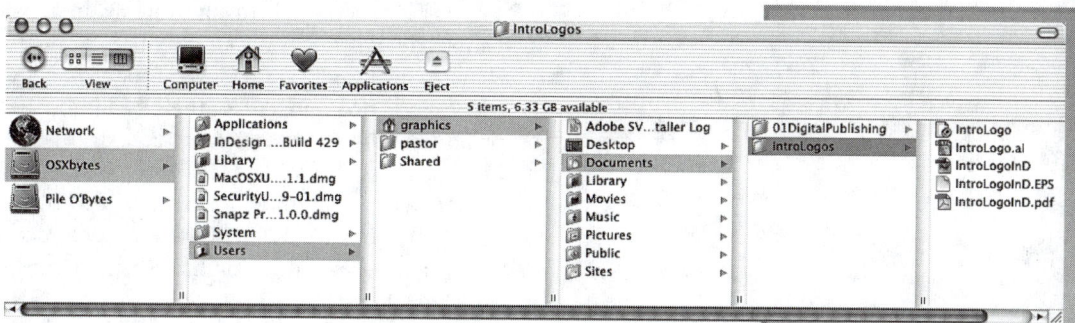

using this more and more, but some of my students hate it. There really is only one right view — can you find the folder or file you need to find quickly. The corollary to that is can your replacement (the days you have to call in sick) find that file easily.

What is comes down to is your personal choice. You must learn your operating system. That is not the subject of this book. For Mac, you cannot beat *The Little Mac Book* series by Robin Williams, PeachPit Press. She is constantly putting out a new version for the latest operating system. There's a *Little iMac Book* and so on.

For Windows, you are dealing with a much more complex problem. You will need to take a course at the local community college, purchase a video or CD teaching series, or study one of those amazingly huge tomes on Windows. I saw one the other day that was over three inches thick. *Gad, what you people put yourselves through to save a few bucks on your computer!*

Naming restrictions

This is one area where Mac formerly had a huge advantage, beating the pants off DOS, Windows, and the others. You can use up to 31 characters in naming. No extensions are required. You can use any character except a colon. With the advent of Windows 95 and up, the number-of-characters lead was taken by Windows with 45. And in OSX, you can no longer use the slash (and maybe other computer-command keys). But in practice, the Mac advantage is still there.

In actual practice, you will find that there are no restrictions except the 32-character limit on a Mac. PCs supposedly no longer need the extensions (.doc, .eps, .FH8, and so on). But in fact, the operating system still needs them, it can just make them invisible — if you choose. At this point, the only naming restriction is intelligence and common sense. Because you can now name in English and you speak English, the sensible thing would be to name your files and folders in English.

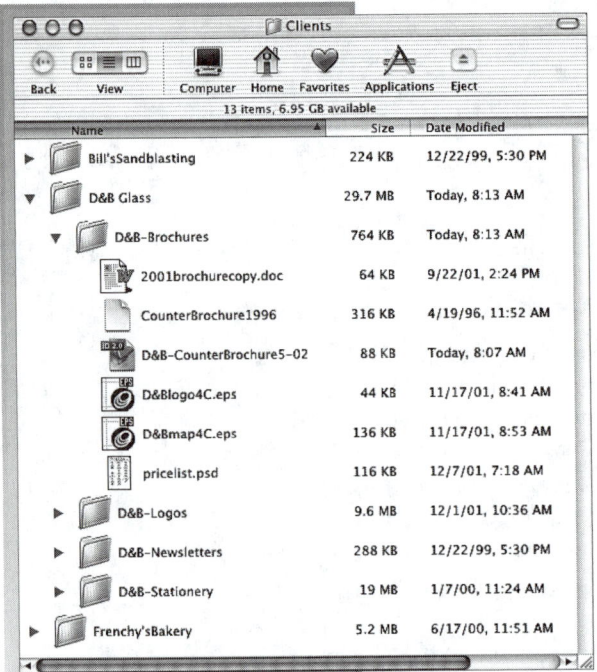

This seems to be a concept beyond most people, though. Let's take an imaginary example. I have a client called D&B Glass. They are a good client, and I do almost all of their designing. So, on my hard drive I have a folder (directory) called Clients. Inside that folder is another folder called D&B Glass. Continuing, inside the D&B Glass Folder are several folders. One for logos. One for stationery, invoices, purchase orders, and so on. One for brochures. One for newsletters. One for every type of normal project I do for them. My next project for them is a counter brochure to be used on the checkout counters of various companies around town who recommend D&B to their customers. So where do I put my new brochure? You can see it to the left. (It has the Today, 8:07 AM date.)

Your filing needs to be at least this clear. Importantly, it needs to be clear to other people who will be trying to use or print your files. There is a time for paranoia, but file management is not that time.

Drag'n'drop

Drag'n'drop is a descriptive term concerning one method of file management. When you are working in Finder or Explorer, filing, copying, and deleting are accomplished by simply clicking on the icon and holding down the button while dragging it to the location where you want the item to be stored, copied, or deleted.

To rephrase the procedure:

1. You click on the icon of the document, folder, or drive to be filed.
2. Holding down the button, you drag the icon to its new location.
3. When the icon of the new location is highlighted, you release the button.
4. The appropriate action will be taken.

This procedure works for many different tasks.

1. Copying from one drive to another. Dragging the icon from the window of one drive and dropping it in the window of another drive causes the document or folder to be copied from

the first to the second drive. Dragging the icon of a drive to the window of another drive causes a copy of the drive to be placed on the other drive (this is how floppies are copied onto hard drives, for example).

2.   File management and storage. Dragging an icon onto a folder or drive icon causes the document or folder to be stored "inside" that folder or drive.

 Holding down the Option key while dragging produces a copy that is filed into the destination folder or drive — this is used for copying within a drive.

3.   Backup production. Dragging an icon to another drive produces a backup copy of the document(s), folder(s), or drive on the destination drive.

4.   File deletion. Dragging an icon onto the Trash Can or Recycle Bin allows you to delete everything the icon represents. Even if you drag a huge group of nested folders (like the System Folder, which may have several dozen folders in it, each of which has folders in it, each of which in turn may have many documents in it), you can delete them with one command. You better not, though. The System Folder contains the pieces that control your entire computer and the computer won't run without it. (In OSX it is the scattered all over.)

A sample setup

How this stuff is used

Every employer you work for will have a different filing setup. Sometimes these setups are very complete and complicated. At the local newspaper, you are given two days of training when you are hired to learn their filing system. You are not allowed to work until you have the filing system and procedures mastered. They catalog their incredible quantities of ads by client name in lettered folders: A, B, C, and so on. When they have filed all the ads for a week, they move them into the Current Month folder, then the Past Month folder, then by month and by year, and so on. Yours will probably not need to be so complicated.

The one suggested on the next page is the one I use in my classroom/lab at school with Mac OS9. We use several basic folders. As you will see, there is plenty of room for variation within the structure. The concept you need to grasp is the essential need for the structure. Whatever setup you use needs to be set up — **NOW!**

What goes in a folder

When you save a job, you make a folder to put it into. Into that folder goes one page layout document and all the graphics used in that document (plus the word processing files used).

You really do need a separate folder for each page layout document. This will make it much easier to deal with when taking it to the printer. It can save you a great deal of unbudgeted expense as you hand your hard work off to someone else to print who has never seen it before.

If you are working on a project that has several page layout documents, make a folder to hold all the folders for each document. If you have a client with many projects, make a folder for the client, to hold the folders for the projects, which hold the folders for the individual page layout documents.

The only exceptions should be folders that hold graphic pieces used to develop special recurring graphics, like logos.

As you can see, I use periods in front of the names so I can make sure that the top folder is always Current Jobs, and the second folder is Official Logos. That way students (who are stressed enough) can always look at the top of the list.

1. periodperiodperiod(Term)Jobs(year) {...FallJobs02} — This is the storage for customer projects: all placed scans, logos, text documents, and graphics. If a job has more than one document (for example, a program that has one document for the cover and one for the guts), each document will be placed in its own folder inside the specific job folder, which is inside the Term Jobs folder on the hard drive.

2. periodperiodOfficialLogos {..OfficialLogos} — This folder copy has to be on one of the hard drives or partitions of every computer. It contains copies of all the official logos we use for our course and our normal customers.

3. period(Last term)Jobs(Year) {.SummerJobs02} — There may be several of these old Jobs folders gathered together by the single period in front of the name.

4. Apps — This folder contains all the folders of all the applications installed on the hard drive.

 Starting with System 9 on the Mac, these folders are made automatically by the operating system. In Mac OS system 9 the folder is called Applications (Mac OS9). When you graduate to OSX, there will be a folder named Applications on the drive used to hold the system for OSX. If OSX and Classic are on the same drive, Applications and Applications (Mac OS9) will both be there together.

5. StudentStuff — This folder contains all the practice work of students. Every student creates his or her own folder under his or her own name inside this folder as needed.

6. System Folder — This folder should not be touched without permission and instruction. You can easily move things around so that the computer won't run anymore.

 Again in OSX this has changed. System Folder is the folder used to run Classic (OS9). The OSX folder that contains the same things is called System. If you are running both OSs on one drive, System will be right above System Folder.

 System folders on a Mac contain the fonts being used, Preferences files, Control Panels, Extensions, and so on. These things change as you load utilities onto your computer. You need to learn what is here and how to control it. But, this is where those operat-

ing system books come into play. You really need to get one of those books, for your own personal use.

It is very important that you use these folders appropriately, with planning and forethought.

The key to this is saving where you intend rather than where you default.

Saving on purpose

When you look at the Save dialog box, you find three key areas that you need to control. First, and probably most important, is the bar over the window that shows the name of the folder into which you are saving the new document.

This folder will normally default to the last used. For example, if you launch PageMaker 6.5, it loads the program out of the PageMaker 6.5 folder, which is in the Apps folder on your hard drive. When you save your new document, the computer will attempt to save into the PageMaker 6.5 folder because that was the last folder used.

 You need to watch this very carefully. Every program is a little different, and they all have their default settings (which you cannot change in most cases).

Here's a list of the common locations:

FreeHand: the English folder inside the FreeHand application folder

Quark: the Quark application folder

The Adobe model: InDesign, Illustrator, and Photoshop (and maybe PageMaker 7, I don't know anyone with a copy): the last folder you saved a document into.

Word: the last folder you saved into

You always check first!

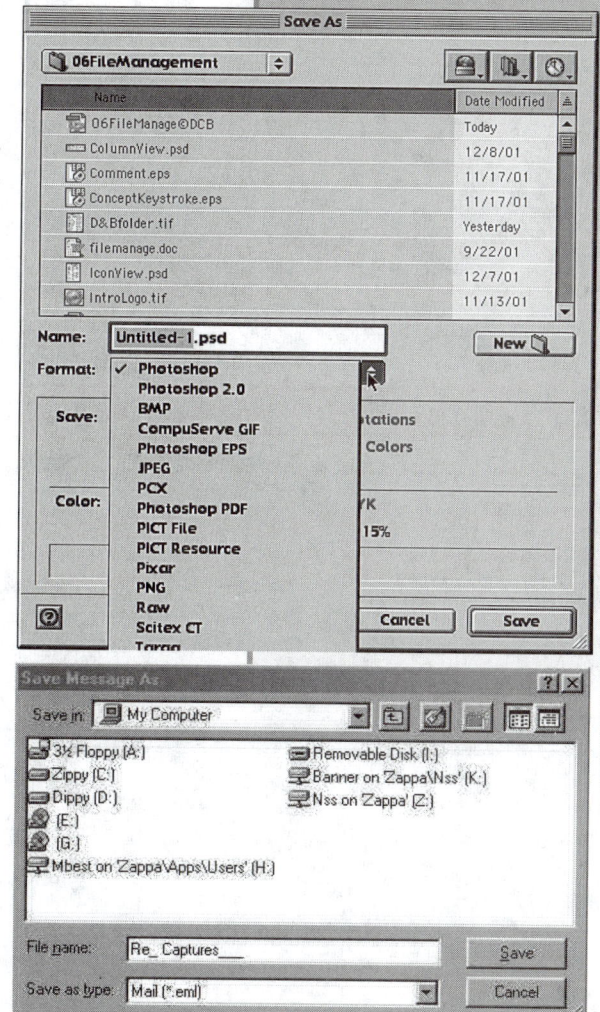

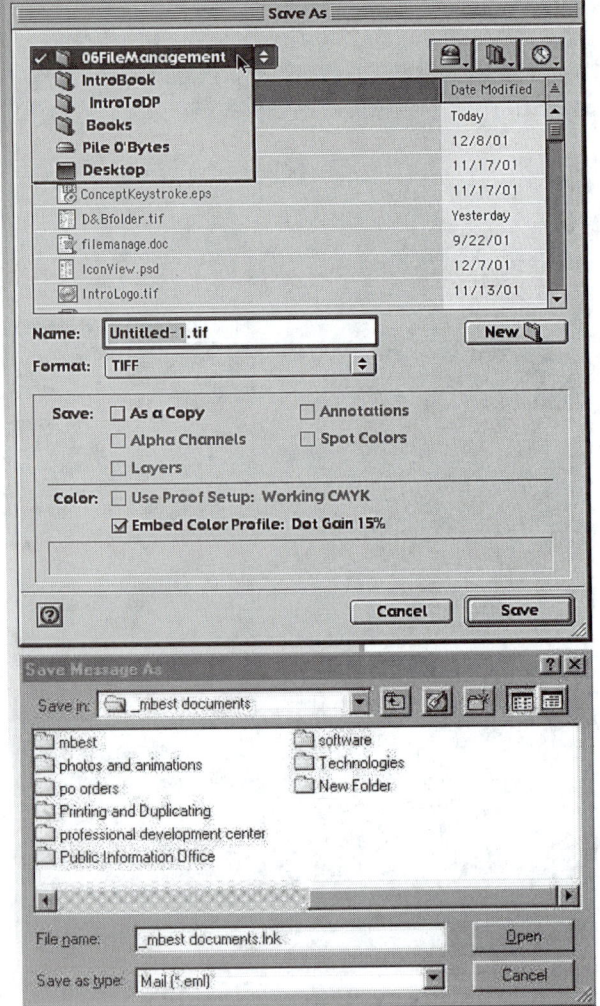

Save As

As you know, Save As is the method we most commonly use to save a file to a location we desire. It is also the way to save a copy of the file to a backup location (but backups are usually done by dragging an entire folder to the backup location). So, the question becomes, *"How to you determine which folder will be saved into?"*

The answer, of course, is the folder name at the top of the Save As dialog box. Windows even has the words *Save in:* next to the location. In both OSs, you need to click on the folder name bar and hold the mouse button down (or on the little arrows to the right of the name). As you can tell, this bar is a pop-up menu. This means that clicking and holding the mouse button down causes the bar to open up as a menu showing the nesting hierarchy of the folder. In the newer operating systems, you don't even have to hold the button down anymore, just click.

This pop-up menu gives us what Mac-ites call the nesting hierarchy and what Wintel calls the path. It is the layering of folders as you put one inside another inside another. The top of the chain is the desktop. This is where you are when the computer is started up and you see the icons. As far as the computer is concerned, the hard drives and everything else are inside the desktop folder. In the example above, you see a hierarchy as follows:

1. The document "o6Filemanagement" (this chapter) is in the IntroBook folder
2. The IntroBook folder is in the IntroToDP folder
3. The IntroToDP folder is in the Books folder
4. The Books folder is in Pile O'Bytes (which is what I call my Classic OS9 partition)
5. Pile O'Bytes is an icon on the desktop (notice that the mini-icon on the pop-up menu is the hard drive icon and the mini-icon in front of Desktop is a miniature desktop.

All the different drives are icons on the Desktop.

Telling the computer where to file the new document

If the Save As dialog box does not show the folder you want to save into:

1. Click on the Desktop button, or go back up the directory hierarchy until you can see the drive you want to save to.
2. Select the hard drive to save to and click Open.
3. Click on the first folder you want to save to and click Open or double-click it.
4. Click on the second folder destination you want to save to and click Open or double-click it.
5. Continue the process, making a new folder if necessary. until you are storing the document where it needs to be.
6. Type in the name of the new document.

Now when you click OK, the new document will be saved into the specific folder you have chosen. You must be certain that you have picked the correct folder before you click OK. If not, the new document will go to wherever it happens to land. If we were to continue this process, the next new document created would automatically be placed into the same folder you just picked.

Normally, you always go to the last folder you were working on, but you cannot count on it. ALWAYS check the folder destination bar before you click OK. This will save you from many nasty surprises as you search through hundreds or thousands of folders trying to remember what you called that thing and where you put it.

Always save on a hard drive!

One of the major things you need to keep in mind is simple: you always want to save on a hard drive. First of all, this will be much faster, because hard drives are much faster than any cartridge. Secondly, by using ZIP and JAZ cartridges, CD-R, CD-RW, or DVD-RAM for backup, you will have that backup for that inevitable day when your hard drive fails. It will happen. Now that Mac is using the cheaper PC standards like ATA or worse, the life expectancy for hard drives is around two years. Long gone are the days of SCSI drives that lasted many years.

Removables

The most common file management error I run across is working off a ZIP or JAZ disk. It wasn't nearly the problem with SyQuest cartridges, because they were actual hard drives and the drives were well made (hence the higher prices). This is definitely not true with Iomega's offerings. I am not saying that you shouldn't use their products. I am saying you need to save everything on your hard drive and then just copy stuff to your ZIP and JAZ cartridges as a backup.

Not only are both cartridge types too slow to work on, you will ruin the actual drives if you try to work on them. I know people who have worn out four ZIP drives in one year — that's the drives themselves not the cartridges used in the drives.

By this time you should be producing simple projects. Make sure that the entire project is located in one folder. Folders made within that folder to hold pieces like graphics may also be a problem. Make sure that all of your graphics used in the document are in the same folder as the document (making copies if necessary).

DISCUSSION

You should be discussing the file management setup you use at school, at work, and at home. Quite probably there is room for improvement.

Talk amongst yourselves...

Making it real

Obviously, these instructions must be tailored for your situation. They are intended mainly to make the concepts clear. It is not so important what the plan is. What is important is that you have a plan that anyone can understand. If no one else will do it and if no one else has already done it, come up with a plan, show it to everyone involved, make any necessary changes, and get it working. Some plan is necessary.

Probably the most important concept to grasp at this point is consistency. Even if you do not have the best plan, if you are consistent everyone else will understand it. This means that mistakes will be reduced, morale will be improved, and your jobs will be printed better.

Knowledge retention and thought provocation

1. Why is file management important?
2. Where do programs automatically save to?
3. What problems does working on removables cause?
4. Why would you want to put a space or a period at the front of a file or folder name?
5. Why do you link graphics?
6. Why would you want to use 8.3 naming?
7. What will happen on those days you have to call in sick? Will people be able to figure out your naming systems?

Chapter 7

Graphic Design History

Concepts

1. Marketing

2. Graphic design

3. Rectilinear construction

4. Broadsides

5. Brand name

WHERE WE CAME FROM

How marketing took over our culture requiring the aid of professional graphic communicators

Chapter Objectives:

By giving students a clear understanding of the graphic design history, this chapter will enable students to:

1. explain the place of color in graphic design
2. explain the significance of the digital paradigm shift

Lab Work for Chapter:

1. Complete miniskills chosen.
2. Begin skill exams.
3. Read chapters 8 and 9 for next week.
4. Work on projects.

THE CENTURY MAGAZINE.

VOL. XXXIII.   NOVEMBER, 1886.   NO. I.

ABRAHAM LINCOLN: A HISTORY.*

By John G. Nicolay and John Hay, Private Secretaries to the President.

EDITORIAL PREFACE.

THE CENTURY MAGAZINE has never entered upon a more important enterprise, nor one in which we have been surer of the sympathy and support of the public, than in engaging to present in these pages the first full and authoritative biography of Abraham Lincoln, together with a history of the times in which he lived. It is hardly necessary to explain that this long-expected history is by no means solely a sifting and re-editing of already printed records and memorials. Its originality is, however, especially notable in its account of Lincoln's administration, in dealing with which will be given to the world important details that have hitherto remained unrevealed, in order that they might first appear in their proper connection[s] [in this] mental work.

The advantages enjoyed by the writers of this history are not only incom[parably greater] than those possessed by any predecessors, but they are also beyond the rea[ch of any future] historian. Both of these biographers grew up in the same region with Mr. [Lincoln, and] were intimate from boyhood with his friends and companions. Mr. Nicolay [managed] his correspondence before his election to the Presidency, and the very f[irst paper] Lincoln signed as President was that of Mr. Nicolay to be his official Pr[ivate Secretary.] He held this position throughout Mr. Lincoln's term of office, and enjo[yed his entire] intimacy and confidence. Mr. Hay, like Mr. Nicolay, accompanied the [President from] Springfield to Washington, where he remained several years as Assistant Sec[retary. He then] entered the army as an Assistant Adjutant-General of Volunteers, and after a bri[ef period of] service was ordered back to Washington and assigned to duty as aide-de-ca[mp to the Presi-]dent, where he remained till the war ended. One of them, and generally bot[h, were] at Mr. Lincoln's side every day from 1860 to 1865; Mr. Nicolay was his [medium] of communication with Congress and the Cabinet; both were continual[ly employed by] him in delicate and important missions to every part of the country; both s[aw him inaugurated] at his two inaugurations; one saw him die.

During all these years of official service at the Executive Mansion, the au[thors conceived] the idea of writing this history. At an age when the faculties of memory a[nd observation] are at their best, they made frequent notes and memoranda of important e[vents and the men] about them. The President was himself aware of their intention, and e[ncouraged and] assisted them in their work. Some of his most precious manuscripts were [copied by] his own hand. Their notes and memoranda taken during the war fill sev[eral manuscript] volumes, the value of which, from an historical point of view, is inestimable.

After the war was over, and the triumph of the national arms had received its pathetic

The history of graphic design

Graphic design history is a very interesting phenomenon. Until very recently in human history graphic design didn't even really exist, although the skills were known, in part. Conceptually, it was not even considered until the latter part of the nineteenth century.

The recognition of personal expression

As you know, hopefully, artists in general made a major leap into self-expression during the Renaissance. Prior to this, artists were craftsmen (extremely few women) in subservience to the nobility of the day. Often, this nobility was the hierarchy of the church. Basically, artists were decorators. They were completely unknown. At best, they were pampered peons. If they signed a name to anything, it was probably the name of the noble who kept them.

They were not supposed to express themselves. They were expected to produce what the nobles wanted, and the nobles wanted portraits of themselves. The church wanted symbolic storytelling. But pictures took immense amounts of time and a great deal of money. The only people who could afford the luxury of pictures and sculpture were people and organizations who could afford to not only completely support people to do the work, but also afford all the materials. It might help to know that ultramarine blue was ground lapis lazuli, for example.

Plus, education was rare and only found among the monks. Even nobles often could not write. Paintings were all symbolic because the viewers usually could not read. What would they read anyway? There was very little of stuff like that available, and then only in the few libraries maintained by the kings and the church.

Into this world, printing exploded. It caused fundamental changes to civilization. Being coupled with the freedom of a Judeo-Christian society, where we are all made in God's image and therefore of equal worth, printing brought art and education to the masses. Of course, it took a while. Cynics might argue that it hasn't happened yet. But, in our European culture, education took the highest place, and that was a direct result of printing.

The addition of graphics

By the turn of the century (1500), there were thousands of books in print. Novels and popular fiction became a popular entertainment. Books reached the middle class and self-education became possible. The only problem was the physical limitations of letterpress. Because everything had to be cut, carved, or cast out of metal or hardwood, printed graphics were relatively rare.

Even though the first book to combine type and graphics was produced within a decade of Gutenberg's 42-line Bible, the difficulty of producing excellent graphics meant that they were not often added to ordinary books. Excellence in graphics almost required printed engravings (fine art prints) that were bound into the books as separate pages. Sometimes they were simply pasted onto (or *tipped in* to) blank pages in the book. Even woodblock prints, like those by Dürer, were usually full page. Even though the 42-line Bible was brightly and colorfully illuminated, the illuminations were hand-painted individually.

The separation of art and words

At this point, the world was almost completely segregated into artists and writers. Printing served writers primarily. Graphics took too much skill, too much time, and too much money. Early printing was almost entirely type. In this context, early printing has to include the first four hundred years up to the Civil War in the United States. Graphics were left to artists who pampered the aristocracy. The books people read were all words. Graphics only began to become relatively common around the time of the Revolution.

The restrictions of letterpress

Much of this was due to the nature of the craft. At this point we can't even speak of an industry, for industries did not exist. Almost everything was controlled by the physical limitations of printing technology. For example, hand-drawn type was virtually impossible. Type was laboriously carved out of metal to make masters that were then converted to molds used to cast the letters, individually, piece by piece.

All printed pieces were assembled letter by letter, block by block. We will talk about that more in chapters 8 through 10. All spacing was accomplished by inserting blank rectangles of metal. Everything had to be locked into the chase or it would slip during printing (worse yet, it might fall out on the floor while being carried around). The rectangles had to fit tightly, and they definitely had to be rectangles.

Letterpress illustration

This illustration would have been impossible to print the way it looks below until the late twentieth century. Why?

Composition

The name given to the process made it obvious that design played little part in the production process — composition. Composing pages was a very rigid process with very strict rules. These procedures were enforced by the sheer physical difficulty of graphic creation. Everything had to be cut into metal or wood blocks. These blocks had to be exactly rectilinear with an exact thickness. The entire process took a great deal of care, skill, and experience.

Rectilinear rigidity

Because everything had to lock together like building blocks, rectangular structures controlled the compositions. Great masters like William Morris, in the late nineteenth century, could make these limitations serve their purposes, but generally, the results were dictated by the methodology.

The few graphic techniques available were restrained by the difficulty of the materials. Engravings are beautiful, but the beauty of the engraved art on a dollar bill is hard to compare with a monochrome ink landscape, let alone a fully developed oil painting. Printing techniques, in general, were used to enable mass reproduction of fine art images. Graphic elements were relatively rare until just before the Civil War. Often they were not used at all. If they were used, they were full-page show-off pages.

Verbal skills dominated. In large part, this was due to the fact that words were relatively easy to deal with. Everything was made up of horizontal lines of type arranged in vertical columns. This is merely fact; there is no quality connotation attached to this fact. Rectilinear construction, left to right, top to bottom, is merely the European method. As most of you are aware, other cultures have very different arrangements. Hebrew is written right to left, top to bottom. Chinese is written top to bottom, right to left.

The entrance of typography

The beginning of graphic design was when type was separated out as an art form. This is attributed to Claude Garamond and Jacob Sabon in the mid-sixteenth century. As we will cover later in this book, these original typographic designs are still the standard by which many judge elegance and style. It's not an accident that Apple uses Garamond Light as its corporate font. But type design was incredibly difficult and dependent on extremely skilled carving abilities. Ornamentation was often still hand-painted. Type design became a respected skill and type foundries (who made type founts) appeared.

Most of you will not read this little message simply because it is at a 90-degree angle. Some would have read it if it were 90 degrees clockwise instead of 90 degrees counterclockwise. That is too bad. Many pearls of wisdom are found in unusual places. Something like this is simply too unusual for the intellectually lazy to pursue. It might require thought. Horrors!

The effective use of normality

Rectilinear construction is neither good nor bad — it simply is. We all learned to read and write in rectangles. Well over 95 percent of everything we have ever read was lined up in horizontals and verticals — left to right, top to bottom. Simply understanding this fact helps us communicate. When we use *normal flow*, people read our message more easily. Normal usage is one of the major tools in design. We discuss this repeatedly throughout this book and in my more advanced books.

From the artist's viewpoint

The Industrial Revolution

The nineteenth century revolutionized printing as much as the fifteenth century did 400 years earlier. Major inventions and new technologies transformed everything. The results were entirely new categories of printing — daily newspapers and monthly magazines among others. Plus pictures were added, then photos, then color. Our economy was taken over by the advertisers and marketers. There was lots of change.

Newspapers had started in the eighteenth century. The first daily paper was in 1784 in Philadelphia. But there were forty-three weeklies by the end of the Revolution. They were usually a single sheet that was predominantly used for advertisements. In the beginning, the ads regularly had cuts of product — pictures of furniture and sailing ships were seen in the first daily in New York in 1785.

Ben Franklin had done some beautiful work, incorporating specialized engravings for favorite customers and adding fanciful ornamentation. One of the major driving forces of these newspapers were the advertisements. Because they were often repeated without change, they greatly reduced the amount of typesetting needed to produce the paper.

However, during the early 1800s printing in the new republic was severely handicapped by a huge paper shortage. It was so bad that by the 1830s, the standard 9×12 inch sheet was down to six-point type with six columns and no graphics of any type. These ads were all type and usually simple lists of products, real estate, or shipping schedules. Newspapers started making a rule that all ads had to be type only and very small and short — much like our classified ads of today.

Broadsides

What this did was force the development of the broadside. These were single sheets that were usually the same width as newspapers but twice as long. This gave the customer room to add all kinds of fancy type and elaborate engravings and wood cuts. The skill level developed for these cuts was incredible. These broadsides were tacked on public bulletin boards or hung in bunches at stagecoach stops and riverboat docks. They were hung by twine threaded through a hole at the top of the sheet so travelers could snap off a copy to read while they traveled.

Papermaking machines

In the 1830s French papermaking machines began to arrive in America. All paper was still 100% cotton made from rags. About that same time chlorine bleach was developed. This enabled the supply of cotton rags to greatly increase. Prior to this, paper had to be made with white and off-white rags — which were not nearly sufficient.

The Civil War had such demands for news and paper that wood pulp newsprint was developed. Huge machines that could grind up trees were necessary. With these new supplies of paper, newspapers sprang up all over and the first advertising agencies appeared. Originally, their main service was as sales agents who made lists of the newspapers available: where they printed, how often, and so on. They bought standard areas from the newspapers and then found advertising to fill them. However, as mentioned, advertisements were very different from what we know today. What we would consider display ads (or large ads with pictures) were mostly still broadsides. The concept and common use of brand-name products was only developed over the next few decades.

The rotary press

About this time the rotary press was developed. The rotary press enabled printing speeds to increase hundredfold. Instead of measuring in impressions per day, the industry now measured in impressions per hour. By the end of the century, the number of prints per hour reached five figures: 13,000 per hour for sheet-fed paper and over 50,000 per hour for web printing on rolls. The presses grew physically until many pages could be printed on one sheet of paper. This brought page production into six figures per hour.

The Linotype and Monotype

The problem was the artwork. Type was still assembled by hand, one letter at a time. What we now call art departments were dirty, smelly, and hot. The Linotype in 1886 enabled an entire line to be set at one time. Because the molds were recycled, lines could be kicked out of the machine as fast as the lead could harden. The monotype machine came out in 1897. It set type with a paper tape. This allowed for editing, cor-

Century magazine

This was the most graphic literary magazine of its day. It was a monthly with no advertising. It had one to five exquisite engravings per two-page spread. It was the first major magazine to use the photographic halftone in 1887. It was book-sized at 6.5×9 inches.

THE CENTURY MAGAZINE.

VOL. XXXIII. NOVEMBER, 1886. NO. 1.

ABRAHAM LINCOLN: A HISTORY.*

BY JOHN G. NICOLAY AND JOHN HAY, PRIVATE SECRETARIES TO THE PRESIDENT.

EDITORIAL PREFACE.

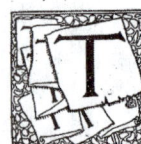

THE CENTURY MAGAZINE has never entered upon a more important enterprise, nor one in which we have been surer of the sympathy and support of the public, than in engaging to present in these pages the first full and authoritative biography of Abraham Lincoln, together with a history of the times in which he lived. It is hardly necessary to explain that this long-expected history is by no means solely a sifting and re-editing of already printed records and memorials. Its originality is, however, especially notable in its account of Lincoln's administration, in dealing with which will be given to the world important details that have hitherto remained unrevealed, in order that they might first appear in their proper connection in this monumental work.

The advantages enjoyed by the writers of this history are not only incomparably greater than those possessed by any predecessors, but they are also beyond the reach of any future historian. Both of these biographers grew up in the same region with Mr. Lincoln; they were intimate from boyhood with his friends and companions. Mr. Nicolay took charge of his correspondence before his election to the Presidency, and the very first commission Lincoln signed as President was that of Mr. Nicolay to be his official Private Secretary. He held this position throughout Mr. Lincoln's term of office, and enjoyed his closest intimacy and confidence. Mr. Hay, like Mr. Nicolay, accompanied the President from Springfield to Washington, where he remained several years as Assistant Secretary; he then entered the army as an Assistant Adjutant-General of Volunteers, and after a brief period of staff service was ordered back to Washington and assigned to duty as aide-de-camp to the President, where he remained till the war ended. One of them, and generally both, were on duty at Mr. Lincoln's side every day from 1860 to 1865; Mr. Nicolay was his official medium of communication with Congress and the Cabinet; both were continually employed by him in delicate and important missions to every part of the country; both stood beside him at his two inaugurations; one saw him die.

During all these years of official service at the Executive Mansion, the authors cherished the idea of writing this history. At an age when the faculties of memory and observation are at their best, they made frequent notes and memoranda of important events occurring about them. The President was himself aware of their intention, and encouraged and assisted them in their work. Some of his most precious manuscripts were given them by his own hand. Their notes and memoranda taken during the war fill several manuscript volumes, the value of which, from an historical point of view, is inestimable.

After the war was over, and the triumph of the national arms had received its pathetic

VOL. XXXIII.—1*.

rections, and resetting. It could be fed by several keyboarders at once, setting type at the then phenomenal rate of 150 characters per minute or more in the smaller sizes.

These two inventions were the enabling technology for the daily newspaper. By the end of the century, daily papers were common. Magazines were also developed during this period, but they didn't really come to full fruition until the twentieth century. Many things still had to fall into place before magazines as we know them were profitable.

Advertising and marketing

The largest change as far as we are concerned began to develop in earnest right after the Civil War. Advertisers became much more aggressive, but there was little access to the public except broadsides. Plus, there was nothing really to market. Up until the Civil War, whatever you could get together to produce and sell was sold almost immediately in your local community or state.

More than that, soap came in blocks and a hunk was cut off by weight, Crackers came in a barrel and were commonly stale and wormy. The only real identifiable products were the sermons of the Methodist circuit riders and patent medicines. Patent medicines, in particular, developed this field. The manufacturers started sending casts of woodcuts and engravings of their product to every newspaper in the country, no matter how small. Sometimes these casts, like the image of Lydia Pinkham, became an informal sort of clipart. Her face was used in ads and news articles whenever a woman was needed. Art was expensive so the smaller papers used what they had.

The brand name

Following the Civil War, several things happened. During the war, mass production started in earnest with uniforms, underwear, and shoes. With the men gone to war, the women went out to earn a wage. As wage earners it was now acceptable for them to buy bread from a bakery, soap from a store, and clothes off a rack. Advertisers jumped on the new source of revenue.

Manufacturers of soap and typewriters were the first to put pictures in their ads. But advertising warfare started in earnest in 1867 with Macy's and Lord & Taylor in New York and Wanamaker's in Philadelphia. They spent so much money that they were able to demand large picture ads in the newspapers, and we were off and running. With the large source of money, advertising became America's culture.

Early brand names

One of the nicest stories of the time concerns a high-quality soap maker along the Ohio River. One day, the man running the huge mixing vat forgot to turn off the mixer when he went to lunch. When he came back the soap was more or less whipped to a froth. He tried to cover the evidence, but to his surprise the soap floated. His boss had a great idea. Now they had a special soap that could be distinguished from their competition. They began with cut bars and special wrappings. They developed a slogan, "99$^{44}/_{100}$% pure, and it floats!" They called the soap Ivory because of its color. The partners who owned the company were Mr. Procter and Mr. Gamble. Possibly, you have heard of them.

Prior to the war, there were no products as we understand them today. Everything came in bins, slabs, crocks, and barrels and was put into a container after sale (often your own, brought from home). After the war, packaging and trademarked products appeared. Crackers were packed in wax paper for freshness by Uneeda Biscuits and then Nabisco. Henry Heinz started putting his 57 varieties into jars. (From the beginning there were more than 57. He just thought that number was cool.)

Kellogg and Post were health food nuts selling ground grain as medicine. And names started popping up like weeds. A short list would contain names like: Campbell's Soup, 1869; Levi Strauss, 1873; Eagle Pencils, 1877; Ivory Soap, 1879; and on and on. It was a good thing. The trademarked brands were genuinely better products. The advertisements touted the benefits.

Beginnings of graphic design

Peter Bridgewater in *Design*, Wellstreet Press, 1988, states that William Morris was the founder of graphic design. That could certainly be argued pro or con. It is probably true that Morris was one of the first to make graphic design a conscious choice of purpose. However, it is undeniable that the last half of the 1800s was the time this development started. At this point, designers were still trying to make things beautiful and attract customers with beauty. Increasingly, artists established the trends that production people followed. The basic attitude is well expressed with the following short quote from a socialist paper by William Morris.

> Yet I repeat that the chief source of art is man's pleasure in his daily necessary work, which expresses itself and is embodied in that work itself; nothing else can make the common surroundings of life beautiful, and whenever they are beautiful it is a sign that men's work has pleasure in it...

His idea, and it became a common one of the era, was that we all needed to work and that work should be enjoyable. It was assumed that the result should be a life surrounded by beauty. To that end, he founded the Arts & Crafts movement in 1884. He was known for designs in wallpaper, stained glass, textile, architecture, and furniture. In 1890, Morris founded Kelmscott Press in an attempt to raise the standards of printing and book design. In that pursuit, he designed three typefaces, and so on.

Blue Acanthus from
webclipart.com

Illustrators

Not to belabor the point, the Victorian era in general was a time of exquisite design – although extremely overdone to our modern tastes. This era was the first time that graphic design was seen as a career. Food can labels from that era are gorgeous. This was helped a great deal by the prices willing to be paid by advertisers. In 1888, the owner of Pear's Soap paid Sir John Millais twenty-three hundred pounds (nearly $10,000) for a painting he used very effectively for years to advertise his soap. (Remember, just before the turn of the century, you could buy an entire two-story home in kit form from Sears and Roebuck for less than $1,000.) This seemed to remove the stigma of commercial prostitution for fine artists, and from that time many respected artists worked as illustrators for advertising on the side.

Chemical reproduction

Photography

As mentioned, photography began in the first half of the nineteenth century. A version of photointaglio was experimented with very early. Photoengraved letterpress graphics were an obvious step. The problem was (and remains) the fact that presses are only capable of printing ink or no ink, black-and-white, color or no color.

Talking About
California Service

A 10-Section-Drawing-Room-Compartment Sleeping Car leaves every day from Minneapolis and St. Paul for LOS ANGELES, becoming, west of Omaha, part of the famous LOS ANGELES LIMITED, the all-steel train equipped with Observation Car; Library; Men's Club Buffet Room; Ladies' Sun Parlor; barber and valet service, capped by a-la-carte dining car service.

Leaves Minneapolis 7.30 p. m.; St. Paul 8.05 p. m.; via North-Western Line—no change of cars. Please remember this is daily service. No need to consult the calendar.

UNION PACIFIC SALT LAKE ROUTE
Daily Service from Minneapolis and St. Paul

Descriptive booklet and all information will be gladly furnished if you will call on, phone or address

H. F. CARTER, District Passenger Agent
505 Marquette Avenue, Minneapolis, Minnesota
N. W. Phone, Nic. 109;   Auto 37 109

The need was for a method that would allow the continuous tonal changes of a photograph to be reproduced on a press. By the end of the century, that problem was solved with the halftone. We will cover this technique in much greater detail in other books. *Publishing with Photoshop* covers it the most thoroughly. It is sufficient here to say that by breaking up a photo into small dots that vary in size, it is possible to fool the eye into thinking that those small dots are really a gray.

The result is an area filled with tiny dots that looks very much like the original photo (as long as you are far enough away from the dot collection). As long as the dots are smaller than one-seventieth of an inch and your eye is farther than fifteen inches from the page, the

Letterpress ad

This old ad from 1917 looks suspiciously like the drawing is photographically reproduced. What do you think? Look at the lines in the face and rose. Don't they look like they were drawn with ink?

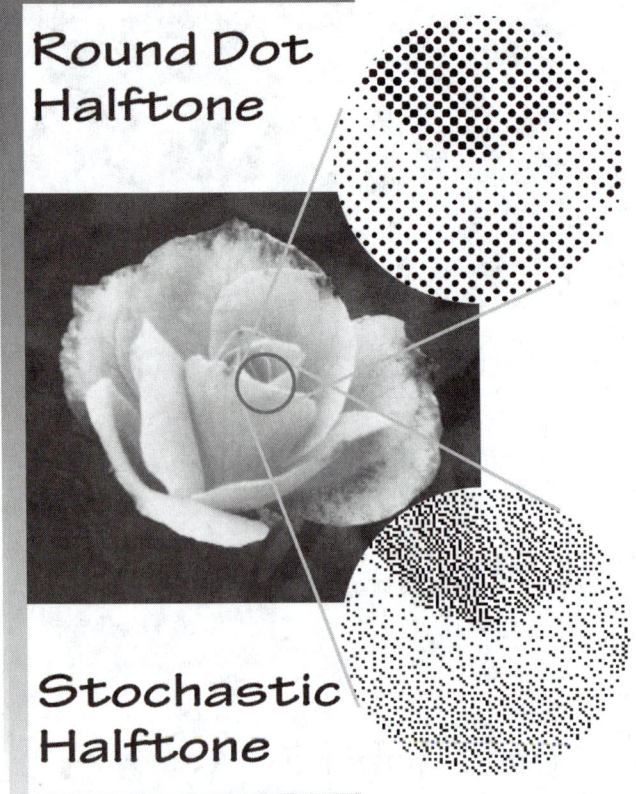

Round Dot Halftone

Stochastic Halftone

illusion works very well. Much coarser dots work if your eye is far enough away. Halftone dots on billboards are commonly one-eighth inch or larger. The two enlarged circles in the sidebar look identical when seen from more than about six feet or so.

The first successful commercial use of the technology was in *Century* magazine (at the end of the century). This magazine used some of the finest engravings ever printed. Photographic technology was a major leap. By 1893, Frederick Ives invented a process using cyan, magenta, and yellow plates to print full-color photographs. In 1890, a process was developed that enabled an emulsion to be applied to a copper cylinder and photogravure came into being.

The use of pictures

The whole concept of using pictures for advertising was developed to an art by a traveling salesman named A. Montgomery Ward. He worked for a dry-goods store in Chicago. He was convinced that what we now call catalogs would be a powerful selling device. In 1872, he borrowed some money and started a catalog operation. The first catalog was three and a half inches wide and seven inches tall, with 100 pages, listing several hundred items for sale.

Very quickly he discovered that a carefully cut woodcut next to the listing could greatly help sales. He mounted a major R&D effort into fine illustration in mass-produced printing. Once he solved those problems, he moved on to color reproduction. An early test run proved that four pages in color moved as much merchandise as twelve pages in black and white.

Ward's illustration techniques were eagerly embraced by the magazine industry. By 1900, front and back covers were commonly produced in color and the quality of illustration in the interior ads had greatly improved. In the last half of the 1890s, work by artists like Remington, Parrish, Whistler, and many others ushered in the golden age of illustration. In the first half of the twentieth century, Norman Rockwell is merely the best known of a host of amazing illustrators.

THE WORLD TO-DAY

The Strength of the Soil

air and sunshine is in every grain of barley that grows. Not without good reason the ancients called it **"The Gift of the Gods."** When skillfully malted and its nutritious juices mingled with the tonic essence of Bohemia's Saazer Hops it produces the health-builder, famed as

ANHEUSER-BUSCH'S
Malt-Nutrine

It creates new blood and sends it pulsing with healthy life to every weakened organ. Containing phosphates and iron organically combined it conserves and feeds the whole nervous system. Its medicinal value to women is incalculable.   **Order of your Druggist or Grocer.**

For 12 tops of Red Metal caps from Large Malt-Nutrine Bottles with **Gold Trade-mark** or 24 from Split Bottles with **Black Trade-mark** and 15c for postage, we will send one of our Vienna Art Plates to any address in the United States.

ANHEUSER-BUSCH,
St. Louis, Mo.

When writing to Advertisers kindly mention "THE WORLD TO-DAY."

Brand names

Some just don't make it — and we thought non-alcoholic beer was new. This one is from 1908 in the *WORLD TO-DAY* magazine from Chicago. This ad looks quite modern. Even its health claims have modern appeal.

Please notice that this artwork is not a halftone screen. All the grays are stippled or crosshatched. This is excellence in letterpress illustration.

In the beginning their work was often printed separately on high-quality color presses and hand-tipped into the magazines (pasted onto blank sheets). Many of the better covers were enlarged to poster size and sold separately. Fine design was seen as a definite benefit. This is where the idea of subcontracted freelance illustrators had its origins. That practice exists to this day. It wasn't until the Depression with its restricted budgets that any of this artistic expertise moved in-house.

Editor domination

The fact of the matter was that editors (who were writers, of course) completely dominated the industry. This is still true to large extent. Roger Black suggests that this is simply caused by the fact that writers are more verbally persuasive than illustrators. This simple fact enables them to dominate meetings, memos, email, and so on.

Editor domination was absolutely true until the 1930s. Artwork was in the advertising. It rarely reached the editorial copy. One of the star magazines of the 1920s, for example, was *The New Yorker* magazine. Its innovation was to build up a large stock of excellent quality, very funny cartoons and use them to fill the blank spaces left by the type. The idea of illustrating stories with pictures was still in the future. There were many stock graphic devices available to the typesetters. But they were rarely specific to the story. Magazine content, other than the ads, was mostly type, all black and white. In general, the production times for graphics rarely allowed journalistic graphics.

This time it was a mere concept that changed things — the picture story. The idea was introduced by Tinsel Town gossip rags and steamy fiction magazines like *True Confessions* and *Police Detective*. It was developed into a powerful communication tool by the magazine giants of the time — *Time*, *Newsweek*, *Life*, *Look*, and many others. The idea was, and still is, that you can more powerfully affect people emotionally with a series of photographs than you can with words. This may be even more true today, as many people are only semiliterate now. Of course, we know the impact of television.

The impact of color

As you have surely noticed, up to this point color is very rare. You may have seen a little color in the large budget magazines. But even there it was only for the covers and a few very expensive ads. We mentioned Mr. Ward's research results. However, printing can barely handle color — and it is extremely expensive. Although most of us assume color now (because of our monitors), color printing is still extremely expensive. This is changing — slowly.

The graphic designer

The 1930s and the picture story brought in an entirely new career – the art director. This was the first time that graphic design reached the masthead. Formerly, only editors were listed; now, artists joined the ranks of the elite. Before this point, artists were mere illustrators, at the beck and call of the editors. Graphic designers did not reach equality until very recently, but it started here.

Development of market research

Coupled with the growth of graphics were the contortions advertising agencies went through because of the Depression. Ad revenue dropped from a high of $3.4 billion in 1929 to $1.3 billion in 1933. Advertisers started asking embarrassing questions like, *"How do I know all this advertising money is doing any good?"* As we know, our economic climate changed radically during this time as those who kept advertising started grabbing huge portions of market share.

One of the main results of this turmoil was development of market research and polls. Gallup Polls started in this period of time. Techniques were radically refined, and messages became extremely hard sell. It got so bad that government came after the industry. The "Depression that business caused" cast the same cloud over advertising and there was a strong negative reaction. The Roosevelt legislative agenda tromped down hard with the Pure Food, Drug, and Cosmetic Act of 1934 and much more. The Consumers Research and Consumers Union groups started in an effort for honesty and accuracy.

Photographic freedom

Photographic reproduction had much wider repercussions, however. By the end of World War II, plates were being produced with the fanciest of new technologies – film. In the 1930s, film was commonly explosively flammable and never dependable as far as dimensional stability was concerned. Until film, photographic plates were exactly that – plates of glass. Sheets of glass were spun, emulsion was poured on them, and centrifugal force flattened the emulsion into a smooth coating. It was almost as physically difficult as cutting metal was.

World War II saw the development of Mylar. That film is completely dimensionally stable and makes an excellent substrate to hold the photographic emulsions. Offset lithography developed thin, flexible aluminum sheets which were coated with a photographic emulsion, exposed using the new film, developed, and wrapped around the plate

cylinder. This greatly simplified plate production. More than that, it enabled photographic art production.

Pasteup

Composition was wiped out in the 1950s by photo-reproduction as thoroughly as pasteup was in the 1990s by digital production. Roger Black called it the "Age of the X-Acto." #11 blades became one of the major drawing tools, along with technical pens using India ink. Photographically produced art and type galleys were cut and sliced into position. It wasn't as physically demanding as cutting metal, but the level of craft was equally high. You would think that rectilinear limitations would have been shattered — not so.

Because most humans follow the course of least resistance, angled text was risky, at the least. In addition, designers began to realize the power of normality. The useful portions of letterpress form were codified into principles taught at design schools. Once codified, these principles caused many design schools to degenerate into legalism. The problem is that it is very hard to teach creative freedom without falling into the pit of anarchy. It is a very fine line that we walk in our creative pursuits: creative taste and style.

There are many guidelines, but taste is a very personal reaction to current cultural style. It is very important to remember the following proverb in the midst of your design decisions:

Habitual reactions are desired in a reader. They are disastrous to a designer.

In general, photography brought little graphic freedom. Mainly, it enabled many more graphics to be used. Photographs became commonplace and graphic design flourished. However, pages and page components continued as rectilinear constructions.

Illustrated ad

This ad from a symphony program in Minneapolis in 1917 should give you a good feel for a basic illustrated ad. It is very difficult to tell how this image was done. I'm guessing a photocomposite by the hard, hand-cut lines around the roses. It's a two-color duotone, with a hand-cut orange negative blocking the color in the gray areas.

Handwriting became fashionable

One loosening in graphic design came with the fad for calligraphic headlines. Handwriting could now be included in normal printing. You could even photograph a signature to place at the end of a printed letter. Ink drawings of any kind (as long as they were black-and-white — no grays) could now be used directly as camera-ready artwork.

Here are some common scripts like those seen in the fifties.

The development of transfer lettering (presstype) in the 1960s brought #11-blade design to its highest form. Now each individual letter could be placed, cut apart, and reshaped at will. By using ultrasmooth, clay-coated board, presstype, technical pens, and Windsor Newton Series 7 sable round brushes, the knife and single-edge razor blade created white shapes as easily as the pens and brushes drew the black ones. It was a remarkable freedom, but everything was put in place and squared up with parallel rules and triangles — rectilinear normality still ruled.

The creative revolution

This is what Goodrum and Dalrymple call it in *Advertising in America: The First 200 Years*, Abrams, 1990. In the 1950s and 1960s, advertising agencies grew incredibly powerful and transformed our entire culture. One of the major changes occurred because of the War. Many of the highly skilled designers (and radical modernists) fled the Nazis and ended up in America as art directors for magazines like *Vogue*, *Harper's Bazaar*, and *Esquire*.

The designs of these very strong personalities, like Mehemed Agha, Alexy Brodovitch, Herbert Bayer, and Paul Rand, began to overwhelm the words. Strong copy was needed. The result was the development of copywriter/designer teams. Because these designs were so tied to individual designers, the appearance of designer boutiques was a natural result. The flexibility and creativity of these new small agencies took over the industry.

Inkwork

Although the color was added later, the black parts of the drawing below were all hand-drawn with India ink, a large sable watercolor brush, and a technical pen — every single dot was drawn by hand.

The marketing economy

As agencies became so incredibly successful, they had to do something with all their money or the IRS would steal it as tax on profits. So they poured millions back into marketing research again. They built audition rooms for TV spots and packaging laboratories for determining customer reaction. They added entire departments of behavioral psychologists to determine how to present product more effectively with shelf position, colors, size, smell, and on and on.

Our culture developed under these market pressures. The arbitrators of our lives were increasingly people whose job survival was based on their success selling us items of little intrinsic value or differentiation. Everything we use is now marketed. Without mass response, items are no longer available. Marketing still relies largely on printed materials. Even the Web has made only small inroads.

The growth of color

Color, in printing, was always a problem. Multicolor etchings, for instance, were horribly frustrating. The desired images required breaking up prints into many colors printed with a different plate. This required the paper to be run through the press many times. Every plate had to fit the others precisely. Making everything fit by hand was an almost impossible challenge. The entire printing industry had the same desire and the same problems. Reality is made of trillions of colors. Anything less than that is definitely less than that. It is obvious to the casual viewer.

The theory and practice of printed color are covered in my more advanced books. Here we'll just note that almost simultaneous with halftone development was separation theory. By taking the subtractive complements of light — cyan, magenta, and yellow — the eye can be fooled into seeing full color in a pile of tricolored halftone dots. The theory is marvelous, the practice is a little more difficult.

Throughout the early twentieth century, camera separation was developed into a salable skill. Early on, separations were very expensive. Three photos had to be exposed through different color filters. If the camera was bumped, the size changed enough so the three no longer fit. Even if they fit properly, registration was a real problem. To keep the three halftones lined up well enough to create the illusion, presses had to be able to print the three images with tolerances of a few thousandths of an inch. If the images were out of registration by more than that, the illusion fell apart.

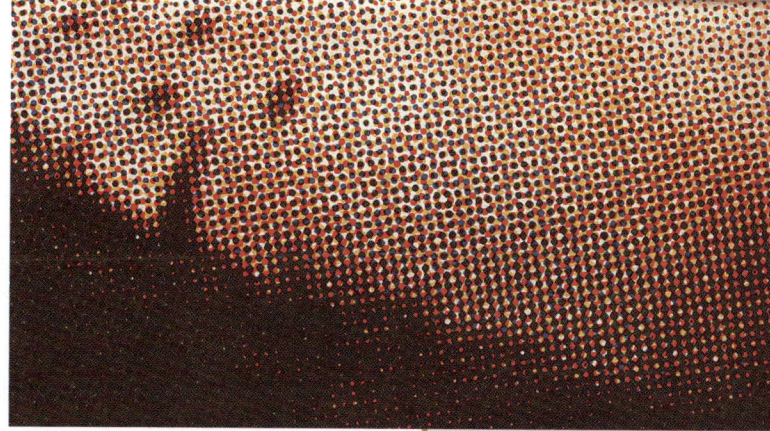

To make things worse, the three commercially available pigments closest to theoretical cyan, magenta, and yellow (CMY) were impure (and not very close). The cyan was particularly weak. As a result, three-color process was not enough. The fourth color, black, had to be added to make the shadow areas neutral and/or black. CMY, in the pigments used, made muddy, ugly brown. CMYK became the standard for full-color printing.

Standardized color

In the 1960s (about the same time as presstype), color production became much more available. It was chaos with thousands of ink companies and no standardized color. Largely due to the efforts of a company in New Jersey — Pantone, standardized color became the norm throughout America and much of the world. Their main work was in the area of what we now call spot color: two- and three-color printing without color photos.

The main impact of this was twofold. First, it became possible for a printer in California to duplicate a color printed in Boston. Secondly, because designers could now control color to a much greater degree, they tended to ask for it more. Spot color is still 30 to 40% of printed output of the entire industry today.

Color usage experienced phenomenal growth that has not peaked yet. Digital production is finally making full color CMYK available to the masses. This means that use of color will grow even faster.

The rosette

Virtually everything you have ever seen printed in color (except for those trashy inkjet prints which are not reproducible) has had a rosette pattern like you see above. This pattern is caused by the overlap of the four halftones of the four colors of ink.

Spot color menu

This is an example from the 1980s of a menu done in two spot colors (PMS) on a mauve paper. The only thing remarkable about it is that it exactly matched the color scheme of the restaurant back then. The newer marketing is in CMYK and very fashionable, and the restaurant remains one of the best in town. It is in an old, restored, Pueblo Deco adobe fire station.

It is an example of a colorful solution to a very limited printing budget. This two-color work cost less than half of a four-color menu equivalent.

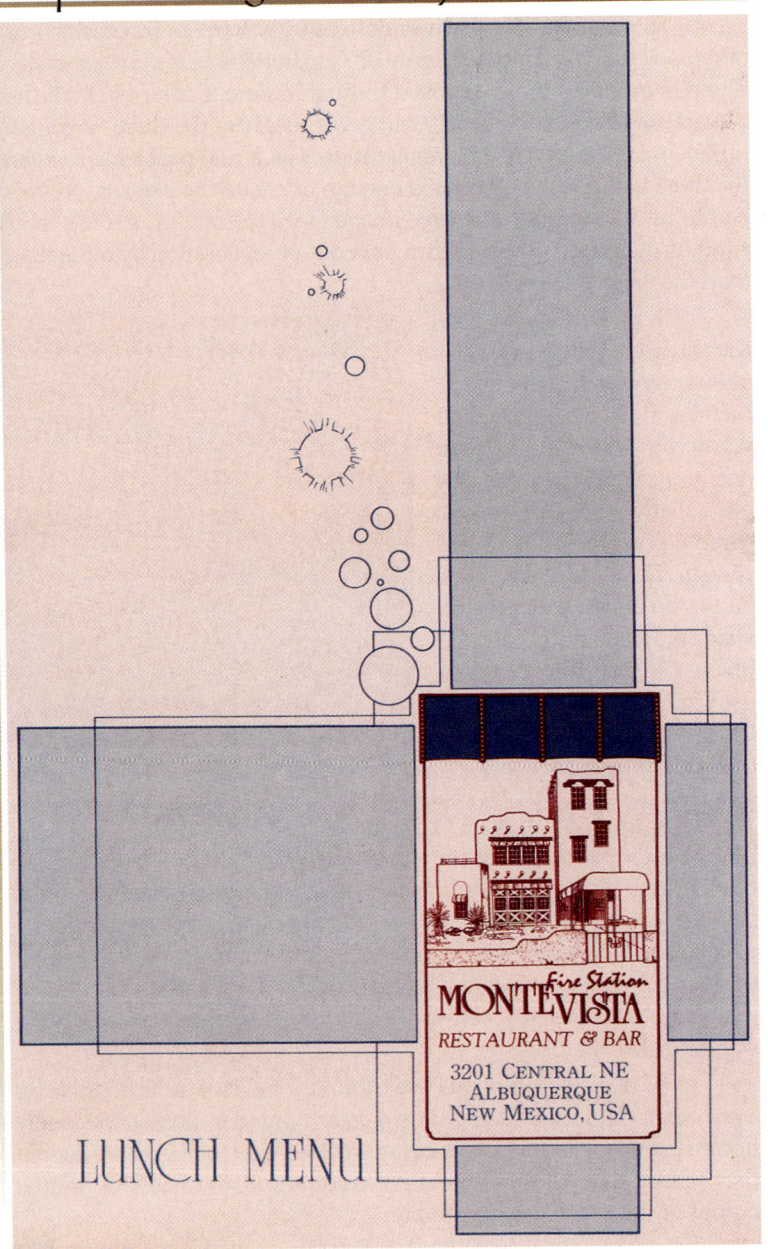

The perfection of offset litho

By the 1970s, printers were commonly producing work that was absolutely amazing. Six, eight, twelve, or more colors became common. Presses that had four to sixteen color-heads became common. Magazines were printed with eight-color presses that could print full-color CMYK on both sides of a web of paper flying at hundreds of thousands of pages per hour. Commercial printers commonly used six-color, 40-inch presses of incredible quality.

Marketers were (and are) constantly striving for new ways to grab the reader's attention. Ridiculously difficult printing became almost commonplace. Printing was becoming almost as labor-intensive as it had been before the industrial revolution, but now labor cost real money. Centuries ago, you sold materials, and the labor was kind of tossed in. In the late twentieth century, labor costs became a real problem. The cost of printing went through the roof. Jobs often took hundreds of hours simply to assemble the pieces of film and plate. Press technology improved to the point where jobs were commonly rejected for flaws that were printed better than the available technology could produce in the 1950s. Tolerances were reduced to thousandths of an inch. Projects were examined with strong magnifying lenses and micrometers. It became normal to print 20,000 identical brochures, with only very minor color variations and possibly a dozen rejects for dirt or scratches.

Virtual perfection

The man who hand-cut all the pieces of film to fit for this 9×16 rack brochure was upset that he missed the little white spot you can see at the end of the double-ended arrow on the edge of the red area that indicates Monument Valley. He had spent over 50 hours assembling the film. He considered it a big deal, but the boss decided that it wasn't worth a reprint (and the client paid for the job, so he was right).

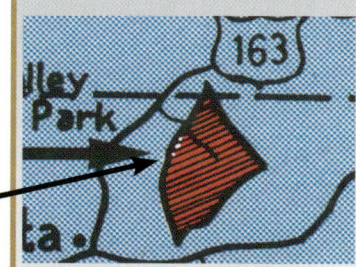

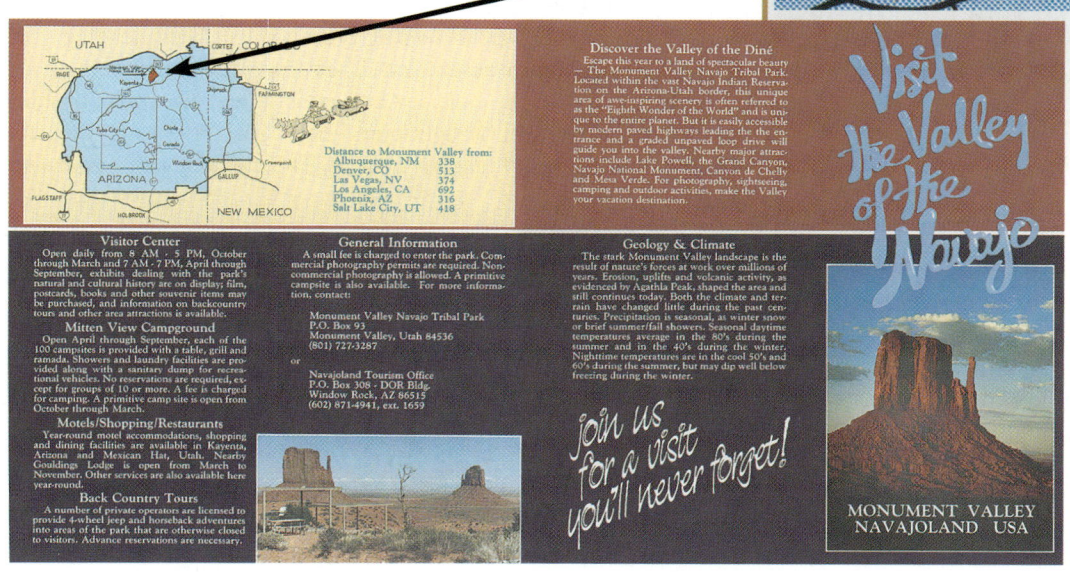

Laser scanners

Color separations then became the domain of computers. The original laser scanners cost several million dollars. When I was working in the late 1970s, there were only a couple dozen in the entire country. Even so, digital scans were much faster, much more accurate, and cheaper than the old camera seps. In addition, the color could be corrected by tweaking the data. Fast, cheap seps greatly accelerated the growth toward full-color printing.

In addition, they set the groundwork for the coming revolution – digital production. As mentioned earlier, these early digital pioneers used mini-mainframes or workstations (which were much slower and had less memory than a G4). Everything was proprietary and limited to those people and companies with huge resources of capital.

The new crafts guild

The result of all this was a labor force that was increasingly skilled. Top-end color printing could not be done without a talented, skilled, and experienced team of professionals. I never even interviewed anyone with less than five years experience for my art departments. More and more, printshops came to resemble technical laboratories. The rough-voiced, cigar-chewing, vulgar, hard-drinking printshop stereotype gave way to men and women in suits driving luxury cars who inspected printed pieces and proofs in luxurious, carpeted rooms with piped-in music.

The new skills were increasingly technologically challenging. Film strippers became image assemblers. The composition room became the art department. It was a whole new ball game. When desktop publishing burst onto the scene, it brought brand-new capabilities to an industry already in the throes of massive change. The digital revolution was set to roll.

STAYING IN CONTEXT
What does all this have to do with design?

Simply stated, without understanding the history you cannot design effectively. All of us experience hundreds or thousands of printed designs daily. The sheer quantity has resulted in a habitually trained readership. As stressed throughout this section, "normal" is the most powerful influence in design today. Even the current fad for "professional ugly" work is simply a reaction to normality.

It is close to impossible to produce excellent designs that work without historical knowledge. You have to know the difference between

Victorian, Art Nouveau, Art Deco, Arts & Crafts, and the others. You must know the graphic styles of the 1920s, 1930s, 1940s, 1950s, 1960s, and 1970s on up to current fashion. You certainly do not have to be fashionable. In fact, my serious counsel is to avoid fashion wherever possible. You absolutely must know whether you are fashionable or not. Don't try to fool yourself.

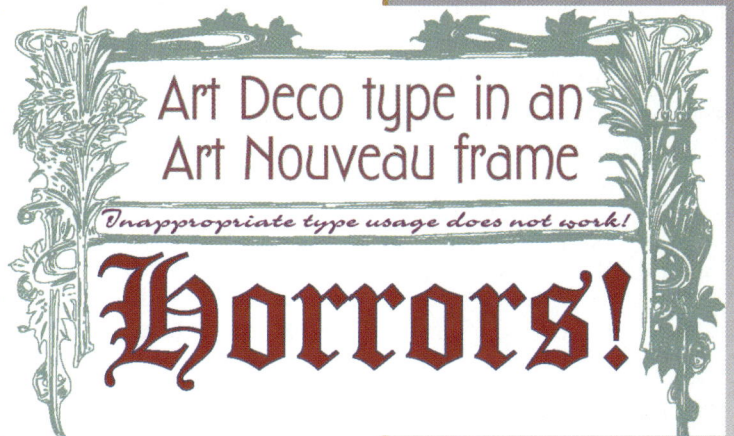

An extremely tough job

It may be sandbagging to let you get this far, but, here goes. Many people get into desktop publishing because they "*like to draw.*" This is not sufficient. This will give you an enjoyable hobby — it will not sustain you in this very difficult career. Design as a profession is impossible without constant study, undying curiosity, and an insatiable drive for excellence. Graphic design is almost certainly one of the most difficult job descriptions in terms of complexity, at the very least. Most of the skills present in those offset litho powerhouses of the 1980s are now your responsibility as a digital designer.

Some argue that fine art is even more difficult, because there you have to invent the rules in addition to developing skills. However, graphic design makes that look easy when you consider that first you have to figure out who is making the rules, what the rules are, and who determines which set of rules will be used in a particular situation. Then you have to make yourself conform to the rules someone else made and produce designs that they are proud of. Fine artists please themselves. Graphic designers have to please themselves, the client, and the reader, in reverse order, all at the same time. Plus you have to handle all the technical issues and you're responsible for most of them.

Design responsibilities

As a graphic designer, you are responsible for every mark on the paper. You need to have a reason for everything. That reason can rarely be whimsical. It has to increase accurate communication. All of this has to be done in an environment run by people who rarely understand creatives. In fact, that last statement is not only true, it is also a good thing. When designers gather together and pat each other on the back, design quickly degenerates into that pit called "art for art's sake."

Where should you be by this time?

By this time you should have a general overview of most of the design applications we use, at least the ones you own or the ones found in your lab at school. You are hopefully itching to get started with something real.

DISCUSSION

You should be discussing design styles, past and present. Try to figure out where things are going. What are the good and useful elements of current fashion? How do they fit with your personal sense of style?

Talk amongst yourselves...

There is no room for the egomaniac in graphic design. This is a service industry. Properly viewed, we are hired guns who provide the creativity others lack for a fee. Our services are as valuable and at least as difficult as the services offered by doctors and lawyers. It has been said that the only equipment a doctor or lawyer needs is a phenomenal memory. Designers, in contrast, have to tread where others fear to go.

More than that, designs are such an integral part of our personal character that critiques can be taken personally far too easily. We have to become persons who use our skill professionally. It helps a great deal to remember that you are offering your creativity for the client's use to serve that client. In most cases, she couldn't care less what you want. What she wants is for you to express her ideas and concepts — clearly, accurately, and beautifully — the way she would if she could.

The real problem with the new paradigm

One of the things that most designers like to avoid is the fact that they have much wider responsibilities in the new world of digital design. You may be able to pass off the sales responsibilities to another person, but you are now required to handle all the production of layout, type, graphics, halftones, separations, and so on. Plus, you have to design for the equipment that will be used to have excellent results. That is what my books are about. Helping you through the complex maze that is modern digital publishing. Let's get to it!

Knowledge retention

1. Why do you think graphic design would be difficult?
2. Why do writers dominate the graphic design industry?
3. What is the major reason photography became so dominant?
4. Why was handwriting fashionable in the 1950s?
5. When did daily papers appear and why?
6. What is a picture story?
7. Why are advertising and marketing so important to us as graphic designers?

Albuquerque Technical Vocational Institute
525 Buena Vista SE
Albuquerque, NM 87106-4096

David Bergsland
Business Graphics Instructor
Business Occupations Department

505 224-3867
FAX 224-3850

graphics@tvi.cc.nm.us

Albuquerque Technical Vocational Institute
525 Buena Vista SE, Albuquerque, New Mexico 87106-4096

David Bergsland
BUSINESS OCCUPATIONS DEPARTMENT INSTRUCTOR
BUSINESS GRAPHICS DEGREE IN DIGITAL PUBLISHING
http://w3.tvi.cc.nm.us/~graphics

graphics@tvi.cc.nm.us

505.224.3867
FAX: 224.3850

Albuquerque Technical Vocational Institute
525 Buena Vista SE, Albuquerque, New Mexico 87106-4096

David Bergsland
BUSINESS OCCUPATIONS DEPARTMENT INSTRUCTOR
BUSINESS GRAPHICS DEGREE IN DIGITAL PUBLISHING
http://w3.tvi.cc.nm.us/~graphics

graphics@tvi.cc.nm.us

COMMUNITY
COLLEGE

FAX: 224.3850
505.224.3867

TVI business card

This is my card at school. The top image is the official style of a couple of years ago. It is almost unusable. All the type is the same font, the same size, the same color.

The second style is approximately the same. However, as you can see, the cream card stock has added a great deal of saturation to the red. It is the same spot color as the original card above. The typography is quite a bit better — emphasizing the only things that matter to me: name and email address. It's still very boring though.

The one on the bottom is pretty radical (as far as the bureaucrats are concerned), but it is the one I use — until they bust me. It breaks many of the norms, but I like it — and that's the bottom line. After all, it is my card.

The original

This was done in Publisher by a person untrained in typography or design. It's not too bad, really. Especially in color, the sunset would have been pretty, at least. It was very hard to read though, and the organization of the copy needed a lot of help.

Smith Brasher Hall Lobby
Corner of University and Coal Ave SE

Tuesday Nov. 13th, 2001
9:00 AM to 1:00 PM

Job Fair

Come join TVI's Business Occupations Department and Student Job Placement Job Fair. Visit with prospective employers and investigate employment possibilities.

GUEST SPEAKER: Listen to well known businessman Kim Jew and share his business and employer perspective at 9:15 in room SB100.

Register for door prizes.

If you have questions please call TVI's
Business Occupations Department 224-3811 or
Student Job Placement 224-3060

Up to 20 Employers,

Including

♦ Sandia National Laboratories
♦ University of New Mexico
♦ City of Albuquerque
♦ Wal-Mart
♦ Staffing Solutions
♦ Wells Fargo
♦ U.S. Department of State
♦ Presbyterian Health Services
♦ Public Service Company of NM
♦ Isleta Casino
♦ NM Relay Network
♦ Blue Cross Blue Shield
♦ Albuquerque Publishing

This is the original I was given. I was told the stock photo was some sunset from Word. I don't know, it didn't seem to help the concept of looking for a job. I was told to do whatever I wanted to do (nice).

Tuesday, November 13th

Job Fair
Smith Brasher Hall Lobby
CORNER OF UNIVERSITY AND COAL SE

Register for door prizes

The doorway to the rest of your life!

9:00 am to 1:00 pm
Come join TVI's Business Occupations Department and Student Job Placement Fair. Visit with prospective employers and investigate possible employment opportunities. Listen to well-known businessman, Kim Jew, share his business and employer perspective at 9:15 am in Room SB100.

Up to 20 employers, including:

- Sandia National Labs
- City of Albuquerque
- University of New Mexico
- Presbyterian Health Services
- Public Service Company of New Mexico
- Wal–Mart
- Wells Fargo
- Staffing Solutions
- U.S. Department of State
- Isleta Casino
- NM Relay Network
- Blue Cross Blue Shield
- Albuquerque Publishing

If you have questions, please call:
TVI's Business Occupations Department: 224-3811 or
Student Job Placement: 224-3060

The poster done in color and typeset. If you look, the typesetting does more than the color.

Typeset

This version was done in InDesign 2. I had color printing available (which was one of the reasons I got the job).

The photo is from Patrician Stock. the *Santa Fe Textures CD*. The open door seemed more appropriate to me. (It really doesn't matter that much — as long as the designer has a plan.) The transparent Door Prize sign draws the eye to the door. The headline uses the door.

The type is much better organized and readable. The client was ecstatic even for the letter-sized version which had the same proportions as the original on the other page.

Please notice that the color simply sets off the type (after it grabs the reader's attention). This is appropriate usage. The picture is not important; the Job Fair *is* important. They had the largest attendance ever — that is the best testimony.

BUSINESS OCCUPATIONS AND
TRADES AND SERVICE OCCUPATIONS

OPEN HOUSE/CAREER DAY

FRIDAY, APRIL 6, 2001
9 am – 1pm

OPEN TO THE PUBLIC

LOCATION: TVI MAIN CAMPUS
TED CHAVEZ HALL
S.E. CORNER OF COAL AND UNIVERSITY

"HIGHLIGHTED PROGRAMS TRADES AND SERVICE"

Machine Tool Technology	Culinary Arts	Cosmetology
Plumbing	Welding	Criminal Justice
Carpentry	Automotive Tech	Fitness Technician
Electrical Trades	Fire Science	
Air Cond./Heating	Truck Driving	
Environmental Technology	Diesel Equipment Tech	

"HIGHLIGHTED PROGRAMS BUSINESS OCCUPATIONS"

Accounting	Court Reporting	Office Assistant
Bookkeeping	Hospitality and Tourism	Pre-Management
Business Admin.	International Business	Retail Management
Computer Info. Systems	Judicial Studies	Stenotranscription
Financial Services	Business Graphics/Comm.	Legal Assistant
E-Commerce	Office Admin.	Call Center Operations

PLEASE LET YOUR FAMILY AND FRIENDS KNOW ABOUT THIS
GREAT EVENT!!!

FOR MORE INFORMATION, CALL 224-3763- TRADES AND SERVICE
OR 224-3870- BUSINESS OCCUPATIONS

This is the original document done in Word. It is acceptable, even expected, secretarial design. The front office thought nothing of it. It didn't even occur to them that it was destined for the trash from the moment it came out of the printer. Would you read it?

ALBUQUERQUE TECHNICAL VOCATIONAL INSTITUTE
BUSINESS OCCUPATIONS DEPARTMENT
TRADES & SERVICE OCCUPATIONS

Open House • Career Day

Friday, April 6, 2001 • 9:00 AM–1:00 PM

OPEN TO THE PUBLIC

Location: TVI Main Campus, Ted Chavez Hall
SE Corner of Coal & University

Highlighted programs: Trades & Service Occupations

Machine Tool Technology	Culinary Arts	Cosmetology
Plumbing	Welding	Criminal Justice
Carpentry	Automotive Technology	Fitness Technician
Electrical Trades	Fire Science	Air Conditioning/Heating
Truck Driving	Environmental Technology	Diesel Equipment Technology

Highlighted programs: Business Occupations

Accounting	Court Reporting	Office Assistant
Bookkeeping	Hospitality & Tourism	Pre-Management
Business Administration	International Business	Retail Management
Computer Information Systems	Judicial Studies	Stenotranscription
Financial Services	Business Graphics	Legal Assistant
E-Commerce	Office Administration	Call Center Operations

Please let your family and friends know about this great event!

FOR MORE INFORMATION:

CALL 224-3763: Trades & Service or 224-3870: Business

TVi
COMMUNITY
COLLEGE

Here's exactly the same copy — typeset. A tasteful amount of color was added — just enough for impact. It is much more inviting. Plus, the first thing you see is Open House and Career Day. On the original the first thing you see is the logo — but it is on TVI bulletin boards.

The gradient-filled Highlights box is almost unreadable on the wall. The color behind the type reduces contrast to the point where it can barely be deciphered at three feet.

The sample above is normal two-color work done in Word, by the lead instructor of the degree. All heads are in color so the impact is greatly reduced. The worst mistake is putting the Highlights in a tint box — especially one with a gradient fill.

Color contrast only works if there is contrast between mostly grayscale and a little color. Highlights should be in a white box set in a gray-tinted field to make it stand out.

ALBUQUERQUE TECHNICAL VOCATIONAL INSTITUTE
BUSINESS OCCUPATIONS DEPARTMENT

Office Administration
Certificate and Associate of Applied Science Degree

Marketable Skills in Demand
Computer Applications • Interpersonal relations • Office Technology • Office Accounting • Written Communications

Office Technology Concentration

Four-Term Certificate
Five-Term Associate of Applied Science Degree

LEARN:
» Microsoft Word
» Microsoft Excel
» Microsoft Access
» Microsoft PowerPoint
» Internet
» Office accounting procedures
» Business English
» Interpersonal skills
» Business procedures

Office Assistant

Two-Term Certificate

LEARN:
» Microsoft Word
» Business telephone techniques
» Working with the challenging customer
» Interpersonal skills

Medical Concentration

Four-Term Certificate
Five-Term Associate of Applied Science Degree

LEARN:
» ICD-9 coding
» Current procedural terminology (CPT)
» Medical terminology & anatomy
» Medical insurance

Legal Concentration

Four-Term Certificate
Five-Term Associate of Applied Science Degree

LEARN:
» Legal terminology
» Microsoft Word
» Transcription
» Interpersonal skills

Highlights

• Tuition **FREE** for occupational courses (supply fee for some)

• Excellent salaries ($13,000 to $26,000)

• Student internship program at Sandia National laboratories

• Associate degree transfers to University of New Mexico toward a bachelor of science degree in education in technology & training

*NM RESIDENT REGISTRATION FEE IS $22.25 PER TERM

BUSINESS OCCUPATIONS DEPARTMENT CONTACTS:

DAN VALLES, Associate Dean
Office Administration, Business Information Technologies, Business Graphics
505.224.3819 • dvalles@tvi.cc.nm.us

MARILYN KONNICK, Program Chair
Office Administration Program
505.224.3886 • mkonnick@tvi.cc.nm.us

Chapter 8

Fonts

Concepts

1. Small caps

2. Ligatures

3. Swashes

4. Fractions

5. Font

6. Italic

7. Oblique

8. Optical weight

9. OpenType

Learning the terminology and attributes of the various parts of a font and its hundreds of characters

Chapter Objectives:

By giving students a clear understanding of what a font is, this chapter will enable students to:

1. define true small caps and recognize them
2. explain the usefulness of swashes
3. label the measurement points of a typeface
4. define the common terms of fonts, like: leading, ascender, descender, x-height, baseline, point size, and many more

Lab Work for Chapter:

1. Complete miniskills chosen.
2. Begin skill exams.
3. Read chapter 9 for next week.
4. Work on projects.

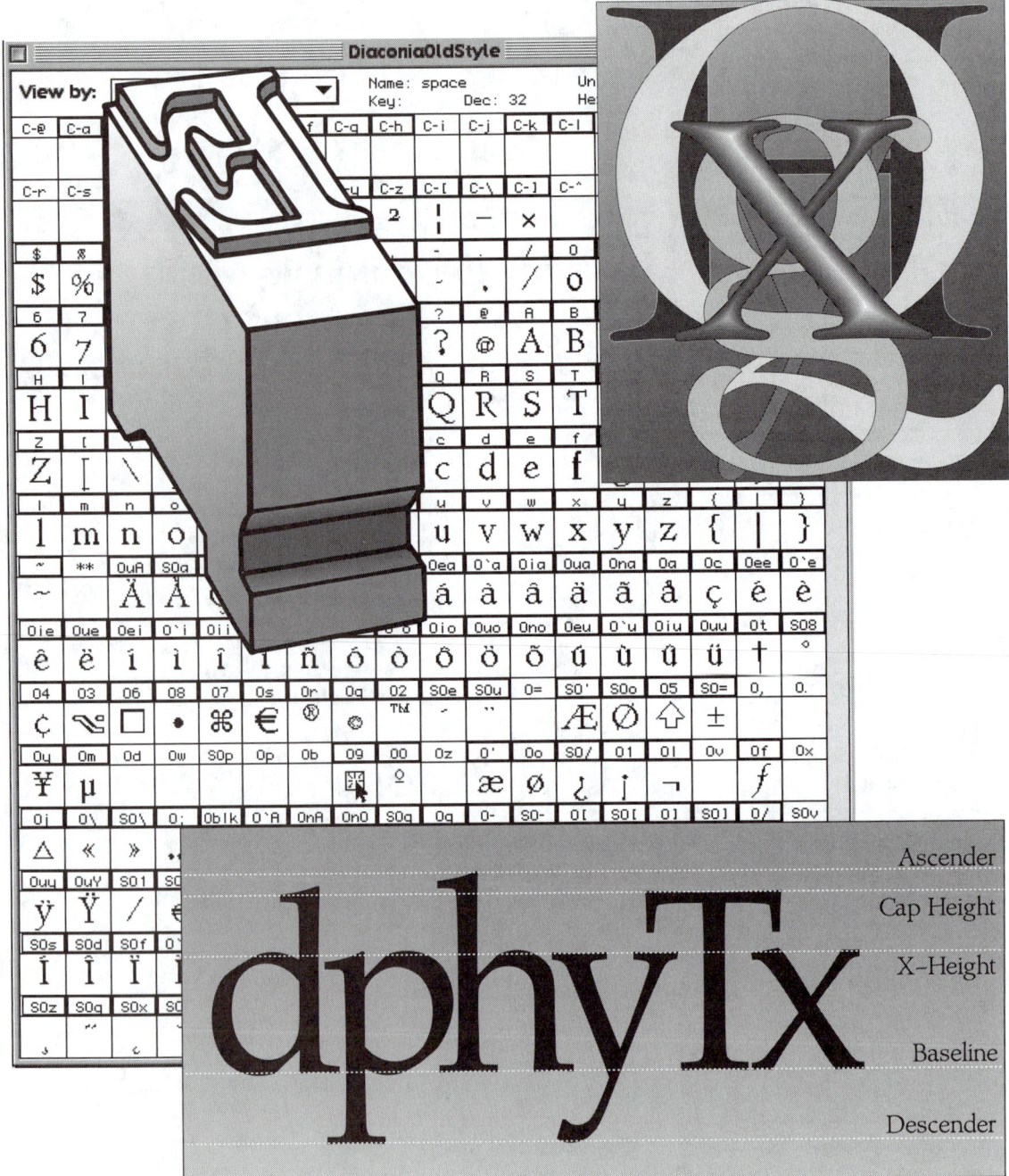

Type is not typed!

One of the major concepts of graphic design (often lost in the shuffle) is the centrality of the copy. Our entire idea is to communicate the client's product as the solution to the reader's need. More than 95% of this communication will take place through the words you place on the document. (If you don't understand this, you need to read books on advertising and design. This textbook is just a barely sufficient introduction to the field. Those written by David Ogilvy, among many others, are highly recommended.) In fact, most of the documents you design will have few graphics, and they will often be supplied as logos and the like.

This is why this book emphasizes type so strongly. The Graphic Artists Guild is solid in their assertion that typography skills are one of the main basic entry-level skills needed by graphic designers. Without type knowledge you will have a hard time communicating. Type is typeset, and that is one of the major skills you'll need in your career.

The old proverb is that a picture is worth a thousand words. This is true, but it takes an exceptional picture to express exactly the thousand words necessary to produce the desired action on the part of the reader. We are not dealing with fine art, but specific communication. These pictures can be produced. However, they will take you lots of time and money plus the services of an exceptional illustrator or photographer. Even exceptional designers can rarely pull it off without needing additional explanatory verbiage. Most clients simply do not have the budget for graphics, illustrations, or photos of that caliber.

In reality, writers are much more common than illustrators although Norman Rockwell skill levels in copywriting are just as rare as they are in illustration. However, in general, the level of competence available in wordsmiths greatly exceeds the accessibility of visual accuracy among illustrators when it comes to communicating ideas. So, in the real world, you will be dealing with words, but we are talking about typeset, not typewritten, words.

So, who cares?

Actually, you do. One of the things most beginning designers are not aware of is the extreme (but usually subconscious) distinctions between what I call secretarial type and professional typeset copy. You are very aware of the differences — just not on a conscious level. You have been making decisions about companies, products, and services

David Ogilvy

Over the past fifty years, Ogilvy has helped to build some of the most recognizable brands in the world: American Express, Sears, Ford, Shell, Barbie, Pond's, Dove, and Maxwell House among them, and more recently, IBM and Kodak.

His best known book is: Ogilvy on Advertising for under $20.

1,000 word pictures

Here's a picture:
I wish you could tell me what the 1,000 words are. In nonprofessional work, graphics are often just dumped in place with no reason at all — just like the sad mutt above.

for years that are at least partially based upon their perceived honesty, integrity, trustworthiness, and so on as seen in their advertising and marketing efforts.

Many of those perceptions come from reactions to type used in their public personas. You probably cannot explain the difference at this point. However, you can tell at a glance whether something is bureaucratic, cheap, top quality, and so on by the typography of the advertising you see. Even the type chosen for logos makes a major statement. It is not a mistake that companies like Compaq use Helvetica almost exclusively for their brochures. This font is the epitome of business usage, just as Times is that font, bureaucratically.

The democratization of typography

The problem, of course, is that everyone now has the capability to do type. It can be done in Word or almost any word processor, and that covers almost everyone. It is very difficult to generate professional typography in a word processor though. It is confused by the fact that all now have access to the same fonts, and the same basic capabilities. Most people simply do not have any idea how far typography goes beyond word processing.

Fonts are not typography — fonts are used to make typography.

Before we can get into this, though, we have to start with a lot of terminology. Typography speaks a new language. Much of this is based on historical letterpress usage. However, without these terms you will be lost. This has been complicated now that all of the digital terms have been added to the mix.

A specialized language

You must learn to use type as one of your major graphic elements. To begin with, most typographic terminology comes from letterpress. This is changing somewhat, for some unimportant words, but most of the present terms will remain. Before you can set type, you must be able to speak the language and understand the concepts.

You can tell how severe this is as we begin by learning a new measurement system. Type is not measured in inches or millimeters. It is measured in points. This is not going to change for many reasons. So, let's start with a little history of where points came from.

A different ruler

The first aspect of sizing type is the ruler. Those who are terrified of metric can relax — type sizing is much more irrational. What happened was this. Until the mid-1800s, all type foundries had their own sizes. These sizes were given common names, but there was no universal standard. Some of the names will still be familiar to you. Agate, for example, is a small size used for classified ads (5.5-point). Other common type sizes were diamond, minion, brenier, long primer, great primer, and canon.

Around 1875, a type salesman named Nelson Hawkes decided to rectify the problem. He came up with a measurement system based on one of the more common sizes, the pica. It happened to be 12 points high. In the early 1700s, King Louis XV had established the point as the standard type measurement for printers in France.

By the time Nelson made his plans, there were two points: the European point, which was .0148 inches; and the American point, which was .0138 inches. This made 72 European points be a little more than an inch, and 72 American points were a little less than an inch. Using the American point, Hawkes decided that 12 points should be called a pica and built an entire type sizing system upon picas.

Today all type is sized in points.

Points were an excellent sizing tool. At approximately 72 points per inch, the smaller sizes of body copy could be clearly differentiated. Type that is one point larger or smaller is almost the smallest increment of size that can be distinguished with the naked eye. We can see, with the naked eye, the differences between 9 and 10-point, 12 and 13-point. We cannot see the difference between 11 and 11.5-point type.

Within a few years, picas and points became the American standard. Today all type is sized in points. The distinctions between European and American points have disappeared, but all use points (and will for the foreseeable future).

The computer has helped

One of the developments in type sizing that eased things a bit for Americans was brought about by Apple's Macintosh. When Apple came out with the Mac and its GUI, they set the screen resolution at 72

Points

The European point: .0148"

The American point: .0138"

The digital point: .0138889"

A Point is now exactly a seventy-second of an inch. Which is nice for those of us still working in inches.

pixels per inch. In the years since 1984, the 72-point-per-inch standard has become universal on desktop computers. This is true even though high-resolution monitors make this measurement meaningless.

The nice thing, for us Americans, is that this is exactly 72 points per inch whereas, under the pica system 72 points came to .9936 inch. This insignificant difference meant that 66 picas was not 11 inches, but 10.93 inches (a little more than 10-7/8 inches). This caused amazing havoc for traditional pasteup artists and designers, whose art never fit the way they designed it. For years, many artists drew all their boards in inches, set all their type in picas, and tried to force things to fit (they often didn't).

At this time the pica is disappearing. In fact, we can safely say it is gone in most cases. But points may never go away. Software manufacturers still make points their default measurement, but no one uses it any more except old traditionalists. One of the first things you do when you install a program is decide which measurement system you are really going to use: inches, pixels, or millimeters. As far as I know, the only industry still using picas is newspapers, and they only use it for column widths.

Letterpress terminology

As you would suspect, much of our type terminology comes from letterpress. After all, this printing technology was dominant until a few decades ago. I could give you dozens of letterpress terms that would be of historical interest only. However, it is enough that you recognize the source of many of the terms we use.

A typical example is leading (pronounced like the metal). It would be better (or at least more accurate) to change the term to line spacing. For a number of reasons, that probably won't happen. Leading came from the letterpress practice of increasing the space between lines of type by adding strips of lead between the rows. These strips came in standard thicknesses: 1/2-point, 1-point, and so on. In letterpress usage, you could only increase leading and could never have line spacing that was less than the type size. That is no longer true with digital type, but the term remains.

We have gotten ahead of ourselves, however. Before we can continue, you need to know how letterpress type was sized and assembled. Just getting a visual in your mind will straighten out a lot of this. The major fact to remember is that hot type is cast metal. The letters are cut into dies and cast into blocks of metal.

They all have to be the same height, thickness, hardness, and so on. You have to be able to fit them together into blocks that can be locked into place in the chase. If any letter is a lower height, it won't ink up as you roll the brayer across the surface of the type. Much of our present type usage comes from factors that were determined by the physical nature of letterpress.

A *slug* of type was always .918 inches high and left enough room for all the characters in a font of type. This was because all type had to fit into evenly sized rectangles to line up properly on the composing stick. Some specialized terms no longer mean the same things. A slug now what we call the black bar highlighted when you select type indicating the leading.

Face, for example, used to mean the actual printing surface of the letter. Now, in common usage, face often means a type style such as Helvetica or Times. Although in that case, the word typeface is often used. As is lamented by grammarians, American English is a living language under constant change.

The same is true of the word *counter*. A counter was the recessed area around the letter above which the face of the character protruded. Now it is usually used (if at all) as a term for the open areas inside a *P* or *e* or *g* or even an *s*, for example. I will give you a diagram in a little bit that covers most of the old terms.

 Many of you are probably grumbling to yourselves at this point. "Who cares?" You say in your twenty-first-century superiority. Actually, you do. Most of you will find that the longer you design documents, the more you will fall in love with type. Type will become the most important graphic tool at your disposal for most of you. This tendency will increase throughout your career. Many of you will begin using all of the esoteric letterpress terminology.

Composing type

The stick

We need to remember how type was set. All the slugs had to be placed in rows on the composing stick — one letter at a time. There's a drawing of one on the top of the next page. This is where the rectangles of letterpress were built, and they had to be precise. If anything was out of size, the slugs would move or fall out as they were printed. There are hundreds of specialized terms used for all this equipment. If you are curious, read almost any book written on printing up to the end of the twentieth century — like The *Lithographers Manual* by GATF.

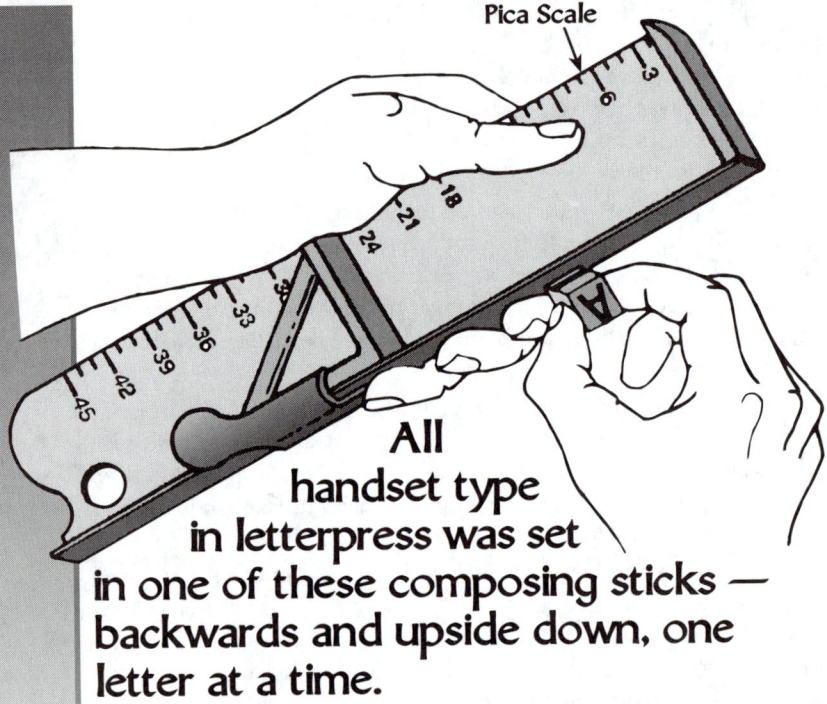

Pica Scale

All handset type in letterpress was set in one of these composing sticks — backwards and upside down, one letter at a time.

Nevertheless, many terms in your software are from letterpress. For example, the sizing of type remains the same — from top of *ascender* to bottom of *descender*, with the capital letters being slightly shorter than the ascenders. This was determined by the necessities of the composing stick. But there are more words to define.

Type parts

The baseline is the imaginary line that all the letters and numbers sit on. The x-height is the height of the lowercase x (the x is the only lowercase letter that is normally flat both top and bottom). However, I saw it called a *mean line* in a diagram on a typography Web site the other day, although I have never actually heard anyone use that term. Ascenders are the portions of lowercase letters that rise above the x-height as in *b*, *d*, *f*, *h*, *k*, and *l*. A *t* doesn't ascend far enough to be called an ascender, usually. Descenders are the portions that sink below the baseline as in *g*, *j*, *p*, *q*, and *y*. The cap height is the height of the uppercase letters.

The reason that x is specified is that curves have to extend over the lines to look the proper height. Yes, it is an optical illusion. The

same is true of letters such as *A* or *V* that have points. If the point does not protrude past the guidelines, the letter looks obviously too short. Even people who know nothing about type will know that something is wrong. Type design has many of these understandings that have become rules.

If you look above, you will see that even the *x* does not fit exactly in the x-height for this font (Palatino). You can even see that for this font the ascenders of the *d* and the *h* are different. You will discover that this optical alignment is crucial to excellence in type. You need to even align the sides of the columns optically to make them seem straight, clean, and perfect.

You can see below a font that fits the way it is supposed to. It's Futura. However, it is a little boring, don't you think? This is the dilemma. If you fit the mold too well, you lose most of the visual interest. However, if you are too far outside the mold, you look unprofessional.

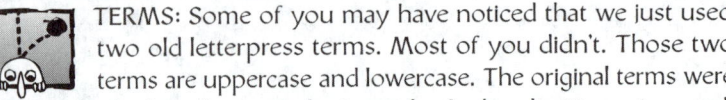

TERMS: Some of you may have noticed that we just used two old letterpress terms. Most of you didn't. Those two terms are uppercase and lowercase. The original terms were majuscules for large letters and minuscules for handwriting using small letters. Majuscules came to be called capital letters. Minuscules remained a mouthful. Uppercase and lowercase come from common typesetting practice where two wooden cases of letters were used in a standard setup. The upper case contained all the capital letters. The lower case contained all the minuscules. In other words, the common phrase caps and lower case (or C&lc) is just one of those things we do in English.

The major point to remember is that all letters of a given typeface and a given size fit into rectangles that are the same height.

AaBbGgQ

Everything has to fit in the same height!

There's another way to look at it in the sidebar.

We've spent a lot of time on this because it is an important concept to understand. Often paragraphs or lines of type look very different in size, but in fact they are the same point size. This is primarily due to variations in x-height and built-in leading. Any letter that goes exceptionally high or low changes the size of the entire typeface.

For example, examine the graphic on the top of the next page very carefully. As you can see, there are huge differences in x-height between Diaconia and Bernhard Modern. Bernhard Modern has a lot of built-in leading also. Even though Diaconia and Futura have very similar x-heights, you can see that Futura has no extra leading built into the font, whereas Diaconia has some. The result is that 10-point Futura will look as large as 11-point Diaconia (and maybe 13- or 14-point Bernhard Modern). These things must be taken into account when you pick your fonts for your projects.

This will be confusing for a little while. However, if you remember these few ideas, you'll be able to understand much better how type works in your software. The options will begin to make sense. They are something you need to control.

dpdpdpdpdpdp

DIACONIA   FUTURA   BERNHARD   BODONI   BERNHARD   TREBUCHET
MODERN

These fonts are all the same point size.

Typesetting measurements

1. **Type size:** Type size is measured from top of ascender to bottom of descender in points (plus the built-in leading). Capital letters are usually approximately two-thirds of the point size, but a little shorter than the ascender. The x-height is normally around one-third. The most important factor in visual or comparative size is the x-height. Sans serif faces, in general, have larger x-heights. Many fonts have some amount of line spacing built in above and below the characters that is included in the point size.

2. **Leading:** Sometimes called line spacing, leading was traditionally measured from baseline to baseline. In other words, leading was the distance advanced to leave room for the next line, measured from the baseline of the original line to the baseline of the following line. To use typewriter imagery: when you hit the carriage return, the roller advanced the distance necessary to allow the next row of type to be typed without overlap. It was simple to calculate leading in traditional typesetting by using a pica gauge.

 **Type speak:** Point size and leading are usually written as a fraction. The point size becomes the numerator and the leading the denominator. It is written **10/12**. This would be spoken *ten on twelve*, meaning ten-point type with twelve points of leading.

As mentioned, many fonts already have built-in leading. You need to be aware of things like this when you pick a font, as mentioned. A font like Futura has almost no built-in spacing and therefore needs to be set with extra leading for readability (as if you could read Futura anyway). A font like Bernhard Modern has so much built-in leading you might be tempted to use negative leading as in 14/13. If you are using a font that is all capital letters, you may want to set the type as 24/18 or so. There would be too much space between the lines with a third of the point size blank because there are no descenders.

Here software developers have messed us up. At present, every application seems to use different definitions for leading. They all still use the term, but you should be careful to find out what they mean. In PageMaker, for example, you must choose between three different possible measuring systems for leading (none of which is baseline to the baseline of the next line of type). Most applications use the measurement from the baseline to the baseline of the line above — which makes little sense traditionally. You just learn to deal with it.

The leading slug

The leading slug

I mentioned that the meaning of the word slug has changed. While you are getting used to your software, it is helpful to highlight your type and examine the result. The height and vertical location of the box containing the reversed-out type shows the leading. After a short while, you will understand how the specific software you are using handles leading. This is also the easiest way to see how your font fits the leading. Built-in spacing can also be seen in this manner.¶

TIP: The main thing about leading is that is greatly affects read.

The black lines of highlit type show you the leading slug.

I mentioned that the meaning of the word slug has changed. While you are getting used to your software, it is helpful to highlight your type and examine the result. The height and vertical location of the box containing the reversed-out type shows the leading. After a short while, you will understand how the specific software you are using handles leading. This is also the easiest way to see how your font fits the leading. Built-in spacing can also be seen in this manner.

The main thing about leading is that it greatly affects readability. Normally, the longer the line length, the more leading is required. We will talk about workable line lengths in chapter 12.

Another old letterpress term you will hear is *set solid*. Type with no extra leading as in 12/12 is referred to as being set solid. That is, in letterpress, the character slugs were set on top of each other with no extra strips of lead.

Fonts

There are many more things you need to know about typefaces. First, as you have surely noticed, this book uses typefaces, type styles, and fonts interchangeably. This is common practice; but it is not entirely accurate. My goal is to give you the common language spoken by your peers — not to be a grammatical Gestapo.

A font, for example, is a very specific thing. A font is the entire set of characters for a given type style. In the days of letterpress, a font was all the characters in a given point size. You had Times 12-point,

Times 14-point, Garamond 18-point, and so on. In some old fonts, this was hundreds of characters.

When phototype became available, a font came in several sizes. The common machines charged you about the same for a font as was paid in the 1800s (several hundred dollars). But these film strips could be enlarged through various lenses to give you a dozen or more sizes for your money. A common setup, using twelve lenses in a turret, was 6, 7, 8, 9, 10, 11, 12, 14, 18, 24, 30, and 36 point. Zoom lenses were the most exciting. For example, one phototypesetting machine went from 6-point to 72-point in half-point increments and 72-point to 144-point in one-point increments.

Today, in the digital arena, a font is simply a complete set of characters for a given style. Below is the font used for this book, showing all the characters available in it.

Diaconia Old Style

ABCDEFGHIJKLMNOPQRSTUVWXYZ

abcdefghijklmnopqrstuvwxyz1234567890

ABCDEFGHIJKLMNOPQRSTUVWXYZ1234567890

1234567890!@#$%^&*()_+{}|:"<>?,./;'[]\=-¡

½¼1¾32¦–×~ÄÅÇÉÑÖÜáàâäãåçéèêë

í""ïñóòôöõúùûü†˚¢✌■•⌘€®©™´¨ÆØ⇧

±¥µ⌦⚲ºæø¿¡¬ƒ×△«»…ÀÃÕŒœ––""""÷ÿŸ/ €◊fi‡·‚‰

ÂÊÁËÈÍ"Ï"ÓÒÔÚÛÙı ˆ ˜ ¯ ˘ ˙ ˚ ˝ ˛ ˇ

Hundreds of characters

However, hundreds just barely begins to cover the characters needed for typesetting. Typewriters were limited to about 88 characters, although that varied a little. We had the QWERTY keys and then those same keys with the shift key held down. The shift key was called that because it shifted the entire set of letters high enough to use the second set on all the keys.

Many of you still think that these are all the letters we need. This is not true. This is not even close to being correct. In fact, we need access to several hundred characters, as professional typesetters. You'll need several thousand characters if you set in other languages. We haven't even mentioned double-byte languages like Japanese, Korean, Chinese,

Western style

An interesting sidelight is the "western style." This is extremely easy to duplicate once you understand what was going on. A font in the Old West was extremely expensive. One cost several hundred dollars in the mid-1800s (or about the price of a small well-built house).

Printers out West could afford only a few display faces. They might save up and buy a copy of Clarendon 96-point, for example. A couple of years later, 72-point Franklin Gothic might be purchased. Gradually a fair library of styles would be built up. However, if you wanted Franklin Gothic, you got 72-point — if you wanted 72-point, you got Franklin Gothic. So, every different size was a different typeface. All you have to do is remember to pick type styles that were available during this era (Victorian) and use a different one for every display size. A fair selection of body copy sizes was usually available — but don't go wild and certainly not modern.

QWERTY keyboard

The story I have always heard was that our current QWERTY keyboard was originally designed to be difficult to use because they had to slow down typists. They had to type slow enough so that the keys didn't hit each other and lock up the machine. This was evidently a major problem when typewriters were first invented.

and so on which have over 30,000 characters — each. Just in English we are really limited, and here we come to one of the major differences between PC and Mac.

7-bit ASCII: the PC limitation

When Bill and the crew designed DOS, they knew nothing about typesetting. As a result, they were very pleased to offer 7-bit ASCII. ASCII is just an acronym for a regulating group setting a standard numbering order for letter characters, but the key here is 7-bit. Remembering your digital code, 7-bit is 128 choices. So, with 7-bit ASCII, PCs had 128 characters.

Good, you say. That is much more than the 88 found on a typewriter. And, in fact, these machines were used only as glorified typewriters. In truth, there wasn't much glory there, but that's another story we have already covered briefly.

8-bit ASCII: the Mac limitation

When the Mac came out, it supported 8-bit ASCII. We Macophiles have used this for years to lord it over our poor restricted buddies using PCs. However, even the 256 characters of 8-bit ASCII do not even come close to what is needed for typesetting. It does enable us to set type professionally in one language at a time — sorta.

Upper ASCII

8-bit ASCII is essential for desktop publishing. Without all 256 characters, there are many things that are a real pain. As a PC user, you will run into that pain very quickly. As we will discuss in chapter 10, there are many special characters that you will need to use all the time. On a PC, these characters are called upper ASCII characters and are only available by holding down the Alt key and typing four numbers on the numerical keypad. The chart shows all 128 upper-ASCII characters. Those from 129 and up require the Alt+four-number routine. The number is in the gray bar above the character. The code under the gray bar is for the Mac keystroke: O = Option, S = Shift.

This is not to say the Mac is much better. However, all these extra characters are available with the Option key. You do have to memorize the shortcuts. But, Option-8 for a bullet is much easier to remember than Alt+0149. Plus, once you learn the double-stroke combinations to add accents, they are simple to remember: Option-n, then n gives you ñ, for example; Option-e, then any vowel will add the accent (é); Option-u adds the Umlaut; and so on. In fact, if you have a strange letter that looks like another letter, try it with the Option key. ø is just Option-o.

0129	0130	0131	0132	0133	0134	0135	0136	0137	0138	0139	0140	0141	0142	0143	0144
	SO-0	O-f	SO-w	O-;	O-t	SO-7	SO-i	SO-r		SO-3	SO-q				
	‚	ƒ	„	…	†	‡	^	‰	Š	‹	Œ				

0145	0146	0147	0148	0149	0150	0151	0152	0153	0154	0155	0156	0157	0158	0159	0160
O-]	OS-]	O-[	OS-[	O-8	O--	OS--	SO-n	O-2		SO-4	O-q			OuSy	
'	'	"	"	•	–	—	~	™	š	›	œ			Ÿ	

0161	0162	0163	0164	0165	0166	0167	0168	0169	0170	0171	0172	0173	0174	0175	0176
O-1	O-4	O-3	SO-2	O-y		O-6	SO-u	O-g		O-\	O-l		O-r	SO-,	SO-8
¡	¢	£	€	¥	¦	§	··	©	^{a}	«	¬		®	–	°

0177	0178	0179	0180	0181	0182	0183	0184	0185	0186	0187	0188	0189	0190	0191	0192
SO-=	(Cu)	(Cv)	SO-e	O-m	O-7	SO-9	SO-z	(Cy)	O-0	SO-\		(Cx)		SO-?	O`-A
±	^{2}	^{3}	´	µ	¶	·	,	^{1}	^{o}	»	¼	½	¾	¿	À

0193	0194	0195	0196	0197	0198	0199	0200	0201	0202	0203	0204	0205	0206	0207	0208
Oe-A	Oi-A	On-A	Ou-A	SO-A	SO-'	SO-C	O`-E	Oe-E	Oi-E	Ou-E	O`-I	Oe-I	Oi-I	Ou-I	
Á	Â	Ã	Ä	Å	Æ	Ç	È	É	Ê	Ë	Ì	Í	Î	Ï	Ð

0209	0210	0211	0212	0213	0214	0215	0216	0217	0218	0219	0220	0221	0222	0223	0224
On-N	O`-O	Oe-O	Oi-O	On-O	Ou-O	(Cz)	SO-o	O`-U	Oe-U	Oi-U	Ou-U	(Cg)		Os	O`-a
Ñ	Ò	Ó	Ô	Õ	Ö	×	Ø	Ù	Ú	Û	Ü	Ý	Þ	ß	à

0225	0226	0227	0228	0229	0230	0231	0232	0233	0234	0235	0236	0237	0238	0239	0240
Oe-a	Oi-a	On-a	Ou-a	Oa	O'	Oc	O`-e	Oe-e	Oi-e	Ou-e	O`-i	Oe-i	Oi-i	Ou-i	
á	â	ã	ä	å	æ	ç	è	é	ê	ë	ì	í	î	ï	ð

0241	0242	0243	0244	0245	0246	0247	0248	0249	0250	0251	0252	0253	0254	0255	0256
On-n	O`-o	Oe-o	Oi-o	On-o	Ou-o	O/	Oo	O`-u	Oe-u	Oi-u	Ou-u			Ou-y	
ñ	ò	ó	ô	õ	ö	÷	ø	ù	ú	û	ü	ý	þ	ÿ	######

≤ ≥ Ω ◊ ≈ π Π ß Σ ∫ ∫ ≠ These Option characters are not available on a PC. On a PC, hold down the Alt key and type the ASCII number in the gray bar above the character on the numerical keypad. The blank Mac keys are Control characters not normally available. For a Mac, S = Shift and O = Option.

Small caps

THERE IS

NOTHING NEW

UNDER THE SUN...

THERE IS

NOTHING NEW

UNDER THE SUN...

Old style figures

1234567890

1234567890

1234567890

This last instance is a set of small caps numbers, which are quite rare.

The cross-platform issues

Not only are PCs 7-bit and Macs 8-bit, but PCs cannot read Mac fonts and Macs cannot read PC fonts. If you have identical fonts on both platforms that are named the same, you will not have too many problems. In the real world, though, that rarely happens. However, as we will see, the problem is so huge that a solution had to be found, and it has been.

Additional characters

Small caps

One of the typesetting options in most professional software (and many word processors) has been the use of small caps. Most of you are probably familiar with this from tutorials of any of the professional publishing programs. Small caps are capital letters that have been reduced to the x-height and used in place of lower case letters.

The problem is that you may have never seen true small caps. What we normally get is proportionally reduced caps. THIS MAKES SMALL CAPS LOOK MUCH THINNER AND LIGHTER THAN THE CAPITALS THEY ARE WITH. WITH TRUE SMALL CAPS, THE STROKE WEIGHTS OF THE SMALL CAPS ARE THE SAME AS FOR THE CAPS AND LOWERCASE OF THE NORMAL FONT. There are quite a few specialized fonts that have no lowercase — just caps and small caps. There isn't room to fit true small caps into an 8-bit font that already has lowercase letters.

Old style figures

Some of you may have noticed that the numbers used in the copy of this book seem to flow with the type a little better. That is because the font I am using has old style figures. Most of you probably think that numbers always look like this: 1234567890. These are called lining figures. Actually, I tend to call them bookkeepers' numbers, because I think that is the only place to use them. But that is another story. For Diaconia Old Style, the font used here, the numbers look like this: 1234567890 — instead of the lining figures.

Lining figures are appropriate for use with capital letters, but nothing else. In fact, they look like capitalized characters in the flow of regular C&lc copy. Oldstyle figures are far less intrusive and flow much better when reading. They flow so much better that it is likely that many of you didn't even notice that I was using them. There isn't room to fit oldstyle figures into an 8-bit font that already has lining figures.

Ligatures

In some cases, letters simply do not fit very well. The typographic solution has been to make special composite characters where two or more letters are made into one character that looks better. In Gutenberg's 42-line Bible, since justification hadn't been invented yet, he used over 3,000 ligatures to help justify his copy. However, in many fonts, through the years, ligatures have been essential to the beauty of the type. Again, the problem has been the 256-character limit. Usually there are only eight ligatures in most fonts: fi, fl, ffi, ffl, Æ, æ, Œ, and œ. Many of the more graceful fonts have many more.

In the sidebar you see a sample of Caflisch Script Pro. This font has dozens of ligatures.

Swashes

With some of the old fonts, especially those that mimicked handwriting, specialized character variants were created to add grace and style to the type. These swashes also were lost when we went to the 256-character limit.

In the sidebar you see the twenty-third psalm set in Caflisch Script Pro. This font has dozens of swashes.

Fractions, superiors, and inferiors

To typesetters, fractions are a real problem. Most PC fonts have $\frac{1}{2}$, $\frac{1}{4}$, $\frac{3}{4}$, plus $^1\,^2\,^3$. However, these are horrible looking things. The spacing is all strange and what do you do about 61/64 or something like that? In reality, that should look more like this $^{61}/_{64}$.

Fractions are best done with superior and inferior numbers. These are numbers that are designed small, but with the same stroke weight. Superiors line up with the top of the caps and inferiors with the baseline. The problem is the same as with true small caps: these numbers need the same stroke weight so they look like they fit. There isn't room to fit fractions, superiors, and inferiors into an 8-bit font.

> **Myriad Pro SemiExtended**
> This OpenType font has built-in fractions:
> $\frac{1}{2}$, $^4/_5$, $^{23}/_{27}$, $^{142}/_{348}$, and so on.

The Lord is my shepherd;
I shall not want.
He maketh me to lie down
in green pastures:
He leadeth me
beside the still waters.
He restoreth my soul:
He leadeth me in
the paths of righteousness
for His name's sake.
Yea, though I walk
through the valley
of the shadow of death,
I will fear no evil:
for Thou art with me;
Thy rod and thy staff
they comfort me.
Thou preparest a table
before me in the presence
of mine enemies:
Thou anointest my head
with oil;
my cup runneth over.
Surely goodness and mercy
shall follow me
all the days of my life:
and I will dwell
in the house of the Lord
for ever.   PSALM 23

Superscript and subscript

These are conceptually the same as superiors and inferiors except that they apply to all the caps, lower case, and numbers. The most common place you see them is in mathematical and chemical formulas. An algebraic expression might be something like this: $a^3 + b^4$. A chemical formula might look like this: N_2O_3. This type of thing obviously does not work very well with oldstyle figures. The problem with this is the same as with true small caps: these characters need to be designed smaller but with the same stroke weight so they look like they fit. There isn't room to fit all the superscript and subscript characters in an 8-bit font.

Expert sets

The only solution, up till now, has been what are called Expert set fonts which have all of the oldstyle figures, true small caps, ligatures, swashes, and so on for the normal font. These are a pain to use and they are very rare. If you find one, you are faced with constantly changing fonts. There is certainly no automatic substitution. They do add additional 256 characters to the mix, but even that is not really enough. Plus, as you have probably guessed, it would take several Expert sets to give us the characters really needed. We'll talk about the real solution at the end of the chapter.

Font families

Over the years, typography has developed groups of fonts that are obviously variants of the same basic font. They are called font families. These families can have differences in weight and width. For a couple of centuries, they have also had italic variants, but that is really a special case, as we will see in a bit.

Font weight

Weight is the thickness of the stroke. Here are the common weights arranged in order from thin to thick: Extra Light, Thin, Fine, Light, Book, Regular or Medium or Plain or Roman, Semi Bold or Demi Bold or Halbfett, Bold, Heavy, Extra Bold, Ultra Bold or Ultra Heavy, Fat, Display, and Ad. Book is probably the most elegant. It is designed for use in books. It is a little lighter than regular (medium) and a little narrower. This makes it possible to get more words on a page.

These radical weight variations are very new to fonts. The first to appear was Bold, and that did not show up until the eighteenth century. As advertising became a major force in graphic design, many specialized

Kabel Book
Kabel Medium
Kabel Demi
Kabel Bold
Kabel Ultra

Bodoni Book
Bodoni Roman
Bodoni Bold
Bodoni Bold Condensed
Bodoni Poster
Bodoni Poster Compressed

fonts were developed for the ads. Because these ads were commonly called display ads (as opposed to classified ads), these fonts became known as display fonts. Many of these display fonts showed extreme weight variations, but they were not linked to normal fonts. As far as I have ever been able to tell, extended font families are primarily, and maybe exclusively, a late twentieth-century phenomenon.

Optical weight

One of the aspects of old letterpress type is that each font (that is, each point size of a given type style) was carved individually. This allowed the designer and carver to make very subtle weight changes as the point size grew larger. As you can imagine, these metal characters took a beating — literally. Any portion of a character that was too thin was smashed flat by the pressures of the repeated pounding against the paper.

To solve this problem, optical scaling was used to aid in printability. While keeping the thickest strokes constant, the thinner strokes were made just a little heavier at the smaller point sizes and they were made a little lighter at the larger display sizes. As a result, 72-point type was quite a bit more elegant and refined than 6-point type. I suspect that this is obvious when you think about it. Imagine carving a letter out of steel that is an inch tall or one that is a twelfth of an inch.

Font width

There also used to be separate fonts for width, as in the following:

There are narrow, extra-condensed, condensed, expanded, wide, extra-wide, and so on. At this point, the demand for fonts with these variations has diminished because any decent publishing software can do what was done to that poor O above (to the horror of traditionalists). However, this is certainly one of the descriptive characteristics of a font.

In the sidebar on the opposite page, you can see the difference between Bodoni Bold and Bodoni Bold Condensed. The Poster Compressed is even narrower.

Heed a few words of caution, however. A font in which the horizontal strokes are thicker than the vertical ones looks very strange. When you make a font narrower, the vertical strokes get narrower and the horizontal ones remain unchanged. This can happen very easily if you make extreme adjustments to the horizontal and/or vertical scale. In general, unless you have a good reason, the set

Jenson Pro

Jenson Pro is an OpenType font with opticals.

ggg

14g   8g   36g

On the left is the regular font which is best for 10- to 18-point type. In the middle is the Caption version which is best for type smaller than 8-point. On the right is the Display version which is best for type over 24-point. As you can see (hopefully), the Display version is much more elegant and stylish.

Chiseled Roman
Academy Engraved

MAJUSCULES
CHARLEMAGNE

minuscules
Papyrus

Italic
Garamond Pro Italic

Diaconia
Diaconia Italic
Diaconia Oblique

width or horizontal scaling command should be set no narrower than 85 percent. Many purists are horrified at any width adjustments. However, if you keep it to plus or minus 5%, no one will be able to see it. Wide set-widths are not so much of a problem, but discretion is always in good taste. Deformed type is not an indication of sophistication.

Italics and Obliques

One original standard for type is the carved type in Roman columns honoring emperors' great deeds. They are still the classic standard. You should check out fonts like Trajan, Augustinian, and their ilk. To our eyes, they look extremely elegant, and they are. The name has remained in the fact that many people call vertical type roman, to this day.

The problem with these carved letters was that they were all caps. What we now call lowercase letters crept in as people wrote the words. As they wrote faster and faster, monks and scribes developed minuscules. These forms were roughly codified by the scribes and officially adopted by Emperor Charlemagne in the late 900s. Called Carolingian minuscules, he made them the standard for education. They are definitely recognizable as what we now call normal letter shapes.

The second time this happened was in Italy in the early Renaissance. In Venice, a man named Aldus Manutius developed a font based on the handwriting of his day, which he called *Italic*. It became very popular, but because of the narrowness and tight fit of the letters, it was not as legible – and still isn't. Italics were completely separate fonts and they were not used on the same page as roman fonts until the pomp and ebullience of the Baroque.

In this day and age, every normal vertical style has a matching italic – Diaconia Old Style Roman, *Diaconia Old Style Italic.* As you can clearly see in these four words, italic is a very different font. The *a* and *y* show the most obvious differences. With some fonts, the matching of these two type styles is done very well and elegantly. In other cases, the two fonts are seemingly just forced into the same bed.

One of the aberrations of the digital age is a new phenomenon of fake italics called *oblique*. These are not true italics, but merely slanted roman characters – for example, NuevoLitho and NuevoLitho Italic. This is not a true italic. Obliques have been known to drive type purists nuts!

I tend to think they should get a life and simply not use the ones they don't like, but then that's just me. In some cases, obliques are a good solution. For the radical geometric sans serif fonts of the 1930s, a true italic would be foolish. This should be the choice of the type designer. What you definitely do not want are the faux italics produced by software (like Photoshop) that simply skews the letters. Thankfully, current versions make this optional in most cases.

All those pretty curves

Type crammed into grids of squares

The headline really says it all. As we have discussed, type is an extremely sophisticated art. Even sans serif faces like Helvetica or even Futura are built with subtle curves. This is the major reason why the original computer type was a mere guffaw for type professionals.

72 dpi is crude

As mentioned, Apple made an extremely helpful move by making the screen resolution 72 ppi. This has enabled nonindustry designers to work in points and inches at the same time (as there are now exactly 72 points per inch). However, 72 dpi is a disaster for output. All you have to do is try to read copy directly off a Web site. It's very uncomfortable.

The original printer available for the Mac was the ImageWriter at 75 dpi. It made some kind of sense because it was a QuickDraw printer. This meant that the printer directly outputs what was produced for the monitor. The screen image looks pretty good — until you examine it closely. The main reason it even looks acceptable is that a pixel can be any color allowed by the bit depth. With 24-bit monitors, a pixel can be any of 16.7 million colors. This allows what appears to be photorealism on the screen. Digital printers are a very different breed, however.

The image to the right is a simple screen capture of 48-point Bodoni Book. It didn't look too bad on the screen, but you can see what it looks like printed. In

Check this out!

fact, this is really pretty good quality. It is a capture of a custom bitmap rendered by ATM (which we will discuss in a little bit).

City name fonts (Mac only)

One of the early results of the combination of this bitmap technology with low-resolution printers was the development of cityname fonts. These are modifications of normal type that force the crude bitmaps into a more legible form on dot matrix printers. They are all named after cities. Often the name makes a connection with the original. For example, New York is a modification of Times, which was a typeface designed for *The New York Times*.

These cityname fonts are unacceptable for professional typesetting. However, they look very good on the screen. This is really what they were designed for. This is a Mac-only aberration, but these fonts are still used for dialog boxes, alerts, and the defaults for browsers and email. The three specific fonts are Chicago, Monaco, and Geneva. My students use them all the time. They look horrible in print — IMHO.

The originals

Bitmapped fonts

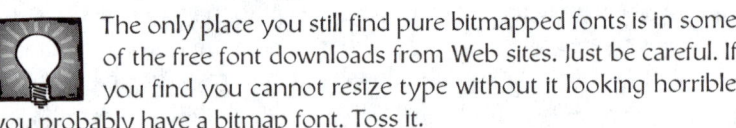

In fact, all the original fonts were bitmapped. This put type back to where each font was a specific point size. When you bought a typeface, you purchased a specific group of fonts in specific sizes. You might get 10-point, 12-point, 14-point, 18-point, and 24-point fonts. It gave you reasonably good-looking type as long as two requirements were met: (1) the bitmapped font had to be at the same resolution as your printer; and (2) you had to have a bitmapped font for every size you used. If these two attributes were not in place, you ended up with a horrible case of the jaggies.

The only place you still find pure bitmapped fonts is in some of the free font downloads from Web sites. Just be careful. If you find you cannot resize type without it looking horrible, you probably have a bitmap font. Toss it.

This didn't seem like much of a problem to most people. They only used a few typefaces and those in limited sizes. Each bitmap ran about 10K. Large sizes with complete character sets could reach close to 100K, but they were almost never used by "normal" folk. So, the situation was handled fairly well.

The problem was (and still is) us — the printing industry. We are used to type in unlimited sizes, with hundreds of faces — each face being a family with two to two dozen or more styles. A type library of this size could easily run into many megabytes of data. This could choke the RAM of any available computer at the time. Plus, there was no way to deal with page layout programs that could set type at 36.798 point, for example. Any professional publishing program can set any font in thousands of sizes.

Adobe to the rescue

PostScript fonts

The trusty engineers at Xerox PARC came to the rescue again. You may remember that they invented stuff you might be familiar with like the mouse, windows, icons, and so on. Since the late 1970s, they had been playing with a page description language (PDL) that would allow machine independence. It never made it to reality, but several of the developers (including John Warnock and Chuck Geske) formed a company that wrote the PDL that has become the standard of our industry — PostScript. The company's name is Adobe.

PostScript made its debut with the LaserWriter in 1984. Its major impact was high-resolution printing of all graphics on a page. PageMaker was the first software to write PostScript. By 1986, Linotronic had come out with the first PostScript imagesetter. Illustrator was the first to enable us to simply draw with PostScript.

The bitmapped problem was solved. PostScript fonts were included with all LaserWriters. Apple got licenses for fonts you are certainly familiar with by now: Bookman, Palatino, Courier, Helvetica, Times, Century Schoolbook, and so on. Because the fonts could now be described with mathematical equations, any size type could be created easily. Until this time, any type more than an inch tall was very rare. It usually required a photographic enlargement from the galley output.

Now, 10-inch type became easy. In fact, 709.25-point type was just as simple. Everything was enlarged from the one-point-high outline stored in the printer font. Yes, printer font — for now it was necessary to have two files (at least) for every font. There was the screen font for the monitor and the printer font for the printer. The computer used the bitmapped screen font to create the image on the screen. Thankfully, this data was ignored when the type was printed. The jaggies were not gone on the screen.

As the computer sent the document to the printer to be printed, the printer font was included along with the sizing specifications. The printer took the specs and RIPed a custom bitmap at the size specified

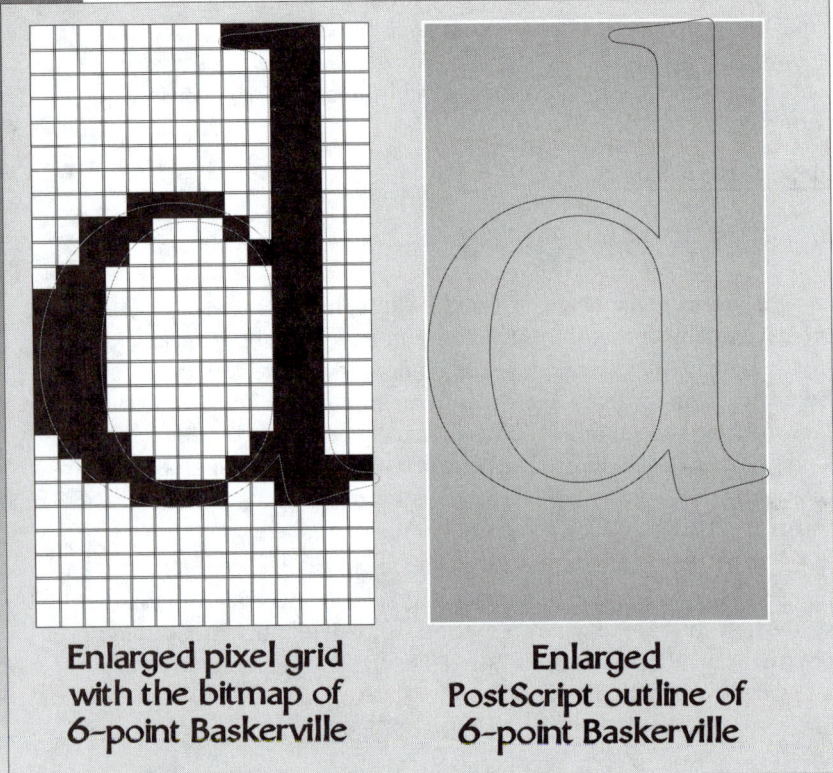

**Enlarged pixel grid
with the bitmap of
6-point Baskerville**

**Enlarged
PostScript outline of
6-point Baskerville**

that used the resolution of the printer. So, type rendered at 72 ppi on the monitor could be printed at 2,400 dpi or more by the printer. This illustration shows how the outline compares with a coarse grid.

This caused a real problem, however. WYSIWYG was destroyed. Again, digital designers could not expect the screen image to have anything to do with the final output. In fact, the screen images were often unreadable. Adobe solved this dilemma in 1989.

Adobe Type Manager

What Adobe came up with was a utility that read the printer font and created a custom screen font. If you need 67-point type, ATM draws a 67-point font, creating each character as needed. This brings back WYSIWYG. The screen image looks pretty close to the printed one – again.

As you can see at the top of the next page, this solved a real problem. In fact, it solved many more problems than the obvious one on

Type Century Schoolbook from 12-point bitmap without Adobe Type Manager

Type Century Schoolbook from 12-point bitmap with Adobe Type Manager

the screen. By the time ATM was released, there was a real war going on among the font manufacturers. Agfa Compugraphic (arguably the king of phototype) had developed its own outline font system. So had Adobe's leading digital competitor, BitStream. Even the game designer Brøderbund had come out with SmoothFonts for its headline manipulator, Type styler. They all had hopes of adoption.

ATM crushed these efforts. It would only work with a certain kind of PostScript font called PostScript Type 1. Type 1 fonts used *hinting* to create fonts in smaller sizes that fit the grid better on the screen. Hinting was a set of rules that told the computer what to do when troubles arose.

It was an almost instant success. Within months, publishing had a new standard – PostScript Type 1 fonts. It took until the early 1990s for the conversion to be complete. Because all of our high-resolution output devices were focused exclusively on Adobe PostScript, we were

NOT

An off-center line is moved left and results in this

a double line or a line moved to the right.

Hinting

virtually dependent as publishing professionals. This caused some competitive problems very quickly. Actually, it made Adobe's competitors very angry, which inspired them to do something about it.

Apple/Microsoft ire

The TrueType fiasco

Apple and Microsoft were fed up with the licensing fees. Adobe would not reveal the hinting technology, so, no one else could compete. Apple/Microsoft developed Royal using different mathematical equations. This format created outline fonts that had a couple of advantages over PostScript Type 1. First of all, only one file was required. The screen fonts were built into the printer font.

Second, the hinting could be more complicated, and optical scaling could be used for the first time in production digital type. This had been lost since the advent of computer type. The idea is this: hinting worked fine for smaller sizes, but larger ones were distorted. Since the early days of letterpress type, the larger sizes were commonly refined — slimmed slightly and made more elegant. This new font language made optical scaling possible.

Apple released a partial execution of the technology with System 7. It is called TrueType. Microsoft made it the core of Windows and that almost ruined the possibilities. It was not because TrueType is an inadequate technology. In fact, in several ways it is a superior one.

TrueType problems

The first and worst problem with TrueType originally was simple: it was not PostScript. Professional printing required PostScript and those printers and imagesetters refused to print TrueType. This is still an issue with printers who use equipment with old RIPs (and there are many). PostScript Level 1 will not print TrueType at all. Only the more recent PostScript Level 2 RIPs can handle TrueType. PostScript 3 RIPs should be no problem. The key is to ask your printer before you use any TrueType fonts. For years, the best counsel was to throw away all TrueType fonts. Now they can be used, but always ask first.

TrueType is not PostScript.

Another part of the problem was Microsoft's commitment to low cost software (which has caused many similar problems). Very soon Microsoft's volunteer clone crew was selling fonts for a price so cheap that quality was out of the question. Low prices usually eliminate the time necessary for quality.

Another portion of the problem can be laid at the door of the new desktop paradigm. One of the primary things software creators have marketed is the illusion that anyone can design documents. "Our software makes it easy to do... and so simple that..." As a result, there are many new users of digital publishing who literally cannot see the difference between quality type and junky copies. This is not the major reason for the dilemma, however.

Copyright loopholes

The real source of cheap type

Type design is a very difficult craft. We have all read for so long that we know what type should look like. Everyone knows! This makes type creation extremely touchy. A simple change, such as making the horizontal strokes heavier than the verticals looks wrong, and this is a very obvious error. Many other changes are equally erroneous but much more subtle. As a result, it is very easy to design a new face, but very rare to create a beautiful one with classic elegance.

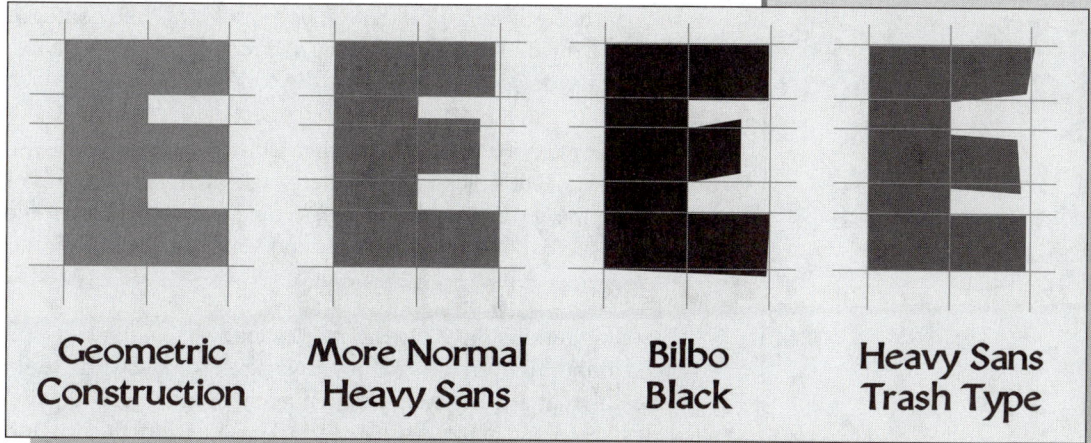

| Geometric Construction | More Normal Heavy Sans | Bilbo Black | Heavy Sans Trash Type |

This very simple illustration of heavy sans serif capital *E*s might help you understand. The one on the left is what most people with no type design experience come up with – purely geometric. The second example is typical. The third one is probably better – at least more interesting – but still within the rules. The final example on the right breaks most of the rules for an *E*. The top bar is longer than the bottom, the middle bar is lower than the middle and the end of the middle bar slants the wrong direction.

As you can see, these have relatively minor variations. A capital *E* is a very simple letter compared to a cap *R*, a lowercase *r*, a lowercase *g* or an *8*. It can take a couple of weeks to finalize a concept for a new font and nearly an hour per character (on average) to create an entire set of 200-plus characters. Then you start on letterspacing, which takes months to do well.

Even this is very fast. In the days of carved metal, it would often take years to develop a font. Families of faces often took decades. There are very few people with both the design skill and the tenacity to produce excellence in typography or exceptional type designs.

The loophole

Type cannot be copyrighted in the United States. Names can be trademarked. The software written for a font can be copyrighted. But the style itself cannot be protected. Why and whether this is either reasonable or rational makes no difference. It is certainly unethical to simply steal a design without at least acknowledging the creator. However, it is done all the time.

It is particularly easy now that we have programs like Fontographer, which can trace a scan of a typeface and recreate it. Many people do it. As long as you do not simply take the code and rename the face, it is legal. As a result, it is very simple to "create" new fonts.

The vast majority are simple tracings with new names. These can be done in a day. Auto-adjusting the letterspacing can take an hour or two. Finalizing the kerning pairs (there are often 1,000 of them) can take a couple days more. Forty hours of work and you have a "new" font.

The foundry's dilemma

These gyrations drive type foundries crazy. (Yes, they are still often called foundries even though they have never worked with metal.) The problem is that a truly excellent, genuinely original face remains a major design project often lasting years. These designers earn and deserve a decent royalty. These fonts are masterpieces of graphic design. They are certainly worth at least $20 a font and $80 a family, minimum. Traditionally, they were worth several hundred dollars a font.

The TrueType trash problem (the problem now includes PostScript Type 1 fonts also) means that fonts sell for pennies. In the mid-1990s, I purchased a CD with a thousand unlocked fonts for less than $40. That's

4¢ a font — more accurately, that's obscene. Out of those thousand fonts, I found about a hundred that I didn't recognize as renamed copies and two that I considered good enough to use. I assume that those two are also renamed copies that I had simply never seen before. A year or two later, Adobe put them out of business with a copyright lawsuit for millions of dollars, but that is very rare.

Quality type still exists. I sell mine on MyFonts.com. But, I am pretty much a hack, designing type for a hobby. The type design superstars work for places like Adobe, BitStream, P22, Émigrè, and dozens of small foundries. If you pay less than $20 for an individual font, be wary. Always install with care to make sure the font works.

TIP: A corrupted font can crash your computer. At the least, it can make your document refuse to print. In fact, that is the first thing to look for when you create a document that will not print for some unknown reason. If the links are okay in the Links Palette, check by changing fonts. This is one of the main reasons to get font management software that will check for corrupt fonts.

The OpenType solution

This relatively new font format promises to solve most of these problems. In 2002, it is not supported in many places. Windows 2000 was the first operating system to support OpenType. InDesign is the first professional application to do so.

OpenType is built out of some of those advanced capabilities we mentioned with TrueType. A conversion mechanism is available to convert any PostScript font to OpenType. More than that, OpenType is completely cross-platform. For the first time you can use the same fonts on a Mac and on a PC. But the new format goes far beyond that.

So, what does it do?

First, it completely solves the number of characters limitation. OpenType fonts can have over 65,000 characters. Few do, but they can, if needed. What this means on a practical level is that almost all of the options we have talked about are available (or can be made available): oldstyle figures, optical scaling, true small caps, inferior and superior characters, automatic building of true fractions, ligatures, swashes, plus Greek and Cyrillic alphabets. All of these are optional settings in InDesign 2. They will become available across the industry soon. Adobe and Microsoft won't have it any other way. (But then you never know for sure. Multiple Master fonts are now gone, for example.)

Where should you be by this time?

You should have at least half of your grade earned by now. If you don't, shame on you!

Get busy!

DISCUSSION

You should be talking about benefits of various specialized characters. You should be checking out what the fonts you are using have available.

Talk amongst yourselves...

Several of these new font technologies have been tried over the years. So, why do I think this one will work? Because they're Adobe. Adobe has the market nearly tied up. With PageMaker, FrameMaker, InDesign, Illustrator, and Photoshop in their stable, they can offer the benefits to every graphic designer in the world (almost).

Knowledge retention and thought provocation

1. Why are small caps usually a problem?
2. What is optical scaling?
3. What problems does OpenType solve?
4. What was the original problem with TrueType?
5. What problem was solved with ATM?
6. What is the advantage of oldstyle numbers?
7. Why does typesetting need so many more characters than typewriting?

Chapter 9

Type Styles

Concepts

1. Serif

2. Sans serif

3. Display

4. Script

5. Blackletter

6. Typist

7. Typesetter

8. Typographer

THE DIFFERENT STYLES

Learning the reasons and history of the different styles of type, what they are used for, and why

Chapter Objectives:

By giving students a clear understanding of what different type styles are available, this chapter will enable students to:

1. explain the history and usage of sans serif faces
2. explain the usefulness of serifs
3. define decorative or display fonts
4. pick appropriate fonts for their projects

Lab Work for Chapter:

1. Complete miniskills chosen.
2. Continue skill exams.
3. Read chapter 10 for next week.
4. Work on projects.

Script and text have one thing in common **Illegibility!**

type type type — Correct
Too tight — Too loose

Classic Sans

Strongly
BAUHAUS

Strongly
FUTURA

Strongly
KABEL

Strongly
UNIVERS

Strongly
GILL SANS

Strongly
FRUTIGER

Strongly
CORINTHIAN

SOME CLASSICS

Dashingly
CASLON

Dashingly
BEMBO

Dashingly
GARAMOND

Dashingly
BASKERVILLE

Dashingly
CHELTENHAM

Dashingly
CENTURY
SCHOOLBOOK

Dashingly
BODONI

Lots of type...

Now that we have briefly discussed what makes up a font, it is time to look at type styles. Type has been around for a long time. In an attempt to get a handle on the different styles, many different classification systems have arisen. Most of these are of mere historical interest. In truth, many of you will find these distinctions increasingly important as you grow further in your career as a digital publisher.

One of the things you will discover early on is that traditional typographers really ought to get a life. I can say that because *I are one*. Even from the inside, I find most typographic wranglings to be far beyond nitpicking and well into anal and/or compulsive. Some of the lists I have been on spend months wrangling over insignificant details that will never be noticed by the reader. But then, you should be aware that in one of my other books I dared to ask, *"When was the last time you refused to read a brochure and threw it in the trash because the color was a little off?"*

A little word definition is in order. As far as setting type is concerned, there are three terms used: typist, typesetter, and typographer. Typists are those secretarial folk we have already mentioned. A typesetter is what you must become in this career. You will take typed copy and set it into type. Typographers are the professional type designers who design the fonts and determine the standards of excellent type. They are concerned with the most nitpicking details, but their type is gorgeous and easy to tread.

One of the major attributes of typographers is that they are truly concerned about beauty, elegance, appropriateness, and so on. The fact that they can take it to extremes does not eliminate the fact that they have a lot to offer you in your designs. People like this are, by necessity, highly opinionated. You have to be to set standards.

However, many typographers live in that ivory tower inhabited by academics. Even though the author of one of the best books on the subject actually writes that an appropriate typographic design might be to use one font and one point size for an entire project, reality is a little different than that. This man sets beautiful type. Does it apply to us as we produce thousands of projects a year? Actually it does. His projects may be a little different from ours, but his solutions are elegant.

My goal in this book is to give you a quick handle on what you have available in our tools of choice: software and hardware. Plus, I want you to end up with the beginnings of a procedure to pick fonts on purpose to help with communication. Font choice is one of the prime determinants of your personal graphic style.

For the purposes of this book, there are four general classifications: serif, sans serif, handwriting, and decorative. It would probably be acceptable to split handwriting into script and text; but these four have served well over the years. We will break these categories down into subdivisions to help you see what choices you need to make. However, these are your four basic choices.

Most books will give you many more classes. For example, they'll break serif into three to nine subcategories; the same with sans serif. These breakdowns are mainly historical. I'll show you quickly what the historical categories are (and give you my ideas about usefully restructuring them), but in reality there is little functional difference between fonts designed in the 1500s, 1600s, or 1700s. These nitpicking details have little to do with reader reactions. They are mainly driven by the Occidental compulsion to neatly categorize everything.

 Historical appropriateness is usually only important to historians. If it makes you happy, do it. However, readers are looking for comfort and ease while reading. Because design is often best when spontaneous rather than structured, this book avoids the legalistic approach as much as possible while still trying to make your choices clear. After all, they are *your* choices.

Bringing it into perspective

Out of the tens of thousands of typefaces mentioned earlier, only 1,000 or so are used all the time by many people. Out of those, there are about a hundred or so serif fonts that a majority use for body copy and another hundred for heads and subheads. There are a huge number of decorative faces. Most of these are unsuitable for serious work. Many are totally illegible on a practical level. Probably 30,000 are multiple-derivative, differently named copies of the 200 most popular fonts. So it isn't as scary as it sounds — quite. However, you will have to learn to recognize several hundred fonts by sight. It will help a lot to learn some of the history.

First, we must define a serif.

A serif is a flare, bump, line, or foot added to the beginning or end of a stroke in a letter. Originally, they were the finishing touches

Serifs
Type
No Serifs
Type

added to the end of strokes produced by pens in the hands of scribes. They have become very stylized. There are hundreds of different serif stylings, but do you know their importance?

They seem totally insignificant, but they certainly are not. They strongly influence how we react to type. In fact, on a subconscious level, serifs can be one of the most powerful influences on the reader's perception of the product. Most people are totally unaware of the effect type designs have on their lives.

Reading has many habitual associations. The type read during or about an occasion takes on the flavor of those events. Many of these typographic reactions are very personal. For example, you may find that your favorite script font happens to be the font on the menu the night you became engaged. It is hard to avoid Caslon for patriotic documents, because the Constitution, Declaration of Independence, and the Bill of Rights are all set in Caslon. No matter what, to be functional in modern American society, we must read, and we do it constantly. Each of us reads thousands of pieces every day. In fact, the literate are rapidly becoming the ruling class in the United States as the masses become increasingly illiterate.

Reading has many habitual associations.

In our homogeneous, franchised society, most of us see the same things every day. The result of all of this is that virtually every person in the United States has similar reactions to various type styles. However, there are large differences between the habitual viewers of Fox, MTV, and Disney when compared to the habitual viewers of HGTV, A&E, and the History Channel. The fonts used to promote pickup trucks are very different from those used for Lexus and Cadillac.

The dominance of serif

Almost every good book you have ever read was set in serif type. Virtually every textbook was also. This one is set in a font I designed called Diaconia Old Style. Virtually all body copy before the 1950s was serif. Because of these things, serif typefaces are perceived as warm, friendly, nostalgic, and easy to read. Some of the more modern serif fonts have that edge that was in style in the 1990s, but most are beautiful, quiet, and comfortable. Designers began to use these connections consciously during the 1950s and 1960s. The marketing research boom in the 1970s simply reinforced this trend.

Literacy

One of the things that will face you increasingly in your career is the question of whether your client's customer can read or not. While it may be true that those with the money can all read, it is also true that mass marketing is increasingly dealing with an illiterate audience. Of course, in America this also has to include those who simply cannot read English. Increasingly, reading is for the power elite.

Baskerville

ABCDEFGHIJKLMNO
PQRSTUVWXYZ
abcdefghijklmnopqrst
uvwxyz 0123456789

One of the great
classic serif faces
by John Baskerville,
cut in 1757.

As a result, serif faces are used almost exclusively in ads promoting quality, stability, good value, integrity, and warmth. They are also used to reinforce family values, patriotism, and the emotional content of character traits considered positive by our culture. They are the main choice for elegance, quality, and high society. Serif faces produce these types of reactions in the reader (at least subconsciously).

Sans serif is relatively new

Even though sans serif faces (without a serif) have been around since at least the early nineteenth century, they were never popular until the 1950s. Some like to tell us that the original alphabets from the Greeks were sans serif. But that has had little influence on our modern culture. There was no printing back then.

Up until the 1950s, sans serif faces were used extensively only by groups like the modernist, Bauhaus movement in Germany during the 1930s, where geometric type was promoted as modern. Futura, Bauhaus, and Kabel are classic examples of this style. Most people saw them as plain and unadorned or aggressively modern. The ties to Germany during the time of Hitler's ascent are not friendly. The ties to the modern art movements of the 1930s does not help either.

There was quite a bit of large extra-bold sans serif used in the wood typefaces cut for the Victorian explosion of advertising. But those connotations again had little to do with readable copy. Hucksters shouting at us like they did in those broadsides with that huge type usually do not bring pleasant memories except for nostalgia. Associations with people like P. T. Barnum didn't help much either.

In the 1950s, Helvetica became extremely popular. It was designed by Max Miedinger in 1951 and was quickly accepted as a new standard type style by many in the business, scientific, and advertising communities. Most logos from that period (like CBS, Exxon, Texaco, and many others) were created with Helvetica Black or a modified Helvetica.

Sans serif faces, in general, became de rigeur for scientific publishing. It is likely that many of you have bad memories from physics and math books set in sans serif. Most of the reading associations of sans serif type are anything but warm and friendly. The only exception would be within the youth cultures like extreme jocks who, in cultivating rebellion and adrenaline rushes, have made sans serif their "normal" type classification.

Businesses of the time saw sans serif type styles as modern, clean, cool, unemotional, and businesslike. Recently, there has been a fad among the avant garde computer byteheads of setting body copy in sans serif. They use distorted, condensed versions, but they fit the stereotypical usage pattern. Their usage is more a rebellion from convention, which fits nicely into the gestalt of sans serif usage.

Again, graphic designers have consciously reinforced these reactions. At this time, sans serif faces can be used effectively to produce these feelings and responses. The usage was almost unanimous until desktop publishing brought in designers with no design education. So the reactions are predictable enough to be very useful. Sans serif faces are clean and modern. Serif faces, in general, are more elegant and beautiful. These distinctions are being greatly muddied by new trends toward very readable sans serif fonts designed for body copy.

Helvetica

ABCDEFGHIJKLMNO
PQRSTUVWXYZ
abcdefghijklmnopqrstu
vwxyz 0123456789

The first widely fashionable sans serif typeface.

The Times/Helvetica problem

One of the more interesting phenomena of digital publishing is the use of Times and Helvetica. Although these are fairly well-designed typefaces, their excessive usage resulting from their specification as the default fonts in so many nonprofessional applications and operating systems has completely changed their perception in the mind of the typical reader. Most professional typographers consider these fonts to be abominations of boredom, at best. That's a bit strong, but at best they are a little too common.

At this point, most serious graphic designers avoid these two fonts like the plague. As a result, the only place people see them is in output by people who are untrained in publishing and simply use the software defaults — think schools, bureaucracies, the IRS, collection agencies, and the like. Because of this uncaring usage, Times, Times New Roman, Helvetica, and Arial have been virtually ruined for serious use by designers. They bring up too many bad associations.

If you want people to avoid reading the copy you are setting, these fonts might be a good choice. For fine print in contracts or long-winded warranties, for example, they work well if your client wants you to limit reading of the legalese. Even cars with 100,000 mile warranties do not want you reading the fine type (you might figure out how much it is going to cost you to service the car to keep that warranty active). If you set them in all caps, less than 8-point, in colored or gray type, no one will read them. In fact, you will have a heck of a time trying to proof them. If that is not enough, reverse them out of a gray background.

The importance of readability

We mentioned that serif faces are considered more readable. This is probably due more to their overwhelming use as body copy than any other factor. However, there is good reason to believe that the serifs do provide more distinctive letter shapes. The serifs also help the eye follow the line of type across the column, making body copy easier to read. Whatever the reasons, serif typefaces are clearly easier and more comfortable for most people to read.

Studies have shown, though, that sans serif faces are more legible (as opposed to readable). What this means is that for short bursts, sans serif type can be grasped more quickly. As soon as several lines are read, this effect is lost. The eye becomes tired, wanders, and loses the ability to easily find the beginning of the next line. You can compensate for this effect, to a certain extent, by increasing the leading, shortening the column width, increasing the point size, and so on. Typically, people just quit reading sans serif body copy.

Self-exam — do this with two pages, Garamond and Futura

It is an interesting exercise to take a page full of copy, three-column, 10/12 (point size of 10 and leading of 12 points). Set it once in some classic style such as Baskerville, Times, or Caslon. Print it out again set in Helvetica, Futura, or (maybe best) Avant Garde. Then, doing your best to analyze yourself objectively, read each. If you observe yourself carefully, most of you will find that it takes effort to make it through the sans serif sample. It is very hard to remain focused. Usually the mind will wander, by the third or fourth column. In fact, you will just come back to yourself from thinking about something unrelated, not knowing how you got there. You will not make a conscious decision to stop reading. The reason you have to watch carefully is that this mental wandering just happens without conscious thought. A few seconds ago you were reading, now you are thinking about something else.

Your brain has several thousand ads a day competing for your attention, so it is just looking for excuses to skip on to the next one. Because one of your major tasks as a designer is to encourage the reader to read your ad, sans serif body copy is risky at best. The result of all these factors is that serif and sans serif have very strong "normal" uses. Sans serif is normally used for headlines, subheads, bursts, and exclamatory phrases; serif is used for body copy.

Typically, you should pick a serif for body copy and a sans serif for heads and subheads.

For things like billboards and outdoor signage, sans serif is often the best choice (especially with billboards, where the rule is a maximum of eight words). The difficulty, of course, is finding a sans serif font that is warm and friendly with trustworthy overtones. The clean look of sans serif type makes copy much quicker to grasp for the reader who is flying by at 55 miles per hour (or more). However, if you are selling quality over price, you probably need serif type.

Categorizing serif fonts

As I said, there are many of these classification systems. Robert Bringhurst, in the currently accepted standard reference on typography, *The Elements of Typographic Style*, Hartley and Marks, 1992, uses historical markers. He sets up categories based largely on what I was taught were the historical periods of fine art: scribal or Carolingian, Renaissance, Mannerist, Baroque, Rococo, Neoclassical, Romantic, Realist, Geometric Modernism, Expressionist, Elegiac Post-Modernism, and Geometric Post-Modernism. It is, indeed, a fascinating journey through history. Robert presents his case extremely well. He's an excellent writer and a poet. You will acquire a great deal of useful knowledge by reading his book.

It is a bit over the top, though. Plus, he skips a lot. Bringhurst clearly does not like Victorian letter styles, so he does not mention them. He skips all of the modern variations like Art Nouveau, Art Deco, and the more extreme elements of the early twentieth century. He barely mentions the slab serifs of the late nineteenth century because he thinks they are coarse. In other words, he presents the type he likes in an excellent setting. It is not very useful for us though.

Thomas Phinney, now of Adobe, wrote a nice little historical piece I found in *redsun.com/type/.* In it, he uses the more common set of categories currently taught in many design schools: Old Style, Transitional, Modern, Slab Serif (or Egyptian), fat faces, wood type, Art Nouveau, synthesis, and grunge. This covers everything nicely and we will follow that basic lead. However, let's get real. The important thing is not historical accuracy, it is readability and decorative style.

The importance of style has to do with appropriateness. Bringhurst is still over the top here when he suggests using French type for French products and so on. His focus is book design. Our focus is marketing. You cannot pull off a Western "Wanted" poster with anything but type from the late 1880s. All of the recent Retro looks have specifically used fonts from a historical period placed in a hip, fashionable setting. Within a few months there were Retro fonts to match the style. At this point, in graphic design, the fonts appear along with the new fashion.

Some font terminology

Before we get into specifics, we need to define a few descriptive terms to help you see some of the differences between the categories. The terms are a little esoteric, but I think you will find them helpful to categorize things in your own mind. They will also help when buying fonts to make good choices.

- **Stems:** the vertical strokes in letters like *b, k, l, r* and so on.
- **Bowls:** the rounded parts of letters like *b, d, g, o, p,* and even *c* and *s,* according to some.
- **Crossbars:** the horizontal strokes on *A, H, e,* and so on.
- **Head and foot serifs:** the serifs at the top and bottom of a stem as in *b, l, k,* and *d.*
- **Adnate or bracketed serifs:** serifs that flow smoothly out of the stems.
- **Abrupt serifs:** cross strokes at the end of stems with no bracketing.
- **Terminals:** the endings of the curved portions of letters like *a, c, r, C, G,* and so on.
- **Lachrymal:** terminals that are tear-drop shaped.
- **Stroke:** the lines that make up the characters from the old assumption that letters are calligraphic and drawn with separate strokes of a pen or brush.
- **Modulated stroke:** a stroke that varies in width as it proceeds around the letter form.

- **Axis:** the angle the pen was held at to produce the modulated stroke of calligraphers.
- **Humanist axis:** the axis for normal right-handed calligraphic penmanship.
- **Contrast:** how much the stroke is modulated.
- **Aperture:** the openings of curves on letters like *a, c, e, s,* and so on.
- **Slope:** how far italic and oblique letters slant in degrees.

There are more, but this will be enough for our purposes. As you can see, type gets very technical. The differences will seem insignificant to you now, as you start. But they are really very important. Aperture, for example, tends to control the friendliness and readability. The axis changes from humanist to mechanical vertical strongly influence our reaction to the warmness or coolness of a font. But we'll discuss these things as we go, giving you examples so you can see the differences.

Old Style fonts: readable and beautiful

The fonts we are most comfortable reading are those based on Old Style forms. These start with the earliest fonts from the Renaissance that were first converted from scribal forms shortly after Gutenberg's Bible and continued for a century or so.

These original serif fonts are exemplified by the work of Claude Garamond in Paris in the early to mid-1500s. This type of font is the standard to which all other fonts are compared. They are full of smooth sensuous curves. They are light, and open — beautiful, comfortable, and elegant. The stems are vertical. The bowls are nearly circular. The crossbars often rise to the right. The axis is always humanist. The aperture is comfortably open. They are direct descendants of the incredible calligraphic work of the fourteenth and fifteenth centuries.

As font design began, italics were completely separate. The first italic font cut was by Griffo, commissioned by Aldus Manutius, in 1499. These early italics seem very condensed to us, with elliptical bowls and very calligraphic stroke endings (as opposed to actual serifs). This was the cursive handwriting of the period. They do not make good companions to modern fonts. They were closer to what we now call script, which we will cover after discussing serif and sans serif.

Through the 1500s and 1600s, these old style letter forms went through gradual changes. Designers began playing with the forms. Sloped capitals were added to the italics. Paired roman and italic fonts appeared. As Europe was caught up in the extravagance and luxury of

Bembo
Garamond
Jenson

abcdefghijkl
abcdefghijkl
abcdefghijkl

Galliard
Caslon
abcdefghijkl
abcdefghijkl

Baskerville
abcdefghijk

Bodoni
abcdefghijkl

This is the classic revolutionary typeface. **Beware!** The thins are so thin they often do not print.

the Baroque and Rococo, those lavish curves and flourishes made their way into type design as well, as we see in Galliard and Caslon.

Type design gradually became drawn rather than written. Baroque designers played with letter forms, having stems that varied in slope and bowls that varied in axis in the same font. The entire period was extravagant, but tightly based on classical old styles. Even the finishing portion of this entire period we are calling Old Style was merely filled with rigidly defined, carefully drawn forms.

By the end of this period, fonts had appeared with a rigidly vertical axis (usually called a rational axis). This was the time of the Revolution and design was into Retro classical, which was called Neoclassical by the historians. This is the time of Monticello. Franklin was extremely impressed with John Baskerville's designs in England at the time.

Throughout this period, careful adjustments were tried with axis, aperture, serif style, and so on. However, to our eye in the twenty-first century, all of these fonts are minor variations on a common theme. Old style fonts are still the normal choice for body copy. Your personal style will determine which you choose. The variations definitely have their own character and leave their feel in the documents that use them. Beyond that, they are all Old Style letters.

 The main point is that all of these fonts, to the contemporary eye, look very similar. More to the point, they all provoke nearly identical reader reactions. It is true there are major differences in the typographer's eye, but then there are not many of us. Functionally, these all can be used in the same places, for the same clients. The only differences are ones of taste.

Revolutionary styles

Modern and Romantic in the traditional nomenclature

These are type styles of the late 1700s and early 1800s, although their influence remains. To call them Modern, as most of the schools do, is silly. They are 200 years old. To call them Romantic is equally strange for they are cold fish. They are the natural expression of the radical, revolutionary intellectualism of the period.

These are hard, tightly structured letterforms which push out the emotional, warm, comfortable type of the Old Style fonts, replacing it with spiky, carved, structured forms. Serifs lose all bracketing, becoming thin, horizontal lines. The aperture is shut down quite a bit. The axis is rigidly vertical and accented with often extreme stroke modulation. These fonts can be very beautiful, but they are never comfortable. Baskerville led into this but it is conservative, old style compared to these. Most touches of humanity are cleaned out of the revolutionary styles. The best you can do is think of a severe elegance — a cold formality.

Realism: type for the common man

In the mid-1800s, a type design movement began making type for the workers, the common man, the noneducated. They were never really popular with designers, but they have had a lot of influence. They are based on the revolutionary fonts but distinguished by an even stroke weight with virtually no modulation. The aperture is nearly closed. Serifs are close to being unbracketed slabs with the same stroke thickness as the rest of the letterform. There are no small caps, old style figures, ligatures, or any of the other graceful tools of typography.

One of these fonts, Century Schoolbook, is the font most of us used when we learned to read in the first few grades of school. It may be the most elegant of the bunch. In general, heavy, clunky, and old-fashioned are the terms associated with fonts like these. Typical would be Bookman, Cheltenham, or Clarendon.

Art Nouveau

The swirling curves of Art Nouveau were also used to produce type. It seems like a rebellion against the realists, as the entire movement was a rejection of contemporary morality and tradition. These are the first fonts with little ties to traditional designs. They were never really popular, but certain cultures can take them on for a time. They were the absolute standard for the Spanish culture in New Mexico in the early 1980s, for example. Common Art Nouveau fonts would be Arnold Böcklin, Raphael, Artistik, and so on.

Fonts like these need to be used very carefully. From a design point of view, they are very interesting. However, they are usually quite hard to read. The larger problem, though, is their ties to a cultural period known for its depravity. They are used a lot by writers and designers in the occult. You need to be aware of these issues.

Geometric serifs (Egyptian???)

This is an outgrowth of the modernist movement of the early twentieth century. Here letter forms are constructed geometrically, with purely circular bowls, no modulation, slab serifs, closed aperture, and so on. Intellectually, they could almost be considered the scientific extension of the socialist expression found in realism.

Century Schoolbook
ABCDEFGHIJKLMN
OPQRSTUVWXYZ
abcdefghijklmnopqrst
uvwxyz 0123456789

One of the most common fonts for teaching reading.

Cheltenham
abcdefghijkl
abcdefghijkl
Bookman

Arnold
Böcklin
abcdefghi
abcdefghijkl
Raphael

City
abcdefghijkl
abcdefghijkl
Lubalin Graph

Times New Roman
abcdefghijklm

Palatino
abcdefghijkl

Usherwood
abcdefghijkl

Warnock Pro
abcdefghijklm

Kabel
abcdefghij

Avant Garde
abcdefgh

Bauhaus
abcdefghijk

Helvetica
abcdefghij

Geneva
abcdefghi

These are often called Egyptian fonts simply because many of them were designed around the time of the great Egyptian discoveries in the nineteenth century. Typical fonts of this type are Memphis, Rockwell, and City. The readability is usually very low.

Current synthesis

Many recent serif faces play with attributes of any and all historical styles. Often they experiment with distinctive serif stylings, sharp angular features, fanciful modulations. However, these more playful aspects are often very restrained and elegant. They take pieces from all over and show a wide variety from Times New Roman to Palatino to Veljovic. Often, like in Usherwood, the x-heights are very large — strictly a fashion statement from the 1980s.

Sans serif classifications

As mentioned earlier in this chapter, There are not nearly as many options in sans serif type. I am only going to give you four general types. I frankly invented these categories to help you make sense of what you run across in your search to build your own font library.

Geometric

Like the geometric slab serifs, these are largely a product of radical modernism, the Bauhaus in Germany, and the Art Deco movement of the 1920s and 1930s. The letterforms seem to be absolute geometric constructs, but they often have many subtle adjustments beyond that to make them more readable.

The real problem with geometric fonts, whether or not they have serifs, is the readability problem. Because all of the bowls are perfectly round and the aperture is usually almost closed, there is little visual difference between an *e* or an *o*. More than that, an *ol* looks a lot like a *d*, an *rn* can look identical to an *m*, and even a *cl* can seem to be a *d*. They can work fairly well in headlines, but using them for body copy is usually a serious mistake. Typical fonts are: Futura, Kabel, Avant Garde, and Bauhaus.

Populist commoner

These are what I call the normal fonts like Helvetica and Univers. (Arial/Geneva are the Microsoft/Apple rip-offs of Helvetica.) They seem to be outgrowths of the realist serif faces of the mid-1800s. Most of them have many subtle curve adjustments, but the stroke is virtually unmodulated. The aperture is closed up pretty tight in most of them.

Stylized

This is what I am calling those fonts that have a style that seems relatively warm and friendly, even though there is no modulation of the stroke. As a result there is no axis that could be called humanist. Many of these fonts make relatively good body copy in short bursts. They all have a distinctively warm feel — relative to other sans serif faces. Common faces in this genre would be Gill Sans, Frutiger, Corinthian, Skia, and Trebuchet — among many others.

Humanist

These fonts are actually neither fish nor fowl. Instead of serifs they tend to have slight flares, They have a modulated stroke and a humanist axis. They are the most elegant of the sans serifs. Most commonly available would be Optima, Poppl Laudatio, and Zapf Humanist.

 Humanist sans serifs are growing in popularity. They are quite readable. They may well become the fashion for body copy in the near future. Stylized and Humanist sans serif typefaces are very clean, neat, and unobtrusive. You should give them a try.

What about the rest of the type styles?

What about all the type that is outside the classifications we just covered? First of all, proportionally there isn't that much of it. Most of it is either serif or sans serif anyway. However, there is huge variety, in every artistic style, for every historical period. Many are so rigidly categorized that they can hardly be used for anything else. Where would you use Rosewood, for example, except for a circus or carnival? Old Towne has little use outside Western and cowboy items.

Decorative or display typefaces

Decorative is the term for the miscellaneous grab bag. Decorative type is defined as typefaces that are so highly stylized that they cannot be read in body copy sizes. For that reason some people call this category display. Display is the term used for the large, splashy ads in newspapers, as opposed to the classified ads.

You need to be very careful in the use of these fonts. Legibility is the obvious problem. Take a look at Birch or Whassis to the right, for example. But that can usually be solved by size and location. Simply making them 36-point or larger is often enough. Some of the more com-

Nördström
abcdefghijklmn
Corinthian
abcdefghijklmnop
Gill Sans
abcdefghijklmno

Albe Sans
abcdefghijklmno
Poppl Laudatio
abcdefghijklm

ROSEWOOD
ABCDEFGH

Whassis
abcdefghij

JAZZ POSTER
ABCDEFGHIJ

Birch
abcdefghijklmnopqrstuvwx

COPPERPLATE 29
COPPERPLATE 32

Academy Engraved
abcdefghijklmoprst

Arquitectura
abcdefghijklmoprstuwxyz

Locarno Light
abcdefghijklmoprst

Narrowband Prime
abcdefghijklmoprst

TRAJAN PRO
ABCDEFGHIJKL

plicated and/or abstract faces must be used several inches tall. Often they work only for posters and billboards. Here you need to understand that, for these pieces, body copy may have to be two inches instead of 10-point. To be readable at fifty feet, decorative faces might easily have to be two feet tall.

Another problem is that many decorative faces are caps only. There is no lowercase. Others are only caps and small caps, like Copperplate. Copperplate is probably the stereotypical lawyer/CPA font for their stationery and the like. But this does not mean it can be used for their letters or brochures. It is too hard to read.

Old Towne #536
ABCDEFGHIJKLMNOPQRSTUVWXYZ
abcdefghijklmnopqrstuvwxyz 0123456789

Hardwood
ABCDEFGHIJKLMNOPQRSTUVWXYZ
abcdefghijklmnopqrstuvwxyz
0123456789

University Roman
ABCDEFGHIJKLMNOPQRSTUVWX
YZabcdefghijklmnopqrstuvwxyz
0123456789

It goes beyond that, though. Circus type (like Rosewood) and Western or Victorian type are commonly so fancy that they defy classification. Decorative faces can have shadows, fills, outlines, inlines, or any combination of these attributes. Sometimes they provide an illusion of the third dimension. But, even Hardwood is considered decorative, though it is merely a stylized sans serif. Old Towne and University Roman are a bit more obvious. However, they are still relatively legible, especially at the larger (display) sizes.

Many of the more extreme decorative fonts are almost completely illegible like the psychedelic fonts of the 1960s and many of the grunge fonts of the 1990s.

The good thing about decorative fonts is that they almost always have very specific historical or cultural connotations. Fonts are available in Arts & Crafts, Art Deco, Art Nouveau, Victorian, Modernist, Cubist, and almost any other artistic or decorative style of the past several centuries. There are many fonts in the futuristic Star Trek and science fiction genre. There are many Gothic gaming fonts. They are the best (and usually the easiest) method of promoting an instant, emotional, stylistic reaction from the readers to your design.

Typeset handwriting

There are two other general classifications that must be considered. Script and Blackletter fit nowhere and must be dealt with separately. Basically they are both handwriting. Script is modern handwriting. Blackletter is medieval handwriting. Blackletter was used in Germany until the Second World War. How they could read it fast is beyond me. It adds many questions to the readability issues. How many of them are cultural?

Script

The 1950s saw an explosion of script styles. This was primarily due to the fad for hand-drawn headlines brought about by photographic pasteup. The problem with scripts is making the letters match up. This is one place where you have to watch the tracking very closely. The letter forms are designed to overlap precisely. If the letter spacing is too loose or too tight, they miss each other. Most script must be hand spaced to fit well. This is called kerning, and we will discuss this in chapter 10.

type *type* *type*
Too tight   Too loose   Correct

Actually, there are scripts for every historical period also. There are flowery Spencerian scripts from the baroque or rococo periods. There are marker scripts that look like they were drawn with felt tip markers. There are scripts that look like brush strokes. And scripts that look like the work of medieval monks in the more informal styles like uncial. You can find scripts that are obviously from any one of the decades of the twentieth century. Commonly available scripts are: Commercial, Brush, Mystral, Nuptial, Fling, Harlow, Pepita, Tekton, and many more.

Blackletter

This is the type that was used by Gutenberg. In current usage, it is only seen in certificate headers, graduation documents, Halloween events, and horror movies. It is hard for us to imagine that this was normal type in Germany well into the twentieth century. It makes us rethink that whole thing about readability. However, it is certainly not readable to the current American culture.

Blackletter styles are almost totally illegible. They are appropriate for certificates, especially the name imprints, because they are simply meant to look good. No one reads them. They are background information to impress those who come into the room. Have you ever

Brush
Script
abcdefghijkl

Dorchester Script
abcdefghijklmnopqstuv

Pepita
abcdefghijkl

Ex Ponto
abcdefghijklnops

Lemonade
abcdefghijkl

Nuptial Script
abcdefghijkl

Old English
abcdefghijkl
Goudy Text
abcdefghijklmn

noticed how close you have to get to read that doctor's certificate on her office wall? It is just meant to make you feel good about your doctor. You really don't even know if it is real, do you?

Script and text have one thing in common Illegibility!

Because script and blackletter are so difficult to read, both of these categories have very restricted usage. In fact, they are limited to products where people have an extreme motivation to read them, like invitations, greeting cards, and the like. They are also used for products where the look is more important than the verbal content, like graduation certificates. Often scripts or blackletter fonts are the only acceptable option as far as your client is concerned. Occasionally you may find a use for them as headlines or banners or other such items, but you must always be aware of reading difficulty. Use all the tricks you can muster to enhance readability, such as emphasizing with white space, large sizes, extra line spacing, and so on.

The leading requirements are extreme. Scripts have especially small x-heights. Simple body copy in script is normally 18-point or more for sheer legibility. Even at that size, the x-height is very close to 10- or 11-point serif faces. Beyond that, the letter shapes are so stylized that you need a "lot of air" or open white space surrounding the letters to help the reader. As a result, the leading is often 18/24 or even 18/27. These jobs almost always require a formal centered layout. This is one place where drama is definitely frowned on. Keep it simple, clean, and open. Give the type as much room to breathe as possible. For headlines, you may have to go to 72-point or larger.

 A final warning on both these classifications. It has always been a designers' joke to spec these fonts in all caps. Do not fall for it. The flourishes on the uppercase letters make all caps totally illegible. It's not funny.

Faux fonts

One of the real problems you will have on a regular basis is choosing real fonts. InDesign and Photoshop now warn you if you pick a font that does not exist. Copperplate, for example, does not have a bold – it uses numbers. Copperplate 32 is Bold (I think). Most decorative faces only have one or two styles. Corinthian only has Light, at present. There used to be a Corinthian family of sorts in press type, but it is not available now.

A worse problem is using the Bold or Italic styling options (you know, Command/Control B or I). These only work with TrueType fonts – if then. They ask for a font like Caslon (Bold) instead of Caslon Bold. The parentheses are not a part of the name of most bold fonts. So that font simply does not exist, and you will probably get Courier when it prints. Using the italic option simply slants the type into an oblique. Even if that exists (and even if it prints instead of Courier), it will be ugly.

These faux elements are sure signs of laziness, lack of taste, inexperience, or stupidity. Are you sure you want to align yourself with those friends?

Too many rules

Remember, legalism kills

The factors discussed in this chapter have to be considered, but they cannot become rigid rules. If you have a good reason, ignore the rules. Make sure you do it on purpose, though. The relationships described here are real and they work on a practical, predictable level. You ignore them at your own risk.

Some fields, like snowboarding, try to require that you break all rules (but that's just another rule). Many have strict requirements – often unwritten. For example, accounting firms will occasionally ask for something special. But, even then, they usually approve only small formal type, caps and small caps, huge leading, and centered designs (usually Copperplate <grin>). The main thing is to be conscious of what you are doing and why.

As the designer, you are responsible for every mark on the sheet, intended or not. If you follow all the rules, your work will be too boring to be tolerated. You always have to add that little bit of interest, and that means stepping outside the norm. **Just do it carefully – please.**

Where should you be by this time?

You should have at least half of your grade earned by now. If you don't. shame on you!

Get busy!

DISCUSSION

You should be talking about uses for various fonts. You should be checking out the fonts you are using. You need to begin picking fonts you like and trying to determine why you like them.

Talk amongst yourselves...

Knowledge retention and thought provocation

1. Where would you use a blackletter face and why?
2. What are realist fonts and what political philosophy do you think inspired them?
3. The vast majority of type styles belong to which classification?
4. How is readability compromised by geometrics?
5. Which class would you use for a billboard and why?
6. Why are script faces not more commonly used?
7. Do you think we need so many different type styles?

LEAVING TYPEWRITERS

Discovering the differences between typewriting and typesetting

Chapter Objectives:

By giving students a clear understanding of what different type styles are available, this chapter will enable students to:

1. kern type
2. use fixed spaces
3. use appropriate typographic characters
4. eliminate widows and orphans

Lab Work for Chapter:

1. Work on skill exams.
2. Read chapter 11 for next week.
3. Work on projects.

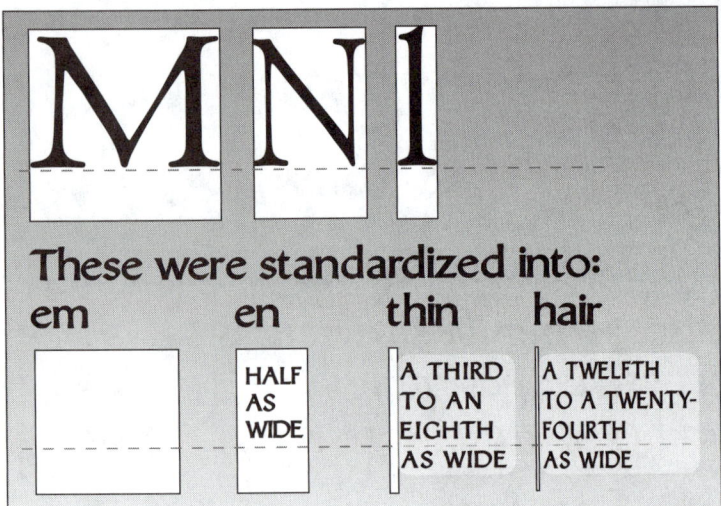

These were standardized into:

em	en	thin	hair
	HALF AS WIDE	A THIRD TO AN EIGHTH AS WIDE	A TWELFTH TO A TWENTY-FOURTH AS WIDE

Normal: Side edges of characters touch
Awkwardly

Tracking: All letters are moved equally
Awkwardly

Kerning: All letter pairs adjusted separately
Awkwardly

Here are several rows of type to demonstrate how justification works in your paragraphs.

Leftover space at the end of a line is divided by the number of spaces and added to each space. Fixed spaces are not adjusted by this.

Here are several sample rows of type to demonstrate how justification works in your paragraphs.

Now we've reached the core of publishing.

In many ways, every page prior to this chapter has merely been an introduction to this chapter. This is the first time I get to talk about typography in the context of tools designed for professional page layout. FreeHand is the master of type manipulation for PostScript, and nothing can touch it (although Illustrator has a few tricks FreeHand has not mastered yet). InDesign is the master of typographic production. We have never had a digital publishing program come close to InDesign's capabilities before. QuarkXPress and PageMaker are only distant competitors to InDesign in many areas. Even Photoshop can do a nice job of basic typesetting in the larger point sizes.

Even though many see this is a large overstatement, it does emphasize that InDesign has typographic controls that have not been seen since the best of the phototypesetters. All of the controls are not available, even yet. However, this is the first desktop publishing program where you can be confident that the type you produce will be up to professional standards. Quark has always lacked some of the basics. Even ems and ens needed a workaround (more on that in a bit). PageMaker did better, but justification controls were always weak. With the new OpenType options, almost all of the old typographic niceties are available again.

However, we are getting the cart before the horse again. First I need to make sure that we are all on the same page. My experience suggests that very few of you have any idea about typography and what it really is. Typographic knowledge, for most people, is based on hunches and feelings derived from experience in observing excellence in graphic design. However, many excellent designs have horrible typography. Most wouldn't know typographic excellence if it bit them. And, at this point, most of you have not yet trained your eyes to even see what is going on. Training your eye is one of the main purposes of this book.

Now, I am not talking about the anal-retentive diatribes regularly seen in the Letters columns of major industry magazines like the lamented *Adobe Magazine*, *Electronic Publishing*, and the others.

Anything can be carried to an extreme. Even though I have over thirty years of typesetting and type design experience, most of this type of nitpicking is merely irritating to me. Many times you will see articles on typographic matters by the national gurus in the magazines where a certain adjustment is declared mandatory when you cannot see the differences in the examples presented. I am telling you that, even with my experience, I usually cannot see the differences either.

However, this avoids the basic statement of truth. Without professional typography, neither your clients nor their customers will take your work seriously. At best, your work will look cheap. At worst, the reader will have an instinctive distrust of your client and skip over the copy. There is a level of typographic professionalism that must be attained. There is a minimum standard of competence. In our marketing culture, where virtually everything is controlled by advertising and marketing, from religion to politics, from tractors to microchips, typographic professionalism is minimal necessity.

Without professional typography, neither your clients nor their customers will take your work seriously.

All of us have had a constant exposure to typography since childhood. Everything you read (except teacher handouts) was professionally typeset: all of the magazines and books, most of the junk mail, and all of the catalogs. However, that does not mean that you know how to produce it yourself. It does mean that typesetting which does not follow the norms produces an uneasiness in you when you read it.

Bad typography usually results in a vague first impression of discomfort or distrust by the readers of your digital documents. I am convinced that it is one of the reasons why many have trouble taking the Web seriously. With everything in Times and Helvetica, with no typographic controls, the online reading experience is very uncomfortable. All of us give that sigh of relief when the Web page is printed out in a decent font, chosen by us in our browser preference (even though the column width is usually far too wide for readability). Bad type is very hard to read, even on an emotional/psychological basis.

Your job is to train your eye to see bad type and to learn how to produce excellent type. Typesetting does have some strange requirements for the newcomer. However, there is a good reason for everything. All it takes is a completely new look at type.

Typesetting is very different

This is not Typing 101!

You have, by this time, realized that type has nothing to do with typing. It is obvious that even the terminology is different. However, we have hardly begun. Much more significant than the new language are the actual mechanics of typesetting. The rules have changed! In fact, one of the difficulties in publishing classes today involves a paradox.

1. To get a job, desktop publishers have to be able to type well.
2. Learning to type in a keyboarding class teaches students so many bad habits that you wonder if it is worth it.

Most of you will find, to your dismay, that many of the things you thought you knew about typing and word processing are simply wrong, as far as professional type is concerned. Things you were taught as necessary now become typographical errors. Your clients can refuse to pay for your designed projects because of one typo (or typographic error). This is where the rubber meets the road.

At this point, we're going to talk about some major differences. By the time we finish this chapter, I hope, you will be into the new paradigm enough to notice the rest as you read the materials you come across in daily living. It is very important to realize that these differences are not minor quibbles. They have a major effect on your ability to communicate with type. They are absolutely necessary for professional document construction and career advancement.

Type color

First, we need to discuss one of the most important attributes of excellent type — the smoothness of the color of the type. What is called the *type color* is created by the design of the font character shapes, the spacing of those characters, the spacing of the words, the leading between the lines of type, and the paragraph spacing.

This is one of those places where you want an excellent font. In fonts like these, the characters fit very evenly and smoothly. This character fit is called letterspacing. Beyond that is a very careful use of spacing throughout your documents, in general. This is your responsibility. This is one of the major places where word processors are left in the dust. Even excellent fonts will not help a word processor.

The professional page layout programs (InDesign, PageMaker, QuarkXPress, and to a certain extent FreeHand) have very precise letterspacing and word spacing controls. Leading can be controlled to a minimum of a tenth of a point and usually much finer distinctions than that can be made. Baseline shifts up or down of individual words and even entire lines of type can be adjusted very precisely.

Paragraph spacing is controlled to a ten-thousandth of a whatever (inch, millimeter, point, kyu, cicero, pica) by the space before and space after fields in the paragraph formatting dialog box or palette. In addition are the margin and column gutter controls, plus the ability to make optical margin adjustments so the edges of the columns appear cleaner. One of the major complaints about early versions of PageMaker was that it could only make adjustments of a tenth of a whatever. Pros found this to be much less control than what is necessary.

Smooth type color needs to become one of your major concerns.

Professional type should have an even color when seen from far enough away so that the body copy can no longer be read and becomes gray shapes. You will come to see that this even type color is imperative. It is what allows the control of the reader's eye that you need for clear and comfortable communication. You will learn to keep your type as smooth as possible, stepping outside of that only to make important points that the reader really needs and wants to know.

This smoothness is what makes headlines, subheads, and our specialized paragraph styles work. The white space surrounding specialized paragraphs like these stands out from smooth type color. This white space attracts the eye and leads it to that statement. Without smooth type color, you are forced to make your headers much stronger and the reader often feels like you are shouting at him or her. That is definitely not a comfortable reading experience. Smooth type color needs to become one of your major concerns.

On to specific typesetting concerns

1. No double spacing

Typing classes teach that one should always double-space after punctuation. This was made necessary by the typewriter characters themselves. All characters on a typewriter are the same width. This is called a monospaced typeface. The result is that punctuation becomes hard to see. The double space emphasizes sentence construction and makes it visible. When you are using monospaced fonts, this type of extra spacing is necessary.

This typing rule is taught even though most people using word processors have not used monospaced type for years. The rule is just taught, without thought, because *"We have always done it that way."*

```
If you look at this paragraph closely,
you will see that the spacing looks far
different from the paragraphs above and
below.  It is set in Courier,  which is a
monospaced font.  As you can see,  the
spacing is horrible.  Much of this is
because of the letter shapes themselves.
But the main problem is that all
characters have the same width —
including spaces and punctuation. As a
result, everything lines up vertically.
This is what monospacing means.
```

Typesetting, in contrast, is done with proportional type. This means that every character has its own width that is designed to fit with the other characters. Typeset words form units characterized by even spacing between every letter. In fact, professional typesetting is judged by this smooth type color, as we just discussed. Double-spacing is not needed because the better-fitting words make punctuation a major break. In addition, there is extra white space built into the typeset punctuation characters themselves. Double spacing after punctuation puts little white holes in the type color. These speckled paragraphs are not nearly so elegant, beautiful, or clear.

2. No double returns

No multiple text blocks, if possible

Keeping your type in cohesive text blocks: One of the major difficulties you will have as you begin setting type is keeping your copy in coherent blocks of text. Ideally, all of the copy on a page (except for the sidebars and possibly the captions) needs to be in a single text block. In some layouts, it may be a single frame per column, but the concept is clear. If you use multiple text blocks, you lose alignment control.

The reason for this is that spacing in typography uses adjustments that are so small, you cannot control them by eye. Although you can clearly see the relationships, hand-adjusted consistency is impossible on a 72 dpi monitor because most of the adjustments are less than a point — or smaller than a pixel. You can only adjust type relative to itself in increments of small portions of a point.

Monospacing

In the sample to the left, the paragraph in Courier was a real pain to typeset. There are so many automatic controls in InDesign that the monospaced characters would not line up correctly. I had to make a separate text block and turn off all the controls to make this little demo. Even yet, the monospacing has been modified a little.

Paragraph spacing

Spacing between the paragraphs is not done with the Return key. It is done with the Space Before and Space After fields in your Paragraph palette or dialog box. In Quark, the dialog is found under Formats, for Paragraph Formats.

The extra space between paragraphs helps the lines of type in the paragraph hold together in a unit. It is especially important to do this in bulleted lists where the paragraphs are short — two or three lines.

The first place you will run across this dilemma in our current discussion is with paragraph spacing. Space between paragraphs is controlled with the space before paragraph and space after paragraph options. It is not controlled with multiple returns.

 Opinion: Here we come to a place where there is major disagreement between typographers. It is quite possible that your instructor has a different opinion than I do. You will have to decide. Your decision on most of these matters will help determine your personal sense of style. Just remember, please: spacing is to be used to help communicate, not just to make a pretty page.

Some of the more anal typographers demand that you put no space between paragraphs, and that all vertical spacing be a direct multiple of the leading. This is to produce that prime virtue, in their minds, of text blocks that are lined up horizontally top and bottom. Beyond that, they want all lines of type in parallel columns to be lined up. Type should fit a tightly defined grid.

IMHO, that type of rigid structure is deadly to clear communication. I do not want all of the lines of type to line up horizontally. That is one of the ways that my readers can easily stray from the column they are trying to read. This type of symmetrical rigidity contributes to the boredom of many layouts. Yes, we must have spacing in control. Yes, we must maintain consistency in our layouts. But rigid grids are as stifling as prison bars.

Spacing is to be used to help communicate, not to make a pretty page.

Double return problems

With these concepts in mind, how should we set up our paragraph spacing? First, be aware that double returns add huge, horizontal white bars that run across your pages — disrupting type color. When cleaning up secretarial copy, you will regularly come across multiple returns — maybe a dozen or more. This is because most secretaries have no clue about the flow of copy. These things are not taught in word processing classes. So they simply type multiple returns to get to the next page.

You want to establish a rhythm to your pages that makes the paragraphs easy to see without being obvious. A couple of points before or after each paragraph is enough. If you do not use a first-line indent, you will probably need to use four to seven points before or after your paragraphs. Try to use as little extra spacing as possible while still making your structure easy to follow while reading. To keep it consistent, this spacing needs to be built into your paragraph styles. They are covered in depth in my advanced page layout book, *Publishing with InDesign*, Delmar Learning, 2003.

For headlines and subheads, their positioning is controlled to a large degree by the space before and the space after a paragraph. You want more space before a header and less after so the header is tied to the copy that follows. For this reason, I usually use a couple of points after my body copy paragraphs to help with the lead-in space to the next paragraph style — especially headers.

3. Space, space and a half, or double space?

None of the above! This is why we use leading instead of spacing. In almost every case (unless you are trying to mimic a typewriter) a single space is too close, a space and a half is too far, and a double space is ridiculous. Again, the focus has to be on readability.

 Before we go on, a little review of typespeak is required. Point size and leading is expressed as **10/12** or **21/21.5** plus the align-ment. This is pronounced ten on twelve or twenty-one on twenty-one and a half. In these cases, **10** and **21** are the point size and **12** and **21.5** are the leading in points.

So, a common statement would be something like this: body copy is normally 10/12 justified quad left. This would be a paragraph with 10-point type and 12-point leading set justified with the last line flush left — like this paragraph and all the body copy in this book. When the point size and leading are the same, as in 16/16, it is referred to as being set solid.

Leading is determined by font design, point size, line length, and reading distance. In our sample in chapter 8, we noticed that all fonts have differing built-in line spacing. As you recall, Futura had none and Bernhard Modern had a lot. Bernhard Modern also had a very small x-height. As a result, if we accept that normal body copy is 10/12 (and it is), then Futura should probably be set at 10/13 and Bernhard Modern at 11/12.

Some leading norms for normal reading distance:

- **Tiny type:** Type smaller than 7 point is usually set solid. With type set that small, you usually don't want people read-ing it. It is used for the small type on legal documents.
- **Body copy:** This is the normal reading copy in your docu-ments. It is rigidly required to be 10/12 by many publishers, as

mentioned. However, when you have the control, those figures should be adjusted by x-height and built-in line spacing. Larger x-heights require smaller point sizes. A large amount of built-in spacing between the top of the ascenders and the bottoms of the descenders in the line above takes less leading. Long line lengths require more leading. In general, bold, sans serif, or condensed fonts need more leading. This is your job: to figure out what reads best.

- **Headers:** Headlines and subheads are commonly set solid. The larger the point size used, the less leading is needed.
- **All caps:** Setting type in all caps often requires negative leading. This means that the leading is less than the point size. If you think about it, the reasoning should be clear. All caps have no descenders. Descenders are about a third of the point size. So headlines in all caps might well be set 36/28 or so.

THIS HEADER IS SET WITH NEGATIVE LEADING: 24/20

Autoleading: One of the things you need to get under control is autoleading. The factory default is 120%. This means the leading will be 120% of the point size. This sounds good, and works well for body copy (10/12). However, it is disastrous for headers. I usually have the autoleading set at 105% (or less) for them.

Even worse is when you drop in an inline or anchored graphic as a character in your paragraph. The autoleading adjusts to give room for the graphic. In these cases, you will need to turn autoleading off. This also happens if you make a letter, a word, or words larger in a paragraph.

4. Tabs and fixed spaces

Spaces cause many other problems for people trained in typewriting. On a typewriter, the spacebar is a known quantity. This is because every character in monospaced type is the same width — even the space. This is definitely not true for type. In fact, in type, the space band is often a different size than it was the last time you hit the key.

This is caused by several factors. First, the word space character in various fonts varies in width. There is no standard. This space also changes with point size, of course. This is not a problem with typewriters because they only have one size and one font. As a result, most people accustomed to word processors do most of their horizontal spacing with multiple spaces. This is one reason why the first thing you usually have to do with secretarial copy is eliminate the double spaces.

More than this, word spacing is one of the defaults that should be set to your standards. Page layout programs give you very precise control over word spacing. Finally, word spacing varies with every line when setting justified copy. The way this works is as follows.

Justification

When you are setting a line of justified type, you determine a justification zone. When the last word that fits in a line ends in this justification zone, any remaining space in the column width is evenly divided and added to the word spaces in the line. If the last word does not reach the zone, the length of the zone is divided and added to the spaces in the line (any additional space is divided and added as letterspacing between every letter in the line).

What this means is that the spaces on every line are a different width in justified copy. Look at the gray boxes on the first and third line to the right. InDesign works hard to minimize this on a paragraph basis, justifying several lines at a time. The other software, like Quark, Free-Hand, and PageMaker, do not even have this capability. More than that, the word spaces are different from paragraph to paragraph whenever size, font, or defaults change. As a result, you never really know how wide a spacebar character will be.

The problem of predictable spaces has been solved by using some more letterpress solutions. When type was composed, it was brought out to a rectangle no matter what the alignment was — right, left, centered, or justified. The characters used to do this were blank slugs, called quads, that were a little lower so they would not print accidentally. These quads came in three widths: em, en, and el, plus what were called hair spaces. The el space is long gone; it is now usually called a thin space. InDesign has all four types. PageMaker has ems, ens, and thin spaces. Quark has one definable fixed space.

Here are several sample rows of type to demonstrate how justification works in your paragraphs.

Leftover space at the end of a line is divided by the number of spaces and added to each space. Fixed spaces are not adjusted by this.

Here are several sample rows of type to demonstrate how justification works in your paragraphs.

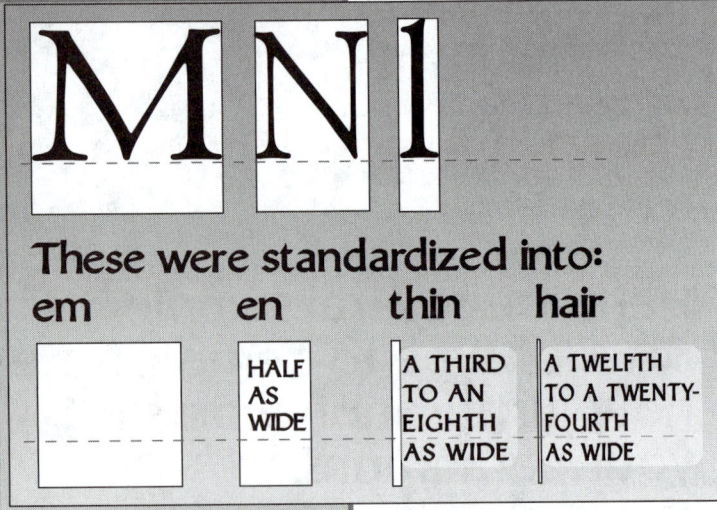

These were standardized into:

em	en	thin	hair
	HALF AS WIDE	A THIRD TO AN EIGHTH AS WIDE	A TWELFTH TO A TWENTY-FOURTH AS WIDE

Originally these characters were blanks the width of an *m*, *n*, and *l*, respectively. Of course, they were standardized. This is something you need to memorize. These spaces are now defined as follows: an em space is the square of the point size; an en space is the same height, of course, but half as wide; and a thin space varies. The thin space can be either one-fifth em (PageMaker and FreeHand), or one-eighth em (InDesign). InDesign's hair space is one–twenty-fourth of an em. As mentioned, Quark only has one space that you define — so it is not a standard.

These fixed spaces are used a lot. For example, they should always be used for custom hand-spacing, because the spacebar can vary proportionally if you change the point size. Fixed spaces remain proportionally consistent. Another fact to bear in mind is that lining numbers are normally an en space wide. This means that an en should be used as a blank when lining up numbers (an em for two numbers) for accountants and bookkeepers.

Tabular construction

Custom spacing should normally be done with tabs. Typesetting tabs are much more powerful than typewriting tabs. They come in four kinds: left, right, centered, and decimal (FreeHand even offers an auto-wrapping tab). All tabs can be set up with leaders. These leaders can be lines, dotted lines, or any repeating character you need. The following shows the four tabs and some leaders:

...Name and 456.7 .... Name and 456.7...Name and 456.7 .... Name and 456.7
...Name and 56.78 .... Name and 56.78.....Name and 56.78..... Name and 56.78
.....Name or 6.789 ..... Name or 6.789........... Name or 6.789 .. Name or 6.789
........................Right .... Centered......................Decimal. .... Left

Secretarial tab use

One of the additional problems you will have with secretarial word processing copy is poor tab use. A single tab is often used for the first-line indent. You will have to delete that. Because many word processor users do not know how to set tabs, they just use the default tabs that come every half inch. As a result, you will often find several tabs in a row – used like multiple spaces. They will all have to be changed to a single tab. In addition, because most do not know how to do bulleted or numbered lists, every line is commonly returned manually using multiple tabs. You will have to get rid of all of them. You will get very fast with Find & Change.

There is no legitimate use of the double space.

In general, get used to the idea that the spacebar should only be hit once. It cannot be used to line up portions of different lines. They will constantly be out of alignment. In fact, you need to be a little careful. On a computer keyboard, any key that is held down will automatically repeat, including the spacebar. Publishing students fight this, but in typesetting there is no legitimate use of the double space. The same is almost true of the tab, but there are exceptions here.

5. En and em dashes

The next major change we need to discuss is dashes. Typewriters only have one – the hyphen. Type has three – the hyphen, the en dash, and the em dash. All three have very specific usage rules.

HYPHEN   EN DASH   EM DASH

Hyphen. This is the character used to hyphenate words at the end of a line and to create compound words. For example, 10-point is the normal point size for book publishers' body copy. In fact, hyphenation is used no other place.

En dash. This dash is an en long. It is used with numbers, spans, or ranges. For example, pages 24–39 or 6:00–9:00 or May 7–12. It is a typo to use a hyphen in these cases.

A special case: In rare cases, hyphens and en dashes need to be mixed for clarity. I used one a few paragraphs back when presenting the width of a hair space for InDesign. It seemed easier to read and understand one–twenty-fourth of an em with the en dash between the one and twenty-fourth. This is the typographer's decision to make.

Em dash. This dash is an em long. It is a punctuation mark. Grammatically it is stronger than a comma but weaker than a period. Other than that, there is no standard anymore. American English is a living language in constant flux. These changes have accelerated in recent years. In many cases, there are no rules anymore. Em dashes are used more every year. In many ways they are very helpful — but traditionalists tend to have knee-jerk reactions to anything outside the grammar books (written decades ago).

Typewriters use a double hyphen for the em dash. This is an embarrassing error to professionals. In fact, it is one of the sure signs of amateurism. However, on the Web, because there are no cross-platform special characters, you have to go back to the double hyphen instead of the em dash.

Finally, do not think you will not be caught. Hyphens are about a thin space wide. They are higher above the baseline than en or em dashes. Also, they are commonly slanted up with little swashes on the ends (although you see swashes for all three in Diaconia Old Style).

6. Real quotes and apostrophes

Here is another place where typewriters are limited by the lack of characters. All typewriters have is inch and foot marks. Quotation marks and apostrophes look very different. This is another typographical embarrassment when used incorrectly.

Inch/foot ' " Open/close quotes ' ' " "

Again it is important to use the right characters. I have seen printed projects rejected because of not using curly quotes. An apostrophe is a single close quote. These are keystrokes you should learn. Again they are different cross-platform.

Character	Mac	PC
Open single	Option-]	Alt-[
Close single	Option-Shift-]	Alt-]
Apostrophe	Option-Shift-]	Alt-]
Open double	Option-[	Alt-Shift-[
Close double	Option-shift-[	Alt-Shift-]

There is a modern American abomination called reversed apostrophes. They are found in many decorative fonts used for display faces. There is no historical precedence so I am not giving you a sample. The question is academic, however, because their use is very obvious and readable — more typographic variations.

Language differences

One of the more disconcerting things to keep track of in this increasingly global society is usage differences in the languages. For example, in America, we are taught to use double quotes for a quote and single quotes for quotes within a quote. British usage is the opposite. Other languages use completely different characters or changes like open double quotes which look like close double quotes on the baseline – to our eyes.

Increasingly, we are designing documents set in multiple languages. It is important to keep track of these things. Consider, for instance, the Spanish practice for questions, ¿Que pasa? or expletives, ¡Vámonos!

Guillemets: ‹ › « »

Single and double guillemets are used by several European languages in place of curly quotes. For French and Italian, they point out like «thus». In German they often point in, according to Bringhurst. German uses »this style« also, but then I am not a linguist so I don't know the ins and outs. The point is to be careful. Bringhurst's work, *The Elements of Typographic Style*, has a great deal of information on specific typographic usage in other languages for those of you doing a lot of this work.

7. No underlines

The next difference has to do with the physical nature of typewriters. Because they only have one size of type, there is no way to emphasize words except for all caps and underlining. Underlining is necessary for these antiques. In typesetting, underlining ruins the carefully crafted descenders. In addition, the underlines that come with the type are usually too heavy and poorly placed. They also compromise readability and type color by messing with the white space between lines.

If you decide that an underline is an appropriate solution, please use a narrow box or a hand-placed line, as in the following example.

Typing not Typing

The goal of typesetting is to make clean, elegant type that is read without distraction. Underlining is almost as bad as outlines and shadows, as far as professionals are concerned. They ruin the unique characteristics of the font. Notice how the descender of the *g* is ruined. At times they serve a useful design function, but this kind of modification should be used very discreetly.

Software styles

In general, you should never use the character styling built into outdated software like PageMaker and Quark: bold, italic, outline, underline, or shadow. They are a sure indicator that you have no typographic understanding. These styles were developed for crude, non-PostScript printers. Instead, use the actual bold and italic versions of the fonts.

Especially bad is the bold styling, which originally just printed the type twice slightly offset. It is very dangerous to ever use this option unless you design your fonts that way. You'll notice that type styled with a command or check box often looks fuzzy (if it is not changed to Courier). In these cases, if you enlarge the type enough, you will see the double image.

Outline style is often so thin that it won't print on imagesetters (the outlines are set as a single pixel by older RIPs). Shadow is unpredictable, at best — it's always too dark and too close.

Shadows, in general, severely compromise readability. You must be careful with your placement of the shadows. Copy the type and make it very light (10% is a good starting point). Then carefully move it around until it is the easiest to read and looks the best.

Dealing with underlines

When receiving secretarial copy, you will usually find body copy littered with underlines. Our job, as typesetters, is to convert those underlines to the proper usage. **Proper Names** should be set in a bold version of the font. Periodic names like *National Geographic* or *People* magazines must be in italics. Words that are simple *emphasis* should also be set in italic. For strong emphasis, you may want to change fonts.

This is one of the things you are expected to do with copy received. This is why you will be getting the big bucks. If you do not, your client may well decide you are not worth the money. Remember, the normal hourly rate for graphic design is $50 per hour or more — on up to several hundred dollars per hour.

8. No ALL CAPS

As mentioned in the underline section, setting letters in all caps is the other way to emphasize words on a typewriter. Typesetting has many more options. There is *italic*, **bold**, ***bold italic***, SMALL CAPS, larger size, extended, **and so on**.

There is something else, however. Studies have shown that type in all caps is around 40 percent less legible than caps and lowercase, or just lowercase. All caps is also much longer than the same word set C&lc. Because our major purpose is to get the reader to read our piece and act on the message, you should never use all caps (unless you have a good reason). For example, all caps is often used to make a piece of type less legible and therefore to de-emphasize it.

Readability

Readability is an interesting and complicated phenomenon. Everyone has theories. What most agree on is that people recognize letters by the distinctive outlines on the top of the letter shapes.

This is the major reason why setting type in all caps is so counter-productive. Because uppercase letters tend to be in rectangular boxes the tops of characters tend to look very similar.

ATTRACTIVE WOMAN

is not nearly as easy to decipher as

cowardly lion

and the bottom halves almost never work, as in

intellectual snob.

As you can see, the straight line formed by the tops of the caps and the bottoms of the lowercase (even the descenders do not help) are not distinct enough to recognize easily. Please, remember that difficulty is not a good attribute of reading material. By the way, the third example is intellectual snob.

By the way, all caps reversed is even less legible. In fact, text set that way (light on a dark background) will not be read unless you force the reader graphically with size, color, or some other such ploy. Sometimes this can be used to the client's advantage. For example, you will regularly see the antismoking warning on cigarette ads set small, all caps, reversed out of a gray box. The worst, for reading, is type that goes back and forth from positive to negative.

On the Web and for presentations, it is true that light, glowing letters on a dark background can be easier to read. This is true for any type used as a light source or backlit. However, you need to remember that on the Web the backgrounds usually do not print. White type on white paper doesn't read well at all.

These readability issues are primary to typesetting. You really need to keep track. Remember, you can read it because you set it. Your readers do not have that benefit.

Reversed subheads

After saying that reversed copy is harder to read, you might be asking why I used that device for my subheads.

My assumption, and I may well be wrong, is that you are a more sophisticated reader. Since you are more visually attuned, my hope is that the reversed heads will not cause any problem. I hope I was right.

9. Letterspacing, kerning, and tracking

Here is another typesetting capability that cannot even be considered by typists. We mentioned letterspacing earlier. Letterspacing is the built-in spacing between characters in a font. The basic idea is that the white space between letters should be identical for all letter pairs. Obviously, this is not simple or easy. AT, OOPS, and silly have very different spacing problems — especially the ill. The better the font, the better the letterspacing. In very cheap fonts, individual letters may be far to the left or right. I bought one once where the lowercase *r* was always at least 9 points to the left — as in da ing.

Tracking

Tracking is the official term used to replace letterspacing in digital typesetting now that we can move letters either closer together or farther apart. In reality, either term can be used and understood. The actual procedure for tracking simply inserts or removes an equal amount of space around every letter selected or affected.

Although tracking is used all the time by typographic novices, it is despicable to traditional professionals. Quality typefaces have the letterspacing carefully designed into the font. Changing the tracking for stylistic reasons or fashion changes the color of the type at the very least. A paragraph tracked tighter looks darker. At worst, it can make the color splotchy.

Tracking suffers from the vagaries of fashion. In the 1980s, it was very common to see extremely tight tracking in everything. I was guilty of it myself, upon occasion. May it never be among you. Tight tracking severely compromises readability.

Kerning

Kerning is a different thing altogether. Here the problem is with letter pairs. There are thousands of different letter pairs. I guess the total would be around 20,000 or 40,000 pairs. There is no way to set up the spacing around letters to cover all situations: AR is a very different situation than AV; To than Tl; AT than AW.

Literally thousands of different kerned pairs are needed to make a perfectly kerned font. Some kern together and some kern apart. Most of them can only be seen at the larger point sizes. Here again

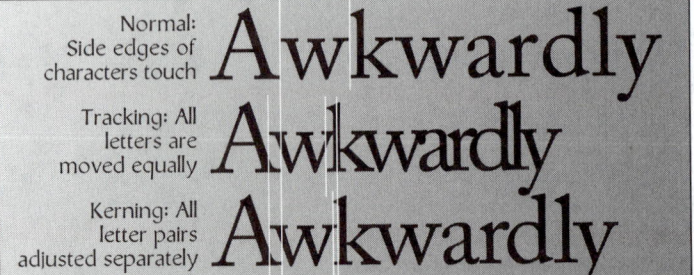

Normal:
Side edges of
characters touch

Tracking: All
letters are
moved equally

Kerning: All
letter pairs
adjusted separately

we see the difference between excellent and cheap fonts. Professional fonts have around 1,000 kerning pairs built into the font metrics. Cheap fonts commonly have a couple dozen or none at all.

As mentioned, quality fonts have kerning designed into about a thousand letter pairs. In addition, all professional publishing programs allow you to adjust kerning for individual pairs. Most give you keyboard shortcuts (most often Option/Alt–left arrow and Option/Alt–right arrow). Adding the Shift or Command key multiples the amount moved.

 We are always expected to check the kerning on all type larger than about 18-point. Yes, you really are required to hand-kern all headlines if necessary. It's the only way, in most cases. Unkerned type looks cheap and unprofessional. In body copy sizes, a quality font will cover it.

InDesign offers Optical kerning which automatically checks the letterspacing and adjusts it for you. It does a remarkable job. Recently I put a font up on MyFonts.com to sell that was unusable outside of InDesign. I had forgotten that I had purposely made uneven and bad letterspacing for the headers in my first book on InDesign to show how well optical kerning worked. Then I used it in another application. Needless to say, I had to take it off the market.

10. Be careful with hyphens.

Because typeset line endings are automatic, so is the hyphenation. You can turn it on or off. Hyphenation can be done by dictionary or by *algorithm*. Always choose the dictionary, if the software gives you an option. An algorithm is a rule, so hyphenation by algorithm means that hyphens are placed according to a set of rules, like: always hyphenate in front of an "ed" ending or always hyphenate between two consonants. Which gives you clean-ed — spell-ed and spel-led are both wrong — you see the problem? Algorithm hyphenation causes many typos, so you have to proof carefully.

Another problem is that automatic hyphenation can create hyphens for many consecutive lines. Here there is sharp debate. Most of us agree that two hyphens in a row should be the maximum (a three-hyphen "stack" looks odd). Page layout software allows you to set that limit. Many set the limit at one.

Yet another problem comes when you run into something like two hyphens in a row; then a normal line; then two more hyphens. The final problem comes when the program hyphenates part of a compound word. **Be careful with hyphens!**

Finally, never hyphenate a word in a headline or subhead. It just isn't done. In fact, almost all headers should be carefully examined if they go to two lines or more. Normally they need to be broken for sense with soft-returns. In your header paragraph styles, simply turn hyphenation off.

11. Eliminate widows and orphans

As Roger Black states in his pioneering work, *Desktop Design Power* (Random House, 1990, out of print) "Widows are the surest sign of sloppy typesetting." The problems arise as soon as we start trying to simply define the words. See the subsection below on orphans.

I am using the most common definitions (also the ones used by Black). A widow is a short line at the end of a paragraph that is much too short. What is too short? Again, there is sharp debate. The best answer is that the last line must have at least two complete words and those two words must be at least eight characters total. Bringhurst says at least four characters. But then his typography is filled with short sentence fragments at the end of paragraphs that look horrible, as far as I am concerned.

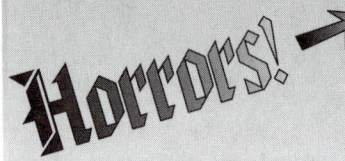

Orphans (paragraph fragments in columns)

The software will really mess you up here, if you are not careful. Programmers usually have no idea what a widow is. Often they confuse widows with orphans. All the major page layout software uses Bringhurst's definitions. I do not know any traditional typesetter who uses these conventions, but then I only know a few hundred or so. I agree with people like Sandee Cohen, Roger Black, Robin Williams, and many others. Actually, everyone agrees what excellent type should look like. There are only semantic differences — word definitions.

An orphan is a short paragraph or paragraph fragment left by itself at the top or bottom of a column. In Bringhurst-speak (and he is marvelously witty), a widow is an orphan at the bottom of a column. An orphan is one left at the top of a column. A classic example is a subhead left at the bottom of one column with the body copy starting at the top of the next column.

Page layout programs allow you to control both of these problems fairly well with their *keeps controls*. A keeps control, off the paragraph dialog or palette, allows you to determine if a paragraph must stay with the following paragraph (in the case of the subhead, for example). It also allows you to set the minimum paragraph fragment allowed at either end of a paragraph. This is normally a two-line minimum, top or bottom, beginning or end. Be careful — all existing software considers a widow to be an orphan at the bottom of a column and an orphan comes only at the top (they are both orphans).

Fixing widows (last lines of paragraphs)

Bad widows mess up the type color. They allow a blank white area to appear between paragraphs that stands out like a sore thumb. There is no way to eliminate them except by hand. The best way is editorially. In other words, rewrite the paragraph! However, graphic designers do not often have such editorial authority. In that case, you must carefully adjust the hyphenation, horizontal scale, point size, or word spacing (in that order).

1. **Hyphenation:** Often you can eliminate a widow by simply adding a hyphenation point to a word with a *discretionary hyphen*. A discretionary hyphen is a character that places a breaking point in a word that is invisible unless a hyphen is needed. The shortcut varies. The norm used to be Command-Hyphen. Sadly, this character is often not available for software on the PC.

2. **Horizontal scale:** Here we get into another of those typographic purist fracases. Using horizontal scaling to condense or expand letterforms makes these guys and gals freak. However, plus or minus 5% is invisible. This is the easiest way to pull back a widow. In InDesign, it can even be set as your spacing default in your paragraph styles under glyph scaling. This simply reduces the amount of widows you are forced to deal with. Even typographers can't see the changes.

3. **Point size:** Here we get into local formatting. As mentioned, all type should be formatted with a paragraph style saved in your Styles palette. This gives you global control over all the type in your document — when those inevitable changes come. However, a difficult widow can often be eliminated no other way than by making the point size a half-point smaller. As you recall, a point is about the smallest difference the human eye can see. An entire paragraph with type that is a half-point smaller is an invisible change. (For those of you who think about it, yes, I have used a special paragraph style set a half-point smaller to eliminate widows by keystroke.)

4. **Word spacing:** In justified copy, the word space is elastic. You'll need to customize this setting because the defaults are terrible. Let's say your software is set at 80% minimum, 100% normal, and 115% maximum. If you change the normal to 95%, you move the words a little closer and might eliminate a widow.

You must be gentle or your corrections will stand out worse than the widow. The point size should never be changed more than a half point, for example. Always make your changes to the entire paragraph. Extremely short paragraphs often cannot be fixed, except to "break for sense." This means placing soft returns so that each short line makes sense by itself (as much as possible). Remember, the best method is rewriting the paragraph to add or subtract a word or two to get rid of the widow.

The absolute worst orphan is a widow at the top of a new page — especially if it is the hyphenated back half of the last word. Other horrible typos are: widow at the top of a column; subhead at the bottom, as mentioned; a kicker separated from its headline; and a subhead with one line of body copy at the bottom of a column. These errors must be eliminated at the proofing stage. This is what we mean by massaging a document into shape. Corrections like these are among the primary factors that cause people to react to a design. If they are missing, your design will be classed with amateur productions like school and bureaucrat output.

12. Use bulleted lists.

The use of bullets and dingbats is unknown to typists. Bulleted lists are an extremely effective means of attracting the reader's attention. In fact, there has been a lot of study to find out what readers see and respond to. These are the paragraphs you use to attract the reader's eye or to re-attract it if it is wandering in boredom. The readership order goes like this:

- First, **picture captions** — everyone looks at the pictures first. Photos are checked out before drawings, unless the illustrations are exceptional. The caption should be the synopsis of the major benefit in the story to the reader.

- Second, **headlines** — primarily because of size and placement. The headline should also be the synopsis of the major benefit in the story to the reader. No reader reads everything. You need to tell them why this story is important to them.

- Third, **callouts or pull quotes** — these are quotes pulled from the copy or statements about the copy that are enlarged to the point where they become interesting graphics in their own right. They are exceptionally valuable in pages of nothing but body copy to capture the wandering eye. Care must be taken. An improperly pulled quote can change the editorial focus of the article. Get all pull quotes approved by the client.

- Fourth, **bulleted lists** – like this one. Bulleted lists are read by scanning readers before subheads, drop caps, or any of the other graphic leads commonly used. The assumption is that lists are synopses of the surrounding copy. Readers use them to determine if the rest of the story is worth reading.

Dingbats

With typesetting we have even more options than simple bullets. Dingbats are fonts made up of graphics. Every keystroke is a different graphic. Zapf Dingbats is a font that almost everyone has on a Mac. Wingdings has a similar function on a PC. Almost everyone has several dingbat fonts, even if they don't know it.

Font creation programs allow you to use a logo in a font. Top-quality dingbat fonts are a good way to pick up a collection of clip art that can be used as you type. Recently, dingbat fonts have become one of the best sources of fashionable art. Using dingbats for bullets increases the attraction of the list. Just be careful that the reader is led to read the copy and not simply be amused by your graphic.

 Often dingbats are graphic enough to make excellent starts and/or pieces of logo design. You may want to buy several of these resources. MyFonts.com has a huge collection. Several type designers specialize in dingbat font design.

13. Use small caps.

Small caps are a specialized letterform, as we discussed in chapter 8. Correctly speaking, they are a smaller set of capital letters, a bit larger than the x-height, used in place of the lowercase letters, that are designed so they have the same color as the rest of the font. Here is where you have to be careful, again. Page layout software creates small caps by proportionally shrinking capital letters. This makes them appear to be too light. The best method is to use fonts that have custom-designed small caps. There were few font families like this. But many of the new OpenType font families have real small caps.

There are only a few places where small caps are required. Although, I strongly agree with Robert Bringhurst here. He has many other places where he recommends small caps. What we are basically saying is that strings of caps within body copy should be small caps. Otherwise these acronyms and abbreviations appear to be shouting.

There are several things attached to this position. First of all, this use of small caps is coupled with the use of old style numbers. Second, small caps are often, but not necessarily, used only in body copy. Your

Dingbats

There are hundreds of dingbat fonts. Many of them are excellent sources of fashionable clip art. Here are a few samples from a font called Wingdings.

task, should you accept this venture, will be to convince your copy editor that this is correct procedure. Most of them are using old, newspaper-based, manuals of style. Basing typographic style on newspapers is like basing fashionable dress on Wal-Mart™.

Nevertheless, there are a few places where you use small caps even if you do not have true small caps. For times and dates, the proper use is not A.M. or AM or a.m. but AM. The same is true of PM, AD, BC, BCE, and CE. In these cases, you always use small caps with no periods.

But what about statements like USA 1776? Here the determining factor is whether or not you have oldstyle numbers in your font. In general, you should always use oldstyle numbers in body copy, at least. So, all strings of caps like this should be small caps: ASCII, USA, UN, USSR, CIA, PLO, and so on.

Adding letter space for readability

To increase readability, you will need to add letter space to the small cap strings. This should be designed into the font you use. You should also do this if you are using all caps for headlines (naughty, naughty). Seriously, any time you are using words made up of capital letters you need to add space between the letters until they become readable. The guiding principle is to add as much as you can without causing the letters to separate into individual characters instead of a unified word.

Lining numbers with all caps

Even though we have stated that lining numbers are really only appropriate for bookkeepers, accountants, and CPAs, there are other appropriate uses. One of these is in the midst of all caps. GOD BLESS AMERICA! REMEMBER 9/11/2001. Yes, there are occasions you will be using all caps. You will have to letterspace to help readability. In this situation oldstyle numbers would look foolish.

Readability is crucial; common sense is required.

14. First-line indents

We have briefly touched on first-line indents for body copy paragraphs. This is the preferred method of telling the reader that a new topic sentence is being developed — a new thought expressed. I also mentioned my practice of adding a point or two after paragraphs to help the reader see that first-line indent on a busy page.

The amount of that first-line indent is up to you. You're the designer. The norm is somewhere between a quarter inch and a half inch. Robert says that the minimum is an en, but that is far below what I would call a minimum. An en just tends to look like a mistake. Some say the indent should equal the lead so when using 10/12 you should indent 12 points. Many specify an em, which in the 10/12 example would be 10 points. That is barely over an eighth of an inch — too small.

The first-line indent should equal the left indent of your lists.

I think it is more intertwined than any of those intellectually fine sounding indents of fixed spaces. One of the things to consider as you set up your paragraph styles and page layout is that second consistent interior line which is made by your first-line indents, the left indent of your lists, the left indent of your body heads, and the left indent of your quotes.

As a result, I have personally arrived at a first-line indent of .4 inch. You may want to use less or more, but IMHO anything less than a quarter inch (18 points) just looks like a mistake. It is not really visible; so it merely irritates. Anything more than a half inch makes the eye feel like it has to lunge in to find the beginning.

However, I have seen extreme first-line indents used to real advantage. In an ad for an extremely high quality group (it may have even been for the Santa Fe Opera), one of the local designers used huge margins, enormous leading (like 10/18), coupled with about a half inch between paragraphs, plus a first-line indent of half the column width. For the first paragraph, he used an enlarged initial cap of about 48-point, indented to the halfway point. It was very clean and elegant looking. It worked very well.

15. Drop caps

One of the typographic devices used to indicate the beginning of a story or chapter is the drop cap. In this use, the first letter or letters of the first paragraph is made large enough to be three, four, or five lines of type tall and inset into the paragraph. The first-lines of that paragraph are tabbed around the letter or letters.

First of all, this is very easy with Quark and InDesign. InDesign's implementation allows you to drop as many letters as you want as far as you want — interactively. You can just click the buttons in the Paragraph palette until you like what you see.

If I speak in the tongues of mortals and of angels, but do not have love, I am a noisy gong or a clanging cymbal. And if I have prophetic powers, and understand all mysteries and all knowledge, and if I have all faith, so as to remove mountains, but do not have love, I am nothing.

If I give all I possess to the poor and surrender my body to the flames, but have not love, I gain nothing.

Love is patient; love is kind; love is not envious or boastful or arrogant or rude. It does not insist on its own way; it is not irritable or resentful; it does not rejoice in wrongdoing, but rejoices in the truth.

Love bears all things, believes all things, hopes all things, endures all things.

Often, the drop cap is in a radically different font. It can be set very dramatically in a flowing script that hangs off in the left margin. It is often in a different color. Commonly used are the illuminated capitals of the mediaeval scribes. Mainly, it needs to be dramatic.

The largest mistake with drop caps is overuse. They need to be used very sparingly. As you can see in the first four paragraphs of this page, multiple drop caps are merely confusing. They should never be used more than once on a page. They should only be used once — for the first paragraph of a story, article, or chapter.

16. Proper accents for languages

When you are using a word or phrase from another language, always accent it properly. Some of these things are commonly missed. Words like résumé, moiré, and the like have entered common usage in English. But the pine nuts from the Southwest used in cooking are piñon nuts. Our ubiquitous and unique New Mexican hot peppers are chilé. Chili is that weird stuff with beans from Texas.

This type of typography is only common courtesy. You need to be aware that in the old Commonwealth it is still cheque and lorry. In those countries, corporations get plural verbs — as in: Shell Oil are drilling five new off-shore wells south of Norway.

In America, you need to be very careful of local usage. I mentioned the chilé example all ready. In speech, what is sillier (or more annoying) than an outsider calling the fertile valley south of Portland the Will•i-a•mette' Valley instead of the Will•am'•et as it is locally pronounced? You will find that all locales have local usage. Use it.

We have just gotten started.

We could go on for many pages with typographic niceties. This is just a first introduction to type. The Chinese showed their wisdom again by considering calligraphy to be the highest form of art. Once you understand type, you will see its beauty. Well-drawn type is absolutely gorgeous. After a while, you begin to understand why some of the best graphic designs are simply type.

This goes far beyond simple beauty, though. Excellent type is much easier to read. It eases customer fears. It helps make good experiences (think about a dinner menu at a fine restaurant and a marriage proposal). It is what makes graphic design work.

Typographers

As we have seen, there are three categories of people producing words on paper — typists, typesetters, and typographers. We have been discussing the first two. Typographers go beyond this to make typesetting an art. You should now have an inkling of how difficult that is. They are some of the finest artists in existence.

Becoming a typographer is a worthy goal. It will take you many years. What I want to impress on you is that a surprising number of you will head in that direction. Graphic design becomes so involved with type that you fall in love with it. My only request is that you remain kind and recognize that there are many opinions about type. Strange to say, almost all of them are subjectively correct.

Where should you be by this time?

By now you should be cruising. Make sure you take the time to analyze your typesetting. How can you improve it? What would make it more readable? Are the important words emphasized? What does the reader see first in your composition?

DISCUSSION

You should be critiquing each others' typography. You have to train your eye. Without a critique, you will not see some of your most obvious and stupid mistakes. This takes a while, and it takes conscious effort.

Talk amongst yourselves...

Knowledge retention and thought provocation

1. Why are typing classes a problem?
2. When is using all caps appropriate?
3. What is the problem with double-spacing?
4. Why do typesetters use tabs instead of multiple spaces?
5. How do widows affect type color?
6. Why are drop caps seen so rarely?
7. How is leading determined?

Chapter 11

Producing Type

Concepts

1. Excellent type

2. Meeting deadlines

A step-by-step procedure for producing excellent, functional type

Chapter Objectives:

By giving students a clear understanding of what different type styles are available, this chapter will enable students to:

1. pick appropriate typefaces
2. speed up production
3. design a beautiful and functional page layout

Lab Work for Chapter:

1. Work on skill exams.
2. Read chapter 12 for next week.
3. Work on projects.

Standard production procedures

These tend to be anathema to designers, but they serve a real, practical purpose. If you do it right, you can get set up and running without interfering with the creative process at all. It does take some thought and some practice — but then anything worthwhile does.

How do you get started?

By this time, many of you are screaming, "Uncle!" At least I hope you are. Because you cannot fight it. Ignoring the basics of typesetting only causes severe drops in readership for your projects. And that is the bottom line for your new career.

The content has to be the focus. McLuhan may think that the medium is the message, but it is a very generalized, diffuse message at best. As I discuss in my other books, there is a great deal that can be implied by color, paper, and font choices. The very fact that a client wants a print project says a great deal. We cannot forget that the modern cultural elite are the readers.

But no matter what the medium, the content is the point. How many incredibly entertaining TV ads have you watched where you don't have any recollection of what the ad was advertising? How many direct mail pieces have you gotten where you were so affected with the design, style, colors, or visual impact that purchasing a product never crossed your mind? Maybe you have not been conscious of it, but it has been happening much more than you think.

Excellent type is invisible.

Here we get to the crux of the matter. If readers become focused on the beauty of your typographic masterpiece, you have totally failed your client. The reaction to your design is supposed to be something like: *"This product looks like it could really help me"*; or *"That is a great concept. I can use that to make this work"*; or *"This seems to be a company that will answer my questions and fix my problem"*.

Type becomes the frame to display the content. It is the structure that presents the process. It is the channel that carries the message. Graphics are merely the embellishment to attract attention and explain the details. Everything must be focused on clear, accurate communication. College degrees for this industry in the bad ol' predigital days were often called graphic communication. That is what we do.

Bad type hinders communication.

If you set a piece in Times, double spaced, heads in all caps Times Bold, readers will be instantly turned off. Your design will be classed with all of that other bureaucratic output like IRS forms, legal notifications, class rules, and the like. If you make all of your headers blue, you greatly reduce the readability of those headers by lowering the color contrast. Setting in Helvetica causes the same reactions as Times, but adds that layer of cold disinterest.

You are looking for basic competence.

This discussion of excellence or ugliness misses a crucial understanding. There is a certain level of competence required by the reading public. The beginnings of typography that we covered last chapter are an assumed minimum. You cannot be seeking to produce award-winners. You are looking for basic competence. Once you achieve that, the award-winners come as a normal percentage of your output as a graphic designer. Without that basic competence, anything you do is doomed to failure before you start designing.

The message is not yours.

In most cases, you will have little choice about the actual writing used. The copy will be provided, usually on a ZIP disk, or attached to an email. Your task is to present that message clearly and accurately. Yes, part of the reason we get the big bucks ($50 to $100 per hour or more) is because we help the client craft her message. Yes, we often have to help him figure out what he is trying to say. Yes, writing and editing skills are a huge part of our careers. However, the message itself is usually supplied.

A basic typographic approach

So what we need is a basic set of tactics. There is a general procedure you will follow as you begin to set your type. It is a very fluid guide — one you are normally not conscious of using. However, as we begin this quest to superior type, it is good to look at some basic things you always need to do.

1.   Read the copy.

One of the most common mistakes for experienced designers is to be so sure of what is necessary that they do not bother to read the copy. May it never be among you. The copy is not a graphic element to be arranged prettily on the page. I know you are not that stupid, but I see the results of it every day in newspapers, magazines, and ads of all kinds. You are trying to present the copy for someone else. Their viewpoint and their needs must be primary.

There is no way you can design a typographic frame to set off the copy without reading that copy. You do not know what to emphasize. You do not know the real benefits to the reader. You are designing blind. You must read the copy. After reading, you need some time to digest it — no matter how boring, opaque, or disgusting it might be.

Reading the copy will inevitably bring questions to your mind. Write them down. Get answers before you start designing. I know you cannot believe how much space I am wasting on this. However, I can hardly believe how large a problem it really is.

2. Organize the copy

Usually the copy you receive will not have subheads, bulleted lists, sidebars, captions, or any of the typographic niceties that help the reader digest the materials easily. Often you will have to write them. Usually you will need to have these additions approved. Here are some things to consider as you begin to set up your document.

- What does the client want the reader to do? What is the closing action, the desired response? Call an 800 number? Visit the Web site? Email your client? Bring in the coupon? Visit the store? Remember the client as the best source for the product?

- Does the chosen format fit the need? Are they asking for a brochure when they need a catalog? Are they asking for a Web site with no commitment to staffing it? Does the brochure fit nicely in a standard file folder?

- What is the entry thought, the headline, the cover page? What is the major benefit to the reader? Why should they pick this product over the competition?

- What are the benefits? Is the product cheaper, better, faster, more convenient, more beautiful, stronger, longer lasting, more comprehensive, more effective?

- What are the disadvantages? How do you sell the product honestly without mentioning the flaws in its design? Remember, if you fool the customer, your client suffers. Angry customers are worse than no customers — for they'll tell their friends.

- Do you have all the information you need?

It is only when you have a firm grasp on what is important and what is required that you can effectively set up paragraph styles, pick fonts, determine layout, and so forth. This time spent organizing and prioritizing is the key to typographic excellence. This is the purpose of good type.

3. Develop a structure.

If the type is the most importance element of your designs — and it usually is — it is still very important to plan on its interactions with the graphic elements of the project. Again there is a series of questions to ask yourself.

1. Is there an existing layout or a company style manual? For larger corporations you may not have a lot of choice. A new company or client may need a style manual developed.

2. Are there existing graphics and logos? Often, supplied graphics and logos provide crucial clues to the fonts and typographic style needed.

3. How are you handling captions? Do you have to write them? These are the most important part of your copy. Clients often do not know this and leave them to you to write.

4. Do you need sidebars? Do you have to collect and produce them? If you are designing a new newsletter, your clients probably do not realize that the life of a newsletter is in its pictures and sidebars. You may have to use a book of quotes or jokes to get them jump-started. You will need to design an appropriate place to locate them.

5. How will you handle bylines and author's bios? Increasingly, bylines are expanding into a short paragraph at the end of an article with a little bio and an email address or phone. Authors are often very touchy about what you put here.

6. Are there footnotes or scientific equations? These are a real problem to add to professional page layout. If you do a lot of these, you may need to get something like Ventura Publisher or FrameMaker to handle them.

7. Are there ads? Do you have to produce them? In many projects, these are the income that pays for the production. The quality of the ads submitted is often very poor. To maintain the quality of your project, you may want to redesign many of the ads. Set up a structure to make that happen.

8. Do you control the size and placement of the ads? If you produce the ads, you have a lot more control. If they are supplied, you need to make sure there is a standard press kit to be given to the ad designers to follow. You may have to produce that — as well as develop the deadlines. Often salespeople will promise a specific location in the booklet — sometimes to several different ads in the same issue.

9. Is there a masthead, and do you have the legalese required? For magazines and newsletters, there are some legal requirements for the masthead — where the names and functions of the people involved are listed. For non-profits, make sure you have that legal copy that goes at the bottom about publication dates, delivery quantities, and so on.

10. Do you need a table of contents? This needs to be designed into your paragraph styles for easy collection. A space needs to be left. If you are doing a catalog, you may need to hide it to force the reader to wander. (If this is true, the goal is to get the reader to call the 800 number.)

11. How will you handle photo and art credits? Often these are spelled out by contract with the photographer or illustrator. Make sure you fulfill the contract and keep them happy. You may need to use them again. Do you need a list of illustrations? If so, make sure you have the artists' names and legal copyright data.

12. Is there a separate color section? These color sections are a real problem with many projects. They are determined almost entirely by economic criteria. Often it is hard to make them fit the actual layout needed. They are a jolt to the flow of the type. They must be handled very carefully. Readers do not like to be forced to reference other pages while they are reading.

13. Do you need a glossary or index? These are difficult to keep track of. An excellent index is very hard to write. Often it will be better to hire a professional.

14. Do you need tables? There are times when the size and quantity of the tables completely controls your layouts. If you have several large landscape tables, you may need to make a landscape booklet. Readers get very irritated if they have to turn the book 90° to read a table — usually simply skipping it.

15. Will articles be continuing onto other pages? If so, you may need to rewrite the articles or have them rewritten. Most readers do not go on to the continued page. I have seen statistics that suggest less than 25% do so. I think that is a little low, but it is not disputed that more than half will not go to the continued part.

16. Do you need diagrams, charts, or graphs? Do you have usable artwork to start from, or will you need to redraw from scratch? PowerPoint files are not usable here. Copies of copies usually won't work either.

17. Are you setting in multiple languages? If so, you may well need professional translation and proofing help. Do you need multiple columns, multiple pages, or multiple documents?

18. Is there a companion Web site? You need to keep the two projects tied into each other as much as possible. Even though the layout and writing style must be very different to meet the requirements of the media, they need to look like they are products from the same company.

19. Is there a lot of poetry? It has very definite and wildly varying layout and typographic needs. Will you need to go to a smaller page size to keep a single poem per page?

20. Are there many long quotes? If so, you will need a definite paragraph style to set them off while leaving them readable. Again, most quotes and poetry are skipped. It is usually the fault of the typesetter.

All of these questions and more need to be covered. More importantly, they should be covered before you even start making font and layout decisions. How can you set up a structure if you do not know the building blocks you will have to work with?

After you have answered these questions, you need to take time to reflect and ponder. You will never have a boss who likes paying you for leaning back on your chair with your feet on the desk. In fact, many of your best ideas will come while driving home or in the middle of the night. Creativity requires processing time. Make sure you allow for it.

4. Place the document in historical context.

This is probably true for books more than anything else. But, most businesses have that context also. Banks, like Wells Fargo for example, often like to tie back to historical roots — mythological though they might be. Insurance companies use historical ties to project strength and stability. For most marketing, you need to put the product into the current vernacular — adding that modern edge.

Designers can make major mistakes by ignoring historical roots. The change for Levi Strauss to that modern, slick look and Dockers™ has caused them major problems according to several observers. It turned out that the leather patch on the pocket, with the old drawing, was much more important than they thought.

Like I said, almost all companies like to look current and part of contemporary culture. The roots of that company are important, however. They can give you valuable clues about positioning their products and image. You are trying to create a unique feel and look for your client that distinguishes and separates the products and services from the competition. You will usually find yourself unable to avoid adding that modern touch. We are visual people very involved in our marketing culture. That always shows.

5. Pick your fonts.

By now you should have a good sense of the style, culture, and history of your client's company and product. Now you want to pick an appropriate style. If they are a hip, sophisticated company, you will need to use the latest style for that culture. If they have strong historical roots you may want to tie in directly to that. If they are aggressively modern, you may want to give an edge by using one of the Revolutionary fonts, like Bodoni.

The main thing to consider here is how you plan to make things readable. Readability is the number one virtue, no matter what the style of the font. If it is highly decorative, you are going to have to work hard to help readers around that reading difficulty.

Try to pick fonts with style. One of the major things you are selling, personally, is your own sense of taste. You must be working on your personal font library, picking fonts that fit your taste. You will need a wide variety to enable you to work with a wide variety of clients. However, every period of font design has examples of excellent design.

There is no such thing as a bad font.

There are fonts with very limited usage. But even Times is useful to sneak in and look like a bureaucrat when that is required. If you need copy to look like a typewriter, what are you going to use – Benguiat or Usherwood? Of course not! You will need American Typewriter or maybe even the dreaded Courier.

However, you will develop strong likes and dislikes for various font styles. This is good. That is why you are unique as a designer. Develop that sense of style into a personal expression of grace and elegance – strength and purpose – fashion and sophistication. Most designers are more like lemmings following the lead of the trendsetters. May it never be among you.

6. Shape the page to set priorities.

This is so obvious that I hesitated to cover it. However, you need to make sure you are emphasizing what you think you are emphasizing. One of the ways to do that is to make a proof and hang it on the wall.

Benguiat abcdefghji

Usherwood abcdefghijk

American Typewriter abcdefg

Courier abcdefgh

Back off fifteen to twenty feet so you can see the structure of the design. What do you see first? What is your eye drawn to? Gather some friends or colleagues and ask them those questions.

Also, make sure that you know what is important. You may have very different ideas than your client does. In many catalogs, for example, the only thing that matters is the 800 number. It is well known that if the reader will only call, a sale will occur most of the time.

In newsletters, the only thing that matters are the pictures. The copy makes the organization and the authors happy. The readers are usually looking for pictures of their friends, the new hires, the new babies, and so on. If the writing is really the most important, you are probably needing a book designed for comfortable reading as opposed to a newsletter filled with warm fuzzies used to build morale.

Sometimes the focus is far different than the client thinks it is. I know several people, for example, who subscribe to *The New Yorker* magazine for the cartoons and the sense of cosmopolitanism that it adds to the rural setting where they live. Fifty years ago, countless teenage boys talked their parents into subscribing to *National Geographic* for the pictures of the bare-breasted beauties found within. I know people who subscribed to *Wired* because it looked hip on their coffee table — they rarely read it.

7. The details really matter.

All documents have peripheral information: page numbers, running headers or footers, photographers' credits, and so on. To make a page sing, these must be carefully designed as well. A single jarring element can make the page look cheap or forced. These elements need to be carefully put in their place. They are subservient — but they are part of the presentation.

All headlines and subheads must be checked for badly kerned letter pairs. No font can cover them all. Even InDesign's Optical kerning misses some things. Also, you cannot optically kern scripts because the Optical kerning algorithm will force the letters apart.

The internal alignments of the page are critical to a professional look. The first-line indents, left indents of the lists, and left indents of the quotes and body heads normally are the same to provide continuity and tight organization. As mentioned, many demand that all horizontal rows of type line up exactly across the page. When you flip the corners of a finished book, the page numbers and margins should not move.

Professionalism requires perfection.

What many forget is that their competition is not the worst, but the best. Madison Avenue has made perfect typography the norm. Yes, there are signs that this is being lost. However, the reader will still be jarred when they hit a blaring typo. Inconsistency looks unprofessional. Sloppiness looks cheap. Even the grocery ads are carefully crafted to give the appearance of low prices — without compromising the image that the store sells quality products.

Although it is true that you can now find typos in national magazines like *Time*, *People*, *Style*, and *Cosmopolitan*, you do not find many. Maybe it is true that thirty years ago you found none (if there were any, the producer of the typo was often canned). However, this type of sloppiness always compromises the quality of the image of the document. This means it is less trusted. This is critical.

Even on the art proof you give the client to check layout, one typo per four pages is about the most that can be tolerated. More than that and the client will start wondering why you are being paid so much.

Well-crafted type inspires confidence.

One of the things that you must never forget is that the better your type is, the more the reader will believe the copy. Well-crafted type inspires confidence in the reader (and in your client). It is the bottom-line minimum of graphic design.

Where should you be by this time?

By now you should be cruising. Make sure you take the time to analyze your typesetting. How can you improve it? What would make it more readable? Are the important words emphasized? What does the reader see first in your composition?

DISCUSSION

You should be critiquing each others' typography. You have to train your eye. Without a critique, you will not see some of your most obvious and stupid mistakes. This takes a while, and it takes conscious effort.

Talk amongst yourselves...

Knowledge retention and thought provocation

1. What should a caption contain?
2. Why does copy sometimes need to be rewritten if it is continued on another page?
3. How should the type be noticed?
4. Why is it important to list the pieces you will need for the document (at least in your mind)?
5. What is the importance of historical context?
6. Why is well-done type necessary?
7. What is the standard for typography?

Typographic Norms

Concepts

1. Gutter

2. Gripper

3. Indents

4. Norms

5. Defaults

Learning the basic setup decisions needed to set type

Chapter Objectives:

By giving students a clear understanding of what different type styles are available, this chapter will enable students to:

1. pick appropriate margins, indents, and column settings
2. set paragraph styles that do not jar the reader

Lab Work for Chapter:

1. Complete the required Skill Exam #1.
2. Read chapter 13 for next week.
3. Work on projects.

CLEARANCE SALE!

The typical temptations to spend more money than you have! Plus luscious pictures and supposed cash savings.

 Logo/address

The dashed line is the actual trimmed size of the document.

BLEED   TRIM

Page 5

Page 4

Page 7
Page 6
Page 3
Page 2

Trimmed 8 page sig

Printer's spreads

Outside

Page 5	Page 4
Page 8	Page 1

Inside

Trimmed Area

Page 3	Page 6
Page 2	Page 7

Putting it together

One would think by now that we've covered all the pieces, finito. Not so! In fact, we have just gotten started. All we have done is talk about history, fonts, and type characters. We've talked briefly about the software used to produce graphics. A complete document has not been described yet, except for how and where to store it.

As we begin to put together complete documents, assembling graphics and type into a communication tool, we move on to the digital publisher's favorite programs: page layout. This is where the heart of graphic design beats. This is where designs become reality. Illustrations are nifty — sometimes spectacular — but they don't communicate specific messages very well. The copy contains the meat of the matter, but it won't be read without excellence in design to capture the attention of the reader. Even copy and illustrations put together are a waste without an overall design and direction. This is the fruition of typography.

Page layout software is where this all happens. It is true that FreeHand also has Style palettes, multiple pages, find and change, spell check, and so on. But, its main function is illustration, not page layout. Page layout applications are designed to assemble pieces, according to plan, with incredible control to shape and mold automatically. This is where indices and tables of contents are generated; where pages are numbered; where headers and footers can become strong graphic elements. Here different automatic page setups can be made available for editorial copy, display ads, chapter heads, regular columns, articles, stories, classified ads, and the like. This is where illustration and photography are added to accent the typography.

This chapter takes you through some of the basic page layout decisions, step by step. It's not a tutorial, but a conceptual analysis of how to produce documents, plus lots of tips and warnings. Basically, I am going to give you a relatively complete set of normals, along with the reasons why they became the typical solution. These will give you a place to start and a procedure to use as you put documents together.

Printing software

It is very bad practice to print from Photoshop or Illustrator. Even FreeHand has some real limitations in this area. They are designed to produce complicated graphics. Graphics are designed for insertion into page layout software for printing. Photoshop and Illustrator don't even do pages. For consistent reproduction, page layout software, with its printing controls, is essential.

Where do we start?

The defaults

The most powerful aspect of page layout software is its ability to prestructure the program so that much of your formatting occurs effortlessly. Defaults are those things that happen when you click a com-

Required skill exam

Nouveau riche design

A major digital design problem is nouveau riche design with its random fancies that eliminate all contrast and focus. The most commonly understood image of the nouveau riche is the Texas oilman with lots of money and no taste who gold-plates his Cadillac and the longhorns on the hood. In our arena, we are talking about designers who add every option: color, borders, boxes, shadows, rules, and so on — just because they can, with the click of a button. It is the natural outcome of software tutorials promoting graphic software as a fun video game. The attitude is pretty much, *"Hey, Mom! Look what I can do."*

mand, draw a shape, or type in copy without controlling its immediate outcome. Defaults control type, margins/columns, colors, everything page layout is capable of. There are three major areas that you have to control for efficient production: application defaults, document defaults, and interface setup. These control how the program reacts, how the specific document reacts, and what is available at a mouse click or keyboard command (in that order).

Interface control is one of the focuses of my other books: *Publishing with InDesign, Publishing with Illustrator and FreeHand, Publishing with Photoshop,* and *Digital Drawing.* FreeHand and InDesign, in particular, enable you to customize the interface to the place where your production is much faster and in greater control. Setting up your interface to fit your working style gives you a huge competitive advantage over those who don't do it.

One of the most important things you must learn about document construction is the principle of prepared production. You must have all the pieces, jigs, and templates readily at hand. One clear analogy is that of a fine art painter who squeezes appropriate amounts of carefully chosen colors on his palette. He makes choices from the hundreds of colors available based on appropriateness, harmony, compatibility, and physical characteristics. The artist is trying to avoid the chaos of color that turns an entire painting into mud. This is what almost invariably happens when too many colors are allowed on the same palette.

Fine artists control this by picking a specific media and limiting their palettes. Digital designers take control by designing within the limitations of a specific output technology and specifying their defaults. On the CD that came with this book, the Defaults Skill Exam is one of the most dreaded, because it cannot be passed without thinking or without a strong basic knowledge of the program. However, students unanimously say they learned more from this one skill than all the rest.

Application defaults

Application defaults are settings that are changed, with no document open, that affect every document opened from then on. The defaults available for control vary from program to program. You can tell which ones can be altered by the commands that are black in the menu bar of the application when no document is open.

You can determine the page size, margins, and number of columns. Plus, every attribute of type (font, size, leading, set width, color, small cap size, superscript size and location, subscript size and location, indents, spacing [word, letter, paragraph], alignment, style, OpenType options, and so on) can be predetermined, along with presets for text wrap, hyphenation, tool performance, paragraph styles, character styles, color swatches, and many other features. Needless to say, you have to know what all of these options are before you can effectively control them.

 If you do get lost and want to bring back the "out of the box" preset factory defaults, the easiest way is to close the application. Then you simply find the defaults document or documents and throw it or them in the trash. When you open the program again, all the defaults will be what they were when you first installed it. The defaults document will be called something clever like FreeHand Defaults, Toolbar Setup, or PageMaker Preferences. You will need your user manual to find the defaults documents to trash them. Many of the newer programs have several files to delete: custom shortcuts, toolbar setups, plus the basic Preferences files.

The idea is to set your application defaults so that you can begin working in a new document by simply typing Command/Control N, and then Return/Enter. When the document opens, everything should be basically set up for your working style. You can just start typing with your favorite font, using your favorite column setup, with a color palette that looks good to you, with Styles palettes you can apply confidently, and so on.

Document defaults

One problem is that you probably have a different setup for all your normal documents such as letters, invoices, newsletters, envelopes, and the like. The way to do this is to develop sets of standard document defaults (commonly called templates).

Document defaults are the same as application defaults except that they are changes made with a document open. These defaults can be made first thing with a brand-new, blank document, or they can be changed as needed during the production process. All you have to do is deselect everything and make changes with nothing selected and no insertion point active. This way you can customize the defaults to the specific project you are working on.

In my advanced page layout book, *Publishing with InDesign*, I discuss a strategy for setting up paragraph and character styles. These incredibly powerful settings allow you to save paragraph and character styles so you can format type habitually with memorized shortcuts. This is a goal you will want to pursue as you grow in your career as a designer. The Web equivalent is CSS (Cascading Style Sheets) – if you still have the fallacious notion that you can do type on the Web.

By taking control of your defaults, you can get to the place where your documents are formatted subconsciously. You think headline and your hand automatically presses the proper shortcut to format that paragraph into the style you have set up for your headlines. You think bold and your hand automatically double-clicks to select the word, adds the shortcuts to select the other words needed, and types the shortcut to make those words bold from your Character Styles.

By setting up your defaults to fit your personal working style, you can save phenomenal amounts of time. One example would be a simple twelve-page newsletter. The first time you set up a brand new newsletter, a simple black-and-white twelve-page document can take three to ten days or more. You will need to pick fonts, set up page layouts, specify ad sizes, design flags and mastheads, design master pages, and much more. By the time you are on the fourth or fifth month of the contract, your defaults should be so complete that you can now produce that same document in five or six hours — or less.

Templates

After you have set your document defaults, you have the option to save the document as a template. A template is a locked document that normally allows you to open only a copy of the template (keeping the original template on file, unchanged). As an example, I have and regularly use all of the following templates: my school degree letterhead, my business letterhead, my wife's church letterhead, and personal letters. There are templates for this book, one each for the other three books I am working on, school handouts, syllabi, outlines, the student newspaper, the department newsletter, lesson plans, invoices, purchase requests, bookstore orders, and several others. They have been developed over a ten-year period.

Templates are normally supplied documents when producing a corporate image package. You will need to set up a letterhead template, with a set of paragraph styles and custom designed margins. This is the only way a secretary will be able to use a document that forces him to type a letter without overlapping those carefully constructed spaces in the letterhead design. You will probably have to set up a Word template with carefully sized TIFFs for the graphics. You should do the same for fax cover sheets, second sheets, press releases, and so on.

Templates are extremely handy and save a great deal of time. Everything you do on a regular basis should be available as a template. You can literally open a document, place an insertion point, and start typing or importing copy and graphics. Everything will automatically appear as it is supposed to look.

For jobs that repeat only once or twice, it is usually easier to open the file for the most recent job completed and Save As under a new name into a new folder. Then, place your type insertion point, Select All (Command/Control A), and Delete all the old type. Then Delete the transitory graphics. This gives you a new, clean document that is set up exactly like the last one was. It is a little slower than a template, and for jobs that repeat often, it is too easy to open the wrong file and get the wrong defaults.

It is usually best to wait for the second or third version of a document to make the defaults. You will not catch all the intricacies of the design for the first few pieces. Usually, by the second or third time through, you have a set that you can use, without changes for a long time. Newspapers and magazines only change defaults rarely. Once or twice a decade is very frequent. For a large magazine, changing the setup is a rare event that can take nearly a year to accomplish.

The best method for producing any template is what I just mentioned. Open the finished document, delete all of the nonrepeating copy and graphics, and save as a template to a spot you can remember. If you find pieces that don't work as well as expected, just change the template as necessary.

A normal procedure

Setting defaults should become habitual. It should be the first thing you do on every job. Application defaults usually have to be set only once or twice a year, if you are the only person using the computer. If the computer is used in shifts, check these defaults at the start of every shift. You can save your own set of preferences files that you can use to replace the files changed last shift. This shifts the program back to your personal working pattern. Even if the company has a strict set of standard setups, all you have to do is keep a set of company defaults to return the programs to their setup before you leave for the day.

There is not a set of defaults that works company-wide. Everyone has a personal way of working. I have found that I can save great amounts of time by setting up my applications so they work better for left-handed operation. Just moving my docked palettes to the left side of the screen saves me about five percent in production time. All documents out of the box are set up right-handed. Since a much higher percentage of creatives are left-handed than in the general population (we are in our right mind), this is a major consideration.

Application defaults tend to change in broad cycles. This is especially true of font choices. There is a strong tendency to use your favorite fonts for most documents. The reason they are your favorites is that you think they are the best solution. As a result, your favorites get boring after a lot of hard use.

In addition, as you learn more, your tastes change. As you begin designing, you will change monthly. Gradually that will change to semi-annual and annual revisions of your basic style palettes. There is nothing good or bad about this, as long as you use well-designed classic fonts. The only reasons to change are fashion, personal style, or boredom. If you produce a thousand documents or more a year (that's about normal), changing your default font helps. (My final solution, personally, was to start designing my own fonts — but that is not typical.)

Taste and style are learned. We cannot teach how to be creative — you either are or you are not. Taste and style are a cultural thing that changes through time. Just remember *My Fair Lady.* You will have to study and observe to learn good taste. Taste and fashion are very different — somewhat like comparing a fox and a lemming. Of course, you are allowed to be as tasteless as you like. But please, don't show your junk to the general public.

When you open a new document, you should either use a template, copy styles from other documents (which can be simply loaded into your Styles palettes), or set new document defaults. Many students complain because setup takes so much time. "*Setting defaults takes longer than it would to produce the entire document,*" they whine. This happens primarily because they are slow, but it also has some truth.

Setting defaults does take some time, but it does not take nearly as much time as producing a document ad hoc, using local formatting. Just watch yourself as you try to make changes to your basic font decisions in an ad-hoc–formatted file. Of course, setting defaults saves time only in a mass production setting where you are producing a lot of documents. Let's say — maybe — a desktop publishing professional might need to set defaults?

Getting started:

Basic settings for every project

Many parameters have to be covered for every document. Many of these are set up as you go through the Preferences for your applications. You might want to consider setting your measuring system to inches or millimeters, for example. Only die-hard traditionalists use points. You should work in whatever measurement system works best for you. Every application has important decisions to be made in Preferences. To repeat, the point is to set up your applications so they work best for you.

Document size

Often document size is a given. Sizes for magazines and newspapers are commonly not under your control. They are limited by publisher choice or the printing presses used. If your printed product is going to be filed, it had better be 8.5"×11" (unless, of course, you are in Europe where you need A4, which is taller and narrower). If it must be inserted in a standard business envelope (4.125"×9.5"), it should be 4"×9" for easy (or mechanical) envelope insertion. If it is a business card, it must be 2"×3.5". The dimensions of the display rack control the size and orientation of many other projects.

If you have any options, make sure that you design for an economical cut out of the paper stock you choose. As you will discover, most of the printing papers do not come in letter-sized reams, or even in tabloid (11"×17"). These are called cut sheet sizes. Only the cheapest paper comes from the mill in cut sheet sizes. The rest are trimmed from parent sheets. Parent sheets are the paper sizes carried in stock by your paper distributor. When you pick a paper to use, find out what parent sheet sizes are readily available in your area. They are sold by the carton, unwrapped, about 1,500 sheets per carton.

I won't speak for sizes available outside the United States. Here almost every paper is available in 23"×35". However, for projects where you want or need to get outside the 8.5"×11" module, there are papers that come in 25"×38", 19"×25", 20"×26", 26"×40", and several other parent sizes. Check your paper suppliers' catalogs to find out what is available in your area.

 One of the first things you need to do when you get set up as a professional designer is to contact some of your local paper distributors. You will usually have several to choose from. You need to get a copy of their price book and swatchbooks of the papers you intend to use. Every printing process has different paper requirements, and it is important that you pick a paper stock that will work well and easily. In addition, there are tens of thousands of different papers. One of the major things you need to do as you establish your style is pick paper stocks that you like, that fit your sense of style. Picking your standard papers is as important as building your personal font list. This is an essential part of your personal style.

Trim size

The trim size is the size of the final document that the reader sees when reading it. The digital document must have the page size set to this trim size. The size of business card document, for example, is 2"×3.5" not more, not less.

Determining economical cuts

Calculating number out

This seems like a simple problem, but many simply have not seen it done. You divide a number into the width and the height of the parent sheet to come up with appropriate size measurements for a custom-sized project.

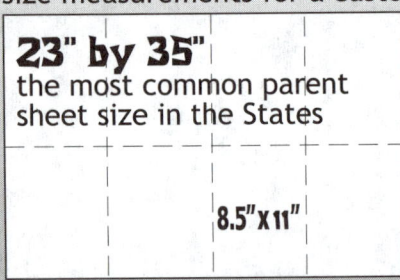

23" by 35"
the most common parent sheet size in the States

8.5"x11"

As we all know, 11" goes into 23" twice, and 8.5" goes into 35" four times. Two times four equals eight out — or we can get eight 8.5"x11" sheets out of a 23"x35" parent. However, 8.5 only goes into 23" twice and 11" goes into 35" thrice which gives us only six sheets out.

Often it is easier to divide the width and height by whole numbers to determine unusual sizes. For example, 23 divided by 3 equals 7.67", and 35 divided by 6 is 5.83". So, a little flyer or postcard set at 5.5"x7.25" would give me 18 trimmed out of a 23"x35" parent even with a full bleed.

Some interesting cuts out of 23"x35"

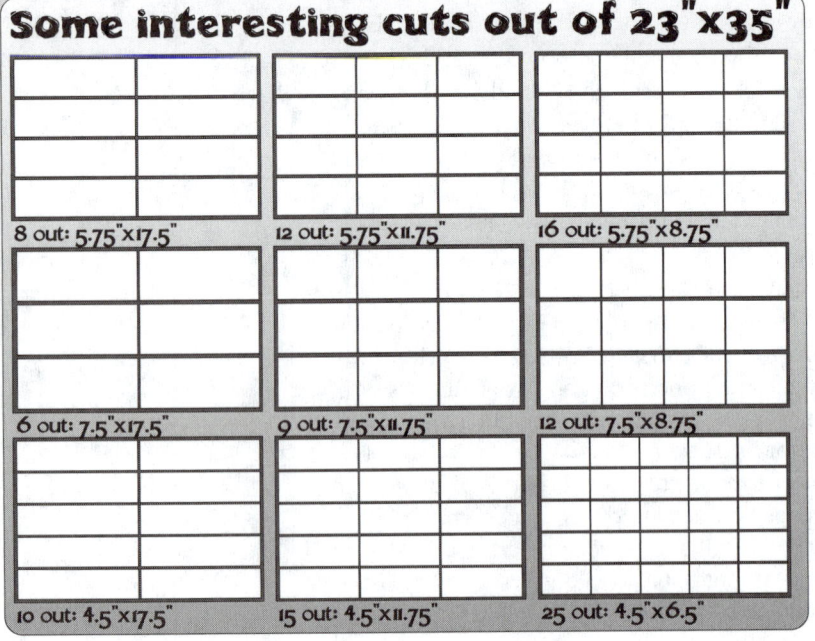

8 out: 5.75"x17.5"   12 out: 5.75"x11.75"   16 out: 5.75"x8.75"

6 out: 7.5"x17.5"   9 out: 7.5"x11.75"   12 out: 7.5"x8.75"

10 out: 4.5"x17.5"   15 out: 4.5"x11.75"   25 out: 4.5"x6.5"

There is a simple way to determine economical use of paper without a lot of waste. You divide the length by a whole number and the width by a whole number. Then you multiply the two numbers to get the number of cut sheets you can get out of a parent sheet. The numbers arrived at by division give you a maximum sheet size. Your projects need to be at least .125" smaller than the divided figures, on all four sides, to allow for trimming.

Economical cuts are very important. For example, if you only have 23"x35" sheets available, 9"x12" pages are a horrible cut. Instead of having eight 8.5"x11" sheets, you can only get four 9"x12" sheets (12 goes into 35 twice, and 9 goes into 23 twice). With 25"x38" stock, however, 9"x12" works well (12 goes into 25 twice, and 9 goes into 38 four times, for 8 sheets out).

Here are some interesting cuts out of 23"x35": 7.5"x11" gives nine out; 11"x11" gives six out; 7.5"x16" gives six out; 5.5"x17" gives eight out. You can get a four-page, 4"x9" rack brochure out of a standard 8.5" x11" sheet. If you come up with some really wild cuts or folds, check them out with your printer or bindery before you show them to your client. There are some terrific folds that have to be done by hand — but handwork costs a fortune! A quick conversation with your bindery can save you lots of money and uncounted heartache. There are times when that custom hand-folded job is the perfect solution. Normally, forcing the bindery to do a lot of handwork is one of the quickest ways to a blown budget.

 I remember a complicated brochure we received at one of the commercial printers I worked for. Normal folding would have been less than a thousand dollars. This is what we quoted. He came in with this amazingly beautiful fold, but we could not do it on our equipment, nor could anyone in town. We had to ship it to Mexico to be hand-folded. It cost an extra $35,000. This was a very determined designer with a client who had deep pockets. In most cases, it would just be a horrible problem and a monumental financial loss.

 Be especially careful when you find a gorgeous color or texture in your paper supplier's swatchbook. No distributor can afford to carry every color of every product line in stock. Many of the prettier colors and weights are only available as a mill order. Mill orders can require a minimum of five to fifteen cartons and a three-month wait. I'm not saying that you shouldn't use these gorgeous papers. I'm saying that you need to plan ahead to budget both the time and the money necessary for a mill order. Often it is a wonderful solution for your client's need for a stand-out brochure or presentation folder.

In the graphic at the bottom of the previous page, you can see some simple mathematical cuts of a typical 23"×35" sheet of paper. They are merely meant to give you something to think about. The 12 out: 5.5"×11.75 cut makes a beautiful 5.5" square four-page sig for a little booklet or brochure. It also makes an excellent 5.25" square booklet, full bleed. The 6 out: 11"×11.5 gives an eight-page signature of that same booklet, and the full 23"×35 sheet gives you a 24-page signature. Neat, huh?

Signatures

If you don't know what a signature is, here's a quick explanation. A signature is a sheet of paper with multiple pages arranged on it so that, after it is folded and trimmed, the cut pages end up in the proper order. They are commonly used and the norm for newsletters, booklets, programs, magazines, books, and newspapers. There are thousands of signatures. Each folding machine has some it can produce and some it cannot. Check this out with your printing company before you start designing. There is an eight-page sample on the top of the next page.

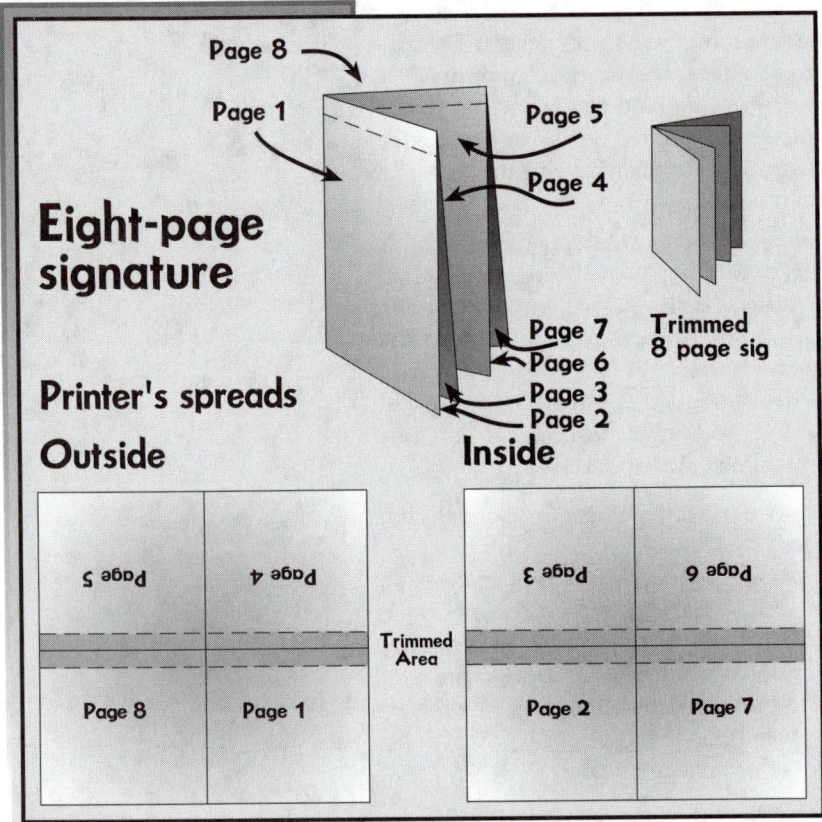

Eight-page signature

Page 8

Page 1

Page 5

Page 4

Page 7
Page 6
Page 3
Page 2

Trimmed
8 page sig

Printer's spreads

Outside

Inside

Page 5	Page 4		Page 3	Page 6
		Trimmed Area		
Page 8	Page 1		Page 2	Page 7

Bleeds

A bleed is needed when you produce a design where you really need the ink to go exactly to the edge of the paper. To produce a bleed, you make everything that reaches to the edge of the page extend one-eighth inch beyond the edge and then trim the piece back to finished size after printing. That's one-eighth inch, nine points, or a little less than four tenths of a millimeter (.375 mm to be precise).

You may discover that the printing company you are using asks for a different bleed. For my second book, *Digital Drawing* in the summer of 1999, my publisher's printer wanted a quarter-inch bleed because it fit their digital imposition better. However, that is very unusual. You will almost never go wrong in making the bleed exactly an eighth inch.

The power cutters used in the industry are the reason a bleed is necessary. These huge guillotine cutters slide their knives through stacks of paper several inches thick. They can cut 1,000 to 3,000 sheets at a time. These stacks of paper are called lifts. There are three problems.

1. The knife slides down at an angle with the edge remaining parallel to the cutting table. This side pressure requires clamps with a ton of pressure or more to hold the paper and keep it from sliding sideways with the blade.

2. Blades able to cut paper piled this high need to be very thick to avoid warping and breakage. The blades are of tool steel and about an inch thick. For strength, the edge is at a wide angle – nearly 30°. This wedge of steel pushes the cut paper

forward. Under the pressures necessary, this cut portion of paper pulls the lower sheets forward.

3. These lifts of paper commonly weigh several hundred pounds. It is a difficult physical challenge for the cutter operator to keep the paper stacked evenly. This difficulty is intensified by the fact that the sheets being cut start at 23"×35" or maybe 35"×45". As you can imagine, stacking sheets that are several feet wide and deep only adds to the problem.

The result of these limitations is that cuts are only accurate to plus or minus a sixteenth of an inch or so. Older equipment or hung-over operators can easily add another sixteenth. So, the eighth-inch bleed is often barely enough. With better shops, and care, you can get by with the sixteenth inch required by the machinery. But always ask first and constantly remind them.

The typical temptations to spend more money than you have! Plus luscious pictures and supposed cash savings.

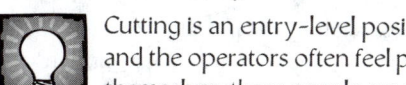

The dashed line is the actual trimmed size of the document.
BLEED **TRIM**

Cutting is an entry-level position and the operators often feel picked on. As soon as they prove themselves, these people are promoted out of the position. So, you are often dealing with slightly hostile, under-experienced personnel on top of everything else. They'll cut an eighth inch for the bleed, even if you have carefully set up a sixteenth, and gotten it approved. I've seen it happen dozens of times.

Bleed production problems and tips

The most common problem is seen when the submitted artwork goes exactly to the trim (the edge of the finished size). If you do that, you force your printer's people into four bad choices:

1. They can print it as submitted, leaving little slivers of blank paper on one or two of the four sides on almost every finished piece. These are caused by the cutter variables.

2. They can enlarge everything by 102%, or so, which changes the appearance and messes with the margins. The margins at the ends become smaller than the ones on the sides.

3. They can bounce the job back to you to be fixed, which can blow your deadlines. It also ruins your reputation with them and convinces them that they cannot trust you because you have proven yourself to be an amateur.

4. They can fix it themselves, which can be a couple of hundred dollars of nonbudgeted expense out of your pocket. (You don't really expect the client to pay for your stupidity, do you?) They charge $150 per hour, more or less.

The second major problem shows up when you have forgotten to tell them that there is a bleed when getting your estimate or price quote. A bleed requires oversized paper to enable trimming back to size. Commonly, a bleed bumps the paper costs up 25% or more. For letter-sized pieces you can only cut six-out instead of the normal eight-out from a 23"×35" sheet. The only other solution is to print it as submitted and cut it undersized. An eighth inch on all sides means your precious 8.5"×11" is cut back to 8.25"×10.75".

The worst scenario, as far as you are concerned, is to have the service bureau or printing company fix it for you. First, they charge from $75 an hour to $250 an hour for the privilege. Secondly, they will now assume that you are yet another of those incompetent desktop geeks who are the bane of their existence. Thirdly, because their focus is production, the way they modify for bleeds will almost certainly change your design in horrifying ways.

Finally, there is that subtle area that will probably catch many of you smug ones who are belittling all of the others in your mind. If you make your margins too small, not allowing for gripper and/or image area considerations, the printer will be forced to print it like a bleed regardless.

If you do not give them enough room to pull the sheet through the printer or press, the machine will crop your image — uncontrollably. The only solution is to print on oversized paper and trim it back to size. Many digital presses cannot feed oversized paper. These problems can completely eliminate all of your profit on the project and even cause a sizable loss, if the project is large enough.

Margins

This seems to be too obvious, but many ruin their job here. The most common amateur mistake is to make margins too small. All printers and presses need blank areas around the edges of the sheet. That area on presses is called *gripper*. The gripper is that blank portion of the sheet needed for the press to physically grab the paper and pull it through.

Ask the printer what their gripper is; it differs for almost every press. It's never smaller than a quarter inch and is often nearly a half inch.

On a digital printer, this is what necessitates the difference between maximum sheet size and maximum image size. You need to be very careful to stay inside the maximum image area. You can assume that you need to leave .375" margins, minimum. On digital printers and presses, you often need to leave half-inch margins (especially on letter-sized printers). Anything less than that is often priced as a bleed because your project will have to be printed on oversized paper and trimmed back to size. On a digital printer or press, this oversized paper is often simply not available. The maximum sheet size will not allow it.

In addition, margins are often a large part of style. If you are trying for the elegant look of an old book, for example, you will need huge margins. There are many formulas, but here's one you can try: 100% inside, 125% top, 150% outside, and 200% bottom (for example, 1.25" top; 1.5" outside; 2" bottom; and 1" inside). Many clients will not allow the margins required for the style, "Look at all that empty paper. I can't afford to waste that space!" You might want to keep some old books of the style to help persuade. Very high-priced products, or very cultured clients like the opera, commonly use one-inch to two inch-margins.

Conversely, if you need to convey cheap bargains – yard sale flyer, grocery store ad, and so forth – you need very small margins, gutters, and a lot of rules and boxes. You need to fill every open white space, making the page look like everything is crammed in to save money. Even if it is not strictly true, readers will think it is.

The point to remember is: the smaller the margins, the cheaper the look. This, of course, must be balanced with the absolute minimum, for everything other than business cards and maybe postcards, of the .375" margin. Quarter-inch margins look terrible after printing. The variables of trimming and registration always cause those tiny margins to be off-center.

Finally, for individual sheets of paper and single pages seen by themselves, the margins are normally even all the way around. For books and booklets, you need to leave extra room at the fold. For three-ring binder sheets, you usually need to leave .75" interior margins.

Columns

Be very careful with your column choices. It is easy to bore your audience to the point of reader rejection. Symmetrical layouts are the worst, unless you need to be formal and reserved. Two or four columns tend to divide in half. In this case, it is hard to make the reader's spreads

Page sizes

If you are serious about trying to make a beautiful page, check out Bringhurst. He has taken those considerations to ridiculous extremes, but a lot of good ideas can be found there. Subtle differences can make a large change to reader reactions.

look like they flow as one consistent unit. Symmetrical layouts with even numbers of columns are really only useful in rigidly formal setups. Even then they should be handled with care to avoid boredom.

An extremely common setup is five, six, seven, or more columns. These are used as grids that can be readily divided into different column structures within the same page to keep things interesting. A seven-column grid can reserve a column for sidebars, and then have stories that are six single columns, three double columns, two triple columns, a double and a quadruple, and so on. Just set up your guides and make the text blocks as needed.

Generally, the more asymmetrical and the more open you can lay out the piece, the better. Of course, you can go crazy and make things totally illegible. Modern style tends to be chaotic, splashy, and overly complex (think Disney™). But your innate taste and discretion should keep these tendencies in check. The problem, of course, is that taste and discretion have become rare. I know you are working hard to learn taste and reduce that trend – thank you.

The basic concept is that we have all become extremely used to "normal" layouts. In fact, these factory default layouts tend to put your piece in the bureaucratic camp or worse. Plus, we are all graphically

NEWSBEAT

TECHNOLOGY NEWS FOR THE CREATIVE PROFESSIONAL

Vio Grand

Applied Graphics Technologies and Vio Worldwide Ltd. have announced an alliance that will result in the creation of a global digital media asset management service. The service, M-Cast, will allow users to build, update and access a database of their digital media assets efficiently and economically from anywhere in the world over Vio's secure network. With corporate brand owners and their graphic arts service providers in mind, M-Cast brings AGT's Digital Link asset management technology and database experience together with Vio's Digital Graphics Network. M-Cast users will pay a monthly service fee, and they will also pay to store their assets on a cents-per-MB per month model.

Vio is also entering into a relationship with Kodak Polychrome Graphics. The two companies are coming together to promote the benefits of remote proofing. To that end, one free year of Vio's global managed network service will be bundled with any Kodak DCP 9300/9500 desktop color proofer purchased before the end of 1999. The Vio bundle includes Vio's two-channel ISDN service, worldwide access through a Vio toll-free number and 300MB of free file transfer per month. After using the 300MB allowance, users will pay only $.40/MB to transfer files. (AGT, www.agt.com; Kodak Polychrome Graphics, www.kpgraphics.com; Vio, www.vio-dgn.com)

Objects-oriented

Whether you're looking for an image of a birthday cake or dental floss, it can probably be found in Corbis' first royalty-free image catalog completely dedicated to objects. *Objects Collection 1* includes every image from its 16 Objects Collection CDs. Each image comes with a handmade clipping path, which allows it to be dropped into a layout without a halo effect. A comping disc lets you search for a specific image quickly and easily, but it might be more fun to spend some time thumbing through the print version, enjoying the images. (Corbis Images, www.corbisimages.com)

Free software is cool

Nikon announces a scanning software upgrade for its Super Coolscan 2000 and Coolscan III film scanners. The NikonScan 2.5 package takes color management to a new level, increases ease of use and adds Altamira Genuine Fractals 2.0 LE scaling technology to the bundle. NikonScan 2.5 ships "in the box" with all new Super Coolscan 2000 and Coolscan III models, and previous users can download the new package free of charge from www.nikon techusa.com. Although the Altamira software is not included in the free download, the site links to the Altamira Group Web site for information on the product. (Nikon, www.nikonusa.com)

Font Savior

A new technology from DiamondSoft promises to standardize the way applications save font information within documents and enable accurate automatic font activation. Font Sense technology allows print publishers to realize a seamless workflow: to open a document in any application, have the correct fonts activate with it and print it without problems. Font Sense makes this happen by saving a precise font specification with documents. This includes information such as the name of the font, its foundry and its version number. In addition, it also contains information about the font's outlines, width tables and kerning tables. With all this information available to it, Font Sense knows to activate the correct font. Font Sense technology is built into Font Reserve 2.5 and Font Reserve Server. (DiamondSoft, www.fontreserve.com)

3-column layout

As you can see, there are two one-column stories, a two-column story, and a story that is one column but the width of two columns. All of this adds interest (and keeps the stories separate).

jaded. As a result, it is necessary to go a little out of the ordinary to allow the reader to even see the piece — boring layouts are invisible and the readers simply skip over them.

 Be very careful of using cheap clip art and the templates supplied with business software. Art and layouts from sources like Word or CorelDraw are instantly recognizable, and subconsciously cause most readers to reject your work as bad quality, bureaucratic, official, or any number of similar horrible epithets. Even the templates that come with PageMaker are boring. My personal recommendation for stock art is Artville or Dynamic Graphics for drawn illustrations. In addition, there are now large supplies of excellent stock photos on royalty-free CDs from companies like Eyewire. All of us use stock art. The important thing is to purchase high quality art, with unlimited use, in current styles. This needs to be a standard yearly line item in your budget. You should plan on $1,000 or more, if possible.

The problem, of course, is that wildly different designs are not read either. There are some exceptions, like the grunge fad; the graphics for *The Practice*; a lot of MTV, Fox, or ESPN2; and so on. Take a look at some of the Web sites and traditional marketing for the Xtreme sports. However, most of these designers frankly admit that their work is illegible. They are selling visual image and rebellion. The very illegibility and destruction of the norm is what calls their readership to their work. It wouldn't work for more conservative products. (And the dirty little secret is that most of these rebellious images are from companies that are unreliable financially — there are not many MTVs, *Wired* magazines, or shows like *The Practice*.) You need clients who pay well and on time. Most of them are more than a little conservative.

Gutters

Gutter is one of those terms that you have to watch. It means different things in different places. Sometimes it means the interior margins of a reader's spread for a book or booklet. Most often it means the vertical gap between two columns. Column gutters provoke many strongly held opinions.

The general rule is that a gutter should be larger than a pica (.167") and smaller than the margins. For most purposes, one-quarter inch works well. The guiding principle is that gutters need to be small enough so the columns of a story hold together as a text block, yet the reader must be able to easily read down the column without jumping the gutter to the neighboring column. The reading order and visual organization needs to be clear.

If there is any tendency to read straight across, from column to column instead of vertically down the column, your readers will get confused. If confused, they flee (turn the page to something else). If you decide that you need narrow gutters, you should separate the columns with a thin (or lightly colored) vertical rule. The only problem with rules, boxes, and borders is their tie to cheapness and low quality because they eliminate all white space, as mentioned earlier. In general, for readability, the use of vertical rules necessitates wider gutters than normal.

Smart, curly, or typographer's quotes

Automatic typographer's quotes are one of those things that sounds good in principle but works less than perfectly in practice. It is important that you learn to access the characters without the smart quotes option turned on. The real problem is the use of inch and foot marks — 8.5"×11". They can get curly without you noticing. Curly inch marks are a far worse typo than straight quotes. If you have to enter measurements, it is usually better to shut off typographer's quotes and enter them by hand. The keyboard access on the Mac and the PC keyboard is different. InDesign has a keyboard shortcut that allows you to toggle typographer's quotes on and off.

Guides

Guides are the equivalent of the nonrepro blue lines in traditional pasteup. They are the non-printing lines that enable designers to line up graphic pieces to keep their designs tidy. More than that, it is assumed that text blocks will line up with each other; that graphics will line up to an assumed grid; that headlines and subheads will relate to that inferred grid. Many designers get very tense if you do not line up the bottoms of the columns as well as the tops. InDesign and Quark have vertical justification, but this causes spacing inconsistencies, however subtle.

Especially when you are learning your craft, shut the guides off on a regular basis (there's a shortcut). Until you get used to the fact that these lines appearing in your design on the screen do not print, you will tend to leave room for them. As a result, many of your white spaces will be surprisingly large. This is a terrible problem with programs that surround text and graphics with nonprinting lines, like InDesign and Quark. Proofing helps a lot, but simply turning off the guides and frame edges occasionally will tend to keep you on track.

One of the major aspects of design excellence is internal alignment. In other words, excellent designs have countless places where type and graphics line up with each other. You need to be consciously aware of these relationships, at all times. It is part of that

great virtue — consistency. However, it goes beyond that into structure. Every time you are aware of looking at graphic design that really pleases you, consciously check out the internal alignments. You'll be amazed.

Coupled with guides are the snap-to controls mentioned next. In addition, most programs have an Align palette where you can make selected objects align by the left, center, or right horizontally, and the top, middle, or bottom vertically. You can also produce even distribution of objects using the same locations.

 About alignments: One of the most common flaws with nonprofessional design is the tendency to have multiple alignments on the same page. This can be done if you are careful. However, in general, items should be all aligned left or right or centered. Different alignments on the same page have to be structured carefully to avoid reader confusion.

"Snap-to" controls

All professional programs have snap-to commands. In all of them, the principle is the same. When you move an item within a specified distance of a guide (or grid or ruler), that item jumps to exact alignment with the guide, ruler, grid, or whatever. Many designers seem to think this is the greatest thing since white sliced bread. Others (like myself) aren't so sure.

In fact, snap-tos often get in the way. Some designers use them very occasionally when creating something with a tight, regular, repeating grid structure. However, the biggest problem with digital design is the computerized, overly perfected images. Snap-to guides are one of the main culprits.

If you use snap-tos a lot, be careful to introduce randomness in judicious quantities. It is extremely easy to produce lifeless boredom with page layout set on autopilot. If you are compulsive about vertical justification, where both the tops and the bottoms of columns line up on a grid, then snap-to rulers are for you. You can easily set up these programs so type baselines snap to a ruler based on your leading. Vertical justification does add inconsistent paragraph spacing. You must solve these problems. Be careful to keep your brain from slipping into neutral as the text flows in so automatically.

 If you cannot move your graphic or text block into precisely the correct position — if it keeps jumping around, out of your control — it is snapping to something. Turn off the relevant snap-to and you will be able to move it exactly into position. It will also help a lot if you enlarge to 400% or more. Sometimes you think things are jumping and you are just moving them less than a pixel. In other words, the low resolution screen image can jump even when things are lined up perfectly. You will be surprised how often InDesign's 4,000% enlargement comes in handy. Even in FreeHand, where you can enlarge 25,600%, I regularly use it all.

Master pages

Some might think that this fantastic ability requires at least a larger subhead, or something. Really, all that master pages do is place repeating elements automatically. Adobe suggests the concept of a background image, and it's not a bad one. Unless you have a large project or a repeating task like a monthly magazine, a journal, or a large newsletter, master pages are only used to place automatic numbering markers for page numbers.

All page layout software allows for multiple master pages, plus InDesign can have parent/child master pages where the child is based on the master (just like in Paragraph and Character Styles). I don't know how many master pages are available (and don't care). It's at least 256 masters — far more than you'll ever need.

The number of masters available might be important if you design a two-hundred–page monthly magazine or a huge daily newspaper, but most of us do not. In fact, multiple master pages are really only help-ful to designers who work with projects that repeat monthly, such as newsletters, magazines, reports, and so forth.

That being said, I use master pages more every year. They are indispensable for newsletters, magazines, programs, annual reports, or any kind of multiple-page book or booklet. I am using two, plus a child of one of them, for this book.

Automatic page numbering

PageMaker and Quark both have shortcuts to insert automatic page numbers. InDesign does page numbering in a method more reminiscent of a word processor than anything else. There is a menu command under the Layout menu: Layout >>> Insert Page Number. You simply use that command or shortcut (with an insertion point flashing in the text block you desire) wherever you want the page number to appear. If you do it on a master page, the page number will appear on all pages where that master page is applied (or its child). If you insert a page number on a normal page, the number will be on that page only. It will always be correct, no matter how many pages you add, delete, duplicate, or rearrange.

Quark and InDesign both offer automatic "continued from" and "continued to" numbering. These are used when you are forced to continue an article in a different portion of a magazine. However, you shouldn't do that regardless, except under duress. All studies suggest that the vast majority of copy continued on another page is not read. Less than half of readers actually go the continued copy — at best.

You are far better off to make it a strict policy to redesign as necessary to eliminate any continued articles. On those rare occasions where it is necessary (like magazines), you'll normally have to go to the online help to remember, anyway. Even magazines do this less and less. They have realized that you can simply delete the rest of the article. No one reads it anyway.

Table of Contents and Index

Here are two more capabilities like master pages. If you need them, they are critical. If you don't — yawn! Professional page layout software can do this. Tables of contents are created from information stored in the Style palette. Indices are created by hand-flagging the entries and then automatically gathering them into an index.

Tables of contents are used quite a bit. Programs, newsletters, magazines, books, and so on all need tables of contents. You simply collect the heads and subheads into a new story and then reformat as desired. The TOC paragraph styles can be generated automatically. All you need to do is fix the formatting.

 Indexing is a very difficult, specialized skill. In most cases, if an index is needed, a pro is needed to write it. A poorly written index is worse than no index. It infuriates the reader.

These features are geared toward the publishing end of our industry — books and magazines. They are specialized abilities that most of you will rarely use. When you are looking for software, make sure that you have the features you need. However, the most important feature is ease of use for your specific projects. If every job is different, you need flexible software that makes spontaneity easy. If most of your jobs are repetitive, you need automation and specialized features. Buy the plug-ins that will save you enough production time to pay for themselves.

Tables

Here is a radical change from my earlier books. InDesign 2 and QuarkXPress 5 both do tables exceedingly well, at this point. Quark has a table tool and InDesign's offering is inserted in a text block. The only point to be made here is that these are the only two options to make tables that are set in type. PageMaker still has Adobe Table, but it is a standalone program that has several weaknesses.

Some table design considerations

- Keep it light! Tables can very easily become cluttered with borders, colors, and tints.
- To make ridiculously long headers fit into narrow columns you often need to go to six- to eight-point type. Many like to rotate the headers, but this causes horrible readability problems.
- In the table cells where you regularly have to put long paragraphs, make sure that hyphenation is turned off.
- Above all, remember that colored backgrounds always lower contrast and make the copy harder to read. Do not make the mistake of putting colored backgrounds or tints behind your most important copy. Make the important stuff pop by leaving the blank paper there.

Sidebars

In general, sidebars are a wonderful idea. As mentioned before, sidebars contain interesting data that is not essential to the document. They add reader interest. They add graphic interest. They alleviate boredom. They contain graphic and typographic aberrations that are added merely for aesthetic reasons.

Some sidebar design considerations

Sidebars need to have definite, sharp contrast to normal body copy. You can do this with different fonts, different alignment, tint boxes, borders, or all of the above. Sidebars (for all of their usefulness) must be lesser than normal body copy. Tint boxes or background graphics lessen contrast enough to be very helpful here. Sidebars are also stored at the sides of the page (duh). In this position, they greatly help in making newsletter or book pages asymmetric and more interesting visually.

The sidebar should be the frame that shows off the normal copy. My sidebar location in this book gives the body copy you are reading more impact. By now you probably don't even see those tints, type, and graphics, but they are still working! Compare this textbook with one that doesn't have such a graphic device.

A final word on consistency

We've called this a major virtue in digital publishing, and this is true. On the other hand, I am not referring to rigidity and absolute rules. While it is certainly true that there is a strong set of normals in graphic design, no design will be effective unless you break some of those rules. The key comes in clearly acknowledging how your readers are reacting and the making specific breaks to the norm to increase their understanding by making specific points.

The callout or pull quote style, for example, is a severe break in the normal flow of the text. It is used to jolt the reader's eye into seeing the specific concept that is most important to the editorial sense of the story at that point. If used too often, they become part of the norm and are seen no more (on a conscious level, at least). Devices like pull quotes work best when they are found sparsely.

The same is true of drop caps. If they are used as intended – to indicate the starting point of an article, section, or chapter – they are very powerful. If they become a mere graphic ornamentation following every major subhead, the impact is lost.

Styles and the basic format settings are used to provide that consistent base from which the graphic devices stand out to make those important specific points. One of my personal problems, for example, is what I would euphemistically call an evolving consistency. Mardelle, my copyeditor, regularly has to rein me in. If she doesn't, the basic style of my books gradually changes every chapter until the last chapter is radically different from the first.

This is why I basically pooh-poohed master pages. It is not that they are not wonderful tools of design and consistency. It is simply that a forty-eight-page booklet with twenty master pages is not going to be very consistent. You must add master pages only when made necessary by the content.

This is a very delicate balance. Graphic design is a very delicate thing, even though we are often using sharp contrasts with massive visual impact. Too much or too little can quickly destroy the flow of communication. This is the key:

All that matters is clear communication!

Standard usage

One of the things you quickly discover as you begin designing is that readers have very strong ideas about what is acceptable and what is not. These standards are what I call norms. They are type usage parameters that almost everyone assumes.

We have mentioned that the only way you can keep your designs from being boring is to break at least a couple of rules in every design

– and that those departures from the norms must be done intentionally and with good reason. However, this assumes that you know the normal assumptions that everyone is using. So, what I want to do now is give you a list of some of these norms. You will find that many of them are quite rigid. When I wrote my first book, for example, I was using a font with a small x-height and extra leading built in. I decided to set it in eleven-point type with twelve points of leading. My publisher bounced that, forcing me to use the standard 10/12.

Typographic norms

Business cards

These standards are pretty rigid. Business cards must fit into a standard business card case or they will be thrown away. Having said that, one of the nice things you can do to make a card stand out is to make it 4"×3.5" folded down to 2"×3.5". This gives you a place to present a lot of copy or even a nice map.

The norms are: 2"×3.5"; .25" margins on all sides; logo .75" at the largest dimension; company name 18–30 pt; name 8–11 pt (often bold); title 6–8 pt (often italic); telephone 9–12 point (often bold); address 6–8 pt; motto 8–12 pt (often italic). The email address is as large as possible (because of its length), but no larger than the phone number.

 Remember, the point of a business card is normally the phone number — or maybe the email address. That is why most people keep a card. So the person's name and the phone number are the two most important pieces of type on the card, and should be seen first.

Letterhead

8.5"×11", .5" margins or larger (unless it bleeds); logo smaller than the business card; company name 14–24 pt; address 7–10 pt; phone 8–11 pt; motto 9–14 pt (often italic) — it's very important to design the letterhead so a letter looks good on it.

It should look empty without a letter.

One of the major considerations for a letterhead is whether or not the secretary is going to use it. If you do not provide a template (and often hands-on troubleshooting), he or she will simply ignore it. Increasingly, of course, the letterhead is simply a template that is printed out as needed. Even so, you need to carefully consider the needs and desires of the person who will be using the template.

Envelopes

#10 business (4.125"×9.5"); logo 12–18 pt; address 6-8 pt. These should be very subdued. You will have enough trouble getting that envelope through the gauntlet of the table and trash can when it arrives in the mail. Make it look like personal communication, as much as possible. By the way, hand-addressed envelopes have a far higher rate of return and are read by far more readers.

Newsletters

The paper size varies widely for newsletters. Just make sure that it is 8.5"×11" if it will be filed. Make sure the size is acceptable to the post office also. Because of the wide variation in size and style, the following are very approximate norms: flag or logo 36–99 pt; headlines 24–36 pt; first subhead 14–21 pt; second subhead 10–14 pt; body copy 9–12 pt; masthead 8-12 pt. But, the almost absolute standard for body copy is 10/12 either left or justified (unless the newsletter is getting federal money for senior citizens; then the body copy has to be 12/14, legally).

Increasingly, newsletters are delivered via email. This is a very dangerous practice. Newsletters' prime purpose is not the articles. Readers are looking for the news, the pictures of friends, the ads, and so on. Online newsletters are very tricky, and very difficult to write well.

Keep it intentionally varied.

Here's a little review. As you format type and lay out the document, consciously prioritize the copy to organize it. What is the most important copy on the page (from the reader's point of view)? What is the most important copy on the page (from the client's point of view)? Often, for example, important information from the client's viewpoint is different from what the reader will choose to read.

If the executive secretary tells you that attendance at meetings is a real problem and he wants that emphasized, this does not mean that the reader will be drawn to read the newsletter to get that information. She's reading the newsletter because she is interested in the background of next month's speaker. So, in a gray sidebar of trivia and required legalese, a strong little graphic splash giving the meeting time, date, and location will serve as a quick attention-getter without competing with the main headline and photo of the speaker on the front page.

The important things are simplicity and clarity.

Where should you be by this time?

By now you should be cruising. Make sure you take the time to analyze your typesetting. How can you improve it? What would make it more readable? Are the important words emphasized? What does the reader see first in your composition?

DISCUSSION

You should be discussing normals in type. You have to train your eye. Without careful observation and training of your eye, you will not see some of your most obvious and stupid mistakes. This takes a while, and it takes conscious effort.

Talk amongst yourselves...

The important thing to keep in mind while you are prioritizing is the need for simplicity and clarity. Too many attention devices function much like the expert roundtables on CNN: that many people talking at the same time is very irritating and causes many of us to switch channels. The same is true of multitudinous headlines, subheads, and specialized headers all competing for your attention on the same page.

Even if it is true that all of these pieces are important, the reader needs help to sort through the chaos. Sometimes you have to arbitrarily assign priorities simply to make the piece readable. This is so even in logo and stationery design. In a business card, for example, which items are most important? To understand that, you need to figure out why you keep a business card in the first place.

Is the logo most important? Maybe, but that is not why you keep a card. You need to be able to instantly recognize that card as belonging to the business you are looking for, but why are you looking for that card? If you are thinking clearly, you'll see that you keep the card for the phone number, email address, and office address — in that order, usually. The most important information on the business card is the telephone number (coupled with the name of the person, so you can call them by name when they pick up the phone). The email address is increasingly important, and the Web site URL might generate some sales. The physical address is rarely why you keep a card. Once you have been there (if you ever go there), you can remember where it was. You need the phone number and email address for reference.

You will need to deal with all of these considerations, and much more, as you begin to design projects. Do not be overwhelmed. Just keep at it, and look at what is around you every day. Your sense of style will take a while to develop. But it may be the most satisfying thing you ever do.

Knowledge retention

1. What is a bleed?
2. Why are defaults crucial to page layout?
3. Why would you use a sidebar?
4. Why must business cards be 2"×3.5"?
5. How do signatures save money?
6. How do you determine an economical cut?
7. How can a bleed ruin your budget?

Chapter 13

Forms, Rules, and Tables

Concepts

FRAMING THE TYPE

Learning the various capabilities to add graphic structure to your typography

Chapter Objectives:

By giving students a clear understanding of what different typographic capabilities are available, this chapter will enable students to:

1. add leaders when appropriate
2. add paragraph rules to a paragraph style
3. create a table for a document

Lab Work for Chapter:

1. Complete the required Skill Exams.
2. Read chapter 14 for next week.
3. Work on projects.

Tabs

X: 1.8472 in   Leader: Align On:

0   1/2   1   1/2   2   1/2   3   1/2   4

#1   »   #2
#3   #4
#5   #6
#7   »   #8

1   2   3   4   5   6

Paragraph Tabs

Alignment: ↕ Right
Position: 6.5
Fill Character: |

Apply

OK   Cancel

Paragraph Rules

Rule Above   ⬍   ☑ Rule On

Weight: 0.5 pt ⬍   ☐ Overprint Stroke
Color: (Text Color)   ⬍
Tint: ▾
Width: Column ⬍   Offset: 0.0764 i
Left Indent: 0 in
Right Indent: 0 in

OK
Cancel
☐ Preview

PARTY SUPPLIES FOR SPRING GRADUATION

PRODUCT NUMBER	QUANTITY	DESCRIPTION	UNIT PRICE	EXTENDED PRICE
24735	3	Industrial strength, 400 amp, handheld blenders with chopping blades	$249.95	$749.85
17356	48	Tank-style garden sprayers, 2 gallon	$19.95	$957.60
46542	7	Tinting sets, aniline dyes, 18 colors	$24.50	$171.50
52394	288	Boxes of gelatine	$.25	$72.00
71492	48	Lucite face shields	$15.00	$720.00
			TOTAL (ALL TAXES INCLUDED)	**$2670.95**

Words are the main thing we do.

We have talked a little about how word processors are not professional software. However, they are an essential part of the production process. Even though the persons keying the words into the word processors may not be design professionals, they should certainly know the basics of typesetting. The problem is that most of them do not.

A certain percentage of you will end up working for firms that are large enough to have a typesetting department. For most of you, the copy you get will only be as good as what the typist has been taught (and most of them have been taught typewriting). A sizable portion of the copy you receive on disk will be littered with double spaces, double returns, double hyphens, headlines centered with the space bar, improper am and pm, all caps, underlined heads, and other typical typewritten abominations. You will find spaces before punctuation, spaces before returns, multiple spaces or tabs for first line indents, and so on.

In addition, much of the copy will suffer from typos, obvious grammatical errors, and inaccurate content. This is one of the main reasons why you should read the copy early in the design process. This is normal. Do not get upset — fix the problems and become a hero.

A word on what we fix

In most cases, as graphic designers, we do not have editorial control. What this means, in practical terms, is that you repair only the horribly obvious grammatical errors and all the spelling. The rest you simply warn the client about. If he tells you that is the way it is supposed to be, bite your tongue, and do it the way he wants it.

Part of this is because we speak a living language. What this means, again in practice, is that things are constantly changing. In this day and age, usage is changing extremely rapidly. In many cases, there is no absolute wrong or right. The only sure guide is this: that the customer is always right — but it's part of your job to make sure that the customer knows the alternatives.

The customer is always right —
after she has heard the options.

When you are paying the bills, you get to do it your way. Until then, it is done as the client requests. Our task is to present the copy readably, with no errors, as the customer approves, on time, and within the budget. Having said all that, our tools are awesome.

This is no typewriter

Editing tools

The basic tool is the text tool (which I'm sure is a major revelation to you). We covered many of these basics. Much editing is done via the Clipboard. Text is highlighted and then cut or copied and pasted to its new location.

Often you can save a great deal of time by copying repetitive elements and then pasting as needed. For example:

Here .... $ _____

The dot leader, $ and space .... $ _____

Is copied .... $ _____

For menus .... $ _____

Fish $1.45

Salmon $9.95

Squid .... $ .35

As you may have noticed, there are two little tricks here that you might not be familiar with. The first is the entire concept of leaders. A *leader* is a repeating character (or group of characters) that fills the space between the last character before a tab and the first character after a tab. These are mainly used for forms, menus, indices, and tables of contents. They are meant to help you read easily across a page when you have elements that are widely separated. However, their use goes far beyond that.

 The second little trick in the leaders above is that the point size of the leaders is controlled by the point size applied to the tab (and often the character before the tab). In the samples above, the space before the tab and the tab itself have been selected and resized to 8-point to make the leader lighter, thinner, and more delicate.

But we are getting ahead of ourselves. We must have a little discussion of paragraphs, alignments, and tabs before we can continue.

The basic unit

Paragraph control

Remember, a paragraph is defined by the Return key. Every time the Return key is hit, a new paragraph begins. This is one of the major characteristics of word processing. If you need to make a line break without ending the paragraph, you must use the *soft return* (the Shift and Return keys). This is how you "break for sense." On very narrow paragraphs, you might have to place a soft return at the end of every line to make it read easily. If you hit a hard return instead, all the space-before and space-after choices will affect every line. The first line indent will also apply to every line.

Alignment

The next thing to be dealt with is alignment, orientation, or justification. We have four to seven choices – flush left, flush right, centered, justified, plus force justified in PageMaker, and justified quad left, justified quad right, and justified quad center in InDesign. These determine how the paragraphs will sit within the column. Many customers request justified copy because they think it is incredibly neat that you can have both edges of a column line up automatically. In many cases, you need to remind them, gently, that justified copy is often less readable. This is particularly true if you are using relatively narrow columns.

One of the major advantages of InDesign is its multiline justification which enables beautiful and very readable justification. You will use justified copy so much more in InDesign that the four flavors of justification become very nice. InDesign is the only program with good justification, however.

For the others, especially the graphics programs of FreeHand, Illustrator, and Photoshop, justification is really not an option. Even PageMaker is poor and Quark is horrible. In those applications, it is usually considered almost mandatory to use flush left body copy (if the client will allow you to do so).

Because all the others justify line by line, the word spacing varies greatly from line to line. Smooth type color is impossible when some lines have word spacing of an eighth of an inch and some a half inch. Only InDesign keeps everything smooth. For the other software, avoid justification entirely, if possible.

Optimum line length

The main factor affecting readability is line length. The basic rule is 30 to 50 characters. But this varies widely according to the width and tracking of a font. Roughly the range of readable line length is a third to half the point size of the body copy in inches. So for 10-point type, the column width would be somewhere between 3.3 inches and 5 inches.

The optimum is probably close to forty percent of the point size in inches, but you actually have to look at the font, set a few paragraphs, and make a subjective decision. That is why we are called designers and typesetters. Our subjective decisions are some of the most important things we do.

Readability

As just mentioned, justified copy can be hard to read. Other things that make reading difficult include: type too small; leading too small; tracking too tight; line length too long or too short; tiny x-heights; decorative fonts; weak color; colored backgrounds; sans serif faces; condensed type styles; all caps; reversed type; and underlines, among others. We've covered many of these all ready.

As was already said (several times), the reader is looking for an excuse to ignore your work. Everyone is so pressured and stressed, lacking sufficient time to do what we are supposed to do, that much reading material is eliminated at first glance. Readers feel that they only have time for important stuff. If something is hard to read, they will keep on looking for other articles or ads that matter to them.

The reader is looking for an excuse to ignore your work.

This is important in books — even with fiction, like novels. My wife is recently tried to read a rather large book with a compelling title, stirring cover illustration, and intriguing back cover synopsis. She loves to read for relaxation. So far, she has complained every day for over a week that she doesn't know if she'll be able to finish the book; it is just too hard to read. It has very long line length. The type is small, old fashioned, and stylized. The leading is so tight that finding the beginning of the next line takes an almost conscious search. She claims the book is excellent. It is just too hard to read! (She finally tossed the book in the trash — unread).

Our first paragraph-level power tool

Indents and tabs

One of the major differences between nonprofessional word processing and typesetting is indents and tabs. It is not that most word processors do not have the indent and tab controls. In truth, they have most of them. The problem is that nonprofessionals do not use what they have, and they are much clumsier to set up in Word™ and its cohorts than in a page layout program. The left and right indents work much as you expect (as long as you remember that they are measured from the edges of the text frame, text block, or column sides).

First line indents

Here is a conceptual change many have trouble understanding. First line indents are not measured from the column or text block edges, they are measured from the left indent. Let's repeat that: **first line indents are measured from the left indent**. A positive number indents the first line farther to the right. A negative number indents the first line less than the rest of the paragraph.

I'm going to repeat that again because this is something that new typesetters have a severe difficulty comprehending. The concept just mentioned is important because that first line indent can be either positive or negative. A normal positive first line indent is set off to the right from the left indent. A negative first line indent is set off to the left of the left indent.

Hanging indents

The first line can be as large negatively as the left indent is positively. In other words, a left indent of one inch and a first line indent of minus one inch would start the first line exactly on the margin, but every other line in that paragraph would be indented one inch.

A hanging indent uses this feature to produce bulleted or numbered lists by setting a tab for the first line that matches the left indent. This sounds simple, but many students have a great deal of trouble with it. The following examples illustrate the differences between simple negative first line and the benefits of adding a tab at the left indent.

Negative first line – As you can see, this looks a bit strange because you are used to seeing all the lines in a paragraph line up to the same margin or having the first line indented to the right a little. This is why hanging indents are necessary. First of all, they are much neater and tidier. We normally like to see things lined up on the left side. Secondly, a hanging indent greatly emphasizes the bullets or dingbats so that the eye is drawn to the paragraphs involved. As mentioned earlier, bulleted lists are one of the better devices used to attract readers.

The example at the top of the next page shows a genuine hanging indent. There is a capture of the palette that was used to create it directly above the sample paragraph. A left tab is placed exactly on top of the left margin, leaving the negative first line. Everything before the tab hangs off to the left of the left margin. Because the left margin is all lined up with this technique, the hanging characters serve to grab attention to the paragraph. The left indent provides the white space to the left of the paragraph that makes this all work.

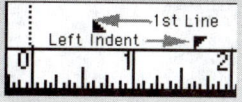

Negative first line

In the sample above, there is a left indent of 1.625 inches. The first line indent is minus one inch or set one inch to the left of the left indent. In the sample paragraph to the left, the left indent is .4" and the first line indent is -.4". That is why the N in Negative lines up with the left margin. However, in this case, nothing in the first line lines up with the rest of the paragraph.

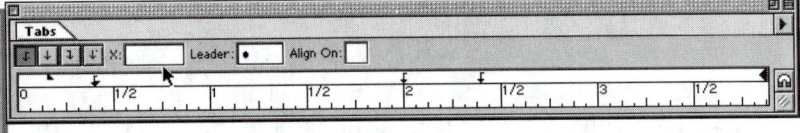

 Hanging indent with tab at left margin: A hanging indent uses this feature to produce bulleted or numbered lists by setting a tab for the first line that matches the left indent. This time everything is neat and tidy. The face is from the font MiniPics LilFaces.

Tabs

Typesetters' tabs are very different from typewriter tabs. First, like alignment, they also come in four or more kinds: left, right, centered, and decimal, at least. FreeHand offers automatic wrapping tabs. InDesign can align on any repeating character.

Left tab —Moves the insertion point to the tab location. The type starts at this point and proceeds normally as it is typed.

Right tab — Moves the insertion point to the tab location. The type grows to the left from that location as it is typed.

Centered tab — Moves the cursor to the tab location, and the type grows in both directions remaining centered on the tab location.

Decimal tab — Moves the cursor to the tab location. Everything before the period extends left, and everything after the period extends right. This style tab is used to quite easily make accountant-style tabular records, where parentheses and asterisks often stick out to the right of the numbers. Like I mentioned, InDesign has a special character tab that lets you align things on any special character.

 All alignments, indents, and tabs are in relation to the column. For tabs to work as you expect, the alignment almost always has to be flush left. All tabs are tied to a paragraph. In other words, they stay in effect only as long as you remain in that paragraph. The only way around that is with paragraph styles, which we cover in depth in **Publishing with InDesign**. These enable you to copy tabs from one paragraph to another.

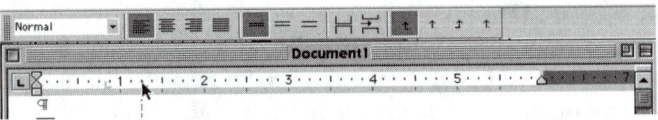

This is the toolbar used to set tabs in Word 98. It is not normally open and you have to look for it.

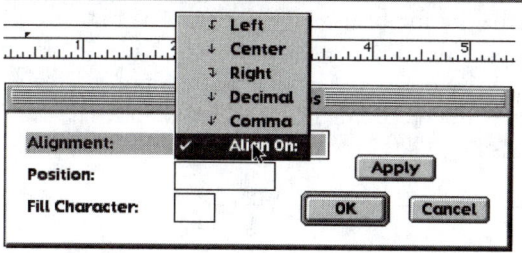

This is the Paragraph Tabs dialog box from Quark.

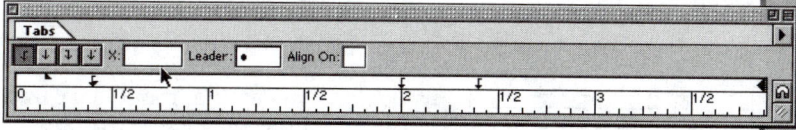

This is the Tabs palette from InDesign.

As you can see, all programs use different icons, palettes, and/or dialog boxes to select the tabs used. However, they all offer basically the same types of tabs. The concept remains intact.

Now we get fancy

Leaders

One of the aspects of tabs that most neophytes do not imagine is leaders. This is where a repeating character leads into the tab. You normally associate these with pieces like menus, where a row of dots connects a name with a price. There are many types of leaders. Any character can be used to repeat (Quark allows two characters to repeat, InDesign allows any combination of eight). Here are four obvious examples.

This is a dot leader produced by a repeating period:

Green Chilé Chicken Alfredo $8.95

This is a line leader produced by a below-line rule:

Black Beans w/Carne Adovada_____ $11.95

This is a dash leader produced by a hyphen:

Buy now! ------------------- Last chance!

This is a decorative line produced by <|>:

<|><|><|><|><|><|><|><|><|><|><|><|><|><|><|><|><|><|><|><|><|>

This is just the beginning of uses for leaders. The best use is probably for the creation of forms. Almost anywhere that a fill-in blank is needed can be done with a leader. Again, a few examples: This is the identical tab set up as the preceding line leader example. The only difference is that there is no price at the end of the line this time.

Name _____

Address _____

City_____

State and Zip _____

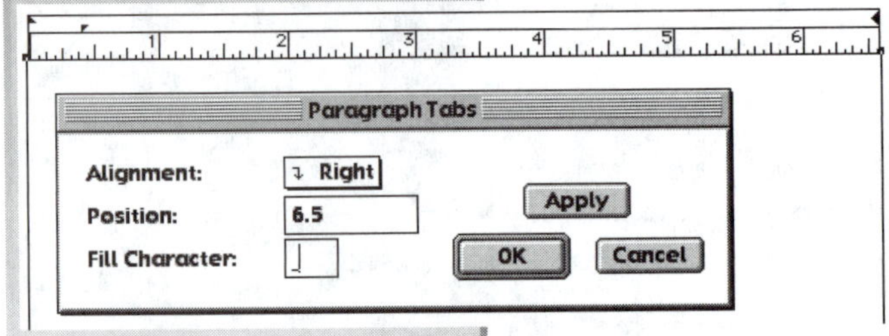

To the left is a capture from Quark that shows the setup dialogs for tabs. Notice that the indents have to be set in a separate dialog (called Formats). The next illustration shows a similar setup in InDesign with double lines and a blank space between the columns – the right tab at 2.5" has a line leader; the left tab at 2.625" has no leader, and the right tab at 5" has a line leader. Notice that InDesign has the indents and tabs in the same dialog box, plus a vertical line appears in the text block to help you line up the tabs. This is a style used very commonly for invoice headings. It comes in handy for such things as City/State/Zip, home and work phones, billing and shipping addresses, and so on.

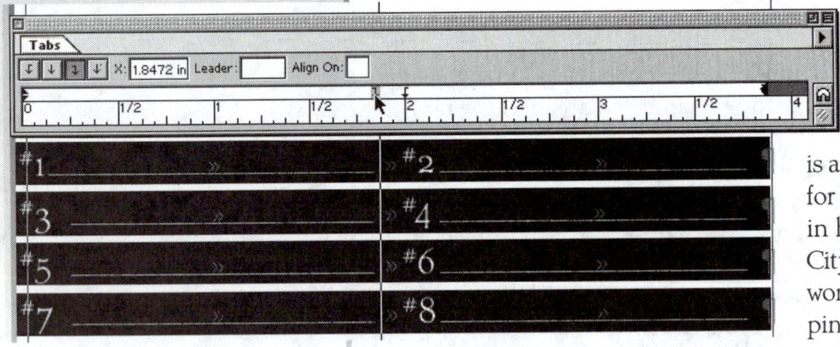

#1 _____   #2 _____

#3 _____   #4 _____

#5 _____   #6 _____

#7 _____   #8 _____

Once you understand the principle, you can easily create forms without having to resort to dedicated table generators or drawing programs. You can have many leaders on the same line. Once you begin using paragraph styles (see *Publishing with InDesign*), it is easy to have different setups for different purposes. The only limiting factor is the time it takes to set up the tabs. Sometimes it is simpler to merely add lines with the line tool (but they do not flow with the copy). This is one place where creativity helps a great deal.

City_____ State ___ Zip_____

    This is the same tab you saw at the top of the previous page except I made it 12-point instead of 14-point. I just typed in State ___ Zip_____ at the right tab insertion point. The stuff I typed in just built out from the right. I typed two below-line-rules after State, and five below-line-rules after Zip. The problem with typing the pieces to the right is that State would not align with anything else. It would be better to set up a set of tabs like the numbers at the bottom of that page to keep the internal alignments and help the form hold together.

    The tab settings on the preceding illustration should be obvious by this point. Another helpful arrangement looks like the following:

Facing tabs

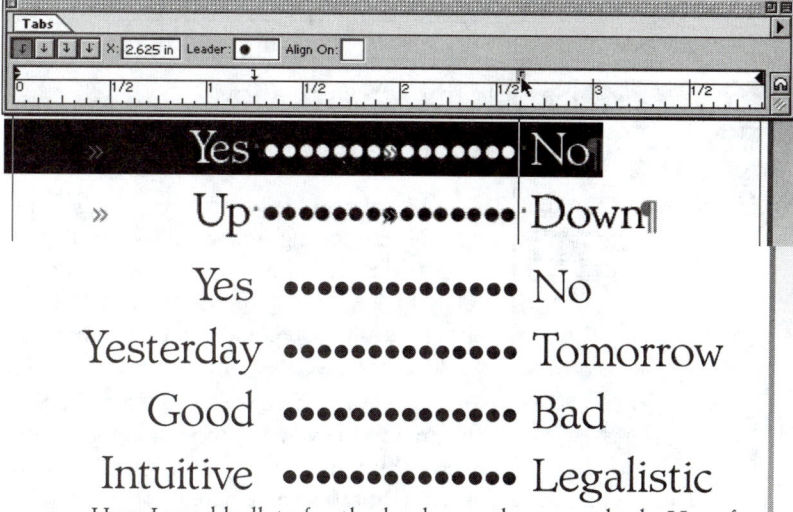

Here I used bullets for the leader on the second tab. Uses for indents and tabs are limited only by your creativity. Simply keep this hint in the back of your mind: *"The solution to this might be a tab."* In addition, file it next to this thought: *"There is no excuse for hitting the space bar more than once."* However, in some cases, another tool common in page layout software comes in handy.

Another paragraph attribute

Paragraph rules

No, this is not a slogan spray-painted on a blank wall by vandals. It is a powerful tool for adding lines in appropriate places. Rules are, like tabs, paragraph attributes. You have the option to automatically add a line above or below a paragraph. Look at the rule under ANOTHER PARAGRAPH ATTRIBUTE above. This is a 2-point rule, set up to be the width of the copy, with no indents, two points below the baseline.

The rule(s) are added when the return is hit at the end of the paragraph. These rules can be almost any width, any color, and almost any length. They can be the length of the line or the width of the column. They can be indented left or right, either positively or negatively, in some cases up to the width of the pasteboard (this enables rules that cross the gutter and the other page of a center spread or even cross a single, double, or triple foldout). Here are some examples (each line is a separate paragraph).

Sample line w/double rule width of column

Sample line w/double rule width of text

Sample line w/black above

Sample line w/single rule w/white type

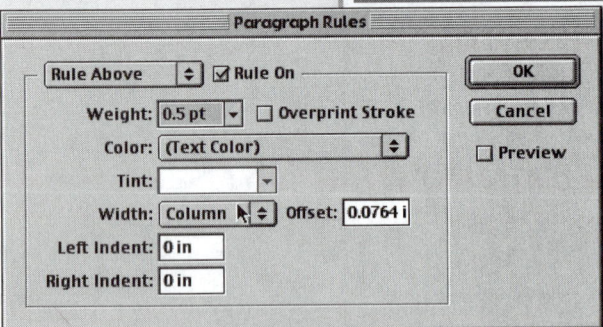

These options for paragraph rules are certainly interesting. You should take the time today to duplicate them. Here is another way to set up a paragraph style so that fill lines appear automatically. You could use this instead of the leaders we started with.

These are five paragraphs set with a half-point rule, made the width of column, 5.5 points above the baseline (.0764"), 6-point type, and a right tab at one inch.

	NAME:
	ADDRESS:
	CITY/STATE/ZIP:
PHONE (WORK & HOME):	

Here's a solution to another common problem: a half-point rule above the paragraph, width of type, with negative 1.5" indents left and right, 6 points above the baseline, with a first line indent of 1.5", centered. This particular setup has countless uses. It can also be used for forms that use tiny names just below the blank line. This is one place where all caps is required.

AUTHORIZED SIGNATURE

Using vertical and horizontal rules

Tables

There are times when rules and leaders are simply not enough. It can be argued (and Bringhurst does) that anything more than simple tabs with no rules or leaders are enough. He is wrong. However, there is certainly a need for restraint. Too many rules, boxes, and borders imprisons type and makes it feel cheap. Sometimes cheap is what you need, but do it on purpose in that case. Especially in the case of tables you need to keep it light and easy to read.

PARTY SUPPLIES FOR SPRING GRADUATION

PRODUCT NUMBER	QUANTITY	DESCRIPTION	UNIT PRICE	EXTENDED PRICE
24735	3	Industrial strength, 400 amp, handheld blenders with chopping blades	$249.95	$749.85
17356	48	Tank–style garden sprayers, 2 gallon	$19.95	$957.60
46542	7	Tinting sets, aniline dyes, 18 colors	$24.50	$171.50
52394	288	Boxes of gelatine	$.25	$72.00
71492	48	Lucite face shields	$15.00	$720.00
		TOTAL (ALL TAXES INCLUDED)		**$2670.95**

Even this table is a little heavy-handed, but it works all right. Styles of tables are hotly debated, like everything in design. What you need to do is work on a style that fits your sense of excellence.

Open to the possibilities

All this is trying to give you a feel for the power available with paragraph formatting. It goes way beyond the ability to cut and paste. Leaders, rules, and tables must be a part of your normal arsenal of problem-solving tools. The governing principle, at all times, is "Does this help the readers of this design read more easily and understand more clearly?" As long as you keep that in mind, these are wonderful tools to that purpose.

Where should you be by this time?

You really need to practice setting up leaders, tabs, rules, and so on. They will seem too complex when you start out; so, practice is essential. It takes a while for these tools to become part of conscious choices for page layout. They are a major help though.

DISCUSSION

You should be discussing the various options for adding lines to your designs. How thick or wide should they be? What color works? What happens if they are too dark, or too heavy? When are they useful?

Talk amongst yourselves...

A little on proofing

There is no way to overemphasize the importance of proofreading and proofing. First, this is probably your greatest tool to convince your clients that you really are a professional. It builds their confidence level to a point where they take your suggestions more seriously. It also prevents unchargeable author's alterations.

Secondly, a careful proofing job gives you the opportunity to fine-tune your design. Many times, relatively major mistakes in layout are caught by the proofers. Having at least two other people proof your work helps you make sure that the phone number is there or the address. Often, there are silly mistakes. If not caught, they can embarrass you, at the very least.

Nonprofessional proofing

Nonprofessional does not mean unprofessional; it just refers to someone outside your field, in this case. Finding a nonprofessional to proof your work often gives you the perspective of the reader. It is often difficult to remember that readers are normally not professional designers. Use the nondesigner to check for readability, comprehension, and attractiveness — things designers often don't see.

The pieces you like the best are often too subtle.

Quite often, the designs that we think are the best merely have personal associations of which the reader is totally unaware. Soliciting several opinions helps objectivity when critiquing your own designs. If you are not sure the design is good, there is usually a reason. Ask someone else to take a look at it.

Knowledge retention

1. Why are tabs set using flush left copy?
2. Why do we need a tab on top of the left indent for lists?
3. Why are hanging indents important?
4. How are tabs used for forms?
5. Why would you want to use a nonprofessional proofer?
6. Why are leaders better than hand-drawn lines?
7. What do you think is the most common problem with tables?

PRESENTING THE TYPE

Understanding the importance of paper choice in publishing

Chapter Objectives:

By giving students a clear understanding of what different papers are available, this chapter will enable students to:

1. pick appropriate papers
2. design within the limits of the paper surface
3. use paper choice as a primary design element

Lab Work for Chapter:

1. Complete the required Skill Exams.
2. Read chapter 15 for next week.
3. Work on projects.

READING PAPER LABELS

wausau papers *Royal Felt*®

White Stone

23 x <u>35</u> – 119M
1000 Sheets-Basis 70

85262

7 59598 85262 0

This is a paper made by Wausau Papers called Royal Felt, color White Stone. The carton contains parent sheets at 23"x35" with the grain in the 35" direction (that dimension is underlined — on some it's bold). 119M means that 1,000 sheets of 23x35 weigh 119 pounds. There are 1,000 sheets in this carton and they have a basis weight of 70# (making this a text paper). It is a recycled

Hammermill
Laser Plus® (Featuring Wax Holdout)
Long Grain   **500 Sheets**
11 x <u>17</u>-24M-S24/60
For Prepress Proofing and Camera-Ready Masters

↑ Print Side

This is a specialized paper made
camera-ready output and paste
White. This carton contains cut sh
out (that dimension is also unde
24M means that 1,000 sheets of
sheets in this package and they
th
p

7 Sigs: 28-page book

36 Sigs: 144-page book

The thickness of paper sets the limit for saddle-stitching before large bulges open it.

---

500 sheets: 60# gloss coated: .75"

500 sheets: 60# matte coated: .95"

500 sheets: 60# smooth offset: 1.15"

500 sheets: 60# vellum offset: 1.30"

500 sheets: 60# hi-bulk offset: 1.56"

The approximate relative thickness of five common papers used in books.

Before

we start winding up this book, there is one final area that must be covered — output media. In our industry, this is normally papers and monitors. Both of these media types are complex, imposing their restrictions upon our designs. Both of these media require planning, for your designs must use these as your base of operation, as it were.

There are thousands of different kinds, styles, colors, and types of paper and printing substrates. Even though monitors seem much more homogeneous, experience quickly shows us that they are even less predictable than paper. However, we have to start somewhere, so let's start with printing substrates and surfaces which are almost always some type of paper.

Your first design decision should be the media.

The first material decision to be made with a publishing project is usually the paper. There are those who simply take what is offered by the copy shop, and that works strongly in your favor. Against that background of cheap, flimsy, white wood pulp, a distinctive paper choice makes a major statement.

Paper manufacturing is huge and capital-intensive.

We have not covered, and won't try to cover, the nomenclature, categorizations, limitations, and availability of paper. Paper machines are extremely expensive and often more than a mile long. Entire trees are now chewed up for the fiber and cooked in vats the size of buildings. The output of these massive machines is logs of rolled paper, feet in diameter and yards in width.

The pulp is poured continuously onto a nonending loop of screen hundreds of yards long. The drying rollers are machined to almost unimaginable tolerances in huge arrays that carry the continuous web of paper while it dries. There are thousands of colors, pulp recipes, embossed textures, and so on.

My intention here is to give you a limited introduction to the huge world of paper, to try to give you enough knowledge to ask intelligent questions. What happens with every designer is that she develops a

Papermaking

It is far beyond our purposes here to get into the discussion of papermaking techniques and machinery. However, you do need to understand the basic process. Fiber is made into a loose, flowing liquid containing 95% water or so. This is called pulp.

The pulp is poured onto a screen so the water can drip out and the paper dry. Modern papermaking machines use Fourdrinier screens which are huge continuous loops of screen many yards wide and a quarter mile long or so. These papermaking machines run 24/7/365, cost billions of dollars to make, and are located where the fiber is found.

At this point, this is almost always in the Northern Woods in southern Canada or the northern United States. There are tree farms for pulp in southeastern United States (Georgia and Alabama), but almost all paper mills are in New York, Michigan, Wisconsin, Minnesota, Washington, and Ontario.

standard selection of papers that meet her needs. There are tens of thousands of different papers manufactured by many dozens of paper mills distributed by hundreds of suppliers. What you will have to do is find the best paper available for the given situation.

Getting samples

Do not hesitate to call your paper supplier. Every city has several. Their expertise goes far beyond a designer's or printer's need. The field is too complex to store in your memory banks unless you sell the material. However, as soon as a paper supplier learns that you are choosing paper choices for your projects, she'll be happy to provide you with a swatch book and idea samples.

Some of the best printing in the world is supplied by paper houses with product line idea books. Many of the swatch books contain a page of every color and texture of paper offered in that line with idea-provoking printing to show you some possibilities you may have never seen or thought of. For years, Warren Paper produced some of the best books available on varnish usage, photography ideas, and many more in a series that was one of the best sources of ideas for designers. Sadly, the whole series is out of print, but keep your eye open for old copies lying around.

Start by finding papers that you like the look of. Then begin asking questions about what papers are kept in stock, get the prices firmed up, and start building your palette of papers. You will find that you come back over and over to certain choices that make the most sense for you, your clients, and your budgets. As you develop your style and reputation, you will find that paper choices are a major portion of that look. Excellent paper is often more effective and much cheaper to use than more colors of ink.

Paper's confusing weights

As we get into paper, there is much confusion about the weights (not to mention the names): 20#, 65#, 100#, bond, text, enamel, tag, pressure-sensitive — the list seems to go on forever. The good news is that paper weights are very simple to understand.

The basis weight of a paper stock is the weight, in pounds, of a ream (500 sheets) of the basis size.

The basis size (the size that the weight calculations are made from) varies arbitrarily with each category of paper. However, there are only three categories that you will need to remember. Unique papers, like newsprint, often have their own basis size. These basis sizes vary for each type of paper. As a result, 24# office paper is about the same weight as 60# printing paper; 140# printing paper is comparable in weight to 55# cover; 90# index is thinner than 65# cover. It seems extremely complicated. The good news is that we only deal with a few categories on a daily basis, determined mainly by the printing technology and the final usage of the printed product.

What you have to memorize is the basis size of the common categories of paper you use every day. Thankfully for most of us, this is only three sizes. Although there are well over a dozen different basis sizes for the various types of paper, there are really only three that you will use regularly. Carefully examine the graphic on page 352.

Papers outside the norm

Before we start, let's just mention the papers that you will come across that you can categorize by name. Newsprint, as mentioned, has a weird basis size and strange weights, but who cares? The newspaper publisher worries about that and you will rarely spec it. Whatever the newspaper uses is fine with you. Neither commercial printers nor quick-printers can feed that junk through their presses or duplicators.

If you have custom printing done by your newspaper publisher, they will show you samples of what they use, and give you the price points and the printing capabilities of the various papers. In general, all you have to know is that it is extremely cheap and very absorbent. You also have to make sure you allow for the fact that everything will print like it's on blotter paper. This is much more important for photos than anything else, so we'll leave that for *Publishing with Photoshop*, my book about the practical uses of Photoshop and fixing scans.

In addition, at the cheaper printers, you will find three papers sold as cover stock that you need to be careful of: *Vellum Bristol*, *Index*, and *Tag*. They are actually the cheapest type of paper – the worst grade of wood pulp. Their only advantage is their price. They look cheap, feel cheap, and cause customers to think your client is cheap. But then if you are making a promo for Billy Bob's Junk Yard, they would work very well. They are very useful, but only if you understand their basic character – **cheap**.

Vellum Bristol only comes in 67# and it is the only 67# paper in existence. Index comes in 90# and 110#, and these are the only two papers that use this weight. You will use these fairly often, simply because they are often the heaviest papers that will feed through a laser printer or copier. Tag is so rare that you will always look for it specifically. It's

Paper reality

Most of you have never seen paper until after it is printed. The stuff sold in the discount office supply megastores and places like WallyWorld is the cheapest office paper available. It is almost entirely unusable for professional print. Even if it was usable, you wouldn't want to use it because it looks so cheap. Cheap paper really compromises the reaction to your projects by both the client and the readers.

Office papers: Basis size: 17"x22"

SURFACES: cockle, laid, linen, parchment, ripple, wove, rib laid
COMMON NAMES: bond, ditto, ledger, mimeo, onionskin, rag, writing
CHARACTERISTICS: *tough, versatile, often beautiful; has personality only matched by text; is designed for writing; prints better on felt side; can be erased*

Printing papers Basis size: 25"x38"

Uncoated sheets

SURFACES: antique, smooth, vellum, wove
COMMON NAMES: book, offset, opaque
CHARACTERISTICS: *easy folding; wide variety of colors; most common paper; used for books and virtually anything else*

Coated sheets

SURFACES: matte, dull, gloss, cast coat, embossed
COMMON NAMES: coated offset, dull, slick, gloss
CHARACTERISTICS: *good ink holdout; produces ink gloss; smooth surfaces (some mirror-like); usually only comes in white*

Text

SURFACES: antique, embossed, felt, laid, silk, linen, rib laid, vellum • COMMON NAMES: text
CHARACTERISTICS: *premium papers for jobs that require "class"; even cheap grades are distinctive; many are very soft and take embossing superbly; deckle edges; wide range of colors, including deep and "fashion" colors*

Cover stock: Basis size: 20"x26"

SURFACES: any of the above as a matching set
COMMON NAMES: C1S, C2S, cover as a suffix
CHARACTERISTICS: *durable, stiff, strong; opaque for cards, folders, etc.*

the paper used for those inspection tags with the reinforced holes held to the pipes with twisted wire. Tag is used so little because even most presses cannot feed it — it's too thick.

The papers you'll use

The commonly used papers can be broken down into three neat classifications (as you can see to the left). For most of your daily use, these will be sufficient. All the other categories are either the extremely cheap specialty papers we just mentioned or expensive papers for a particular use, such as label stock for wine or jam bottles; pressure-sensitive or crack'n'peel paper for bumper stickers and labels; plastic stock for posters and banners; latex-impregnated paper for waterproof posters and durable menus, and so forth. Many of these have different basis sizes. But if you use them at all, you will quickly learn to recognize them by sight.

The three categories of *office*, *printing*, and *cover stock* make up close to 100% of the papers sold. Printing papers, by themselves, probably come to three-quarters of the paper manufactured and sold. You may hear figures like "half the paper sold is 60# offset." It matters not. What you need to know is that printing papers contain all the most commonly used sheets and rolls. Of those, 50#, 60#, and 70# offset are by far the most popular, followed by the same weights in coated stock. Almost all paper sold is white. There are hundreds of different whites ranging from almost cream to brilliant, snow white.

Experience is necessary.

We will describe these papers in a little more detail, but you need to recognize that this is an unregulated industry. You must learn how specific papers behave on the printers and presses you have to use. Almost all printing companies will have a favorite paper stock that they are convinced works the best for their equipment mix. (They usually call it their *house sheet*.) You will save a lot of money, time, and hassle if you can live with this stock.

Your customers may specify other papers that you will be forced to use. You will have to be the person who knows what papers cause problems, when and why. Before you specify a paper, call your printer and ask if this paper choice causes any problems that they know of. Some papers feed well, and some don't. Some curl badly and have a pronounced grain direction. You will have to learn what papers are available in your area, which manufacturers, which of their colors are stocked by the local distributors, and what printers use.

White paper

Almost all paper sold is white. Most of the projects you have seen on colored paper were actually color printed on white paper. To do this you need a press at a commercial printer. Quickprinters cannot print large enough solid areas to cover the paper.

You have to be very careful of colored papers because they severely limit contrast and make type and graphics much harder to read. However, an excellent, gorgeous text paper is often the perfect solution for short-run one- and two-color projects.

Office papers

Thee are many names and surfaces. Office papers are usually light — so letters can be read easily. The surface has some tooth so pens will write normally. They will be called bond, writing, or rag for the better qualities. Ledger is paper especially designed for bookkeepers and such.

Ditto and mimeo falls into the category usually called DP papers for dual purpose. They are trying to make you believe that this paper will work for bond and/or for offset. In reality, they are neither fish nor fowl — they are C***.

Avoid these papers like the plague. They will make your work look unprofessional, cheap, and many other far more derogatory adjectives. DP papers have no real use in professional digital publishing.

No area has all papers. No one stocks all the colors available for all the papers. Sometimes the paper you really want is only available as a mill order which usually requires five to fifteen carton minimums. Paper is simply too bulky, which means that shipping and storage problems are a major consideration. A carton of paper ranges from around 50 pounds for 10 reams of 8.5"×11" precut stock to close to 150 pounds for parent sheet stock (typically 1,000 plus sheets of 23"×35" or larger). Buying partial or broken carton quantities normally almost doubles the price. You should ask your supplier about their pricing policies. Often commercial printers buy enough paper to always receive the 16-carton price for any paper carried by their paper distributor of choice.

Obviously, larger cities have better availability. However, some papers are made on the West Coast, some on the East Coast, most in the Upper Midwest, some in the Desert Southwest. Shipping tons of paper thousands of miles raises costs to the point where local papers are much more cost-effective. The building size required for warehousing all of these papers limits availability. You need to cultivate relationships with your paper sales personnel for help on what is available. It will help more than you can imagine if you find a customer service representative who you can trust for advice.

What you write on: office papers

First we cover the top category in the graphic on page 352. Office papers are distinguished by the fact that they are designed for writing. We do print on them, but they have several characteristics that set them apart. First of all, the basis size is 17"×22"", an exact multiple of 8.5"×11". That seems insignificant, but it means that bleeds are rarely cost-effective on office stock unless you design for special sizes or unusual formats.

Because office papers are designed to write on, they are heavily sized. *Sizing* is a coating that controls absorption. Good examples of unsized paper are blotter paper or paper towels. If bond papers were not sized, ballpoint pens would bleed into and maybe through the paper. However, it is important to note that bonds are sized well on only one side. They are not meant for double-sided use. Paper that is written upon is usually too dented and marked on the back by the pen or pencil to be used for more writing or printing.

In addition to the sizing, writing papers use specially chosen, stronger fibers. This enables erasure of mistakes. It also enables office papers to hold up under the heavy use they receive. They are handled, filed, moved around, copied, and mistreated more than any other kind of paper. The only pieces treated more roughly are things like menus, pocket calenders, and membership cards. Those require either special synthetic stock, plastics, or laminated coatings.

These stronger fibers are not usually diluted with fillers. *Fillers* are used a lot in printing papers to make the paper opaque, but office stock uses relatively little additional fill. As a result, office papers (bond, writing, rag, ledger, and so forth) have what is called *snap* (see sidebar). This is especially true for premium bonds containing cotton fiber. Fillers weaken the paper and dull the sound. Much of the experience of top-quality bond paper is in the feel and sound.

Bonds are usually relatively translucent.

As mentioned, they are sized on only one side, so they normally are printed on only one side. This means that they do not have to be opaque unlike printing papers. This means that writing papers are the only category that can offer *watermarks*. Watermarks are made in the paper pulp when it is extremely liquid (80 to 90 percent water). Wire patterns pressed into the liquid pulp rearrange the fibers, making them more translucent. The watermarks are only seen when the paper is held up for reading, and light shows through the back of the paper. There is no dent or surface mark to be seen.

 You can design custom watermarks. Paper mills will produce custom watermarked bonds for you with relatively small orders. An order of only a couple dozen parent-sheet-size cartons is usually enough. A simple thing like a custom watermark can add a great deal to the perceived image of a firm of CPAs, lawyers, bankers, and others trying to project power, wealth, and influence.

Bonds are usually white or light tints. This is because we write on them and because whiteout is available only in limited colors. This may be no longer necessary now that typewriters are gone. With edited copy, printed on laser printers, the better quality colored sheets can look very classy. At this point, they are still a relatively unusual option that can add a great deal of impact with little additional cost. Make sure you consult with the secretaries who will be using the letterheads before you design, however. Many a beautiful design has sat in desk drawers, unused, because it didn't fit the secretary's normal typing procedures.

Office paper surfaces are often embossed with fabric textures like linen; Chinese papermaking bamboo screen textures called *laid*; unrolled, baked, unflattened surfaces like *cockle*; and so on. The better

Snap

One of the real attractions of cotton fiber paper (apart from the beauty and gorgeous writing surface) is the sound the paper makes when it is held and handled. This snap sounds so good because almost the only 100% cotton paper seen and used by the general public is money. This explains why the major use of cotton paper is accountants, CPAs, banks, and the like. Many designers also like it because of its associations with drawing paper and watercolor blocks.

papers are more conservative. A top-quality, 100% cotton bond has a richness of surface, snap, and feel that is unsurpassed. Remember that this is the same paper used to print our money. You need to read the sidebar to the left on counterfeiting.

You should plan on spending $12 to $20 per ream on bond paper. Nothing makes a company seem questionable more than cheap, thin letterhead stock. In many cases, the quality of the paper used for the letterheads, business cards, and envelopes is the first impression a client, or your client's prospective customer has of quality, ability, and reliability. Your client is trying to convince his customers that the company can be trusted. Excellent letterhead paper helps.

What we print on: printing papers

As you saw on our category list, printing papers take up far more than three-quarters of papers used. Printing papers are the papers you will be speccing most of the time. They are designed to feed well through a press. They are well-sized, equally on both sides, to control absorption. They use a lot of filler so the sheets are much more opaque. This allows double-sided printing without *show-through*, on relatively thin papers. Even on paper stock too thin to feed through sheet-fed presses, like 36# to 50# offset (like this book), the ink on the other side of the paper is not disturbingly visible.

Most printing papers, except text, are smooth and white. You'll get a feel for this if you try to imagine a novel printed on textured pink paper. These papers are used for all books, magazines, programs, brochures, and the like. The two major types of this smooth white stock are offset (also called uncoated) and enamel (also called coated).

Cheapness

Printing papers, in general, are very cheap. Yes, I am using that term to imply poor quality. Good paper, in general, is found in the office papers. Excellent paper must have a large cotton content. Printing papers are almost exclusively wood pulp. Most of them are the cheapest wood pulp, assaulted by the harshest bleaches to bring it to the brightest white. The only printing papers offering quality are the text grades, and even these are usually cheap wood pulp (even though they come in fancy textures and beautiful colors). Quality in printing papers (#1 sheets and #1 premium sheets) concerns smoothness and printability.

Calendering

The smoothness of printing papers is accomplished by a stack of steel rollers called calendering rollers. These highly polished rollers compress and smooth both coated and uncoated printing stock. In fact, calendering is one of the main distinguishing characteristics of these sheets. All offset and enamel papers are *calendered*.

There are two reasons for calendering: smoothness and compression. The second is a definite factor in binding and shipping. The first has to do with requirements most people believe are necessary. Some of this is due to press operators' claims that smoother papers print better. Some of it is due to paper manufacturers' hype. Most of it is due to the fashion for "slickness" in the 1970s and 1980s, which was largely a reaction to the incredible advances in press and prepress technology.

Smoothness

We've discussed briefly how lithography and xerography work. Both of these technologies do print easier on smoother sheets. Electrostatic printing (xerography) almost requires this smoothness, thus the phrase "suitable for laser printing" on the reams in your office supply center. It is true that electrostatic printing does not work well on strongly textured sheets (the surfaces embossed to look like fabric for example).

In fact, this smoothness requirement is actually a matter of taste. As I read the histories of printing technology, I am struck by the oft-stated fact that one of the main benefits of offset lithography is the ability of the rubber blanket to print well on textured sheets. The blanket is a sheet of rubber mounted to an intermediate cylinder to "offset" the image from the plate to the paper. In my thirty years of printing experience, I have often been pleasantly surprised by how well offset litho works with textured sheets.

Even with electrostatic imaging, the problems of texture are rarely severe. The only real problem is that the hot rollers which melt the toner onto the sheet usually flatten any texture on the paper. It takes an extreme texture to cause image breakup. Although the layers of toner found on CMYK sheets printed with laser printers often peel off softer papers like text, all you have to do is cut back on the darkness of the color for spectacular results. My experience has proven over and over that black-and-white laser printers print beautifully with slightly textured and noncalendered sheets of paper.

I have often been struck by how well offset lithography works with textured sheets.

Another factor to consider is that materials like rubber-based inks commonly used in quickprint and the inks used for digital mimeography only dry by absorption. In these cases, excellence in printing demands that you reject coated sheets and heavily calendered stock.

Excellence in printing simply requires designs within the capabilities of the technology used.

 Discussion point: Increasingly, designers like myself are seeing the overly smooth, slick printing done on super-calendered stock as slick, mechanical, unfriendly, and often cheap-looking. To use terms of furniture and woodworking, it is the difference between the slick, super-glossy one-day coat of polyurethane and the patina that can be produced only by years of hand-rubbed oil and wax application.

Process color prints beautifully on noncalendered, slightly textured, uncoated, or text paper stock. Certainly the dot gain requires adjustments. However, the richness of the paper surface is often much more desirable than the glossy, slap-in-your-face gaudiness of paper where you can see your reflection. Try it, you'll like it.

Compression

The second result of calendering is genuinely important. The stack of rollers used to smooth the paper also makes it thinner. Pull up that image from your mind about that sandwich of bologna and that pasty white stuff some actually call bread. What happened when you squeezed the bread? Calendering does a similar thing to the relatively loose mat of fiber that comes off the screen of a papermaking machine.

The importance of this is simple. Let's briefly look at a saddle-stitched booklet. These are booklets, newsletters, or magazines that are folded in half and stitched (printers use wire in rolls that is stitched into place).

There is a real limit on the thickness of such a booklet. If there are too many sheets of paper, the book bulges and separates

500 sheets: 60# gloss coated: .75"

500 sheets: 60# matte coated: .95"

500 sheets: 60# smooth offset: 1.15"

500 sheets: 60# vellum offset: 1.30"

500 sheets: 60# hi-bulk offset: 1.56"

The approximate relative thickness of five common papers used in books.

around the staples. In the printing companies I worked for, we had a rule of thumb that stated that you could not have a saddle-stitched booklet of more than 100 pages. However, this was not really true except for premium grade 60# offset paper. Cheaper sheets, that were calendered less, were restricted to eighty sheets or so. Thinner sheets, like super-calendered 50# coated stock could go up to nearly 200 pages.

As you can see from the illustration on the previous page, calendering has a great effect upon book thickness. Another place calendering has great effect is with mailing requirements. Post cards, for example, have to be seven thousandths of an inch thick in the States, minimum. A cheap, uncalendered 67# vellum bristol is that thick, but it can take up to an 80# cover stock to reach that thickness with a super-calendered coated sheet.

7 Sigs: 28-page book

36 Sigs: 144-page book

The thickness of paper sets the limit for saddle-stitching before large bulges open it.

Offset or uncoated paper

All offset paper is calendered to some degree. The cheaper the paper, the less the calendering in general. Uncoated sheets and rolls are not entirely white. They do come in pastel (think cheap and ugly) colors. Some even come in Day-Glo™ colors (often referred to as neon). Uncoated sheets usually have only two finishes: smooth and vellum (sometimes called antique or wove), depending on the amount of calendering. Basically this paper is smooth and white.

However, there are major differences in price and quality. The better (#1 premium) sheets are often called *opaque* instead of offset. They are usually smoother, brighter, and more opaque. They have a quality feel, especially in the heavier weights like 70#, 80#, and 100#. Often, simply bumping your paper weight from 60# to 70# will set it apart from the competition.

One thing to remember as you choose paper stock is that different technologies require different paper. We've mentioned this already. The extremely smooth, relatively nonabsorbent opaque sheets will print very poorly on many duplicators and all digital mimeographs.

One thing to remember is that there are many situations where printing on printers like Risographs is extremely advantageous. With printing prices of around a half cent per sheet per color, including the cost of paper, digital mimeographs are seriously underused. For simple spot color, loose registration jobs with no continuous tone, the quality is exceptional. In our excitement over the top end of things, we tend to forget that nearly half of all printing fits this description.

Opaque sheets

These better grades of very smooth, very white printing paper are the paper of choice for laser printers. I use a 70# opaque which is the same thickness and feel as a 28# bond — plus it is much cheaper. They print very well and cost less than half the price of the specialized laser papers. However, for art proofs to your clients, the impact of super-white laser paper (with a brightness well over 90) cannot be over-estimated.

The coating

The material coated onto coated offset is kaolin. For those of you with a stoneware background, this is a porcelain clay. It is very white and very fine. It easily polishes to a gloss.

Enamel or coated paper

Coated paper, commonly called enamel, is designed for offset lithography. Its coating is used to increase ink *holdout*. Holdout is the term used to describe the amount that ink soaks into the surface of the paper. The more the ink remains on the surface of the paper, the brighter the ink color and saturation. The super-premium cast coated sheets give a brightness, saturation, and clarity that nearly equals a photograph— at 10,000 to 50,000 copies per hour!

Except for very rare cases, enamel stock only comes in white. There is one premium line of highly saturated hues and another that offers a cream coated sheet, but these are very rare. Enamel, or coated stock, differs from offset in only one way — it is coated with clay! The clay is polished on with the calendering rollers.

All enamel sheets are calendered. The quality levels are usually determined by it. The cheapest are sheets called *matte*. Here the clay is thin and even the calendering cannot give an even surface. They are still smoother than offset and have much better holdout, but they look cheap (because they are).

The next quality level is *gloss* and *dull*. Here there is quite a variation in quality. I have heard many say that dull is a cheaper grade. This may or may not be true. In fact, the dull finish is added by a specially textured calender roller. The amount of calendering and the thickness of the clay is the same. Here is where you reach what printers call excellent quality. In truth, it is hard to beat the image quality and the feel of what is called a #2 Dull Enamel 80# or thicker. For years we used a paper called LOE Dull (for Lustro Offset Enamel from Warren Papers) as our best sheet. It printed better than any other, was easy to read, and had a real quality feel. It was a lot cheaper than cast coated.

The top of the line enamel is called *cast coated*. The clay is laid on so thick that it can be calendered to a mirror finish. They are also called *supercalendered*. These sheets are so smooth you can see your reflection in the surface. Printing firms tend to think of these papers as the best papers, but this really is not true. They are very shiny. They print process color very brightly and colorfully, but, they are just wood pulp paper. The ink color is often amazing, which can cause the reader to notice the printing more than the message about the product.

This is because the clay gives the paper great ink holdout. In other words, the ink does not soak into the surface (hardly at all), so the color is very bright and clean. Because it does not soak in, there is relatively little dot gain on the press. The problem is that the shiny stock tends to be garish, cheap-looking, and overly slick. It is hard to sell elegance and top quality on superslick stock. Think of the difference between chrome-plating and hand-polished brass or hand-oiled furniture and gloss polyurethane. Cast coated sheets compare well with chrome-plating or glossy plastic coatings like polyurethane.

There is a reason why "Slick Willie" was a nasty nickname. Slickness usually has a mechanical feel that is often associated with cover-ups, slick presentations, slick salesmen, and so forth. Because most cheap direct-mail huckstering is done on slick paper, these associations are increasing. It is becoming increasingly difficult to convey quality, trustworthiness, reliability, and so forth with super-glossy papers. (And we haven't even mentioned the readability issues in the midst of all those bright, shiny reflections.)

The truly top-quality papers are 100% rag or pure cotton fiber. These last for centuries without yellowing or getting brittle. They are very strong. Printing papers (except for the extremely rare and very expensive 25% to 50% cotton text) are all pure wood pulp. This means that the papers are relatively limp. They tear easily, plus the surface cracks when folded (especially across the grain), unless it is scored first.

pH: acid and alkaline fillers

Wood pulp papers are extremely susceptible to yellowing and brittleness when traditional fillers are used. These fillers were typically materials such as rosin (the residue from turpentine production). Rosin is very acidic. Most of the great libraries of the world are in serious trouble because the acidic, wood pulp papers used in books are falling apart before they can be put on microfiche. The most recent solution (beginning in the 1970s) has been to use calcium carbonate (think TUMS®) for filler. This is a high pH material used to make papers that are normally called *alkaline*.

The paper mills are claiming that alkaline papers will last about 200 years. That is certainly better than the twenty to forty years for traditional wood pulp sheets. (Of course, there is no alkaline paper over forty years old, yet.) Regardless, alkaline paper still does not come close to the quality of 100% rag stock. Rembrandt etchings are still bright and white. Wood pulp sheets do print beautifully, however. Plus, most printing is trashed within a month of production.

Text papers

However, we haven't even touched my favorite category of paper – text. The text grades have the most fashionable colors, the best textures, the richest feel and look. It is uncalendered, so it works beautifully for embossing and foil stamping (especially in the companion cover weights). It is quite a bit more expensive, but it is well worth it. Text sheets are the only papers that come in the rich dark blues, hunter greens, maroons, blacks, and so forth. Many of them look as rich as the finest fabric. In most cases, for short runs, a rich text paper costs less and looks better than a second spot color of ink. If you need to imply top quality, excellent service, and reliability, you really need to use text papers. Another side benefit is they print extremely well on digital mimeographs — enabling startling quality from the cheapest source of printing.

... for short runs, a rich text paper costs less and looks better than a second spot color of ink.

In many cases, the best way to win your way into the reader's mind is with the rich look and comfortable feel of a text paper. Two spot colors on a beautiful, elegant, luxurious sheet of paper can have much more impact on the readers than the slap-in-the-face, amazing four-color process color of a cast coated sheet. It also costs less to print and holds up better to the wear and tear of busy schedules.

Heavyweight companions: cover stock

Virtually all the papers mentioned so far come in companion cover weights. This is paper that has the same color, the same texture, the same fiber content, and the same look, but is much thicker and heavier. One way to get an idea of the difference is to make a basis weight comparison: 65# cover, about the lightest cover stock worthy of the name, is roughly equal to 120# printing paper or 48# office stock. It would seem to make sense to use these weights, to help us understand. However, cover stock uses a different basis size (20"×26").

This basis size allows for many things needed by cover stock. Because an eighth sheet of 26"×40" is 10"×13", there is plenty of room for the tabs, spines, and full bleeds often found on covers. It probably wasn't planned that way, however. Little seems to have been planned in the entire paper industry. Most developments simply seemed to happen, followed by codification into rather rigid usage. It is nice though that cover stock comes in larger sheets.

Sheet sizes

All printing papers in the United States are loosely based on the 8.5"×11" module used by the American business community. European papers are all metric with sizes like A3, B4, and so forth. The metric sheet sizes have a different proportion. Obviously, care must be taken when comparing the two different sizing systems.

In America, we have an aberration known as legal size. 8.5"×14" paper is only available in the lowest-quality papers. In fact, when a client demands that you design something for the 8.5"×14" format, the first thing you should do is determine if this is a real need. It is possible that the client is ordering a template to be printed out on the laser printer in their office. Many laser printers cannot print anything larger than legal size.

Even with legitimate use, legal size stock is always a waste of money because 8.5"×14" does not cut well out of any parent sheet based on the letter-sized module. The standard parent sizes of 23"×35", 25"×38", and 26"×40" only allow you to cut out four legal-sized pieces with a lot of waste. What you are really doing is cutting each legal size sheet out of an 11"×17" (tabloid or ledger) piece of paper.

The legal size papers commonly available are the specially sheeted dual purpose stock used in copiers. It is given a weight of 20/50# because even the paper companies know that this garbage is neither fish nor fowl. It is only available in the cheapest wood pulp grades and the basic obnoxious pastel colors (with a few poorly done neons tossed into the mix). Is it an office stock with sizing equal on both sides and filler added — or is it printing paper with slightly stronger fibers? The term bastard comes to mind for this unsightly union.

Cover sheet thicknesses

One unusual practice is that cover stock is often sold by the point. There is 8-point cover, 10-point cover, 12-point cover, and so on. Here a point is not a twelfth of a pica. Instead, it is called *caliper*, stands for a thousandth of an inch, and is measured with a micrometer. This is a place to exercise care. Mailing requirements, for example, state that postcards must be between 7 and 9.5 points thick.

Some papers are much bulkier than others, so weight does not matter much here. Often some of the very cheap cover papers like vellum bristol or index are left uncompressed or use bulky fillers so they reach the caliper needed for postcards.

What counts is the calendering. The more a paper is calendered, the thinner it is, as you saw in the page thickness illustration. An uncalendered sheet like text will be more than twice as thick as gloss coated with the same basis weight. If you do not know how thick a sheet is, look in the paper supplier's catalog. Caliper is usually found in the paper listings right below the name of the paper. If there is any question, or if there seem to be too many choices, call your paper rep and ask.

READING PAPER LABELS

wausau papers *Royal Felt* ®

White Stone

23 x <u>35</u> – 119M
1000 Sheets-Basis 70

85262

7 59598 85262 0

This is a paper made by Wausau Papers called Royal Felt, color White Stone. The carton contains parent sheets at 23"x35" with the grain in the 35" direction (that dimension is underlined — on some it's bold). 119M means that 1,000 sheets of 23x35 weigh 119 pounds. There are 1,000 sheets in this carton and they have a basis weight of 70# (making this a text paper). It is a recycled sheet, 15% postconsumer waste.

| HAMMERMILL PAPERS® | Hammermill Laser Plus® (Featuring Wax Holdout) Long Grain   500 Sheets 11 x <u>17</u>-24M-S24/60 For Prepress Proofing and Camera-Ready Masters | ↑ Print This Side Only | 10452-1 |
| MADE IN USA | | White | 0 10199 00452 9 |

This is a specialized paper made by Hammermill Papers to be used for camera-ready output and pasteup using wax, called Laser Plus, color White. This carton contains cut sheets at 11"x17" with long grain spelled out (that dimension is also underlined — on some cartons it's bold). 24M means that 1,000 sheets of 11x17 weigh 24 pounds. There are 500 sheets in this package and they have a basis weight of S24/60 (making this a dual-purpose paper comparable to 24# bond or 60# offset). The printable side is indicated.

Planning for final thickness is often one of the considerations for the designer. It affects the thickness of the spine on perfect-bound books; the legal stock for postcards; the maximum number of pages for saddle-stitched booklets; and so on. It is usually a simple matter of picking a paper and calling the paper house for a dummy. Most suppliers are happy to supply a folded dummy or the paper to make one (knowing that if it works, they have a sale). Sometimes the paper is sent to the bindery to make the dummy.

Reading paper labels

Here is a very short lesson on reading paper labels. If you look at the graphics on the opposite page you will see the basics of paper labels. Notice that they are not labeled office, printing, or cover (although cover stock is usually called cover somewhere on the label). You know the type of paper by its weight and its description. It will definitely take some practice. Thankfully, you usually cannot buy these papers outside of a professional paper distributing house. So, your questions can all be answered there.

One of the first choices in a design

Picking the paper is important.

Paper is often extremely important for small (short-run) jobs. On long runs, paper becomes one of the major expenses. For short runs, paper is often a negligible cost. On huge long-run jobs, setup charges (which include design and artwork) become ignorable. A $5,000 artwork charge means nothing on a $1 million job in which the paper costs might be as high as $750,000. On small jobs (runs of 2,000 or less), setup charges become the dominant factor. For a typical short-run brochure, the artwork could cost $500, the stripping and plates cost $500, the presswork cost $150, and the paper be only $25 or $35.

On these little jobs, going to the most expensive paper on the market would triple the paper cost, but add only 5% or so to the overall cost. In comparing the two preceding examples, the short-run case adds another $50. In the large job, we would be looking at a $1.5 million increase. For short runs, paper quality is a powerful tool to use for conveying quality.

The difference between a ream of the cheapest bond and the best 100% cotton bond is around $30. Top-quality text paper is about halfway between. If you are printing only one ream, each additional color of ink

Where should you be by this time?

By this time you should have earned nearly all your grade. You should be working comfortably in page layout. In fact, software should be ceasing to be such a major issue, becoming a comfortable tool in your hands for designing your projects.

DISCUSSION

You should be discussing differences in personal style with your classmates. Discuss the different papers available, which ones you really like, and why. Pick a stock for your personal letterhead that you think represents your stance best.

Talk amongst yourselves...

will probably cost almost $100 in production costs at a normal commercial printer, and every additional hour of design or image assembly time adds at least $50 plus materials. I cannot emphasize enough how important it is to consider this option for many, if not most, of your printing projects.

For short run projects, paper quality is the cheapest option in quality improvement.

Even on longer runs, paper choice is critical. Glossy paper is often perceived as cheap because of all the newsstand magazines that use it. Simply going to a dull sheet can greatly increase the perception of quality. Often, for that top-quality image, two-color PMS on a top-grade text works much better than process on cheap coated. In addition, it often costs less.

 In general, any project needing fewer than **2,000** sheets of paper is considered short run (unless there are many pages). Projects like these make up half of all jobs printed, according to Frank Romano's *Pocket Guide to Digital Prepress*, Delmar, 1996. That percentage has gone up substantially since then as more and more printing moves into the office. Text papers can help, at relatively no cost, to greatly improve the appearance and quality of your projects.

One of your first, and most important, choices is the paper you will use. It not only sets the tone for the message you are trying to convey to the readers for every piece you design, it also is an important part of your general style of design. Your paper choices provide the environment of your design.

Knowledge retention

1. What should you know about a 28# paper?
2. What is the advantage of text stock for short-run projects?
3. Why is enamel stock often not a quality improvement?
4. Describe the differences between an 80# text and 90# index?
5. Why are paper choices so important?
6. Where do you go to find out about papers in your area?
7. Why are paper weights so different?

CHAPTER FIFTEEN

Web Design

Concepts

1. Gamma

2. Bandwidth

3. Image map

4. Download times

Dealing with low resolution and tiny files

Chapter Objectives:

By giving students a clear understanding of what capabilities are available on the World Wide Web, this chapter will enable students to:

1. design for both platforms
2. keep download speeds low
3. deal with monitor display quality issues
4. explain the monitor differences between platforms

Lab Work for Chapter:

1. Complete the required Skill Exams.
2. Read chapter 16 for next week.
3. Work on projects.

Welcome to the CD-ROM!

This is the CD index for:
Publishing with Illustrator and FreeHand,
OnWord Press by David Bergsland

This CD has several resources that have not been printed in the book. There is a Pedagogy PDF teaching instructors how to teach this material (contact Delmar or David for the password). Primarily there is the Website containing an outline, the reading assignments, theory exams, Miniskills, and Skill Exams that constitute the actual course content of this three-credit course for advanced high school students, vocational students, associate degree digital publishing students, or design students in a four-year school.

There are also installers for Netscape Communicator, Explorer, and Acrobat Reader 4 in both PC and MAC formats. There are also several demo versions of publishing applications. The folders are named: MacInstallers & PCInstallers. Finally, there are several FREE fonts, also in PC or Mac. The folders are named: DD Fonts & DD PCFonts. These are fonts that can be used for your Miniskills and Skill Exams. Each purchaser of a book gets a license to use these fonts however they like, on their personal computer. They are not to be given to anyone else.

Realities of the Web

While this design probably does not excite you, it has several advantages. The main one being that the entire page is around 18K. It downloads very fast. The tables used instead of fancy rollover buttons mean that the links work even for those surfing with the graphics turned off (which is a much higher percentage than you might think). The fact that the graphic is a GIF means that the majority, who have less than 24-bit monitors, will see it as designed.

A different world:

World Wide Web

This is where many designers with a print history will begin having a rough time. On the World Wide Web, we are entering a world of coarse, crude graphics, with little layout control, no color calibration, and no output control. However, like all design problems, this is just another problem to be dealt with. There is hope. Some of the new software applications, like Dreamweaver and GoLive, promise layout control, but it is still dependent on the abilities and defaults of the individual browser which is reading the site.

The software only changes a little.

The best software applications for Web graphic creation are still FreeHand, Illustrator, and Photoshop. Fireworks and ImageReady are more specialized, adding powerful file-size reduction capabilities. Flash offers new and powerful animation abilities, but the download times are still very long. Surely you can recognize that we are still talking about bitmap and PostScript illustration programs. Graphic communication is about using graphics to communicate, and the FreeHand/Illustrator/Photoshop combination is the best, no matter what the medium.

This is the primary reason why Web site design and creation are still dominated by desktop publishers. It is basically the same skill set. The drawing and creative skills are almost identical, compromised only by the limitations of the formats used. The layout and design techniques and skills are still largely the same.

The conceptual difference is the interactivity.

The main thing to remember is that Web design is conceptually different. James Mohler and Jon Duff in their book, *Designing Interactive Web sites*, make a great deal about nonlinear design. Their ideas are very sound, but this is really nothing new when you consider almanacs, encyclopedias, reference books, and so forth.

The basic difference is the interactivity of the Web as a whole. Our rides through cyberspace are all individual searches for content. In fact, due to the present bandwidth restrictions, it may be fairly said that content is at least as important on the Web as in print.

So, exactly like all of the things we have been talking about, the important thing is to determine what the surfer is looking for when they come to your site. Why are they there? You need to meet their needs quickly and efficiently. Unless you are selling games or the like, most of the visitors to your clients' Web sites are looking for solid data about the products or services offered by your client — easily, quickly, and efficiently.

The Web cannot do type.

The reason that the Web has not been mentioned much in this book is plain: type is almost impossible online. For Web site design and creation you need Dreamweaver or GoLive. In fact, you can do as I do and meet all of your Web design needs very easily with PageMill. However, a couple of words about Web design are necessary here. For the truth is that you will regularly be asked to make a Web version of your printed documents.

Page layout's HTML capabilities

The HTML capabilities of all the new version of page layout are very impressive. However, I wouldn't get too excited. As with all page creation on the Web, many rather harsh realities need to be considered. First of all, the completely graphic look of many contemporary designers does not translate well to the Web.

The PDF solution

If you truly need to retain the exact look and feel of your typeset documents, the only true solution is PDF. Taking into account the fact that almost all reading of Web sites is done from printed copies, PDFs are really not a bad solution (except for the file-size load placed on your server). You do need to warn the surfer about the file size and the approximate download times.

If you are designing for an in-house service or intranet, PDFs work exceptionally well. Over an Ethernet connection, PDFs download quickly, print beautifully, and can be just as internally interactive as any Web site.

For traditional Web sites (now there's a silly concept), you will almost always have to rearrange your documents rather radically. On the Web, reading is done in very short bursts. When the needed data is reached, the first reaction is to print the page. All of the other pages need to be clear and concise, offering all the linkage options suggested by the content, so the surfer can arrive at that needed data as quickly and efficiently as possible.

So, what I am saying is this: it is normally best to design your documents for print first because of the far higher resolution and typography requirements. You can always dumb down your pages for the Web. However, to make a truly usable Web site, you will need to spend a lot of time designing the site structure, and it will normally be radically different from your print documents.

Even though InDesign, PageMaker, and QuarkXPress can export their documents into HTML pages that look much like their printed version, you are far better off to think of the conversion as a much more fundamental change. Simply exporting that gorgeous brochure using Cascading Style Sheets (CSS) will usually result in a nonfunctional (albeit beautiful) Web page or site.

Limited by the environment

First of all, the Web is severely limited by its output device – the monitor. Although it is true that the Web looks better on high-resolution monitors, less than a third use them at this time. Even if high-res monitors are available, the graphics are still limited to 72 to 96 dpi. Most people use 800×600 pixel monitors, although there are still nearly 20% using 640×480. The most recent figures I have seen suggest that even though 800×600 has become the norm, the high-resolution portion is only growing slowly from a quarter to a third.

Beyond low resolution is the problem of color depth, or the ability of the monitor to display enough colors to satisfy the designer's desires. The figures I saw in 2001 show that nearly half of the monitors can only produce 16-bit, with more than 25% at 8-bit and around 20% with 24-bit. To make sure you've got it, 80% of monitors are less than 24-bit. Think about that the next time you drop in that exquisite little 24-bit JPEG.

If your client's customers are mostly graphic designers or digital gamesters, then you can almost count on resolutions of at least 800×600 with 24-bit depth. If those customers are small business owners, you'd better design for 640×480 and 8-bit. Don't be suckered by thinking that rural areas or small towns have lesser equipment. In reality, they often have better and newer hardware. However, the subtlety we take for granted in print is simply not available on the Web.

Platform differences with monitors

On the Web, you have to be cognizant of the vast differences between PC and Mac. It sounds like a simple difference. PC monitors use a gamma of 2.2, and Macs use a gamma of 1.8. To translate the gammas just mentioned: Mac monitors are much brighter, and usually much higher resolution. Images created on a high-res Mac, that look great there, often look very dark and dingy on a PC, not to mention that they look huge. Images created on a PC, that look fine there, are often far too light, with all the highlights blown out on the Mac; often they are also much too small. This tends to be true, even when you set a Mac's gamma at 2.2 to try to compensate.

This is also true of type. On my high-res monitors, I use 14-point type or larger to make it legible on the screen. The type looks absolutely huge on a PC. This is also why many Web sites created on a PC are completely unreadable on a Mac, because the type is too small to be read, especially if it uses small, light type on a dark or graphic background.

Huge numbers of people surf with the graphics turned off.

This is probably the place to mention all those who surf with the graphics turned off. In mid-1999, surveys said that there were somewhere between 15% and 30% of surfers who browse with the graphics turned off. The best guess I have heard recently suggests it is still 10% to 25%. This was largely because of the speed of their connection. We have to remember that the average modem is still 33.6 – *and* the average person has a modem. In fact, virtually all of us who access the Web over a phone line are limited to that speed by the phone line. However, many surf with graphics off because everything they are looking for is in the words anyway.

Pretty depressing, huh?

Actually, it's not that bad.

This is an environment where color has no penalty, you can always work in color at no extra cost. Although we are not talking about the impact of process color on cast coated stock with photos popping off the page, highlit by gloss varnish on a dull varnish background, the color available is good enough to get the reader's attention – 256 colors are definitely better than black and a spot color. All we have to do is design within the medium's capabilities. Careful attention to detail still provides excellence of design. Don't fuss about the limitations. Design within the medium.

Color on the Web

The major thing to remember is that color still lessens contrast. A limited color palette is essential to effective communication. The 216 Web-safe colors give you more than enough colors to work with.

However, the same color issues found in print cause problems online. Colored type on a colored background is harder to read *always*. Because color is available so easily, you must exercise restraint.

The limiting factor is bandwidth!

This real problem is actually far worse than the limited palette and low resolution. As I mentioned, the average surfer has a 28.8 to 56 kilobit modem. Normal phone connections max out between 3K and 8K per second. Even the 56 kilobit standard is glacially slow when normal color images are dozens of megabytes in size. At 28.8 kilobits (which is well under 4K per second), a 10 MB graphic would take 42½ minutes — minimum (if there is not a break in communication that requires you to start over).

In general, modem connections over phone lines are slow, no matter what hype sold you your particular modem. DSL and cable are not real solutions although they certainly help. All Web traffic ends up on phone lines, at this point. When we reach small satellite transceivers, then we can talk about true bandwidth change.

Download times

Surveys often state that the average surfer cancels out and moves on if the entire page takes more than 30 seconds to appear. I have read articles that suggest anything over 10 seconds is a problem. An informal study of my students over the past seven years indicates that 15 seconds is a practical limit. This means that the entire page must be under 45K (though many agree with me that under 30K is much wiser). Even at the community college where I teach (where we have a T-1 line on an Ethernet network), I consider myself fortunate if I can download at 50K per second during the day. The norm for off-campus sites is still 3K per second or less, because even this very fast network is too busy.

Of course, there are always the storied cable modems and even satellite modems. I'm sure you have one — right! I know something of that ilk will probably come in the next decade, but we don't know for sure what it look like or work like *yet*. So the sum of the limitations for the next several years is that your Web graphics have to be 72 dpi, usually 8-bit, and always under 30K (3K is obviously far superior).

A reality check

Please remember that, outside our community of designers, the average monitor is still 16-bit or less. Many monitors at poorer schools and smaller businesses are still 4-bit. All of those gorgeous, too large, Web graphics crammed into the sixteen colors available is a sorry sight. JPEGs viewed in 8-bit are still severely compromised. Be aware of your viewers! **Design to communicate, not to show off.**

Calibrated surfing

Pushed by the need for accurate colors to sell clothing online, there are many groups working on free and easy monitor calibration for the Web. At the time of this writing (mid-2002) it is all vaporware. However, it will probably happen. The scenario I am hearing at this point is that we will be downloading software from the Web sites. That remains to be seen.

Dithering

For some, dithering is a big deal. This is the process of making intermediate colors by interspersing different colors of dots. Sort of like pointillism in fine art. As long as the dots are random and not patterned, this is no problem. Pattern dithers are very ugly. Diffusion dither (geekspeak for random dots) looks very nice — almost like mezzotinting.

Those of us in the design community tend to forget how limited the average business PC is. Remember, the Mac is designed by graphic designers for graphic designers, and the PC is designed to be cheap. Always check out your designs on both platforms, and as many different browsers as you can.

System color variances: Web-safe color

The final platform difference we need to discuss is commonly seen when using GIFs. GIFs use indexed color (8-bit or less). Both PC and Mac have a standard set of 256 system colors (8-bit). Of course they are different sets. Actually, there are 216 common colors in the two different systems. This is the fabled Web-safe color palette. Don't get too excited!

Much has been made of using the Web-safe palette. In my humble opinion, it is simply more of that anal-retentive nitpicking commonly found in designers who think that the perfect color/design/layout really matters. Basically, *Web-safe* is an oxymoronic concept. It is barely possible to have a calibrated PC monitor, so you have no idea what the colors are going to look like anyway. The real solution is not a Web *safe* color palette, but clean, crisp design that looks good no matter how the colors are modified. The concern for dithering is more of the same. Design your graphics so dithering doesn't matter.

Software limitations are simply part of the problems we have to solve as designers. Design is problem-solving. On another arena, think of what bridges would look like if we had a material that was so strong that a half-inch-thick plate could span a mile while carrying a full load of cars and trucks.

Your task is not to fight reality, but to use available capabilities to create beautiful solutions that communicate clearly to the selected readership.

Some suggested production procedures

First of all, my suggestion for graphic creation on the Web is to work from FreeHand or Illustrator. The key to small, easy-to-read, functional graphics is that they be clear and communicate clearly. One of the major tests of your design is that your pages download in less than 10 seconds on a 28.8 modem over a regular phone line, so it is imperative that you use no graphics without a good reason. When you use a graphic for a good reason, it has to be **SMALL** (in bytes).

The result of this is that many, or most, of your graphics will be words or will contain words. Photoshop is terrible with type, unless it is very large and high-res. Even with Photoshop 6 and 7, and the much vaunted type tool, type is still clumsy. In print, most know that PostScript illustration is the only real solution for powerful type manipulation. If you don't know that yet, at least now you know why you are always out-produced.

In addition, Photoshop is a lousy drawing program. It is not designed for, or meant for, drawing. I know many of you use Photoshop as your primary illustration program. However, it is better used as an image manipulation program that deals with scans and rasterizes original art from PostScript illustration at specific sizes. It cannot do composite paths, complicated blends, or most of the other path combination capabilities we take for granted in FreeHand and Illustrator.

However, it is necessary for adjusting your graphics to the smallest size after they are created. Now that ImageReady is part of Photoshop, all of us have all the tools needed to make very small, and very effective graphics. The new lossy GIF option is a real help. When combined with color depth and dithering percentages, wonderful GIFs are easy.

Keeping the high-res needed for print

If you start in PostScript illustration, you'll have a high-resolution graphic available for the conversion. They are actually more powerful, in many ways, than the specialized Web tools which are totally incapable of being used for anything other than the Web. Most designers who do only Web design have simply never paid the money necessary to get the good tools that are a normal part of our graphic design experience. Without the graphic knowledge we have begun to cover in this book, they cannot come close to the communication effectiveness we have available with the software we use.

The Web has different design problems.

Do not even try to mimic your incredible page layout on the Web. It is a different medium. Personally, I usually simply copy and paste the copy out of the print documents into the WYSIWYG Web editor being used. It does save the typing time, but its main advantage is the elimination of formatting. I want to make sure that I have eliminated all formatting that might cloud my view toward clear communication on the Web. Converting print projects directly to Web pages rarely works.

I find that I commonly have to eliminate half of my print copy or more. What we see as terse in print becomes verbose online. When all of the copy is necessary, I am leaning more and more toward PDF delivery. I know they are going to print out that copy to read regardless. The new printing quality Flash content may offer some solution, but then that is pure heresy in a book on Adobe software, isn't it?

What we see as terse in print becomes verbose online.

A little more reality

At this point, we are still governed by phone lines and hemmed in by AOL. We have to design for our customers. The only excuse for the fancy stuff would be if our customers are young gamers or seekers of entertainment (as opposed to data). Beyond that, focusing on fancy graphics, wild animations, rollovers, full-page imagemaps, and the rest really misses the point entirely. Most of the Web sites that are done professionally (for money) are greatly inhibited by extraneous graphics and a cluttered interface. You've only got a few seconds to keep them on your site.

The best thing I have ever read about the Web was on one of the Web design sites, and it went something like this:

People do not come to your site to see the killer Web graphics — they come for easily accessible information.

Your customers (or your clients' customers) are not looking for amazing digital dances to amuse and pass the time. They want to know what you are offering, why they need it, and how to get it. The fancy stuff does not help. **It irritates!** It's the same reason why most of your printed projects are still (and will remain) black and white. In printing, process color is the fancy stuff, and even process color is much easier to justify than that incredible animation with the embedded row of changing interactive buttons where you have to wait seconds for each new image to appear (assuming the screen is not blank while waiting).

At school, as I mentioned, I am running a G4 Quicksilver, with 512 MB RAM, on a 100BaseT WAN, to a T-1 line, and I still find the fancy stuff merely mildly irritating (entertainment at best). There are many sites, even with this exceptionally fast access, where pages take so long to download that I simply click off in disgust. Even Yahoo's Home Page was like that for a long time (although they have fixed it). Imagine how a surfer feels on an early iMac or slow Celeron, with 16 MB RAM, using a 28.8 modem through AOL. Heck, maybe your customers even live in rural areas where good phone lines are a luxury that hasn't arrived.

Always preview your site!

I clearly remember my shock the first time I saw my Web site at school on a computer in one of the PC labs upstairs. It was huge, very dark, and in Times New Roman. That original home page didn't even look like the clean, bright page set in Palatino that I had designed on my screen. I ended up redesigning quite a bit of the page, making the logos and the type smaller, changing the fonts used. This is a much larger problem than you might think.

The first major differences are found in the two opposing operating systems themselves. We have already mentioned that the Microsoft and Mac system palettes are different, with only 216 common colors. A much more important difference is the monitors used. As is true in most things PC, the operative word is *cheap*. Whenever you have a product and an entire industry that is primarily governed by price concerns, you have a problem. PC purchasers complain if a computer costs more than $1,000, in fact, many now expect them to cost less than $500. **This is absurd!** They get what they pay for.

Even with a PC, to get a computer that will do what we need it to do as graphic designers will cost between $2,000 and $3,000 or more. You cannot even seriously run a PC before you buy several cards and peripherals that do not come with the machine as standard equipment. However, the real problem here, as far as viewing your marvelously designed site on the Web is concerned, is that any monitor over $300 is considered ridiculously expensive.

Finally, we have the differences in browsers. We assume that there are only two: Explorer or Communicator. But already you can see the problem. About 80% have Explorer available. AOL uses a limited Explorer-based browser, and they are the largest sources of surfers. More than that, we have the different version numbers. All of the latest bells and whistles assume that you are using a version 5 browser or better. Only Y2K got the average up to 4.0. Both browsers and all of the different versions of those two browsers show pages differently; check out as many as you can when proofing your Web sites.

In addition, there are many more browser options. I am not just talking about all of the nongraphic interfaces found on many of the bureaucratic systems. There are also several companies who were eagerly awaiting the alleged Microsoft breakup. I won't even speculate here.

A word on friendliness

How to communicate online

Web sites are unique bits of graphic communication. On the one hand, they are very cold, uninvolved, impersonal assemblages of digital data. For pixel pushers like us, they are great fun and global, on top of that. Some may push the Mac as friendly, but it is not alive and cannot relate to us. The same is true of the Internet, that incomprehensibly vast and intertwined network of most of the computers on Earth. On the other hand, our Web sites reach our customers on a very personal level in a quiet time, where they are isolated within their computer environment, often in the apparent safety of their bedroom, den, living room, or office. Like a Mac, the Web seems friendly, responding easily to our command. More than that, it is a communication medium.

What this means in practical terms is that the Web is a strange type of uniquely personal communication. I've written this book in first person, but none of you really think you are communicating with me. However, if you go to my Web site, find out where I am coming from, and we start an email dialogue, we can develop a pretty tight relationship relatively quickly.

... the Web is a strange type of uniquely personal communication.

In my commercial online school, I have students from all over the world. The farthest one to register, so far, is from the North Island of New Zealand, but I've had many inquiries from most of Asia, all over Europe (especially Italy, for some reason), and the Middle East. Normally, I don't even find out where they are from until we have talked to each other several times. It really does not matter at all. The only differences I have noticed with my student in New Zealand are: their year is very different, being south of the equator; they use metric (but most do that); they hyphenate words differently; and they use plural verbs with companies. Those small differences are merely enough to make things fun.

The other interesting fact is that I know her better than I do most of my students who are in my classroom for a few semesters. The

Web seems to promote that. It seems to have something to do with the safety of distance and the relative anonymity of computer-to-computer communication. When she graduated, she flew here to New Mexico because she just had to meet us!

The visitors to sites you design really need to touch a human there. They want to know names, email addresses, history, background, and so forth. One of the original successful sites (now morphed into deadlock.com) was for a small hotel in London.

It was phenomenally successful via the simple technique of letting prospective guests wander through the hotel in their imagination. If they wondered about meals, there were pictures, menus, a picture of the cook and her background. The designer (who was then in charge of marketing for this little side-street hotel) said he regularly got bookings from people who made statements like, "I've been wandering around your site for nearly two hours now, having a marvelous time, I guess I'll book a room." The last time I heard, nearly 75% of their bookings were coming from the Web site. How did he do that?

The answer is actually very simple. First of all, his writing style is cheerful, friendly, unpretentious, and believable. This is very important. However, more than that, he has a real gift of letting a surfer answer any question he or she might have. Upon visiting the site, you are left with the feeling that the hotel really cares for you, that they genuinely want you to have a wonderful experience staying with them.

The friendliness, openness, and genuine trustworthiness of your site are primary!

This needs to be your focus in Web design. Seems like normal stuff for any type of graphic design, doesn't it? Just as with print, if the surfer reacts consciously to the neat graphics and your incredible design, you've lost him as your client. The best designs are not only invisible, they should also enable the surfer to feel like she can go anywhere she wants and get the answers she needs.

Button bars and communication

By now, you have noticed on the Web site for this book that the communication bars are simple tables with colored backgrounds. Some of you may have even wondered why there weren't amazingly beautiful 3D buttons to guide you on your way through the site. In fact, there are no buttons at all, because tables download like type, *and just as fast*. Not only that, they are clean and easy to understand. I am a little concerned

Where should you be by this time?

Finishing up!

Talk among yourselves...

that they are too dark for PCs, but the goal was ease of use.

"Can't I do buttons?" I can hear your whining from here. Certainly you can. But you need to think it out first. If a page is supposed to be 15K to 35K in size (and 15K is far better), then you really need to plan the button sizes accordingly. If you have seven buttons, for example, 3K each will use up almost your entire graphic allotment for the page!

The other problem with the fancy button approach is a little more subjective. Once a person starts with the fancy buttons, it's very hard to stop. The home page at my school had this problem. After the first page, the buttons did show up very fast. However, the designer couldn't stop there. Every page had large graphics unique to that page. Worse yet, after you got past those new graphics, the typography was very bad, clumsy and difficult to read. It's a little better now, maybe.

Most of your Web design problems will be solved if you simply remember the reason for the site in the first place. If you are getting paid to design the site, the client needs to make income from it. So, you immediately go back to the same old questions.

- What's the product?
- What's the message?
- Who's the client?
- Who's the reader?
- What does the client want the reader to do?

With the answers to those questions, you can design a clean site, that downloads fast, is easy to understand, and is easy to negotiate. The client's readers will happily do what is desired because you will have helped them to see that the client's product is something they really need, plus it is easy to purchase, easy to remember, and/or easy to use.

Finally, typos are absolutely forbidden!

Knowledge retention

1. Why are button bars a problem?
2. How can the Web be friendly?
3. How long do you have to answer an email?
4. Why do you have to be concerned about monitor gamma?
5. What is the average download speed?
6. Why do people go to a Web site?
7. How do you convert a print document to a Web page?

Customer Relations

Concepts:

Oh, my gosh,
the customer
is always right!

*Dealing with employers, clients,
and deadlines*

Chapter Objectives:

By giving students a clear understanding of what the reality is of employment in this industry, this chapter will enable students to:

1. plan with a clear head

Dealing with reality...

The customer is always right?

Of course not! What we have to keep foremost in our minds is that it doesn't matter whether the customer is right or wrong. Our job is to serve him. Our task is to convince him that we are professional and that we really care about his business. It does not matter if he's wrong; if we treat him like he is, he is gone. That may solve the problem (since he is no longer our client), but it is a poor way of doing business.

A service industry

Printing has been referred to as a service industry. As we draw this book to a close, it is imperative that we review a little, and this is the most important fact. Our job is to please the client. We are designers of custom products. We normally cannot just make millions of copies and throw them around, hoping to sell a high enough percentage to stay in business.

We sell custom products for individuals. Even though you may be dealing almost exclusively with large corporations, it is the individuals in the corporation that matter. If we do not make an individual happy, that person will find a printer that does. It is that simple.

The realities of pressure

Deadlines

Our industry is run on deadlines. Many of these time limits are ridiculous. We know it. The customer knows it. It does not change the fact that the deadlines are real. If you are producing an event program, complaining about the deadline will not move the event back a day. If the SEC has a March 1 deadline for receipt of that annual report, March 2 is not good enough.

It is common to blame the client for delays. It is common for printers to lose work because they blame their clients for deadlines. Instead, they should figure out what can be done as soon as the job is brought in. You can do a great deal to help customer relations by simply explaining reality to your clients whenever possible. Your job is to serve your clients and meet their needs if at all possible. The blame game is a waste of time at best.

Sales staff and CSRs

Reality checks are primarily the task of the sales personnel. As they locate and close deals with clients, they must be aware of the deadlines involved. However, more and more, we are all involved with the customers — face to face, by phone, or online. With the possible exception of the pressroom, all of us deal with the clients.

The front office — back shop distinction is almost gone. This is especially true in the digital part of our industry. All of us are working together to meet the customer's needs.

An excellent employee is prepared to do what it takes.

That's a scary thought. What if you are asked to work the weekend? What if you have to come in a little early or leave late? Are you willing to be reliable help? This goes 'way beyond the normal requirements of showing up every day, on time and ready to work. Can you serve?

The proper attitude

We cannot continue until we cover what you should expect to offer an employer (or a client). They do not owe you anything beyond honesty and integrity. Even these are sometimes in short supply. When you are hired, you will be given a list of company expectations — sometimes written, sometimes verbally, sometimes through the grapevine.

Your job is to meet those expectations. If you cannot, do everyone a favor and find a place where you fit. Every position has pluses and minuses. You will want to find work where the positives meet your needs and the negatives are inconsequential. It is not the employer's job to change the company to satisfy you. Their concern is financial survival.

Owners and managers make the big bucks because they have the big headaches. If you want the money, you get the pressure. It is a decision you have to make. You will never be a welcome employee if you are always complaining about reality. Your task is to meet your employer's needs by satisfying the company's customers.

You need to be prepared to work extra hours and to put the company's needs on a high priority. You will discover, as your career develops, that many people do not do these simple things. As a result, they make everyone's life miserable — always complaining, always the bottleneck in production. If you are like that, do us all a favor and find another career.

Publishing is a team sport. All of us need to work together. Many students are almost horrified to learn that they cannot take anything all the way through production. Sooner or later, you have to hand off your baby to someone else. The likelihood is that you will be working on something started by someone else anyway.

The key is communication.

How many times has this been said over the past 400 pages? Experience shows that it cannot be repeated often enough. There must be good communication between the sales staff and the client, between the sales staff and the designers, between the designers and the client, the designers and the printshop or service bureau, and so on.

The job ticket

The first major communication tool is the job ticket. This is the way the sales staff communicates with the rest of the shop. It is extremely important that these forms be filled out accurately and completely. Not only are the complete job specs required, but also the complete client name and address, former job numbers, and the appropriate contact person(s). If you are working for yourself, you still need one.

Just as important as filling out the job ticket is reading it. Most jobs that had to be redone were messed up because someone did not read the job ticket. Do not take anyone else's word for what you need to do — **read the job ticket!** This even covers the bosses' instructions. You make them look good if you discover that what they told you does not match what is on the job ticket. You can save the company thousands of dollars.

Customer proofs

The next most important communication tool is the proof. We need to examine them from the customer relations viewpoint. The most important proofs from a legal and public relations standpoint are the customer proofs. These are sample prints that are marked up with notes to explain what the client might not know.

Three proofs are usually necessary. The first is a laser proof of the artwork. This art or copy proof must be signed off by the client before you proceed to the expense of a color proof. In some cases, it is better to have an artwork proof that has FPO graphics. You might not want to spend the time color-correcting separations if the customer has not even approved the photos yet.

Often, what we are calling the art proof takes the place of what used to be called the comprehensive or comp. The comprehensive was accurate enough to enable the client to approve the artwork (without spending any more time or money than necessary). In many cases, all the budget will allow is a digital color print of the final artwork and the hope that the client doesn't make too many changes.

It is important to make sure that the customer realizes that signing the art proof means that he approves of the graphics and the copy on it — including all typos, spelling, and grammar. If you do not have that, you will find it very difficult later to charge for customer alterations. Supposedly, if the client changes her mind, about copy or layout, she should be charged for the time and materials it takes to make those changes. Without a signed art proof, you have no evidence that she ever liked the artwork in the first place.

Getting customer approval

The signed proofs become legal contracts. You promise to produce the work as proofed. The client promises to accept and pay for the work as proofed. There are ways to ease the approval process. The primary method is thorough proofing. As a general guideline, you are in trouble if you have more than one correction per four pages. Any more than that and you will be considered less than professional.

The basic problem is that clients are used to Madison Avenue, just like the rest of us. Their baseline assumption is perfection, because that is what they are used to. A sizable percentage of clients feel the same about artwork charges as they do about dental bills — and it does not make them happy. Many of them are looking for an excuse to prove that they know as much as you do. You will find, in not a few cases, that customers will use your mistakes to try and leverage a reduction in the charges. What is the simple solution? Do not give them anything to pick on.

The customer is always right!

The old saying, "The customer is always right," is not a joke. It is a truism. In other words, it is so obviously true that it seems stupid to mention it. This is where we started this chapter, but we have not covered it yet. By definition, the customer is right because our job is to serve the client. Our task is to bring what the customers ask for into reality.

There will be many times when you are asked to do something very difficult. Remember that you chose this career to avoid boredom. To develop skill, you have to be stretched. If everything is easy, you get bored, relax into bad attitudes, and begin to dislike your profession. Some of your clients' most ridiculous requests are your best opportunity for growth.

You do not have to like your clients. You do have to respect them. In a very real way, the success of your business depends on the success of their business. Often clients are headstrong or arrogant or egotistical. Some of this is necessary; some of it is simply obnoxious. It is not your job to tell them that their arrogance is simply a projection of their insecurity (even though this is often true). They are in business to make a profit and your job is to help them. They need help, not hassles.

Business relationships are not social relationships.

Even if you do like your clients (and that is always pleasant), you should not expect a social relationship to develop. Friends that you hang around with tend to make poor clients. There is a tendency to give them favors, put their jobs on a higher priority, and do many other things that jeopardize your relationships with the rest of your clients. The friend who allows you to keep business on a businesslike basis is a rare friend. I hope you have many.

Business ethics

There are many lists and several books concerning business ethics and trade practices. For example, there is the excellent book, *Graphic Artists Guild Handbook, Pricing and Ethical Guidelines*. Don't restrict yourself to this list. Ask your employers for a copy of the list they use. In general, these books are concerned with legislating morality, which is always tricky, at best. The basic tenets are always the same: honesty, integrity, keeping your word, and fulfilling written agreements. In this day of constant litigation and adversarial relationships, it is extremely wise to have written contracts for everything.

This is a major pain. However, it is really not optional. Contracts are not about limiting people and keeping them in line. The purpose of a contract is clear communication and mutual agreement. Little is more disheartening than to do exactly what you think you were asked to do and get screamed at for your incompetence. People simply hear wrong, believe it or not.

Your word may be good, but that does not help if clients think you promised something else. This does not count those who are looking to pick a fight to avoid payment. Those people exist also, and contracts help keep them in line. The best thing is a standard printed contract. That way personal friends and disliked clients get the same treatment. It is all in the interest of fairness and communication.

It gets very complicated. The likelihood is that your new employer already has a working set of guidelines in use. If the company doesn't, the book recommended is an excellent resource.

Knowledge retention

This section is a little different from the others; these questions have subjective answers.

1. Do I like publishing as an industry?
2. Do I enjoy beautiful printed work?
3. Am I willing to quench my ego and serve the clients?
4. Can I maintain a tight schedule with pressing deadlines?
5. Do I have a hidden agenda?
6. Am I willing to commit to the industry for at least five years?
7. Am I willing to continuously study the newest techniques, hardware, and software?
8. Do I have the creative gift?
9. How do I feel about the customer being right?
10. Why am I choosing this career?
11. Am I constantly designing, regardless of what I do?
12. Will I need further formal education for design skills?

Curriculum glossary

This glossary is for this series of books. It combines the glossaries from *Digital Drawing, Publishing with InDesign, Publishing with Photoshop, Publishing with Illustrator and FreeHand,* and this book. It should be much more helpful to students of any area of digital publishing.

The alphabetical listing

A

Additive color — A full-spectrum color space in which all three primaries add together to make white.

Aliased — Unmodified bitmap edges that are jagged, stair-stepped pixels.

Anti-aliased — Bitmapped edges that are visually smoothed by adding partial colors to smooth the edges of jagged pixel blocks.

Application defaults — The defaults for an entire application (program). Photoshop does not use them.

Ascender — The strokes of lowercase letters that project above the x-height: in *bdfhklt*, for example.

B

Banding — The bands of color that appear in gradients or blends when the resolution is too low, the linescreen is too high, the length of the transition is too long, or the color differential is too small.

Baseline — The imaginary line that the letters of type sit on.

Basis size —The sheet size used to determine the basis weight (used to define the weight of paper in pounds).

Basis weight — A ream (500 pages) of the basis size; that is, 500 sheets of a 20# bond paper weighs 20 pounds. This is the paper weight written on the packaging.

Bézier curves — The mathematical equations used to describe PostScript paths.

Bitmap — The grid to which pixels are mapped.

Bitmap image — A graphic in which every pixel is separately defined.

Bleed — Printing ink one-eighth inch beyond the trim size to give the illusion that the ink goes exactly to the edge of the sheet of paper when it is trimmed back to size.

Blend — The transformation of one path to another. Not available in Photoshop.

Blending mode — The method Photoshop uses to combine or overlay layers in a document.

Body copy — The basic reading paragraph of a document. This is outside the paradigm of Photoshop.

Bond — The most common name of office, bookkeeping, or writing paper.

Bounding box — The invisible box defined by the vertical and horizontal lines that touch the extreme left, right, top, and bottom edges of a shape or group. The manipulation handles for an image are located by the corners and centers of the sides of the bounding box.

Bridging — When two halftone dots barely touch and bleed together, creating a dot that is larger than the one specified.

Burst — A splashy graphic used to pull the reader's eye to a compelling idea or command (such as "free," or "buy now").

C

Calendering — Using a stacked series of large milled steel rollers to polish and compress paper as it comes off the papermaking machine, used for all printing papers.

Calibration — Adjustment of equipment to manufacturer's specifications to provide the most predictable results.

Caliper — The thickness of cover stock measured in thousandths of an inch.

Callout — A paragraph style of enlarged or emphasized body copy used as a graphic device to recapture a reader's wandering attention. Only possible in a page layout program (that is, not in Illustrator or Photoshop).

Camera ready — Artwork that is black and white, ready to be shot in a copy camera to make a negative or a plate.

CMY(K) — The full-spectrum color space of process printing. Cyan (C), magenta (M), and yellow (Y) are the primary colors, with black added because of the weak cyan.

Color depth — The number of bits assigned to a pixel. This determines the number of colors available to the monitor, scanner, printer, or digital press.

Color management — Establishment of relationships between calibrated machines, using color profiles, to accurately predict the final product's appearance.

Color proof — A proof of the final color output, formerly called a *stripping* or *prepress proof.*

Color reproduction — The ability to reproduce original color in multiple copies; this is theoretically impossible.

Color space — A system of colors defined by a set of three primary colors that are mixed to produce all the other colors in the color space.

Color system — A color environment that is not full-spectrum.

Color temperature — Color defined by its temperature in degrees Kelvin.

Color wheel — The RBY color space represented in circular fashion.

Commercial printing — Custom manufacturing of printed materials of almost any type.

Commodity color — Color that is so common that pricing is based entirely on market value and return on investment (copier color, digital color).

Complementary color — Color pairs of color wheel opposites.

Composite paths — Two or more closed paths that are converted into one path with a common even/odd fill. One of the major things missing in Photoshop's vector tools.

Compression — Replacing patterns in digital code with placeholders, or averaging areas of pixels to decrease file size.

Continuous tone — Images that continuously vary in color or tone, like photographs and scans of fine art paintings, pastels, charcoal drawings, and pencil drawings.

Contract proof — A proof, used as a contract for the client who promises to pay, and the printer who promises to duplicate the proof, protecting the designer and the others.

Contrast — The distance between the two extremes of dot range.

Copydot — Scanning or photographing a printed (screened) piece of artwork as lineart at a high enough resolution to copy the dots.

Creep — The movement of the copy toward the outside of a saddle-stitched booklet, due to the increasing thickness of the paper at the stitched edge.

Cropping — The elimination of extraneous data from an image.

Cross-platform — A workflow accomplished with some of the people working on Windows machines and some on Macintoshes or UNIX machines.

Curves — A line graph used to indicate all of the pixels in an image, which can be modified by click-dragging on the curve.

Customer proof — Used to give the client something to approve before continuing with production.

Customizable shortcuts — The ability to specify personalized keyboard shortcuts for almost all commands. This is a major lack in Photoshop and QuarkXPress.

Cylinder press — A printing press made of two milled steel cylinders with a plate in between the cylinders to carry the plate and paper; has an appearance like washing machine rollers with the metal plate passing between the rollers; developed for pressures necessary for intaglio.

D

Deboss — Using a letterpress platen press with a male and a female die to press graphics into the paper that go below the surface.

Defaults — What the software and hardware do when the designer has made no specific choices.

Density — A measurement of the lightness or darkness of a scanned or printed area measured from 0 (pure white) to 4.0 (absolute black).

Density range — The difference between the highlight and the darkest shadow, as measured by a densitometer using a logarithmic scale from 0–4.

Descender — The portions of lowercase letters that hang below the baseline: as in *gjpqy* for example.

Die-cut — Bending a knife-edged ruler to trace the shape drawn by the designer; used with letterpress to cut shapes out of paper like folders, door hangers and the like.

Diffusion dithering — Giving the illusion of continuous tone with seemingly random dots: the natural output of low-resolution color inkjet printers.

Dithering — A coarse arrangement of relatively small dots that gives the illusion of continuous tone, whether grayscale or color: used with low-resolution printers.

Document defaults — Defaults that apply only to a specific document. The document setup that opens when you hit the NEW DOCUMENT command under the FILE menu. They are not changeable in Photoshop.

Dot — The smallest unit of printing. A dot can vary in size or location but not in color.

Dot gain — The normal phenomenon of dots increasing in size as they are printed. All printers have dot gain except for calibrated electrostatic printers.

Dot range — More appropriately called the *tint range*. The range from the lightest highlight to the darkest shadow in tint percentages.

Duotone — A technique used to give more shadow density by overprinting two halftones.

E

Electromagnetic spectrum — The visible light spectrum.

Electrostatic — A printing method that uses an electrically charged image. This image attracts charged toner that is melted onto the paper. The basic technology of laser printers.

Emboss — The reverse of deboss using the same technique with letterpress to raise an image above the surface of the paper.

Emulsification — The mixing of oil or grease and water. This is the purpose of soap (except that in printing, emulsification is a mechanical process).

Enamel — Another name for coated offset printing paper; also called gloss, dull, or matte.

EPS (Encapsulated PostScript) — A graphic format written in the PostScript page description language. Files in this format can only be printed on PostScript printers.

Export — Writing digital code in a format that can be read by other software.

Extrema — Points placed on a PostScript path at the extreme left, right, top, and bottom of the path.

F

Fill — The interior content of a PostScript shape. The attributes applied to the area enclosed by a path.

Filler — A chemical added to paper for bulk and opacity.

Fine art reproduction — One of the most difficult printing projects, because of the critical nature of the color and detail reproduction necessary. Many fine art colors cannot be duplicated and many details are too fine or subtle.

Flag — The name of a newsletter or newspaper expressed in a banner-style design on the front page.

Flexography — A method of letterpress using relatively soft, flexible plates; dominant in packaging.

Foil stamp — (see Deboss) A letterpress technique using flat graphic shapes, often heated, to stamp foil onto a sheet of paper.

Font — A complete set of characters for a given type style.

Font family — A group of type styles of different weights from light or thin to bold, heavy, or black.

Format, graphic — Code exported from a digital document in a form that can be read by other programs.

Formatting — Arranging copy for readability and comprehension by applying specific paragraph styles.

Frame — A containing shape in PostScript, or an additional window open on a Web page.

Front matter — Pieces of a book or magazine that come before the real content, such as table of contents, foreword, preface, and the like.

Fugitive color — Color that fades quickly to white.

Full-spectrum — A color space that contains colors from all areas of the visible spectrum.

G

Gamma — The slope of the curve indicating contrast.

Gamut alarm — A dialog box that warns when the color on the screen is unprintable.

Generation — A copy of an original.

Ghosting — Making an image, or a portion of an image, light enough in value that type can be overprinted.

GIF (Graphic Interchange Format) — A graphic format with limited colors and good compression, used for low-resolution Web graphics. CompuServe's Web graphic format uses indexed color (8-bit or less) and LZW compression (like TIFFs).

Graphic design — Design in any area of digital publishing production. What was formerly called commercial art; the arrangement of copy and graphics for the purpose of clear communication.

Gravure — The modern printing technology using intaglio; digitally uses huge, plastic cylinders carved by lasers.

Gray levels — A number of available tint percentages.

Gripper — Blank space left at the edge of a sheet of paper to allow the press to grab it and pull it through the duplicator or press.

Group — Constraining two or more objects into permanent relationship. Photoshop cannot do this.

GUI (Graphic User Interface) — A computer interface, like MacOS or Windows, that uses graphic analogies to relate to the data in the computer: mouse, icons, pop-up menus, and so forth.

Gutter — The vertical white space left between columns; also used to describe the center margins of a book or booklet.

H

Halftone — A method for converting continuous tone art to lineart using screens that convert the continuous color to patterns of dots. Breaking up continuous tone artwork into variable-size dots to enable the printing of the illusion of continuous tone.

Halftone cell — A group of dpi dots used to generate a variable-sized lpi (or linescreen) dot. A group of printer dots producing a halftone dot.

Handles — The manipulation levers attached to a point, used to manipulate the tangents of the incoming and outgoing segments.

Handmade stochastic — a random-dot halftoning technique using the Bitmap mode's DIF-FUSION DITHERING option.

Hanging indent — A paragraph style with a left indent that has a negative first-line indent and a tab on top of the left indent to line up the rest of the first line with the indent; used for bulleted or numbered lists.

Hard cover — Perfect-bound or smythe-sewn books covered with hard cardboard covers.

Hard dots — Dots with hard edges, even density, and a specific size.

Head — A paragraph style, normally sans serif, used to capture the reader's attention with a real benefit.

Heat-set web — A printing press that prints on a roll of paper and has infrared dryers to dry the ink, enabling high-speed four-color printing.

Hi-fi (high-fidelity) color — Process color schemes that allow the colors available to more closely reproduce reality. A process color system using more than four colors to produce a much larger color space: Hexachrome, by Pantone, seems to be the standard.

Highlights — The tints in an image from 0% to 25%. The lightest areas in continuous tone artwork.

Histogram — The least intuitive method of interactively indicating gray levels. A graph that indicates the number of pixels for each PostScript level of color (0-255) in a Photoshop document.

HSB or HSV — Hue, saturation, and brightness or value; a color description language that allows accurate communication.

Hue — The name of a color.

I

Imposition — Arranging multiple pages on the front and back of a single sheet of paper so they are in proper page sequence after folding and trimming.

Incandescent or tungsten — An ordinary light bulb which uses a tungsten filament and glows with a very yellow light.

Index — A cheap, low-quality, calendered, lightweight cover stock (90# and 110#).

Ink holdout — The ability of a paper to keep ink on the surface with no absorption; produces much brighter, more saturated colors with much more control of ink densities.

Intaglio (now called gravure) — A printing technology that engraves or etches the image below the surface of the plate. The image is filled with ink and the background is cleaned and polished, then the ink is pulled out by squeezing slightly dampened paper into the recessed image. In gravure the background is squeegeed clean with doctor blades and looser ink.

Interface — What you see on the monitor screen that allows you to interact with your software application.

Internal proofs — Used during and within the production flow to locate problems and errors.

Interpolate — What image manipulation software does when it attempts to guess what color pixels to add when enlarging or which to remove when reducing.

ISP (Internet Service Provider) — A company that lets you use its Web server for a fee.

J

Jaggies — The pixelated edge of shapes or lines that appears when the pixels or dots are large enough to see with the naked eye.

Join — The three manners of rendering the appearance of the bends in a stroke at corner points.

JPEG — The lossy compression scheme used for continuous tone art on the Web. It works for high-res printing, but compressing too far leaves "plaid" artifacts. Compresses by averaging pixel areas.

K

Knockout — A PostScript property whereby the top shape knocks a hole in its exact shape in the colors underneath it.

L

Laser proof — A generic term for a black-and-white art proof.

Layer (Photoshop) — Another bitmapped image added to the Photoshop document that can interact with other layers (or not, according to the choice of the designer).

Layer (PostScript) — A collection of shapes that can be manipulated separately from the rest of the image.

Layer mask — A selection in a layer, which can be soft-edged, that blocks all the pixels outside the mask.

Leader — Filling the space between the end of the type and the new tab with repeating characters; used for attaching prices to items in menus and so forth.

Leading — Typographers' term for line spacing.

Letterhead — The stationery used by a company for printing official documents and letters.

Letterpress — The modern term for relief printing as developed by Gutenberg; currently used almost exclusively for die cuts, foil stamping, scoring, embossing, and the like.

Levels — A bar chart that shows how many pixels are set to each of the 256 colors available in a channel.

Line — A design element that is distinguished primarily by length and direction.

Lineart — Originally, black-and-white artwork, also called camera ready; currently, the output of PostScript illustration programs. Photoshop's equivalent is Bitmap mode.

Linescreen — The number of elements per inch on a printed image. The measurement system for dot patterns necessary to print continuous tone artwork on a 1-bit press. Used to describe the size of the dots in halftones, measured in lines per inch.

Link — The digital pointer that causes the PostScript printer or Distiller to use the high-resolution original instead of the low-res preview that is actually in the document.

Linotype — The first mechanical typesetting machine in letterpress; the technology that enabled the daily newspaper.

Lithography — A printing technology that uses a water-receptive background and a grease-receptive image; the plate is covered with water and then inked with a roller containing greasy ink.

Local formatting — Making changes to paragraph or character specifications without using the Styles palettes.

Logo — A graphic device used to distinguish and market a company.

Lossless — A compression scheme that loses no data.

Lossy — A compression scheme that loses data.

Loupe — A magnifying lens used for examining halftone dot structures, color fit, and trapping. The common name of a magnifying lens used by prepress personnel to examine screens, angles, fit, and rosettes.

LZW — The lossless compression scheme used by TIFFs and GIFs.

M

Marked up — Written on by the designer to indicate color breaks and instructions. Proofs are marked up by the client to indicate problems and errors.

Mask — A path used to cover, hide, or otherwise block out portions of a drawing or image. Photoshop uses selections (which are a type of path).

Master page — A page containing background images that are automatically placed onto pages of a document.

Masthead — The official, legal column listing publication personnel and publishing data required by law.

Matchprint — A color proof made from the negatives of the page made by laminating thin mylar images for each color of the separation: cyan, magenta, yellow, and black.

Matte — The color of the background when a transparent layer is flattened. Matting is supported by GIF, JPEG, and PNG. Its major use is to provide a background matte with a matte color that matches the background of the Web page (giving the illusion of transparency). Layer edges often blend more smoothly into a matte background.

MB (megabyte) — A digital data size measurement for approximately 1 million bytes (8 million bits) of data.

Menu commands — Capabilities and dialog boxes accessed by clicking on the drop-down menus at the top of the monitor screen on a Mac or the top of the application window on a PC.

Mezzotint — A fine art intaglio technique that involves polishing highlights out of a solidly scratched, deep black, copper plate; for our purposes, the look of a mezzotint is a random arrangement of very short lines that produces a very arty halftone appearance.

Mezzotint filter — A very poor approximation of the look of a true mezzotint.

Mill order — Paper not commonly available that must be ordered in multiple-carton quantities from the paper mill.

Miter — The extended point, beyond the corner point, of a stroke that changes direction. The length of this point is controlled by the miter limit option. Not available in Photoshop.

Moiré — Interference patterns that appear whenever two or more regular patterns are printed on top of each other: a major problem when rescanning.

Morgue — A designer's storage and filing system used to keep samples and references for design ideas.

Movable type — This is what Gutenberg invented, primarily by developing metal molds that were reusable: the enabling technology for printing as we know it.

Multimedia — Graphic productions that use video, animation, sound, music, and/or interactive linkages.

N

Nested graphic — An image imported into an illustration and then exported along with the finished illustration: a separate digital file, or an image, within an image.

Neutral grays — Colors that show no hue cast.

Newsprint — An extremely cheap, low-quality, acidic wood pulp paper used for newspaper production.

Nouveau riche design — Conspicuous display of the powerful capabilities of publishing and design software, "just because you can" with little or no taste involved.

O

Offset — Lithography presses that print the image first onto a rubber blanket and then transfer the image to the paper: allows right-reading plates.

On-demand — Storing documents digitally, then printing only what is needed when it is requested, often with variable data so each printed piece is different.

Opaque — A common name of high-quality, offset printing papers (#1 Premium sheets).

OPI (image substitution) — A process developed by Aldus to enable top-end scanners to supply low-res images to the designer for easy manipulation and then automatically substitute the high-res images at the service bureau or printing firm, applying all the changes made by the designer to the low-res image.

Output simulation — Adjustment of the monitor and proof colors to mimic the final output of the production printer or press, using machine color profiles.

P

Page layout — The assembly of prepared pieces, graphics, and copy into a finished document. Contrary to popular opinion, Illustrator or Photoshop cannot do this.

Panels or palettes — An arrangement of commonly used dialog boxes into floating boxes for easy mousing access.

Pantone Matching System (See PMS)

Papyrus — A writing surface made of strips of a large reed that has been soaked and peeled: cannot be printed on.

Paragraph rule — A rule attached to a paragraph, either above or below, applied with the Return/Enter key. Not available in Illustrator or Photoshop.

Parchment — A writing surface made from stretched and scraped hide: usually from kids or lambs: cannot be printed on.

Parent size — The sheet sizes of paper purchased from a paper distributor, commonly 23"×35" or 26"×40" in the United States.

Path — The name of the mathematical description used to define lines and shapes in PostScript illustration.

PDF (Portable Document Format) — A file format of simplified, streamlined PostScript that can be read on any platform with the free Adobe Reader. It contains all the fonts and graphics, so it is truly portable and can be used as the preferred format to send to your printing firm or service bureau.

Perfect bound — As opposed to saddle-stitched, books and booklets that are trimmed on four sides and have a square binding edge with a cover wrapped around.

Permanent color — In printing, color that lasts a year; in fine art, color that lasts a minimum of 200 years.

Photo-direct plates — Plates made photographically from black-and-white original artwork; an enabler of quickprint.

Pixel — A contraction of the two words *picture element*. A pixel is the smallest unit of a digital image. It can vary in color but not in location.

Pixelated — An image in which the pixels are large enough to be seen as tiny squares with the naked eye. This can be caused by enlarging or resizing a bitmapped image.

Place (import) — Putting a picture preview in a document with a link to the high-resolution version for printing; what is done with exported graphics.

Platemakers — A vacuum frame that contacts assembled negatives in traditional printing to expose plates photographically.

Platesetters — A digital press that outputs plates directly from the document.

Platen press — A style of letterpress press using flat palettes to apply the pressure; developed by Gutenberg, still used by Franklin.

PMS (Pantone Matching System) — A standardized spot color ink system that is dominant in the United States. It has 1,001 standard colors mixed out of 14 basic inks according to standard formulas listed on swatch books (you need to buy a swatch book).

PNG — A new Web format designed to eliminate the royalties for the LZW compression used in CompuServe GIFs. Supposedly it has superior compression, but it rarely does as well as Photoshop's new lossy GIF capabilities. It also supports partial transparency (alpha channels). Spotty support.

Point (paper) — Cover stock measured in thousandths of an inch with a micrometer.

Point (PostScript) — A reference location on a Bézier curve.

Posterize — The reduction of an image to only a few gray levels.

Posterizing — Converting continuous tone art to art with severely limited tonal values.

PostScript — A page description language at the core of high-resolution printing; the standard for the printing industry and the basis for PDF.

PostScript illustration — Images drawn with PostScript shapes produced in FreeHand and Illustrator (plus QuarkXPress and InDesign).

PPD (PostScript Printer Description) — A small piece of software supplied with a PostScript printer that defines the capabilities of that printer to the software being used to print, such as resolution, linescreens available, paper sizes, and so forth.

Preferences — Settings for some basic application defaults.

Preflight — Opening up submitted digital documents to see if they are complete, correct, and will work; a checkout to see if it will "fly."

Press proof — A proof created using press output; used as the final proof on a job.

Primary colors — The three colors from which all other colors in a color space are made through mixtures.

Process color — A full-spectrum color space using primaries: RGB for Web and multimedia; CMY for color printing (plus K [black] because cyan is weak).

Proof — A one-off print of the final product used for checking accuracy of copy and layout, color, imposition, and traps. They come with huge differences in accuracy depending on need and price.

Pull quote — *See Callout:* using body copy quotes as a graphic device to recapture readers' attention.

Q

Quadritone — A four-color separation using spot colors to give much greater shadow detail and midtone control.

Quality control — The means of taking control of the production process, using proofs, calibration, and color management along with customer and employee feedback.

Quickprint — Short-run, quick-turnaround printing using paper, plastic or digital plates and limited paper choices. Normally, low-resolution, coarse-registration printing done on cheap plates with limited paper and ink choices using duplicators instead of presses. This portion of the industry was the first to adopt digital technology, so there are now wide variations in quality and capabilities.

R

RAM (Random Access Memory) — The ultra-fast memory used by your computer to work in as it creates files and documents. It is wiped out any time power is cut.

RBY (Red Blue Yellow) — The fine art, full-spectrum color space of artists' pigments.

Registration — The ability of a press to feed paper consistently. The normal standard is a half dot.

Rescreening — Screening artwork that has already been made into a halftone.

Resolution independence — One of the basic attributes of PostScript: PostScript vector drawings and type have no resolution attached to the file, so they print out at the highest resolution possible on a specific printer with a custom bitmap created to best utilize that printer.

RGB (Red Green Blue) — The full-spectrum color space of a monitor. The additive color space of light.

RIP (Raster Image Processor) — The computer in a PostScript printer that generates the custom bitmap of PostScript information to exactly fit the resolution of that printer, imagesetter, or platesetter.

Rollovers — A Java-scripted action where graphic buttons change as a mouse moves over them.

Roughs — A hand-drawn rendering of an idea to establish layout and proportion. Quick proportional sketches used for layouts.

S

Saddle-stitched — Booklets made by folding paper, stapling through the fold, and trimming the three outside edges.

Sample — The smallest image unit of a scan.

Saturation — The intensity of a color.

Scanning resolution — Twice the linescreen.

Score — (see Die-cut) Placing rounded edged steel rules on plates in letterpress (primarily), to dent the paper to enable it to fold easily, accurately, and smoothly with no breakage of the surface of the ink.

Screen — Another name of a tint using linescreen dots.

Screen angles — The angles of the dot grid in the four halftones used for CMYK color (45°, 75°, 105°, and 90°); used to avoid moiré patterns.

Screen preview — What you see on the monitor when you place a graphic into a document.

Script fonts — Fonts that mimic handwriting (specifically modern handwriting).

Secondary colors — Colors made by mixing two primary colors.

Segment — The path portion between two points as defined by the handles.

Self-extracting archive — A compressed archive that will open with a simple double-click of the icon.

Separation — Converting a scan of a color image into CMYK.

Serif — A flare, bump, line, or foot added to the beginning or end of a stroke in a letter.

Service bureaus — Companies with color expertise, high-end color scanners, and top-quality imagesetters that prepare designers' documents for printing.

Shade — A fine-art term to describe hues plus black.

Shadows — The dark areas of a halftone or separation; the tints in an image from 70% to 100%.

Shape — A two-dimensional piece of a graphic.

Sheet-fed — Presses that feed one sheet at a time.

Short-run — Printing 2,000 impressions or fewer, as far as traditionalists are concerned; the primary area of digital printing.

Sidebar — Information placed to the side of a layout that is interesting but not essential.

Sign off — A way in which printing establishments attempt to place output responsibility on the client.

Signature — A sheet of paper with multiple pages arranged on it so that, after folding and collating, the pages are in the proper order.

Sizing — A coating that controls absorption.

Slicing — The cutting of oversized Web images into smaller pieces. Each piece can have its own links and disjointed rollovers.

Smooth — The surface of uncoated, calendered, offset paper.

Smythe-sewn — The highest-quality process for making a book, in which the signatures are hand-sewn together and case-bound, usually with a leather cover.

Soft proofing — Using the monitor for proofing. It is very dangerous without some kind of hard-copy proof to go with it, and requires much experience.

Specular highlights — Reflections of a light source off a shiny surface like chrome or water.

Spiral-bound — The binding of a book or booklet with spiral wire into prepunched holes.

Spot color — Color printed on its own plate or printhead.

Spot color separations — Output of a spot color document so that each color is on a separate print, plate, or negative.

Standard color — A standard pigment mix of an ink company.

Stationery package — Business cards, letterhead, and envelopes.

Stochastic — A recent development in halftone technology that uses irregular dot patterns, precisely placed. The dots remain the same size. Tints are created by the number of dots in a given area.

Stochastic screen — A new digital halftone technique using precisely placed, very tiny dots with frequency modulation. A usable hand-generated stochastic effect can be created by using BITMAP MODE >> DIFFUSION DITHER in Photoshop, a random dithering technique.

Stroke — The color and width applied to a PostScript path or the outline of a PostScript shape.

Stroke and fill — All PostScript shapes give you almost unlimited options to color the outlining path (the stroke), and the area enclosed by the path (the fill).

Style — A recorded format of a paragraph, character, graphic, or applied layer effects available on a palette.

Subhead — A lesser headline.

Subtractive color — A full-spectrum color space in which the primaries add together to produce black.

Swatch book — Standard set of printed colors that shows designers what the color will look like when printed.

Symbols — A shape with attached meaning.

T

Tabs — A soft return with a leading of zero to implement a new indent and alignment setting on the same line of type.

Tag — A very cheap, very thick card stock used for tags.

Tangent — A straight line touching a curve at a single point.

Templates — Saved documents with customized defaults.

Text — What software programmers tend to call copy.

Text fonts — Fonts that mimic medieval handwriting.

Texture — The visual "feel" of a shape's surface.

Thumbnails — A fast sketch (a few seconds) done to note down an idea in a personal shorthand that enables the designer to retain the idea.

TIFF (Tagged Information File Format) — The most reliable format for printing bitmapped images.

Tint (fine art) — A hue plus white.

Tint (printed screens) — A partial color expressed in the percentage of area covered by the linescreen dots.

Tipping in — Pasting the output from another print run into a printed document, usually done by hand, currently used to put process color images onto debossed areas of text covers and the like.

Tools — Software routines that change the abilities (and usually the look) of the cursor; buttons to click that change the capabilities of the mouse.

Transformation center — A target that appears with a transformation tool (in Adobe software).

Transparency — Pixels that print or partially print or output.

Transparency mask — A mask or selection where the pixels outside the mask do not print or output.

Trapping — Building small overlaps into touching color shapes to cover for bad registration.

Tritone — Three halftones printed on top of each other for greater shadow detail and density plus better midtone control.

Tungsten or incandescent — An ordinary light bulb uses a tungsten filament and glows with a very yellow light (or low temperature) light.

Typesetting — The craft of setting type.

Typography — The art and craft of setting and designing professional-quality type using well-designed fonts.

U

Ugly — The current fashion in illustration, accurately presenting the frustrations of the younger generations.

Unsharp mask — A filter that heightens the contrast of edges to make them more apparent.

V

Value or brightness — The lightness or darkness of a color.

Varnishes — Transparent or translucent inks printed to protect or provide texture to underprinted inks.

Vector image — Graphics drawn with outlines in which the curves are rendered with countless short straight lines (vectors). FreeHand and Illustrator (plus InDesign and QuarkXPress) produce vector images. Photoshop has a few vector tools.

Vellum — A surface description of the texture of relatively uncalendered offset paper.

Vellum bristol — An extremely cheap, wood pulp cover stock.

Volume — The illusion of three-dimensional space.

W

Waterless printing — A new high-tech printing technology that uses plates covered with an ink-receptive coating covered with an ink-repelling coating. A laser is used to burn holes in the repellent coating.

Watermark — A slightly translucent image in office papers.

Web printing — Printing onto a roll of paper that is sheeted after printing is completed.

White space — The empty, open, or blank areas of a design: one of the most important factors to control in graphic design. These areas should be planned shapes to increase readability.

Writing — The name of better-quality bond or office papers.

X

X-height — The height of the lowercase X.

Xtras — FreeHand's name for its plug-ins.

Y

Yak — An extremely smelly, ugly animal with a horrible disposition.

Z

Zorro — A hero of Spanish Southern California.

Index

This is the first book in a publishing series

Introduction to Digital Publishing is meant to be the first of a final series of courses students take before they move out into the real world of employment and freelance. It covers the basics of the industry: history and typography. There are three more books and courses to help complete this education.

Publishing with Photoshop

Could be called Image Manipulation. This book covers the daily practical uses of Photoshop — what you will be doing every day and how to meet deadlines.

Table of contents

This book deals with the practical use of Photoshop day-to day under the normally ridiculous deadline pressures. It covers the tools and filters you will be using daily, but focuses on the realities of halftone production, duotones, tritones, and separations.

Publishing with Illustrator and Freehand

This book covers the real need for vector illustrations — more specifically PostScript Illustrations. It covers both FreeHand and Illustrator, pointing out the advantages and disadvantages of each. My position is that you need both. Freehand for production speed and typography, Illustrator for actual drawing.

Table of Contents

The book gives the reasons why any designer needs to add PostScript illustration to their arsenal. These skills are often passed over due to the seductiveness of Photoshop. However, they are essential skills — required for logos and extremely advantageous for Web graphics.

Publishing with InDesign

This is a solid, page layout book. The book proceeds from the obvious fact that InDesign is the page layout program of the future. Quark feels so antiquated that I can no longer get my students to use it except for the required tutorial courses.

The book focuses on the use of the styles palettes, setting up defaults, and streamlining page production. There are hundreds of practical tips for the design of almost all of your daily production of stationery, brochures, booklets, newsletters, magazines, and so on.

By the way, here is the landmark. You made it!